SO OTHERS MIGHT LIVE

Also by Terry Golway

FULL OF GRACE:
AN ORAL BIOGRAPHY OF JOHN CARDINAL O'CONNOR

FOR THE CAUSE OF LIBERTY:
A THOUSAND YEARS OF IRELAND'S HEROES

THE IRISH IN AMERICA *(with Michael Coffey)*

IRISH REBEL:
JOHN DEVOY AND AMERICA'S FIGHT
FOR IRELAND'S FREEDOM

SO OTHERS MIGHT LIVE

A History of
New York's Bravest

THE FDNY FROM
1700 TO THE PRESENT

Terry Golway

BASIC
BOOKS

A MEMBER OF THE PERSEUS BOOKS GROUP
NEW YORK

Hardcover first published in 2002 by Basic Books,
A Member of the Perseus Books Group
Paperback edition first published in 2003 by Basic Books

Illustration credits: © Bettmann/*CORBIS*, pages xvi, 15, 72, 77, 95, 105, 111,
139, 166, 172, 183, 227, 238, 260; © *Bob Crist/CORBIS*, page 335; ©
CORBIS, pages 27, 329; © *CORBIS-Sygma*, pages 287, 314; *Courtesy Mand Fire
Department Library*, pages 31, 92, 198, 247; *Courtesy New York City Fire Museum*,
pages 32, 82, 163, 204, 273; *Courtesy FDNY Photo Unit*, pages *3, 8, 123, 140,
187, 206, 209, 212, 225, 254, 267, 292, 303, 308;* © *Ed Eckstein/CORBIS*,
page 280; © *Medford Historical Society Collection/CORBIS*, page 108; © *Hulton-
Deutsch Collection/CORBIS*, pages 175, 195; © *Museum of the City of New
York/CORBIS*, pages 44, 51, 134, 182; © *Paul Colanglo/CORBIS*, page 319; ©
Sean Cassidy, page 295; © *Steven Scher*, pages xvi, 39, 218, 229, 233, 251, 262,
277; *Terry Golway*, page 345

Designed by Lovedog Studio

A CIP catalog record of this book is available from the
Library of Congress

ISBN 0-465-02740-7 (hc); ISBN 0-465-02741-5

03 04 05 / 10 9 8 7 6 5 4 3 2 1

For my father, Firefighter Tom Golway,
and my mother, Mary Golway; my godfather,
Firefighter Frank Tomaselli; my in-laws,
Firefighter Neil Duggan and Peggy Duggan;
and the families of firefighters everywhere.

Contents

CONTENTS

· · ·

ACKNOWLEDGMENTS

My FATHER spent more than thirty years protecting New Yorkers from fire. My mother protected us when he worked his night tours. I owe both of them my love and thanks.

My childhood memories are filled with images of firefighters sitting around our kitchen table or flipping burgers in the backyard. They laughed a lot, and told great stories. I wouldn't blame them for any of my personal or professional flaws, but I'll thank them and their loved ones for providing me with role models, an appreciation of life and whatever work ethic I might have. Thanks, then, to my godfather, Frank Tomaselli, to my late uncle, Walter Golway, and the gang from Engine 162 and Truck 82, especially Donald and Stella Holton, Tom and Madeline Canterino, Donald and Diane Dillon and Charlie Bruns. I suppose it comes as no surprise that I married into another firefighting family: So thanks, too, to Neil and Peggy Duggan.

Everybody who agreed to be interviewed for this book has my thanks. I owe a special debt to Ed Staines, who was so generous with his time, his contacts and his personal files. John Fox led me to a handful of terrific interviews. Susan Blake put aside a night's worth of studying for the lieutenant's test to answer my questions. Ed Koch and Joe Hynes are among the busiest people in the city of New York, and I thank them for accommodating me. Vincent Dunn gave me a tutorial in Firefighting 101—who better? I spent an unforgettable afternoon with Reggie and Vincent Julius in Cryan's Pub in South Orange, and luckily, I have the whole session on tape.

Chief Jack Lerch and Lieutenant Dan Maye of the Mand Fire Department Library were a great help. Thanks especially to Chief Lerch for his help with getting photos and answering a thousand questions. The man's knowledge of the FDNY is astounding.

Peter Rothenberg of the New York City Fire Museum allowed me to troll through the journals in the museum's basement, and was a wonderful help with photo research.

Thanks, also, for their help and encouragement along the way to Drew Bauman, Dennis Duggan, Joe Conason, Jay Price, Mark Hanley, Dennis Smith, Dan Barry, Mitchell Moss, Kevin Davitt, Dan Janison, George Hunt, Jim Martin, Peter Quinn, The Rev. William Huntley and Frank McLaughlin.

I'm indebted to the staffs of the New-York Historical Society, the Municipal Reference Library, the American Irish Historical Society, the New York Public Library, the Maplewood Public Library, the LaGuardia Community College archives and the Wagner Labor archives at New York University. Special thanks to the FDNY's photo unit and Ralph Bernard. Frank Gribbon helped in a hundred ways, most especially in digging up the videotape of the ceremonies at Engine 73 and Ladder 42 on September 10, 2001.

Josh Benson, Greg Sargent and Mike McLaughlin are researchers without peer. Thanks, friends.

Not for the first time, Arthur Carter, publisher of the New York Observer, and Peter Kaplan, the Observer's editor, were generous beyond belief. I can't thank them enough.

Bob Leonard and Sean Cassidy of Dan Klores Communications offered terrific advice and guidance, and were always quick to answer my calls. And it's because they love the men and women of the Fire Department of New York.

My editor, Liz Maguire, is a jewel. Her assistant, Will Morrison Garland, has a way of remaining calm in the midst of chaos, which is a good thing. The support, professionalism and good cheer from everybody at Basic Books have been wonderful to behold. Thanks to the hard work of Eugenia Pakalik, Sabrina Bracco, Liz Tzetzo and Matty Goldberg in sales; John Sherer and John Hughes in marketing; Scott Manning and Jamie Brickhouse in publicity; Christine Marra, Brian Mulligan, and Stephen Bottum, in managing editorial, design and production; publisher John Donatich and Perseus CEO Jack McKeown.

My wife, Eileen Duggan, and our children, Kate and Conor, are blessed with patience, and that is a good thing for me.

For John Wright, my agent and friend, there are no words.

Finally, a heartfelt thank-you to the heroes of this book and their families and friends. Their courage and sacrifice have inspired the world.

—*Terry Golway*

PROLOGUE

THREE HUNDRED AND FORTY THREE members of the Fire Department of New York died on September 11, 2001, while taking part in one of the most successful rescue efforts in history. In the days afterward, people around the world put names to faces, flesh and bone to numbers. We heard about firefighters who rushed to the mortally wounded World Trade Center from their homes, on their day off. We heard about Peter Ganci and Terry Hatton and Ray Downey and so many others, family men, mostly, with accents that betrayed their roots in the middle-class suburbs of Long Island, or the old working-class neighborhoods of Brooklyn and Queens. So many of them had Irish names, reminding the world of a time when civil service gave the Irish something they didn't get in their tortured homeland: respect, security, and a living wage.

The men who died were surprisingly well educated—surprising, that is, if you assume, as so many did, that this was a job filled by the remnants of blue-collar New York. Yes, there was a time when the FDNY, like other uniformed civil service jobs, drew its workers from the same labor pool as did the breweries of Brooklyn, the West Side docks, and

A classic engine company tactic: While one firefighter works the nozzle, others open a hydrant outside a burning building.

the small factories of the Bronx. But that was a long time ago. In the days after September 11, the world learned just how hard it is to become a New York firefighter. Physical prowess isn't everything—you'd better have college credits, too. The obituaries spoke of firefighters with B.A.'s in fine arts and sociology; of a firefighter who fashioned glass he found that had been melted and twisted by the heat of a blaze into pieces of art; of firefighters who played musical instruments, or who could quote poetry, or who could cook you a meal you'd never forget.

The dead were exclusively male, but only chance prevented the Fire Department from losing its first woman firefighter on that awful day. Alongside their male colleagues the women of the FDNY desperately worked the pile of rubble that had been the Twin Towers, searching for survivors.

The world learned about heroes—real heroes, who lived in obscurity, who weren't going to get rich, and who, with their last breath, reminded us that selflessness, courage, and commitment are not part of some other generation's tale.

It took September 11 to show us what manner of human being joins the Fire Department of New York. But the men and women who responded to the most historic alarm in New York history weren't breaking precedents or going where no firefighter had gone before. Though faced with a catastrophe of historic proportions, they responded with the same kind of professionalism and quiet courage that marked the response to a much smaller fire on Twenty-third Street in October of 1966. When that fire was over, twelve firefighters were dead. The heroes of September 11 reacted as had Chief John Bresnan of the 6th Battalion more than 100 years earlier, on a December night just after Christmas, when he left behind his motherless children and raced to a burning building. He and a colleague were killed when the roof collapsed. More than a century later, his great-grandson Bill Bresnan, newly retired from the FDNY, thought about the fate of his legendary great-grandfather as he watched the Twin Towers burn on television.

When it came to courage and selflessness, September 11 was no different than the hundreds of fires in New York's history that have killed firefighters, sometimes one at a time, and sometimes a handful. The culture of firefighting on September 11 was the same as it always was. Deputy Commissioner Bill Feehan once said of the FDNY, "They have to be ready at a moment's notice to put their life on the line for the sake of a stranger. You can't pay people to do that job. It has to come from something else."

Bill Feehan died on September 11 at the age of seventy-one. Firefighters his age generally are long-retired. But Bill Feehan was an

Generations of New Yorkers joined the Fire Department for job security, but that security often turned out to be an illusion.

old-fashioned firefighter, and loved his work. That's the amazing part of this story. Firefighters love their jobs. They are happy, and they enjoy each other's company. And that's not new, either. Benjamin Franklin, observing firefighters in Colonial Philadelphia, noted that they "took reward in themselves, and they love each other." And they still do.

CHAPTER ONE

SEPTEMBER 10, 2001

ON THE MORNING of September 10, 2001, Father Mychal Judge, the Fire Department's popular Roman Catholic chaplain, was on his way from the Franciscan friary in midtown Manhattan to the quarters of Engine Co. 73 and Ladder Co. 42 on Prospect Avenue in the Bronx. There, he'd join the mayor, the commissioner and the chief of department for a ritual of renewal. The ancient firehouse of Engine Co. 73 and Ladder Co. 42 had been rebuilt, like the neighborhood it served, and on September 10, a ceremony would commemorate not only the building's rehabilitation, but the revival of a borough left in ashes during the 1970s.

Also heading to the Bronx on this bright morning were a few dozen retired FDNY veterans who served in the firehouse when the borough became a national symbol of urban decay. They had witnessed the flight of the borough's middle-class from the old Irish, Italian and Jewish neighborhoods in the 1960s, and they saw firsthand the misery they left behind. By the mid-1970s, the Bronx was poor. It was derelict. It was powerless. It was hopeless. And it was burning. It burned by day and by night; it burned at random, and it burned with malice of forethought. It

So OTHERS
MIGHT LIVE

. . .

1

burned on national television in 1977, when a fire broke out beyond the centerfield wall of Yankee Stadium during a World Series game. Cameras followed the fire's progress from inning to inning, and America saw what the Fire Department of New York faced on a daily, on an hourly, basis.

People died in those fires, civilians and firefighters alike. Sometimes they died in fires that were deliberately set, fires that burned buildings because they were worth more in ashes than as real estate. A new, chilling phrase had entered the lexicon: Arson for profit. Burn your building; collect your insurance. It was all the rage in the Bronx.

And sometimes people died because their local firehouse was empty, the firefighters out chasing the deadly phantoms known as false alarms. In neighborhoods bereft of recreation, where crab grass poked through asphalt playgrounds, kids pulled fire alarms for the fun of it. They knew the firefighters would come, with sirens blaring and lights flashing. They had to come. And they always did. It was one of the few things you could count on in the Bronx. The schools were crumbling, the hospitals chaotic, the police demoralized. But the Fire Department of New York always showed up.

That was the Bronx Tom Von Essen knew as a young firefighter in Ladder Co. 42, two decades before he put on a tie and jacket and became Mayor Rudolph Giuliani's fire commissioner. Amazing though it sounds, firefighters who served in the Bronx during the chaos and danger of the 1970s loved their work. They were trained to put out fires, and when they worked in the Bronx, that's what they did. Whether they worked the day tour, from 9 o'clock in the morning to 6 o'clock at night, or the long night tour, from six o'clock until nine the next morning, they went to work knowing they would be called to a fire. More likely, two or three fires. They loved every minute of it. Years later, they would talk about the excitement of it all, and they would say, almost matter of factly, that there was no better place to be if you were a young firefighter. If you were in an engine company, you would crawl on your hands and knees through burning apartments, dragging hose and throwing water on great, frightening walls of fire. If you were in a ladder company, you'd be on the roof of a neglected

Through the 1970s, entire neighborhoods in the Bronx burned, and the borough's exhausted firefighters often worked through the night, every night.

old tenement, ventilating the building, or you'd be sent into the building to look for civilians who may or may not be inside. You'd put the fire out and you'd return to the street coughing and spitting up black, oily mucus. Maybe you threw up in the gutter. But you were young, you were a firefighter, and you were in the Bronx. You couldn't ask for much more in life.

A quarter-century later, times had changed in the Bronx. The catastrophic fires had been extinguished, and the borough was reviving. Out of the ruins new businesses and homes were rising, and while the Bronx was not and perhaps never will be the way it was at the apogee of the American century, at least the smoke had cleared.

The young firefighters of Engine Co. 73 and Ladder Co. 42 had no memories of that terrible time in the life of the city they served. They heard talk in the firehouse kitchen of a time and a place known as "the war years," but by September 10, 2001, the fires of the South Bronx in 1975 were just another piece of FDNY lore. The story of fire service in New York in the early 21st Century was one of triumph, mixed with occasional tragedy. Modern construction and new building codes had put an end to the era of big, memorable fires; improved equipment and superior training had improved the firefighter's chances against smoke and flames.

The quarters of Engine Co. 73 and Ladder Co. 42 were among the classic old New York firehouses that dated back to the days just after the city swallowed up Brooklyn, Queens, Staten Island and those parts of the Bronx it hadn't already digested. Greater New York, city of five boroughs, came into existence in 1898, and among many other projects, this new metropolis went on a binge of firehouse construction. These turn-of-the-century houses were built for a department that ran on horse power, and required firefighters to be on the job at all times, returning home only for meals and days off—which were granted only after they worked seven straight days. It was hardly a wonder that individual engine and ladder companies took on the character of extended families.

Many of these old houses were made of red brick, with white trim around the doors and windows, and the plaques on their cornerstones bore the names of old Mayors—Seth Low and Robert Van Wyck; John Purroy Mitchel and John Hylan—and forgotten borough presidents. The houses looked charming and nostalgic. They also were falling apart. Von Essen was rebuilding them, and on September 10, 2001, the modernized quarters of Engine Co. 73 and Ladder Co. 42, outfitted with new plumbing and modern wiring, would be formally re-dedicated with pomp, ceremony and firehouse camraderie.

It was going to be a fine day. There would be a ribbon-cutting, speeches and, reflecting the Department's roots as a profoundly Roman

Catholic institution, Father Judge would celebrate a Mass of thanksgiving on the apparatus floor.

BATTALION CHIEF John Fox had been on duty over the weekend, so he had the next couple of days off. A single dad, he had gotten his teenage son up and out of their Brooklyn apartment that Monday morning for the first full week of the school year. Then it was time to deal with Fire Department paperwork, a task that doesn't respect an officer's on- and off-duty days. There was a problem with Fox's time sheets—even chief officers have to account for their time, even men like Fox, exalted winners of the Department's highest award for heroism. For his rescue of a trapped and injured firefighter during the terrorist bombing of the World Trade Center in 1993, Fox had won the James Gordon Bennett Medal, donated to the Department in 1865 by the founding publisher of the old *New York Herald*. On that February day in 1993 Fox lowered himself by rope into a fifty-foot bomb crater in the North Tower's parking garage, and each foot of his descent seemed like one foot closer to hell. Fires burned in the distance, cars exploded, and chunks of concrete were falling around him. But he got the job done.

Fox called the Department's payroll office and explained the paperwork problem to a clerk. She told him what sheets he needed to file. "Listen," he told her, "I'll fax in the sheets tomorrow morning." There was no rush. It would wait.

BILL BRESNAN should have been a lieutenant. That's how he saw it, anyway. After spending nearly twenty years with Ladder Co. 15 in downtown Manhattan, in 2001 he wanted a promotion. But firefighters don't simply ask for promotions; nor do they earn one with, say, great displays of heroism. They take a civil service test. If they pass, they're promoted. If they fail, they stay where they are.

For an ambitious firefighter, the lieutenant's test is considered the biggest hurdle among many. Moving from lieutenant to captain or from captain to battalion chief isn't easy, but the first promotion, the transition from firefighter to lieutenant, is considered the toughest. The incentives are nothing to sneeze at: higher pay, more prestige, and the opportunity to be called officer. But so are the obstacles.

Bill Bresnan studied hard for the test, and passed it, or so it seemed. After the results were announced, however, auditors threw out four questions for which Bresnan had the correct answers, and he ended up with a 72 instead of 76; he needed a 73 to pass. Disgusted, he decided to retire and pursue his first love, painting. With a degree in fine arts from St. John's University, a younger Bill Bresnan had intended to pursue a very different life from that of his brothers and his father, who were firefighters; his grandfather, who was the chief fire dispatcher in the Bronx; and his great-grandfather, Battalion Chief John J. Bresnan, one of the firefighting heroes of late-nineteenth-century New York. Bresnan grew up hearing about his great-grandfather, and one of his earliest childhood memories was of his aging grandfather, in retirement, monitoring traffic on a Fire Department radio he kept near his bedside. He, Bill Bresnan, was going to be different.

And he was, for a while anyway. But after getting laid off from private-sector jobs while trying to launch his career in art, he gave in to his father's arguments: "Join the Fire Department and you'll never get laid off. You'll have a pension after twenty years, and you can do your art on the side." His father knew about the dreams of youth, for he had been a hot minor-league baseball prospect in his youth. But things didn't work out, and he became a firefighter. And so did Bill, in 1981, at the somewhat advanced age of twenty-eight.

He quit exactly twenty years later, in July 2001. He stayed in touch with his old friends, though, enough to know that had he passed the test, he probably would have been due at work as a lieutenant the next morning, September 11.

A VOICE shouted, "Three, two, one!" On cue, with flashbulbs popping, Mayor Giuliani cut the ribbon, formally opening the rebuilt headquarters of Engine Co. 73 and Ladder Co. 42. Fire Commissioner

Tom Von Essen smiling, was on Giuliani's left. Joining the mayor and commissioner was Chief of Department Peter Ganci, who was next to Von Essen for the ribbon cutting photo-op. Ganci was in his dress uniform, with gold flourishes on the beak of his white hat and a row of three ribbons on his chest. Five stars in a circle adorned the collars of his starched white shirt. Trim and younger-looking than his fifty-four years, Pete Ganci held an office that could be traced back to Colonial days, when the head of the Fire Department was called the chief engineer.

The mayor spoke, as did the commissioner and the chief. They unveiled a new plaque, dedicated to the firefighters who came before, and reminded current firefighters of the Department's traditions of sacrifice and courage. Then matters were turned over to Father Judge. He was dressed in white robes embroidered with a green Celtic cross. His congregation sat in blue folding chairs on the equipment floor. Some were standing in the back murmuring to each other. Just like church.

"This truly is a chapel," Father Judge said as he began the Mass. "Thank you, Lord, for life, thank you for goodness, thank you for work, thank you for family, thank you for friends, thank you for every gift. . . . Let us enjoy each other's company, and most of all let us be conscious of all those who have gone before us." There was no mystery about Father Judge's popularity. He loved being with firefighters, and he sounded like one, with a New York accent that paid scant attention to hard *r*'s. And he was a superb speaker. He talked in complete sentences, with the cadence of a poet. Though he seemed modest, he must have taken great pride in his voice, for he was not afraid to break into song, and seemed unaware that the results were decidedly mixed.

In his homily, he talked about the blessings and the tragedies of fire-fighting. "That's the way it is," he said, standing in the middle of a makeshift aisle, in front of a makeshift altar. "Good days, bad days. Up days, down days. Sad days, happy days—but never a boring day on this job. You do what God has called you to do. You show up, you put one foot in front of another, you get on the rig and you do the job, which is a mystery and a surprise. You have no idea when you get on that rig, no

In his white helmet and
turnout coat, Father Mychal
Judge, an FDNY chaplain, was
a familiar presence at fires.

matter how big the call, no matter how small, you have no idea what God's calling you to do.

"You love this job. We all do. What a blessing that is. A difficult, difficult job, and God calls you to it, and he gives you a love for it, so that a difficult job will be well done. Isn't He a wonderful God? Isn't He good to you, to each one of you? And to me. Turn to Him each day, put your faith and your trust and your life in His hands, and He'll take care of you, and you'll have a good life."

The priest recited the prayer of St. Francis of Assisi, which is not part of the traditional liturgy, but Father Judge, after all, was a Franciscan. "Where there is hatred, let me sow love. . . . Where there is darkness, light, and where there is sadness, joy." When Mass was over, Father Judge led the congregants in singing "America, the Beautiful," attacking the high notes with a bravery that matched the setting. The congregation applauded, and retired to trade small talk, handshakes and old war stories.

THE NEXT morning, September 11, dawned sunny and clear, and at the FDNY it was business as usual. The Department's daily orders were printed and distributed to the city's 300 firehouses, and they were as routine as the morning was brilliant: Firehouses were reminded to turn off window air conditioners on September 24, even if summer weather reappeared. Captain Michael Halderman of the Bureau of Training and Firefighters Michael Egan of Engine Co. 26 and Adriene Walsh of Ladder Co. 20 had completed the Health and Physical Fitness Unit's ten-mile run. The Technical Services Division delivered an underscored reminder that no hoses older than ten years should be in service.

An alarm from Box 8087 in Manhattan was transmitted at 8:47. Men and women working the day shift were in the houses already, in keeping with custom and inclination. Firefighters showed up for work early because they were expected to, and because they wanted to. That's why, later, when it became clear that the alarm sounded at Manhattan Box 8087 was for a fire like no other in Fire Department history, engine and ladder companies responded with personnel from both the night and day tours.

Paperwork in hand, John Fox was walking in the summerlike sun on his way to Knapp Street and the quarters of Engine Co. 254 in the Marine Park section of Brooklyn. He figured he'd use the fax machine there to send the payroll department the papers he'd promised to deliver. As he was walking along Avenue U, he saw a huge column of smoke to the west. "Wow," he thought, "they've got some job going in Flatbush." By the looks of the smoke, he figured the fire was nearby. He kept walking, and looked again to the west as he crossed Coney Island Avenue. The sky was filled with smoke. "What the hell is that?" he asked himself. He didn't wait for an answer. He ran to the firehouse.

Bill Bresnan was asleep when the first plane hit. His wife woke him. She had the television on, and Bresnan looked at the images of horror with the detached eyes of a professional. There was no white smoke, meaning that so far there was no water on the fire. The elevators couldn't be working, so the firefighters would have to walk up thirty, forty, fifty stories or more, carrying hose. Sooner or later, he thought, all the heat is going to twist the tower's steel. When you fight fires in downtown New York for twenty years, that's how you think.

And if you're retired, living in New Jersey and watching the fire on television, you think something else: "God," Bresnan said to himself, "I hope the chiefs withdraw everybody."

CHAPTER TWO

"DISCREET, SOBER MEN"

WHEN THE COMMON COUNCIL of New York assembled on May 6, 1731, the honorable members knew they could no longer postpone the inevitable. If they waited even just a few more months to improve fire protection in their growing colony, they risked losing everything. Old measures such as requiring citizens to have leather fire buckets at the ready and placing hooks and ladders—used to tear down walls and roofs to prevent fire from spreading—in strategic places throughout the town would no longer suffice for a city of New York's size and ambitions. Night patrols charged with sounding the alarm at the first sight of fire were not particularly well regarded—citizens referred to them derisively as "the prowlers."

The members of the council knew full well what the price of neglect could be: not just contempt, but catastrophe. Even a city as grand and as powerful as London could be laid low by fire, as it was in 1666. And although the main threat posed by fire in early eighteenth-century New York was the loss of property, lives were at risk, too. Though fatal fires were rare, they were not unknown in the larger cities of the old world. In 1689, more than 350 had died in an opera house fire in Denmark.

Better protection meant buying New York's first fire engines, and buying fire engines meant raising money. The Council ordered a tax on "estates real and personal" to raise 300 pounds to buy two engines "with suction and materials thereunto belonging." If the merchants who were turning New York into a vital center of New World commerce objected to this levy or regarded the council's intentions with suspicion, their opinions are not recorded. In any case, it would have been hard to argue that the decision to invest in state-of-the-art fire equipment was rash. Modern fire engines had been in used in European cities for decades, and nearly fifty years earlier, in 1686, the council had passed a resolution bemoaning the "great damages" that fire was causing. Even then the councilors pointed to the lack of "instruments to quench" the blazes. In the 1680s New York was a city of about 2,000 people and 400 buildings that was only beginning to edge north of Wall Street. In 1731 the population was nearly 9,000, there were about 1,200 buildings and the city's expanse was moving ever-northward. Fire protection, however, had not grown accordingly. It was still the citizen's leather bucket and a few hooks and ladders against a force of nature that destroyed cities much larger and much greater than New York.

So New Yorkers would have to suffer a tax hike to pay for better fire-extinguishing equipment. And what equipment it was! Two brand-new engines, designed and produced by none other than the inventor Richard Newsham of London, were guaranteed to throw a continuous stream of water. Newsham's engineering skills were known far and wide, mainly because he was not shy about publicizing his machines. Sensing an opportunity to create a new market, he dispatched advertising pamphlets to New York, claiming to build "the most substantial and convenient engines for quenching fires." And long before anybody had ever heard the phrase "celebrity endorsement," Newsham pointed out that he "hath play'd several of [his engines] before his majesty and the nobility at St. James, with so general an approbation that the largest was at the same time ordered for the use of that royal palace." So how could New York resist? After all, His Majesty himself had bought a Newsham engine.

The council decided that what was good enough for the sovereign— that would be George II, King of Great Britain, France (so he thought) and Ireland (he also thought)—was good enough for his subjects in New York. And, as a matter of fact, what was good enough for George II was quite a good deal better than the alternative equipment the council had considered. Somebody came up with the idea that if you strapped a large water barrel onto a device outfitted with gunpowder and then rolled the contraption into a burning building, the fire would set off an explosion that would tear open the barrel and send water flying hither and yon. Voilà! End of fire. This intriguing concept had the support of many influential people, until it was pointed out that in some cases, the water barrel might catch fire first, draining off the water before the gunpowder exploded. This would, supporters admitted, complicate matters.

An eighteenth-century drawing showed New York's state-of-the-art fire engines in action.

So it was to be Newsham's machines. The council dispatched two upstanding citizens, Stephen De Lancey and John Moore, to London to complete the purchase—in return for a 20 percent commission; the two also were among the city's shrewdest businessmen. Through the summer and fall of 1731, the city eagerly awaited the arrival of the new engines. Many had heard all about Newsham's successes in front of His Majesty; others may have heard about the 20 percent commission and been eager to share their opinion of the transaction with De Lancey and Moore.

In the meantime, the council continued to attend to fire matters. On November 18, 1731, members appointed two people from each ward to be "viewers of Chimmnies and Hearths"—an eighteenth-century version of a meter reader. Those who refused the viewers access to their homes to inspect chimneys and fireplaces once a month were fined three shillings. As a sign of just how ruthless fire prevention could be, citizens whose chimneys caught fire were fined forty shillings. That piece of legislation was called the "Law for the Better Preventing of Fire." It might have entitled an "Act for Adding Insult to Injury."

As the great day approached, the council designated a committee of two alderman to prepare "A Convenient Room in the City Hall" to house the new hand pumpers, which arrived on December 3, 1731. New Yorkers by the hundreds turned out at the Battery, the southern tip of Manhattan Island, to watch as the machines were unloaded. Volunteers happily assisted Alderman Peter Rutgers, who was placed in charge of the new arrivals in dragging the engines north to Wall Street, where more crowds gathered to see what their tax money had bought. Top government officials, including the mayor and governor, just as curious as the public, were also on hand.

For a city that relied on buckets for fire protection, the machines must have seemed well worth the investment, on first glance anyway. Essentially, they used muscle power, and lots of it, to activate pistons that sent water gushing through a narrow pipe, which served as a primitive nozzle. As many as twenty people had to pump to keep a continuous stream working. Bucket brigades fed the engine's reservoir, forming a line from the engine to one of the rivers surrounding Manhattan, or to a well-placed cistern, or to the increasingly nasty Fresh Water Pond, a body of water whose title would soon qualify as false advertising.

New Yorkers didn't have to wait very long to see whether their new equipment, designated Engine Co. 1 and Engine Co. 2, could match Newsham's promises. A late-night fire broke out on December 7 in a garret where several people were sleeping. The fire was burning fiercely when the engines arrived, pulled to the site by citizens roused from their sleep. Firefighting in early eighteenth-century New York as in other American cities was a communal activity. Not only were all able-bodied males obliged by law to help fight the flames, but so were the mayor and aldermen. Fighting fires was considered part of a citizen's obligation to the larger community, and it helped foster a civic culture in the new world these colonists were creating. It also furthered the idea of self-protection and mutual dependence in the face of a hostile force—indeed, a metaphor for the plight of European settlers in the Americas.

Firefighting in colonial times was a communal activity: Here, a civic-minded citizen directs water on a fire while other volunteers work the pump and others carry buckets.

Brave and civic-minded as they were, the citizens of New York were amateurs in the art of firefighting, and they could not be expected to do much more than haul buckets and hurl water at burning buildings. But on this December 7, they were working an engine for the first time. The results spoke for themselves. A Boston newspaper reported that "by the aid of the two fire engines which came from London. . . the fire was extinguished after having burnt down the house and damaged the next." Although this may sound like a perfect example of a pyrrhic victory—the fire was extinguished, but the building was in ashes—in fact it was a genuine victory, for in those days of wooden construction and narrow streets, it was an achievement to contain a fire to just one or two structures. On their maiden tour of duty, the engines proved their worth.

That's not to say there was no room for improvement. Courage and enthusiasm were no longer sufficient to fight fires; a certain professionalism was needed. In 1732 the council took the step of appointing an alderman named John Roosevelt as overseer of the two engines, at an annual salary of twelve pounds. His task was to become, in essence, a professional firefighter. In addition, demonstrating an attention to spit and polish that would characterize the Fire Department of New York through the ensuing centuries, the Common Council formed a committee to ensure that the engines were properly oiled and maintained. Two sheds were built near City Hall to serve as the city's first, albeit primitive, firehouses.

So now that the city had firehouses, they needed firefighters. Such is the nature of bureaucratic expansion—and the needs of a growing city. In December 1737, the colony's General Assembly authorized the formation of a volunteer fire department in New York. The legislators instructed the city's Common Council to appoint no more than forty-two "strong, able, discreet, honest and sober men" who would hold the title of "Firemen of the City of New York" and report directly to the salaried overseer. No longer would the city's safety depend on an ad-hoc collection of untrained citizens, however brave they might be. Indeed, the General Assembly duly noted that New Yorkers had "justly acquired the reputation of being singularly and remarkably famous for their diligence and service in case of fires." But now the job required specialized skills and training. And so New York's first Fire Department was born.

The firemen were volunteers, just like the regular citizens who turned out so famously to put out fires. But unlike the citizen firefighters, the volunteers would train and drill, keep charge of the equipment, and maintain some rudimentary sense of professionalism. When the bell in City Hall rang, they were expected to leave their homes or jobs and report to the firehouse. From there they dragged the engines and any other equipment to the fire, worked the pumpers as a team to keep the water flowing, and followed the commands of the overseer. Between fires, they were expected to maintain their equipment and practice with the engines to keep them, and themselves, in good working order. They would be obliged to do all of this on their own time, for in the everyday work world these firemen were blacksmiths, carpenters, bakers, and bricklayers, among other trades.

The volunteers quickly became much-admired figures in New York and in other American cities that also were developing fire departments. Observing the firefighters of Philadelphia, Benjamin Franklin wrote: "[He]re are brave Men, Men of Spirit and Humanity, good Citizens, or Neighbours, capable and worthy of civil Society, and the Enjoyment of a happy Government." Franklin was not the most objective source on the subject, for he himself was a volunteer fireman, having helped organize Philadelphia's first fire company. Still, most citizens in Philadelphia, New York, and elsewhere seemed to agree with his assertion that the volunteer firemen were "Heroes and effective Men."

Heroic though they may have been, they were not expected to put themselves in danger without any form of compensation. New York's lawmakers declared that the volunteers would be exempt from such civic drudgeries as militia and jury service. This highly effective recruiting strategy remained in place for more than 150 years.

New York's original firemen came from the ranks of the city's artisans and tradesmen, not from its merchant classes. Many of them bore names that bespoke the city's fading Dutch heritage: There were two van Gelders, along with Johannes van Duersen and John Vredenberg. Also among the originals was Jacobus Stoutenburgh, whose family had been fighting fires and helping to govern the colony since the seventeenth century.

When Peter Stuyvesant, appointed by the Dutch sovereign as the new director general of New Amsterdam, arrived in the colony in May 1647, he found no shortage of offenses against his well-developed sense of order and discipline. The population, numbering about 500, was a diverse group of Dutch, English, and other Europeans, along with the black slaves brought to the city under the auspices of the Dutch East India Company, corporate sponsors of the colony. They liked to drink, perhaps understandably, given the conditions: They lived in a town newly carved out of wilderness, and they were surrounded by hostile natives. Stuyvesant did not approve. Within days of his arrival he ordered that "all brewers, tapsters and innkeepers" could not "entertain people, tap or draw any wine, beer or strong waters of any kind. . . before 2 of the clock" on days when "there is no preaching." Cutting down on drink was to become one of Stuyvesant's crusades.

Another was the prevention of fire. The director general noted that "most of the houses here in New Amsterdam are built of wood and roofed with reeds." They also were built close together, on narrow streets. All in all, it was a bad combination if a serious fire broke out. But the nonchalance of the citizenry concerning this danger appalled Stuyvesant, and, not surprisingly, he was determined to shake them from their lethargy. "It has been noticed and seen by the Director General," read a document from the time, "that some careless people neglect to have their chimneys properly swept and that they do not take care of their fires, whereby lately fires broke out in two houses and further troubles may be expected in the future." The director general was determined to minimize further troubles by asserting civic authority over private property and demanding that building construction comply with basic safety requirements. He and the Common Council ordered that "no wooden or merely plastered chimneys shall be put into any house" in the most populated part of the city. On matters of fire prevention and public safety, Stuyvesant made it clear that the values of marketplace and property rights alone would not rule this intensely mercantile city.

Stuyvesant was under no illusions that the hard-drinking, hard-living, slothful population would improve their habits simply because they were requested to do so. So in 1648 he appointed four "firemasters" who were empowered to make sure the laws were being followed. In a bow to the city's diverse population—at least by seventeenth-century standards—two of the firemasters were Dutch, representing New Amsterdam's founding population, and two were English, part of the colony's more recent influx. These four men, Adrian Keyser, Marten Krieger, Thomas Hall, and George Woolsey, can be considered the founders of firefighting service on Manhattan Island. All citizens were expected to help when fires broke out in Peter Stuyvesant's New Amsterdam, but these four firemasters were hired specifically to help prevent fires. They had the power to levy fines of three guilders on householders for chimneys that were deemed unsafe, and the proceeds served to finance another part of Stuyvesant's fire strategy, the purchase of hooks, ladders, and buckets.

Still, the unruly city did not respond in the manner the director general demanded. Stuyvesant was a battle-scarred veteran of the New World's wars of conquest who had lost a leg in battle and whose peg leg bore witness to his bravery and sense of duty. This disciplined military man found that even as formidable a figure as he couldn't simply command a change in the common citizens' behavior and culture. He lamented that "our former orders" against "intemperate drinking at night and on the Sabbath. . . to the shame and derision of ourselves and the nation, are not observed and obeyed." He saw that men and women were living together without the benefit of marriage. And he couldn't help but note that citizens were still unconcerned about the risk of fire. Peter Gerard Stuyvesant was a man of action, and he acted. When Stuyvesant determined that his fire regulations were "obstinately and carelessly neglected," he prepared his next move.

In late 1657, New Amsterdam witnessed a vision straight out of one of Peter Stuyvesant's cautionary harangues. One of the town's most impressive residences, a sturdy structure far removed from the shanty houses and cabins built elsewhere, was owned by a fellow named Sam Baxter. One evening, a log rolled out of Baxter's fireplace, and Baxter's house was doomed. It was reduced to ashes.

The Baxter fire apparently left an impression, and Stuyvesant took advantage of the public reaction. On December 15, 1657, he ordered that all roofs covered with reeds and all wooden chimneys "shall be taken down and removed." Each house was hit with a property tax hike of "1 beaver or 8 florin[s] in wampum" to import from "the Fatherland. . . 100 or 150 leathern fire buckets and to have some fire ladders and hooks made with the surplus."

After some delay, the buckets were brought into service—made not in the Fatherland but in New Amsterdam itself, after Stuyvesant and the new city legislators, the burgomasters, decided to contract the job out to a local shoemaker who was eager for the work. They were placed in strategic locations around the city.

These measures apparently heightened public awareness of fire prevention, but Peter Stuyvesant wasn't finished improving the city's character and culture. He recruited eight men, armed them with 250 buckets and several hooks and ladders, and ordered them to patrol the streets at night to keep order and to detect fires as early as possible. They carried with them a noisy rattle, which they used as an alarm when they spotted a fire or some other threat to the peace. The night watch—or rattle watch, as it become known—proved so successful that Stuyvesant eventually increased the watch's strength to fifty. And, in keeping with the colony's sense of community and interdependence, Stuyvesant decreed that every house should have three buckets of water placed outside the door every night. When an alarm was raised, members of the fire patrol grabbed the buckets and transported them immediately to the scene of the blaze. When the blaze was extinguished, the buckets were tossed into a heap and the householders were summoned to the scene to retrieve them.

Thanks to these sorts of measures, New Amsterdam was a more orderly city than it had been, and was better protected against the threat of fire, when four British frigates loaded with soldiers appeared in the harbor in 1664, bound to take over the colony for England. Stuyvesant, never one to back down from a fight, was eager to defend the town he served so well. But once again his fellow citizens disappointed him, and this time no edict from the director general could bend the populace to his will. The city's political and business leaders were happy to take the terms the British offered and shift their allegiance, so New Amsterdam became New York without a shot fired. Peter Stuyvesant set sail for Holland to defend his record as the administrator of the lost colony, only to return to Manhattan in 1668 and die on his farm there in 1672.

It was a tribute to Peter Stuyvesant's methods and vision that the city's new rulers quickly adopted his approach to fire prevention and firefighting. The British liked the idea of inspecting the chimneys of private residences and retained the practice. As in Stuyvesant's time, hooks, ladders, and buckets were placed in strategic locations throughout the city. The increased size of newer buildings led to some refinement in fire prevention. Houses with two chimneys were required to have one bucket available for emergencies; houses with more than two chimneys had to have two. Brewers needed six and bakers, three.

The Stoutenburgh family's long connection to New York firefighting began in January 1690, when Tobeyas Stoutenburgh was one of five men appointed as New York's first paid fire wardens. They replaced the hearth and chimney viewers of past decades.

When, despite these precautions, fire did break out, the entire city knew about it. Then, as now, fires often started at night, but whatever the time, an organized system of detection and response was set in motion. Watchmen on patrol shouted the alarm and demanded that citizens hurl their buckets into the street, where they were picked up by their fellow citizens heading for the fire. Church bells rang to help spread the alarm and call out citizens to help. Two lines of civilians formed at the scene, one to pass three-gallon buckets filled with water hand to hand from a river or well to the fire scene, the other to return the empty buckets from the fire to the water supply. Passersby who tried to cut through the line or who declined to help usually found themselves drenched and shamed into assisting. After the fire, the buckets were collected near City Hall and the town crier passed word that the public could fetch them.

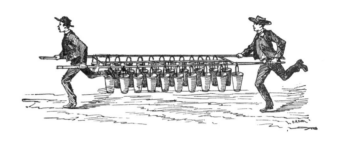

Getting buckets to a fire in eighteenth-century New York required speed and strength.

Though this system was not without charms—it inspired a sense of civic duty, and it promoted democratic values—the city's growth demanded better equipment and a force of trained firefighters. Which is why the Common Council ordered the Newsham engines, and why "discreet, sober men" were given the title "Firemen of the City of New York."

At around noon on March 18, 1741, as the last winds of winter were swirling around lower Manhattan, one of the city's most important buildings caught fire. The volunteer firefighters rushed to the firehouses and dragged their engines south to the governor's house, where the king's representative lived, located near the site of the present-day Battery Park. The house was within the confines of the colony's military garrison, Fort George, and so was in close proximity to several other buildings designed to feed, house, and otherwise maintain His Majesty's troops. It was soon apparent that the governor's house was a lost cause, so the firefighters desperately tried to prevent the blaze from spreading to the barracks and other buildings. It was no use. By sunset, Fort George was in ashes. The city's firefighting force had suffered a tremendous defeat.

There was little time to dwell on this failure, however, as another large fire broke out a week later, on March 25, this one in a building just outside Fort George's walls. The results were much better: The fire was restricted to just the one building. But in quick succession there were more fires: A warehouse along the East River; a stable; two houses. By early April, the sight of exhausted firefighters hauling their engines had become all too familiar. New Yorkers—that is, white New Yorkers—began to speculate that the rash of fires was no coincidence. The slaves, they whispered, were trying to burn down the city. The slaves, they feared, were about to rise against their masters.

It was a common enough fear, born of a mixture of guilt and loathing, in eighteenth-century America, but one associated more with Southern cities, such as Charleston, than northern. However New York was not immune to the fear of a slave rebellion. The first slaves arrived in the city in 1628, and in the ensuing years, most affluent New Yorkers, including Peter Stuyvesant and his family, came to own at least one. Demand was brisk enough to warrant the opening of a slave market in 1709 on Wall Street near the East River waterfront. Within a few years, nearly half the city's residents owned slaves.

There had been a minor slave rising in 1712, when a small group of arrivals from Africa got their hands on muskets and knives. The slaves set a building ablaze and ambushed the whites who responded to the fires. Nine whites were killed. Inevitably, lynchings of the innocent followed. By 1741, as fires burned and rumors of a rebellion circulated among white New Yorkers, there were about 2,000 slaves in the city, living amid a white population of about 8,000. The authors of *Gotham*, Mike Wallace and Edwin G. Burroughs, note that in the 1740s New York City had the highest concentration of slaves among northern cities.

Tensions between white citizens and black slaves worsened when four more fires broke out on a single day, April 6. There were reports of a black man having been seen running away from one of the fires, leading to full-throated cries that the slaves were on the verge of rising. More than 100 were rounded up and thrown in prison, which did nothing to quiet whites' fears. When a sixteen-year-old girl named Mary

Burton, the indentured servant of a white tavern owner who was known to sell liquor to slaves, was promised her freedom in exchange for information, she spun a fantastic tale of a plot involving resentful poor whites, vengeance-seeking slaves, and scandalous relations between the races. On April 11, a Saturday, a frightened Common Council posted "a reward to any white person that Shall Discover any person or persons lately concerned in Setting fire to any Dwelling House or Store House of this city." The reward, to be paid upon conviction, was 100 pounds, and the desperate government was prepared to take information from anybody—even nonwhites. The Common Council decreed that a free black, mulatto, or Indian also could claim the reward, but they would be given 45 pounds. And any slave whose information led to a conviction would be set free and given 20 pounds.

The next few weeks brought a bizarre and tragic parade of confessions, allegations, and court proceedings, the combination of which did little to justify white New York's fears, and little to dispel them. New York's upper classes learned of an underworld in which whites and blacks socialized and consorted with each other in waterfront grog shops. A white prostitute named Peggy Kerry not only sold her services to slaves, but had had a child by a slave named Caesar, a known thief. John Hughson, a tavern owner, along with his wife, daughter, and mother-in-law, were said to have encouraged their slave customers to rebel. And a recent arrival to New York, a schoolmaster named John Ury, found himself accused not only of being a Catholic priest—preaching Catholicism in New York was a crime punishable by death—but of organizing a planned rebellion of poor whites and black slaves. In the midst of these startling revelations, authorities in Hackensack, New Jersey, arrested two black men for starting a series of barn fires. The suspects were tried, convicted, and burned at the stake.

In the name of justice, New Yorkers took action that was equally swift, certain and indiscriminate. The slave Caesar and an accomplice were convicted of theft and hanged. Two other slaves were found guilty of conspiracy and were burned at the stake. As the flames consumed them, they confessed to the Fort George fire and, in their agony, named accomplices. John Hughson and his wife, Sarah, and Peggy Kerry were hanged. Ury, the suspected priest, also was hanged, but not before delivering a stirring speech from the dock: "I depart this waste, this howling wilderness, with a mind serene, free from all malice, with a forgiving spirit. . . praying that Jesus. . . will convince, conquer and enlighten my murderers' souls." Slaves were given no similar chance to proclaim their innocence or display their forgiving spirit. More than a dozen more were hanged; thirteen were burned at the stake.

Prosecutors might have gotten rid of some troublemakers and disreputable citizens, but they never proved conclusively that any plot to burn the city existed, save in the imagination of many white citizens and in the testimony of Mary Burton, the prosecution's chief witness. But when she continued to tell her tales, this time accusing some of the city's more upstanding citizens of conspiracy, her credibility, and the government's, faltered. Investigators declared victory, gave Mary Burton her 100-pound reward and closed the case, which became known in white New York as "the Negro plot," never mind that nothing was ever proved. It didn't matter. And it would not be the last time in New York history that fire and racial tension intersected, with grievous consequences.

Whether or not the fires were the work of conspirators, the city's Fire Department clearly needed additional manpower. On December 1, 1741, the council appointed fourteen more firemen on and also named thirty-six "sober men" to serve as night watchmen over the next year. The events of spring and the loose talk of a "Negro plot" clearly had shaken the city's civic leaders.

Over the next few years, Engine Companies 3 and 4 were organized and given quarters. Greater expansion followed, and within twenty-five years of the fires of 1741, the firefighting force numbered 170; as before, the volunteers tended to come from the ranks of the city's artisans and tradesmen—blacksmiths, carpenters, gunsmiths, and the like. Four more engine companies were founded, giving the city eight, and in a sign of the city's needs and the firefighters' skills, the department organized two hook-and-ladder companies, with their own specialized equipment. This division of labor between engine and hook-and-ladder companies (or, more simply, ladder companies) remains the essence of modern firefighting tactics. Engine companies pumped water on fires;

hook-and-ladder companies pulled down ceilings and walls to ventilate the flames and to identify pockets of fire for the engine companies. These were complementary measures and required close coordination between companies. That was true in the nineteenth century; it remains true in the twenty-first century.

The Department's expansion also saw the development of a command structure: In the 1760s, Jacobus Soutenburgh was given the title of chief engineer of the Fire Department, and the council named two assistant engineers to help him run the Department. At about the same time, firefighters were assigned to individual companies, and companies were assigned to one of the city's six wards. A foreman commanded all the companies in each ward.

With the department's growth and increased sense of professionalism (even though the work of firefighting was still strictly volunteer) came a slowly developing but distinctive culture. It was, from the very beginnings, a culture born of the bonds firefighters shared with each other and nobody else, for nobody except another firefighter could fully appreciate what they did, and why.

For Chief Engineer Stoutenburgh and his men, the years leading to the Revolution were relatively tranquil, thanks in part to further restrictions on building construction and materials. Stoutenburgh found time to augment his annual salary of thirty pounds by supervising the night watchmen and supplying oil for the city's street lamps. According to Common Council records, Stoutenburgh chalked up hundreds of pounds annually through his side jobs. In 1772, for example, he received more than 700 pounds in salary, expenses and reimbursements for duties unrelated to the Fire Department, dating to October 1771. There appears to be no record of any questions raised about this arrangement, perhaps because New Yorkers had gotten used to Stoutenburghs in city government: Isaac Stoutenburgh was an assistant alderman, his son was a fireman, John Stoutenburgh was an assessor from the West and North wards, Peter Stoutenburgh was an assistant alderman, and Tobeyas Stoutenburgh was an assessor from the West Ward.

As anti-Parliament agitation in New England spread to New York in the mid–1770s, New York's firemen were divided on the subject of revolution. Some joined seditious groups and worked for independence; others feared that revolution meant disorder, and disorder meant fire. And they were pledged to fight fires, not start them.

According to Fire Department lore, when war broke out between the colonists and the British, Jacobus Stoutenburgh raised a battalion of firemen to join George Washington's army, and Stoutenburgh himself received a commission as a major. The story is repeated in several histories of the period and of the Fire Department, but there is little reliable documentary evidence. The name Stoutenburgh, misspelled "Stoutinburgh," appears in service records from the Revolutionary War, but no evidence that he was a major has been found. There is little doubt, though, that many New York firemen enlisted in the patriot cause when George Washington arrived in late summer 1776 for what proved to be a very short stay.

Several days before Washington evacuated the city, knowing that his position was untenable with British forces preparing to assault Manhattan from Brooklyn, he held a council of war with his principal aides, including General Nathanael Greene, a promising young strategist from Rhode Island. Alone among Washington's advisers, Greene argued that New York could not be defended, a position that eventually prevailed. Greene then made it clear that the American strategic interests would be best served by leaving New York in ashes, thus handing the British a hollow victory and making it extremely difficult to house and feed the occupying force. As for private property that would be destroyed, Greene argued that two thirds of it was owned by Loyalists anyway. Washington was inclined to agree, but the civilian micromanagers in the Continental Congress forbade the city's destruction. Washington and his army pulled back to the northern end of Manhattan, beyond the city limits, on September 12, 1776.

On September 15 the British took control of the city. Six days later, just after midnight on September 21, a fire broke out in a tavern called the Fighting Cocks. Contemporary accounts indicate that this was not a place where one might hear learned discussions regarding the merits of, say, republican government versus the divine right of kings. Subsequent

The fire of 1776 in lower Manhattan may have been the work of "some good, honest fellow," in George Washington's words.

descriptions suggest a place well-suited to its rough-and-tumble location on the East River waterfront, near the city's wharves.

Depleted of firemen, New York was not prepared to battle a major conflagration. And the tavern fire quickly became just that, as winds from the southwest carried sparks and set fire to houses and businesses to the north. Within two hours the city was ablaze, a "scene of horror great beyond description," according to a newspaper account. Stirred from their bed, frightened New Yorkers grabbed their children and valuables and ran into the street as flames consumed block after block. As winds shifted, so did the fire; areas on both sides of Broadway were in flames. The captain of a vessel four miles away in the harbor saw fire reaching relentlessly for the spire of a church near the waterfront. "The deck of our ship for many hours was lighted as if at noonday," the captain wrote. Trinity Church caught fire and burned to the ground within minutes.

New York's Fire Department was in shambles, with so many members watching the fires from rebel camps at the north end of the island. British soldiers were summoned from their barracks to help beat back the flames, but the Loyalist amateurs soon discovered that some of the city's firefighting equipment had been sabotaged. Bottoms were cut out of buckets, fire bells were missing, and some of the engines were useless. All the while, men and women screamed in horror as they watched their homes or businesses burn and fall to the ground in a fiery heap. As rumors of a rebel plot made the rounds, angry mobs of civilians, not British soldiers, searched for suspicious characters. They came upon a carpenter who allegedly was spotted cutting holes in fire buckets. According to an eyewitness, the carpenter used his knife to wound a woman working with the bucket brigades. "This provoked the Spectators to such a Degree that they instantly hung him up," the witness reported. Other mobs reportedly came upon would-be arsonists carrying "matches dipped in melted Rosin and Brimstone." They were spared the carpenter's fate when British troops intervened.

The flames roared from the East River waterfront near Whitehall northwest to Barclay Street and the Hudson River, a mile-long tract of residences and stores. As he watched the orange glow in the sky from his headquarters to the north, George Washington said, "Providence, or some good honest fellow, has done more for us than we were disposed to do for ourselves." Dawn broke with no end in sight; the fire burned all day and into the night, when a young American patriot, Nathan Hale, was arrested and taken into British custody. Hale was an American spy, and he freely admitted as much. He was hanged the following morning, at 11 A.M., as smoke from the fires of New York drifted uptown, towards the gallows.

When the fire finally was extinguished, the extent of the horror became clear. More than 500 buildings had been destroyed, accounting for about 25 percent of the city's structures. Thousands of civilians, in a city of about 12,000, were without homes, and 300 sought shelter in the city's almshouse. Two hundred suspected rebel sympathizers were under arrest. And a great prize, the city of New York, was turned into a ravaged burden for the occupying forces.

British authorities were convinced the fire was no accident. Major General James Robertson, the city's military governor, issued a proclamation asserting not only that rebels were to blame for "the destruction of Part of the city," but also that they were eager for more. The general authorized a "[w]atch to inspect all parts of the City to apprehend and to stifle Fires." Several civilians volunteered to be part of the watch.

With New York—or what was left of it—secure from Washington's rebels, the British installed their high command in the strategic city. And with the high command came high life, the life to which titled aristocratic British military officers were accustomed. The city's social elites were more than happy to keep the officers entertained, and enthusiastically resumed the elegant nightlife that the war had ever so briefly interrupted. Nathanael Greene's belief that the city's land-owning classes were predominately Loyalist was unassailable. The British were good for business, which meant the British were good for New York's businessmen.

The occupation was not so pleasant, however, for New Yorkers of lesser means, those made homeless by the conflagration. Left to fend for themselves, they built what amounted to a city of canvas tents—made from the remnants of sails—amid the fire's ashes and ruin. There, they huddled together through the long New York winter, fending off the winds that whipped across the island from the rivers and bay. The district in lower Manhattan, soon labeled "Canvastown," was infested with disease.

Little attempt was made to rebuild the ruined portion of the city, although there was some effort to re-form a fire department of some sort. Civilians joined companies with names like Friendly Union and Hand in Hand, which were formed not so much to extinguish fires but to salvage whatever property they could during and after a blaze. Meanwhile, Britain's military government ordered stricter enforcement of rudimentary fire-prevention methods, like regular chimney sweeping, in hopes of preventing another catastrophe. These measures met with some success: Another dangerous fire broke out in 1778, destroying sixty-four houses and several businesses along the East River waterfront. Soldiers and civilians united to prevent even wider destruction, but the loss of more homes worsened the city's housing shortage, and sent more dispirited people shuffling to the discomfort and diseases of Canvastown.

On November 25, 1783, a victorious American army marched into New York a few hours after the last British soldier sailed away. The New York that the Americans had evacuated in 1776 was quite literally in ashes. There had been no recovery since the fires of 1776 and '78. A sizable portion of New York was a mass of charred walls and solitary chimneys, of rubble and ruin. Trinity Church offered terrible witness to the fire and to seven years of neglect—it had not been rebuilt, and all that was left was a blackened skeleton.

The city's fire service was in ruins, too. Most of the department's engines were out of service, and it required no great flight of imagination to understand the dangers the city's new government faced in case another large fire broke out. Two days after the British left for good, four of the city's leading firemen, John Dash, George Stanton, Francis Dominick, and Jeronimus Alstyne, sent a desperate petition to George Clinton, who would lead New York into the new era as the new state's governor. These men had served as "fire engineers" during the British occupation, and clearly they were worried that their association with the defeated regime would be held against them. They took great pains to point out that they had "always gain'd applause from the Citizens for our good Conduct in the Alarming times of Fire in this City—Should it please your Excellency to Continue us in this office under your Administration we will always Act with such Conduct as we make no Doubt will, when Called upon in Time of Fire gain the applause of your Excellency."

His Excellency chose to withhold his applause, for the moment anyway, while he and General Washington inspected what was left of the Fire Department's equipment. It was in appalling condition. Over the next three years, New York's municipal government ordered new fire engines, reorganized engine and ladder companies, and recruited new volunteer firemen, continuing the tradition of offering exemptions from jury and militia service. This massive rebuilding effort culminated on February 15, 1786, when the Common Council authorized the creation of a new Fire Department with 300 men, fifteen engine companies, and two hook-and-ladder companies. The four men who had fairly begged Governor Clinton for their jobs discovered the price of their service during the occupation. Five men with the title of engineer were appointed to oversee the new department, but none of the four petitioners was included among the new leaders. One of the five engineers, William Ellsworth, eventually was named chief engineer.

The independent city of Brooklyn joined the revolution in firefighting with this engine, brought into service in 1785.

Indeed, the department was nearly purged of the 253 firemen who were serving as volunteers under the British when they handed control of the city over to the American army, and new firefighters were named. Many of the new firemen were veterans of Washington's army. Who would expect them to take orders from engineers who once answered to British military governors, or to serve with men who had served the occupiers? Those firemen from the old order who did manage to make the transition to the new regime served as firemen or as part of the new force of fire wardens, who helped supervise the bucket brigades, which were still manned by citizen volunteers.

In keeping with the new nation's spirit of democracy and republicanism, New York fire companies elected their own foremen, rather than allow the council to appoint them. This led to the creation of what Lowell W. Limpus, a historian of the Fire Department, called a "miniature republic" within the ranks of the city's firemen. The phrase is only a slight exaggeration. As the Department grew, it would come to regard itself as a force separate and apart not only from the everyday citizenry but also from the city's political leaders. The bonds of shared danger and mutual dependence, along with the firemen's embrace of republican ideals of liberty and democracy, led the volunteers to demand a direct role in running the Department in 1792. It was a remarkably aggressive position in a city whose leaders were, for the most part, from aristocratic merchant families. The firemen, by contrast, were tradesmen

The Fireman, N°1.

Running to a Fire.
A Collision.

Never get in the way of a firefighter
with a speaking trumpet: This woman,
laden with fruit and vegetables,
learned that lesson the hard way.

and craftsmen, and they owed their appointment to the Common
Council or the mayor.

With the conflagration of 1776 still fresh in the civic memory, the
city's political leaders were in no position to argue with the rank and file.
Administration of the department, until now in the hands of council-
appointed engineers and foremen elected by individual companies,
became an exercise in power sharing between management and labor.
Large fire companies were allowed to elect two delegates apiece to a
new administrative board; smaller companies elected one member. A
single engineer would represent the interests of the department's com-
manders. At around the same time, firemen organized a special fund to
raise money for families of "for the relief of. . . disabled Firemen, or

their families." This fund, too, would be under the control of the firemen themselves, through their elected delegates.

A miniature republic indeed. In these early years of the American republic, the firemen of New York established a measure of independence from the city's civilian leaders and from the opinions of civic elites—even though some firemen went on to serve on the Common Council or in other elected positions. Succeeding generations would guard this tradition of independence and exclusivity with zeal and pride, often in the face of immense political and social pressure.

New York served as the nation's unofficial capital beginning in 1785, and as its actual seat of government from 1789 to 1790. In that time the city's spirit and, more important, its economy were restored. The rubble left by the British was rapidly swept away in a torrent of new construction and growth. The city, thanks to one of its great champions, Alexander Hamilton, became a center not only of trade but of finance.

Fortunately, the post-Revolution fire department found few opportunities to show off its new equipment and sense of discipline, for weeks often passed without a fire, although the firemen continued to drill once a month. But rare though they were, fire alarms certainly added to the city's excitement. Once the alarm sounded, firemen would drag their engines to the scene of a blaze, ignoring the trend in other cities to employ horses for such drudgery. Other groups of firemen raced behind the engines with poles laden with leather buckets. The mayor and aldermen would arrive—by city law, the firemen were subject to the commands of politicians at a fire scene. (This indignity was suffered until their chief was given authority over actual firefighting in 1805.) All the while, company foremen shouted instructions through speaking trumpets or tried to keep the streets clear so the engines could get through.

Fire, financial disaster, and the specter of racial tension once again became a combustible combination in the first real trial of the city's new and improved fire department. Once again, the fire started along the East River waterfront, and as usual, it broke out at an ungodly hour, one o'clock on the morning of December 9, 1796. Firemen arrived to find houses, warehouses and stores already engulfed in flames. Between fifty and seventy buildings were destroyed, at a cost of a million dollars. Fire, it seemed, was New York's curse.

Likewise, the danger of arson fires seemed inextricably linked in many people's minds to the city's minority population. A newspaper called *The Minerva,* published by Noah Webster, warned readers that the flames of December 9 might be part of a wider conflagration. "It is no longer a doubt, it is a fact, that there is a combination of incendiaries in this city, aiming to wrap the whole of it in flames," the paper warned. And who might these incendiaries be? The editors noted that a *black* man—the editors' italics—had been sent to prison on suspicion of arson. "Rouse, fellow citizens and magistrates! Your lives and property are at stake. Double your night-watch and confine your servants." There was no evidence that arsonists of any color were intent on burning down the city.

A renewed effort to prevent major fires from starting and spreading was set in motion. There was another round of stricter building regulations, and the Common Council won the power to order the destruction of derelict structures. Nevertheless, a select committee of the council reported in 1803 that "the means imployed in the extinguishment of Fire are susceptible of considerable improvement." In addition to recommending larger fire engines and other measures—such as ordering the mayor and council members to report to fires carrying a seven-foot staff as identification and a "convenient Speaking trumpet" so everyone would know who was in charge—the council soon began buying the latest craze in firefighting devices: hoses. Made of linen or leather, hoses had been in use since the late seventeenth century, but regardless of what they were made of they were leaky and undependable, particularly the couplings. In the early 1800s, improvements in couplings finally resulted in water-tight connections, making it possible to pump water from engine to engine, and finally to the fire. A relay system of engines, and then, starting around 1815, the construction of modern hydrants, quickly replaced the city's colorful but archaic bucket brigades. It was just as well. New Yorkers, required by law to have three buckets in their homes, were tired of tossing them into the street as firemen passed by, only to have them disappear after the fire was extinguished. Residents in the city's Third Ward finally refused to oblige when firemen raced through the streets shouting, "Throw out your buckets!" Before the hoses arrived, the city bought 1,000 buckets to make up for those the Third Ward declined to hand over.

By the early 1820s, the department had grown to 1,200 firefighters in forty-six engine companies, four hook-and-ladder companies and one company whose job it was to bring hose, lots of hose, to fires. The firefighters, based in nearly fifty firehouses scattered around the city, were fast becoming neighborhood legends. They certainly were colorful characters—literally. Along with their black leather fire caps, they started wearing bright red shirts (which soon became all the rage with the city's young men) along with dark trousers and great, wide suspenders of various hues. Neighborhood firehouses began to function as social halls and political clubhouses, as popular firefighters held court to the admiring citizenry. They were seen as role models, and apparently were expected to carry themselves as such. One firefighter was fined a dollar for referring to a colleague as a "damned old Dutch hog." Authorities did not specify which adjective it was that met with their disapproval.

So popular were the firefighters, and the firehouses, that a no doubt envious Common Council complained about the "disorder and confusion" at fires caused by boys and young men trying to help the firefighters. The extra hands were called "volunteers," leading to a sort of confusion the Council loathed, since the firefighters themselves were "volunteers." In any case, the council ordered the chief engineer to order the companies to dispense "with the services of the Volunteers." The firefighters cheerfully ignored this directive.

But New Yorkers had more important matters to attend to than the volunteer flap. In 1822, an outbreak of yellow fever in a fashionable part of downtown led to a mass exodus of rich and poor from the city, an exodus that included the Fire Department. Their fears were entirely justified, for yellow fever had killed 2,000 New Yorkers in 1798. The *New York Evening Post* of August 24, 1822—the height of the epidemic—listed the names of thirty-five people who had died of the fever since July 17. Two days later, the paper called for "the acid fumigation of the infected district." The newspaper itself moved its offices uptown, to

Broadway between Spring and Prince streets, away from the "infected district" of downtown.

The firefighters soon returned, and they were quickly reminded that for all the firehouse jocularity, they were engaged in a dangerous mission, one made increasingly difficult as the city continued its astonishing growth in population and geography. Two firemen died in the line of duty at a fire on Maiden Lane in March 1827, and another, a year later.

By then, New York had already had entered on a new phase in its history, in which commerce would lead to untold growth and prosperity—and its firefighters would be given the task of protecting ever more lives and ever more property. On November 4, 1825, Governor De Witt Clinton heralded the new era when he poured water from Lake Erie into the Lower Bay, the outermost reaches of New York Harbor. This mingling of waters was a symbolic representation of the opening of the Erie Canal and the creation of a water transport route connecting the American heartland and the Atlantic Ocean.

From this union would spring the mightiest city in the world.

CHAPTER THREE

A NATIONAL CALAMITY

TEN YEARS AFTER THE GREAT "Wedding of the Waters" ceremony that ritually united New York and its harbor with the riches of the west, the city was thriving. By 1835, New Yorkers had realized the promise of the Erie Canal, and then some. A European visitor, observing the city's bustling commercial center in and around Wall Street and Hanover Square, said that New York accounted for "nearly the whole commerce of the country." Not quite, but it was clear that the three-way competition to become America's financial capital was virtually over, for New York was lengths ahead of Boston and Philadelphia.

The city's financial district, home to insurance companies, investment houses, real estate concerns, and import–export firms, had become one of the world's great centers of capital and industry. More than half the nation's exports were shipped out of New York, and more than a third of the goods coming into the country passed through warehouses along the city's waterfront. Railroads, already under construction, soon would link Manhattan north to south and make the city even more accessible to business and trade. Chestnut Street in Philadelphia might claim the Bank of the United States, but it was Wall Street that would become synonymous with American commerce and finance.

As Philip Hone, one of the city's prominent citizens, surveyed the growth and prosperity of this city he so loved, he was not entirely satisfied. Limitless though the city's prospects seemed, Hone, who had been mayor in 1826–27, detected a danger that grew more threatening as New York expanded northward and buildings became larger and higher. "The frequency of fires in the upper part of the city has of late caused serious alarm," he wrote in his diary. "Scarcely a night passes without our citizens being awakened by the cry of Fire!, and it is much to be feared that our firemen will be discouraged by the hardships they suffer." Hone's fears were both personal and professional. One of New York's leading aristocrats, he was a tall, elegant man who took great pride in the city's rise from the ashes of 1776 and the long British occupation. He and his wife, Catherine, also took satisfaction from the company of landed, established families like their own—a "small patrician band" that impressed visiting Europeans. The Hones lived in a mansion at 235 Broadway, where they entertained some of the nation's leading political figures, including Henry Clay and Daniel Webster. Philip Hone's fate and that of his family and fortune was entwined with that of the city he had helped build.

Hone also was a director of a fire insurance company, and was hardly the only leading figure with a financial stake in that precarious, though potentially lucrative, business. Mayor Cornelius Lawrence, elected in 1834, and a number of Common Council members either held stock or served on a company board in one or more of the city's twenty-six fire insurance companies. A catastrophic fire would spell not only the ruin of these companies but potentially also the wealth and prestige of their aristocratic stockholders. One company executive, John Pintard, wrote of a fire in the financial district in 1826 which cost his company, Mutual Insurance, between $30,000 and $40,000, leaving him "totally prostrate. . . God's will be done." In 1834, insurance companies paid one million dollars in claims after a series of fires in the city's dry-goods district, home to stores that sold clothing, fabric, and other flammable materials.

From bell towers like this one in Harlem, New Yorkers in the nineteenth century kept a lookout for flames and smoke.

Hone, Lawrence, and the city's elders took aggressive measures to protect their personal, professional, and civic investment in this fledgling capital of commerce. New bell towers were rising throughout the city to sound alarms, and from a cupola atop City Hall, a watchman monitored the streets twenty-four hours a day, looking for the first signs of fire.

Such precautions, while prudent, would mean nothing without a reliable source of water. This years-old problem would require a long-term solution, one that would be far more expensive and far more difficult than erecting a few bell towers. There was serious talk of replacing the city's brackish supply of fresh water with water from the Croton River in Westchester County, north of the city, but such a massive project, though inevitable, was years away from fruition in 1835. In the meantime, beginning in the late 1820s, the city built forty cisterns in strategic locations for use during fire emergencies. The water supply as a firefighting resource remained dubious at best, and an outbreak of cholera in 1834 proved that the city's water stores not only were inadequate, but could also be lethal.

Hone's worry about the firefighters' morale in the face of almost nightly alarms and limited resources was misplaced, however. The volunteers enjoyed the respect and awe of their fellow citizens, particularly boys and young men, and their sacrifices prompted great displays of civic mourning. When two members of Engine Co. 13, Eugene Underhill and F. A. Ward, were killed at a fire on Pearl Street on July 1, 1834, a huge funeral procession made up of relatives, firefighters, and members of the public escorted the bodies up Broadway and across Varick Street to a cemetery. Engraved on a monument built to their memory were the words, "They were buried as they were found, side by side."

So despite the risks, New York's firemen seemed a contented lot. *America's Own and Fireman's Journal,* an early trade magazine, noted that the volunteer firemen would "not attempt for money what they would voluntarily do for the sake of emulation." The *New York Spy,* a departmental journal, noted the "fondness of firemen for the hazards and duties of their station." The problem was that the hazards and duties were many, and the number of firemen few. The Department's growth did not match the pace of the city's through the 1820s and into the 1830s. With the northern boundary of the city pushing toward Forty-second Street and the population approaching 270,000, there were about 1,500 firemen with fifty-six engines, six hook-and-ladder rigs, and five hose carts, compared with about 1,200 firemen in the early 1820s, when the population was about 125,000. What the firefighters lacked in numbers, however, they made up in leadership. In 1835, the chief engineer was a handsome, curly-haired firefighting veteran named James Gulick, who had assumed the post in 1831.

Gulick's size alone—six feet, two inches—was enough to intimidate not just his subordinates but also the gangs of tough street characters who were beginning to attach themselves to the Fire Department. He was burly, too, and fearless, which made him all the more formidable to friend and foe alike. Even as chief, he shared the risks of his men, and helped save their lives on several occasions with quick decisions and personal bravery.

He was a popular figure from his earliest years as a firefighter. He had been elected foreman of his outfit, Engine Co. 11, before winning election as an assistant engineer in 1824. But his popularity was based on something more than back-slapping amiability. He clearly was a man who could be trusted with the lives of his men. After his election as chief engineer, he embarked on a series of reforms aimed at instilling greater discipline and cooperation among the volunteers. A foreman who lent his company's engine to other companies risked immediate expulsion under Gulick's crackdown, and the chief formed hydrant companies to stop the colorful practice of deploying scouts to place barrels over hydrants to hide them from rival engine companies. These measures, together with Gulick's emphasis on a rudimentary sense of professionalism from men who were getting no pay for their labors, only inspired greater affection. The firemen even forgave Gulick's efforts to introduce horsepower, in defiance of the department's macho tradition of pulling their rigs through the streets. Gulick bought the department's first horses in 1832—not in a full-fledged effort to begin modernizing the department, but as a concession to grim reality. Cholera was on the march that summer and eventually killed 3,000 people in the city. So many firemen were sick that Gulick was forced to use horses rather than sheer numbers of firemen to pull the engines to fires.

Shortly after assuming command of the department, Gulick was presented with a ceremonial silver speaking trumpet as a token of his men's affection. The inscription left little mystery about the root of Gulick's popularity. It spoke of "the high estimation in which we hold his official capacities as a fireman." The following year, he showed just how capable a fireman he was. One of his subordinates, Morris Franklin, was trapped in the attic of a burning building on Park Place. Gulick charged into the building alone, freed the trapped fireman, and brought him out to safety. Franklin, as it happened, was one of the founders of a hardy tradition in New York firefighting. He was the son of a firefighter, indeed, of a chief engineer: Thomas Franklin had been an active fireman for more than forty years and the department's chief from 1811 to 1824. He was known to his men as "Uncle Tommy." Gulick's men gave him a silver pitcher to commemorate Morris Franklin's rescue.

About the only people in civic life who didn't love James Gulick were, ominously, members of the Common Council, particularly those from Tammany Hall, the all-powerful local Democratic club. The Tammany men preferred their fire chiefs to be agreeable and pliable. Gulick was neither. In fact, he seemed to disdain politicians and their

SO OTHERS
MIGHT LIVE

· · ·

41

interference in the Department's operations. And Gulick had the power to act on his disdain, for in a reorganization of the department in 1831, the chief engineer had been given the additional title of commissioner, meaning that he now had unprecedented authority over the Fire Department's administration and personnel. Aldermen accustomed to stooped deference from chief engineers were confronted with the steel spine of Gulick's independence and righteousness. A confrontation was inevitable, and when it came, it was bitter and ugly. Worse, one of its results was that along with their apparatus, firemen would henceforth be forced to drag along their political alliances.

James Gulick's volunteers presented this pitcher to him as a token of their affection.

The last few months of 1835 were extremely busy for Gulick's men, and were fatal for a handful of residents, including a thirteen-year-old boy named George W. Baker, who died in a fire on Fulton Street in September. The worst fire, in terms of property loss if not casualties, broke out on August 12 on Ann Street. Some fifty structures were engulfed, five persons were killed, and nearly 1,000 people lost their jobs when their places of employment were reduced to ashes. City elders were especially disheartened because many of the buildings were fairly new and, in keeping with the city's fire codes, were built of brick rather than wood.

None of the other fires in late summer and throughout the fall was as dramatic, and most were in buildings that the *New York Evening Post* described as of "small" value, though "the inconvenience to the occupants is very great." As an example, the *Evening Post* reported that a routine fire on October 30 in a three-story frame house at 103 Anthony Street left "a number of. . . tenants" without "furniture or clothing." Minor outbreaks, while not threatening the stability of the city's insurance companies or the lives of firemen, could be a catastrophe for poor people with no insurance and no refuge. And even small fires attracted all manner of curious citizens, not all of whom were necessarily interested in watching the firemen go about their exciting business. During a blaze in September, 1835, at Niblo's Gardens, an old New York landmark, firemen spotted a woman emerging from the burning building with an expensive watch chain partially concealed by her shawl. She was arrested after she was found to be carrying $200 worth of jewelry taken from the restaurant. Newspaper reports identified her as Mary McLaughlin, a "most worthless character."

The approach of winter meant that the already harried and overworked firemen could expect to be even busier, as rich and poor alike lit fires to keep their dwellings and businesses warm. On the night of December 14, 1835, two large fires wiped out thirteen buildings and two shops. All 1,500 firemen were summoned to the blazes, and they worked through a freezing, miserable night before returning home wet, cold, and exhausted. Meanwhile, the city's cisterns were nearly depleted.

The weather was even more severe two nights later, on Wednesday, December 16. By nightfall, as shops and businesses in the financial district closed, the temperature dipped below zero. The Hudson River was frozen, and snow was piled up as high as two feet in some places. The editors of a new daily newspaper, the *New York Herald,* on that day had turned their thoughts to the city's less fortunate, and to the perceived indifference of the city's leaders, editorializing: "We pity the poor. . . . They are suffering terribly. Is it not time to call a meeting in every ward for the relief of the poor? Come—bustle, bustle, ye men of wealth. Philip Hone. . . Cornelius W. Lawrence—be stirring for the poor. No muffling up in your princely sables, forgetting the houseless, unfed poor."

At nine o'clock, a watchman named William Hayes was making his rounds through the financial district, doing his best to ward off the cold, made all the more cruel by a howling wind off the harbor. When he crossed the intersection of Exchange and Pearl streets, he smelled smoke. He hailed some of the other watchmen who were patrolling the area, and they raced to Merchant Street (now Hanover Street), where they spotted a fire in a five-story warehouse with shops on the ground level. Forcing open a door, they found the interior "in flames from cel-

Horrified New Yorkers watched from the street as an inferno ripped through the financial district in 1835. When the fires finally were extinguished, New York looked to Washington for help.

lar to roof," as Hayes later recalled. "I can tell you we shut that door mighty quick."

Engine Co. 1 was first on the scene. The fire hadn't spread beyond the warehouse, and the men were soon desperately working the engine's hand pumps, or "brakes," to get a stream of water on the flames. For a few moments, it seemed possible that the evening's only casualty would be the warehouse. But such hopes were short-lived. The fire, whipped by gale-force winds, quickly became an inferno. Within fifteen or twenty minutes, Hayes reported, fifty buildings in the financial district were on fire. As required by law, the city's aldermen hurried to the scene, carrying their staff of office as identification. The city's bell towers began ringing incessantly, alerting firemen still recovering from their ordeal two nights before to return to work. This time, though, the situation was far more dire, and far more dangerous. They left the warmth of their homes and raced to their firehouses, heads down to protect themselves from the cutting wind. Then, the familiar routine, as they donned their leather fire caps and grabbed hold of the ropes attached to their engines. The flickering orange sky told them that this would be a far bigger job than the fires two nights ago, a far bigger blaze, perhaps, than any of them had ever seen.

As quickly as the fire spread, so did word of an impending catastrophe. Catherine Burnhans Wynkoop, the daughter of a merchant who owned a store on Pearl Street, heard shouts of "Fire!" just outside the family's home on nearby Greenwich Street. Her father raced toward the flames, expecting to find his store in ruins. Firemen were deployed along Pearl Street to try to stop the blaze from spreading, but it was a losing battle. Before long, the light from the fire was so bright that it lit up the bedrooms of young Catherine and her family so brightly that they couldn't go back to sleep.

A *Herald* reporter hurried to the fire and filed a terse dispatch in time for the morning edition. "At ten o'clock, when we left that scene, probably thirty or forty of the most valuable and richest dry goods stores in the city were burned down or on fire," the reporter wrote. "It was expected that it would sweep away the whole section of the city. . . . The loss of property cannot be estimated—probably *several millions*."

Chief Gulick's men deployed ladders to rooftops and stretched hose from block to block, but they were increasingly helpless in the face of the fire's ferocity. Samuel Swartout, who held the important political office of collector of the Port of New York (he collected all the port duties), put himself to work with members of an engine company, as, he said, "a good citizen should." Watching the gathering horror around Wall Street, he became convinced that the city was doomed. Hydrants froze, becoming useless; when water could be deployed, the whipping winds often blew it back in the faces of the firemen. The firemen with Swartout were beginning to panic. He saw Gulick and asked, "What is to become of us?" The chief dispatched a dozen engine companies to the East River, hoping they could tap into the water there, get a hose going, and then form a relay of engines to deliver a stream of water to the burning buildings. But a heavy layer of ice covered the river near the piers. Men assigned to ladder companies frantically cut holes in the ice with their pike-like hooks, and finally got water running through the engines and hoses, but the river water soon froze in the hoses. Desperate, firemen dumped alcohol on the engines, hoping to melt the buildup of ice. They used allotments of brandy to keep themselves warm, but not in the usual way. Rather than drink it, they poured the stuff into their boots to melt the ice inside. All the while hellish scenes surrounded them: Buildings caught fire and were reduced to ashes before they could react; new blazes broke out every few minutes; wind-fed flames leaped from block to block. A frustrated Gulick ordered wet blankets placed on a wooden building housing the New York Insurance Company. It was the only protection he could offer. Meanwhile, merchants desperate to save what they could tossed their inventory into the street from upper-story windows. Manifests, inventory lists, and other paperwork swirled in the air; some were found the next day in the New Jersey Meadowlands. Burning embers were carried through the air above the East River, setting fire to rooftops in Brooklyn.

A *Herald* reporter returned to the fire as the city's newspapers prepared extra editions. The horror of the scene (and the press of deadline) was evident in the terse, despairing report under a headline "Terrible Conflagration": "Eleven o'clock—Just came from the scene. From Wall Street to Hanover Square, and from Merchants' Exchange to the East River, all on fire. About 300 stores burned, and burning down. . . . About 1000 merchants ruined, and several Insurance Companies gone. Many lives lost. . . Gracious Heaven! Is it a punishment for our madness? Forgive us our sins as we forgive those that sin against us!"

Firemen in Philadelphia, ninety miles to the south, saw an orange glow in the sky and rushed to their firehouses, assuming the blaze was nearby. When word reached them that the fire was in New York, they packed up their gear and headed north, hoping to arrive in time to help their comrades. Volunteers in Brooklyn and across the Hudson River scrambled to their rigs and began to make their way to the scene without being asked. Eyewitnesses described "an ocean of fire. . . with roaring, rolling, burning waves, surging onward and upward." Walls and chimneys came crashing to the ground, scattering firemen. A series of explosions rocked the South Street waterfront as a warehouse filled with

One of downtown
New York's
signature
buildings, the
Merchants'
Exchange,
burns in 1835.

sperm oil caught fire. Iron shutters and copper roofs melted in the
intense heat.

The blaze moved toward one of the city's great buildings, the
Merchants' Exchange, on Wall Street. During the night, merchants trying to salvage their huge inventories of tea, silk, and other imports had
been hauling what they could to this building, which was built of marble
and was considered fireproof. The Merchants' Exchange was New
York's cathedral of commerce, a great-columned three-story edifice
crowned by an impressive cupola. Inside, in addition to the exchanges,
were a post office, the offices of the Chamber of Commerce, and several telegraph and newspaper offices. A fifteen-foot statue of Alexander
Hamilton, who had done so much to make New York a financial capital,
had been placed in the building's rotunda several months before.
Somewhere out in the chaotic streets, Hamilton's son, James Hamilton,
was assisting the futile efforts to save the city while the larger-than-life
image of his father, holding a scroll in his left hand, formed a defiant sil-
houette against the flames.

The Merchants' Exchange turned out to be no match for the fire.
Witnesses saw flames in the building by 12:30; ninety minutes later, it
was fully engulfed. The inventories burned along with everything else.
Gulick ordered his men, many of them with nothing left to do, nothing
left to fight with, to help merchants move their stock out of other

threatened buildings. The sidewalks near Bowling Green were littered with goods from around the world—linens, tea, crockery—hurriedly removed from stores and warehouses. A hat merchant offered free hats to anybody who would help him move his stock out of danger.

But where would that be? Water Street, Front Street, South Street, and Hanover Square were being reduced to ruins. The heart of New York's financial district, the capital of American commerce, was in flames. Even ships docked along the East Side piers were ablaze. And the Fire Department's hoses lay on the icy ground, stiff, frozen, and useless.

The flames threatened the offices on Pearl Street of one of the city's best-known merchants, a silk importer and Massachusetts native named Arthur Tappan. In recent years, Tappan and his family had grown accustomed to threats of a different kind. As president of the American Antislavery Society and one of the city's leading abolitionists, Tappan knew that his well-being, and possibly his life, could not be assured from one day to the next. A vigilante group in Louisiana had offered a reward of $50,000 to anyone who could spirit Tappan away from New York to face Southern justice. Other Southern groups called for more violent means of silencing him.

Even in his adopted city, where he was one of the business community's most generous philanthropists, the devout and stern Tappan was not a universally popular figure. Tappan's employees were expected to attend church daily, and were prohibited from gambling and going to the theater. The city's business leaders, though they tended to regard the status quo on slavery as best for business, nevertheless read his newspaper, the *Journal of Commerce*.

Tensions over slavery were on the rise throughout the antebellum period, and in the summer of 1834, a pro-slavery mob had set out to attack Tappan's home, but they changed course and invaded his brother Lewis's home instead. Lewis Tappan and his family escaped, but the house was destroyed. The next day, rock-throwing crowds laid siege to Arthur Tappan's store and were not driven off until Tappan's employees produced firearms and were joined by the city's watchmen. Tappan was forced to install iron shutters on his store as protection against future attacks. Despite these measures, and even though his building was built of stone, no fire insurance company would underwrite a policy for Tappan.

Now, the conflagration that was destroying New York was about to do what Tappan's political enemies had only dreamed of. As flames neared Tappan & Co., word of the danger made its way to the crowds gathered near the fires. Several African Americans raced to the store and, at risk of their lives, saved their champion's merchandise and records. Eventually the building was engulfed in flames, but the store's goods were saved.

Charles King, editor of the *New York American,* left his home on Bleeker Street when a young relative told him that downtown was burning. The *American*'s office was in danger, and King arrived to find printers and workmen frantically moving equipment out of the building. King joined the rescue effort until the *American*'s roof caught fire. Assuming command, the editor ordered everybody out of the building. Within fifteen minutes, the offices were in ashes. King, a forty-year resident of the city, had never seen anything so frightening. Worse yet, buildings were catching fire all around him, and there was not a working Fire Department hose to be found. They were frozen solid. King decided that something else, "some other power," he later said, would be required to save the city from destruction. He left the ruins of his office and sought out Mayor Lawrence. The narrow streets were filled with useless fire engines, panic-stricken merchants and businessmen, frustrated firemen, city officials, and piles of merchandise. Vandals took advantage of the chaos and disorder, helping themselves to goods piled in the street. Flames were leaping higher into the freezing night air, reaching for the cupola atop the Merchants' Exchange, the symbol of the city and its grand ambitions. The cupola eventually succumbed, crashing through the building's rotunda and smashing down on the statue of Alexander Hamilton.

At about 1 A.M., Charles King found Lawrence with several alderman and other civic leaders on Garden Street (present-day Exchange Place). Terrified citizens gathered nearby, watching their civic leaders confer. King knew the mayor had the power to blow up private property to check the spread of fire. He told the mayor that he had no choice but to exercise that right. The mayor hesitated. A stockholder in an insurance company, a member of the city's business class, he naturally would abhor the deliberate destruction of private property. No mayor had ever made such a drastic decision. But the aldermen and others in his party, including Colonel Robert Temple, an off-duty army officer, agreed with King.

"Where will I get the powder?" the mayor finally asked. King assured him there was gunpowder to be had at the navy facilities across the icy East River.

"How can I go to the Navy Yard?" Lawrence asked. The editor volunteered to make the journey himself if Lawrence wrote an order to the yard's commanding officer requesting a consignment of gunpowder. Lawrence ducked into a building, wrote out the order, and gave it to King. Meanwhile, Colonel Temple agreed to row to a fort on Governor's Island, just off the southern tip of Manhattan, to look for more powder.

King was rowed across the icy East River to the frigate *Hudson,* where he met with the Navy Yard's commodore, a gout-ridden officer who had been enjoying a quiet evening in front of a fire, while, a mile away, New York burned. The commodore approved Mayor Lawrence's request, and ordered several sailors to sail a barge to Red Hook, Brooklyn, where the powder was stored, and bring it to New York. King and several sailors and marines recrossed the river, picking their way through ice floes. All the while, Mayor Lawrence and James Hamilton formed a scavenging party to search for gunpowder in nearby shops.

Colonel Temple also collected some powder on Governors Island. He put several 100-pound kegs in his rowboat— realizing, he later recalled, what a "crazy little thing" his vessel was as it was nearly swamped during the short journey back to Manhattan. Once ashore, he left the powder with somebody he described only as "a person of authority," and returned to the inferno.

The powder-laden barge from Red Hook arrived at the foot of Wall Street. Charles King arrived with his party shortly afterward, and found Mayor Lawrence back on Garden Street, surrounded yet again by desperate citizens. The mayor hurried to Wall Street to supervise the powder delivery. King joined a column of sailors carrying the kegs to

Flames from the Great Fire of 1835 could be seen for miles, and an orange glow was visible as far away as Philadelphia.

Garden Street, through a terrifying combination of fire and ice. "I was concerned," King later said, "for the ground was frozen and covered with ice, and it was raining fire." The sailors took off their jackets and wrapped them around the powder kegs to ward off burning embers. It meant they had nothing but their shirts to protect them against the gale-force winds and subzero temperatures. But better to be freezing than to be blown to bits.

When the powder was collected, somewhere between two and three o'clock, Mayor Lawrence summoned Captain James Swift, a former general-in-chief of the Army Corps of Engineers, who happened to be in the city that night. He had joined James Hamilton on a mission to identify buildings whose destruction might help stop the spreading flames. Swift and Lawrence conferred in the vicinity of Broad and Nassau streets, Lawrence asking Swift whether he could supervise a planned explosion. Swift said he could, but Lawrence, still anxious about giving an order to destroy property, asked Swift if blowing up buildings in the fire's path really would do any good. Swift reassured him, telling him that 150 pounds of powder would be enough to take down a building without causing damage to other structures.

The sailors were ordered to a grocery store at 48 Exchange Place, the site Swift and Hamilton had settled on. The building was near the intersection of Broad Street and Exchange Place—the great fear was that the fire would leap Broad Street and move west and north. There would be nothing, then, to stop it from consuming the residential neighborhoods outside the financial district. At about 4 A.M., the sailors began placing powder kegs in the store's basement. About an hour later, huddled with the mayor and other officials near the intersection, Hamilton checked his watch and said to Lawrence, "It's now past five o'clock, and if anything is to be done in the matter, it should be done now."

Even at this desperate hour, as the fire licked at the city's residential neighborhoods, Lawrence hesitated. He turned to a man he regarded as better suited to the work of destruction: Chief Engineer James Gulick, standing at Lawrence's side. The mayor said to him, "It is your duty, as chief engineer, to set off the powder." Gulick, never patient with politicians and suspicious of their motives, saw through Lawrence's maneuver. Very likely he knew that the law authorizing this destruction specifically deputized the mayor, and not the chief engineer, to give the order. So Gulick would have none of it, replying haughtily that he dealt "not with powder, but with water." Lawrence turned to James Hamilton, who was eager to get the job over with. He lit the charge— but nothing happened. Hamilton ventured out from the crowd surrounding the mayor and walked to the doomed store to check the charges. He could see that the fuse leading into the basement was on fire, so he quickly returned, anticipating a blast.

Still there was no explosion. Five minutes went by, and Hamilton once again started down the street to check on the explosives. He thought better of it after a few steps, which was lucky for him. There was an explosion, and, to the surprise of skeptical onlookers, the building imploded. But the effect was more spectacular than planned. The building next door, at 50 Exchange Place, promptly caught fire. Within ten minutes, the next building, 52 Exchange Place, was filled with explosives and blown up to prevent the fire at 50 Exchange Plaza from spreading, and to check the blaze as it moved toward Broad Street. Once again the building imploded, but this time it did not spread the fire, but created a hole where the flames found no fuel. The strategy was working. Several other buildings were blown up, and the horrendous inferno, deprived of fuel, began to capitulate.

There was more drama before the night was through. At about 4 A.M., even as preparations were under way on Exchange Place, the shingled roof of the Tontine Coffee House on the north side of Wall Street, another of the district's landmarks, began to burn, the blaze on its roof marking the northernmost thrust of the conflagration. A passerby who spotted the flames offered to make a $100 contribution to the firemen's relief fund if they could get the blaze under control. Engine Co. 13, under the command of Foreman Zophar Mills, arrived to organize a frantic defense of Wall Street under orders from Chief Gulick. Luckily, some water was available, but Mills knew his hoses couldn't reach the coffee house roof. He ordered his men to drag out tables, kegs, and other furniture from a nearby building to make a makeshift tower, and then deployed Engine 13's nozzle man to the top of it. From there he was able to get a stream of water on the roof. The fire never made it past Wall Street.

As dawn broke, the enormity of the destruction became clear, even as scattered fires put up a stubborn resistance. Fifty-two acres, from Broad Street to South Street, and from Wall Street to an area then called Coenties Slip, lay in ruins. Some 674 buildings, most of them shops, businesses, and warehouses, were destroyed—although the shop owned by the father of young Catherine Burnhans Wynkoop was spared. Between 3,000 and 4,000 people were out of work, their places of businesses gone. Two people were dead, an amazingly low figure considering not only the fire's ferocity but the large number of civilians who were on the scene to watch the devastation or save their merchandise and records—or to take advantage of the mayhem to steal and carouse.

Eventually, more than 400 people would be arrested for looting. It sickened Philip Hone: "The miserable wretches who prowled about the ruins and became beastly drunk on the champagne and other wines and liquors with which the streets and wharves were lined, seemd to exult in the misfortune," Hone wrote in his diary, noting that the prowlers' behavior was made all the worse by such taunts as "This will make the aristocracy haul in their horns." Hone continued, "This cant is the very text from which their leaders teach their deluded followers. It forms part of the warfare of the poor against the rich—a warfare which is destined, I fear, to break the hearts of some of the politicians of Tammany Hall."

James Gordon Bennett, the publisher of the *New York Herald,* the newspaper that had challenged Hone to stop hiding in his sables and help the freezing poor, toured the disaster site at around nine o'clock on the morning of December 17. He was not alone—scores of New Yorkers wandered through the financial district, even as firemen continued to battle scattered fires. The district, normally bustling with commerce, had been reduced to a gigantic salvage site, though not much of use could be found. No business was getting done; and trading on the New York Stock and Exchange Board was suspended, and would remain so for four days.

Bennett made his way down William Street toward the site of the Merchants' Exchange. The southern side of Wall Street was devastated, and just the front walls of the Exchange, covered in smoke, still stood. The street itself was crowded with merchandise, furniture, safes, and piles of debris. Even though soldiers patrolled the streets looking for looters, Bennett saw "boys, men and women, of all colors. . . stealing and pilfering as fast as they could." The suffocating smoke gave them cover as they went about their business, but not every thief got away undetected. Bennett watched as a small boy tried to make off with some merchandise and was caught by an "honest black porter" who tried to turn him over to the authorities. Somebody in the crowd shouted: "Let the scoundrel go." The porter did so, but not before delivering a well-placed kick.

Fire engines were still on the scene, and the exhausted firemen were still coping with frozen hoses and insufficient water. They were joined by volunteers from New Jersey, Westchester County, and, eventually, 400 firemen from Philadelphia. There was no shortage of work for them. Fires were still burning, though they were smaller and more contained than during the night. Flames occasionally leaped into the sky along a portion of William Street, and forty buildings, some seven stories high, were ablaze near the corner of Front Street and Coenties Slip.

The darkened area shows the extent of the catastrophe in downtown Manhattan.

Approaching Wall Street, Bennett found all that remained of Arthur Tappan's *Journal of Commerce*'s offices: a sign. His shop on Pearl Street was also destroyed. Bennett walked toward the East River, feeling colder as the wind off the river grew stronger. He saw a group of people gathered around a fire, warming themselves. For fuel they were using "the richest merchandise and fine furniture from some of the elegant counting rooms" in the district. Another group's fire smelled particularly pungent, and Bennett asked what they were burning. "Tea, sir," a boy responded. "Fine Hyson tea; doesn't it make a fine fire." Some young girls wearing ragged clothing were trying to take away some of the tea, placing boxes of it in baskets. Children gathered around hogsheads of sugar strewn around the wharves. "Boys and girls were eating it as fast as they could," he wrote.

Walking south along Front Street, Bennett found "smoke, ruin, hot bricks" and huge crowds blocking the street. He threaded his way to Bowling Green, just outside the area of devastation, and found rows and rows of imported goods—silks, woolen cloths, linens—stacked along sidewalks.

He pushed his way through crowds milling along Broad Street and reached the Custom House, which already was set up as an emergency post office. Clerks told him they had no idea what had been saved from the post office in the Merchants' Exchange, and what was lost. And they had no idea when regular mail service would resume. Bennett wrote: "On falling in with several of our most respectable citizens, I said, 'Awful! Horrible!' 'Truly, truly,' said they, 'we are all ruined. . . New York is bankrupt. New York is put twenty years back. Philadelphia and Boston will now start ahead of us.' "

Estimates put the damage at $20 million, leading to the bankruptcy of twenty-three of the city's twenty-six fire insurance companies. The *Herald,* which had so recently demanded that the rich pay greater heed to the poor, now sounded a lament for the stockholding classes, saying that "the old respectable families, widows, orphans, aged persons who had invested all their property in Insurance Stocks" would be among "the heaviest sufferers."

Operating on little if any sleep, Mayor Lawrence issued a public statement of sympathy and encouragement on December 17 as firemen battled the last remaining blazes. "Our community has been visited by a fearful calamity," Lawrence's statement read. "A large and valuable section of our city is in ruins. . . . Great as our losses [are], and deeply as we may lament the disastrous visitation, it cannot be doubted that the enterprise and activity of our citizens will be found adequate to repair the evil." Lawrence also convened a special meeting of the Board of Aldermen on that day, asking them to consider "such measures as you deem necessary for the protection of the immense amount of property exposed by the dreadful conflagration last night." Three hundred extra watchmen were deployed in the commercial district, and the city accepted the services of 1,000 citizens who volunteered to stand watch over what the popular press began calling the "burnt district."

The *Herald* immediately grasped the enormity of what had happened to the city's commercial center. The destruction of New York was not a local tragedy; it was, the newspaper wrote, a "national calamity" requiring immediate, and unprecedented, government intervention. The paper called on the governor and the state's lawmakers to "devise measures to sustain the credit of the great capital of the Western Hemisphere. . . . Let Congress immediately apply the vast surplus treasure to the like purpose. The credit of New York is the credit of the nation." Whether or not Nicholas Biddle, president of the Bank of the United States and one of the nation's leading citizens, entirely agreed with that radical assessment, he clearly believed that the fire was no mere local matter and hurried to the city from Philadelphia to meet with local officials. The *Herald* reported that Biddle promised that the central bank would follow the government's lead if Washington lent the city or private businesses money to help cover the enormous losses.

The city's political and civic leaders met at City Hall on December 19—the same day Biddle arrived—and resolved to request financial assistance from the national and state governments. Mayor Lawrence chaired the meeting. Never before had the federal government come to the aid of a distressed locality, but the request came at a time when national legislators were debating how best to spend the federal treasury's surplus revenues of $35 million. Lawrence put together a committee of 125 leading citizens to investigate the fire's causes, recommend changes to the city's housing codes, and lobby for assistance.

Cities around the nation rallied to New York's side. Throughout late December, meetings were held in Boston and Philadelphia—the very cities that figured to benefit by New York's loss—as well as Baltimore, Albany, Utica, Brooklyn, New Orleans, Buffalo and even Montreal, among other places. Philadelphia's Common Council approved a message to Congress asking Washington for the "prompt appropriation of Ten Millions of Dollars to relieve as far as possible the sufferings and injuries of our brethren of New-York." The resolution left it up to Congress to decide whether the $10 million should be an outright gift or a loan. During a Christmas Eve public meeting in Fanueil Hall, Bostonians argued that "it would be just and politic" for the federal government to offer "relief and assistance to New York." These and other cities backed up their words of support with their own pledges of financial and material assistance. The citizens of Montreal were of course in no position to advise Congress on the merits of financial help for New York. So they sent $2,000 to Mayor Lawrence as a contribution from the city's concerned citizens.

Not everybody was so generous, not even close to home. Where some saw calamity, many clergymen saw the wrath of a God made angry by the city's values and morals. From a pulpit in the village of Flushing, now part of Queens, the Reverend William Augustus Muhlenberg pronounced that "this terrible destruction" was "a solemn rebuke from Heaven of that inordinate spirit of money-making, which marks our country in general, and its commercial cities in particular."

But it wasn't just the city's love of commerce that the Reverend Muhlenberg found offensive and worthy of fire and perhaps even brimstone. "When I remember the iniquity there is in that city, along with this mad and excessive spirit of money making. . . when I remember how the Sabbath is violated by the rich and poor. . . when I think of the increasing licentiousness of their youth; men in vice while boys in years—their gambling rooms—the depraving influence of their stage, now more vile and indelicate than ever. . . when I think of these clouds of hell in the very sunshine of the gospel, I feel bold in speaking of judgments, and almost wonder that the flames are not curling to heaven to this very hour," he said. Actually, there still were some flames curling to heaven at that hour, Sunday morning, December 20. Small fires would burn and smolder for many more days, and would continue to inspire dozens of similar sermons from clerics near and far.

Many sermons concerning the fire were published in pamphlet form, and some were a bit more sympathetic than Reverend Muhlenberg's. The Reverend William Ware of the First Congregational Unitarian Church in New York took issue with pronouncements like Muhlenberg's, saying in his homily that "this destruction. . . has but obeyed the physical laws of the universe. We do not call it a judgment." But Reverend Ware did ask his congregation to reflect on larger issues, including the aimless pursuit of material comfort. The fire, he said, "reveals to us [in] a most striking manner the instability of earthly fortune, and reminds us of, and urges us to remember, our connection with and our constant dependence on a higher power. . . . In a single night, how many fortunes were laid low! How many years of anxiety and toil all turned to vanity!"

But for the city's political and business leaders, the toil and anxiety had only just begun. They now had a city to rebuild. The speed with which they organized, and the spirit of cooperation they displayed, pleased a frightened public. Commenting on a public meeting of politicians and businessmen, the *New York Evening Post* reported that "the best possible spirit prevailed. . . . The buoyancy of our business community is truly wonderful." The fires were still smoldering when Arthur Tappan told his employees, "We must rebuild immediately." And so he did, he and scores of other merchants and shop owners. Horrible though the fire was, it opened up to the city the opportunity to create a new commercial district on the ashes of the old one, which, a relic of colonial days, had grown outdated with its narrow and often byzantine street layout. The Common Council urged property owners to come up with a plan "for altering the route and width of the streets before commencing any buildings." Soon, new and wider roads were mapped amid the rubble, and new stores and warehouses began to rise. Even as rebuilding was just beginning, merchants set up temporary quarters in the ruins. Meanwhile, plans already were under way to rebuild the Merchants' Exchange—it would be grander, bigger, and more impressive than ever.

Reconstruction began long before Washington took up the controversial idea that it had an obligation to help. New York State was quick to authorize a loan of $6 million to the city, which itself was an unprecedented act of cooperation. But lawmakers on Capitol Hill were a good deal more cautious when the idea of assisting New York came up for debate a few months after the fire. Rather than offer the city outright reconstruction funds, Congress considered a bill that would authorize refunds to merchants for duties they had paid on imported goods that had been destroyed in the fire. Even this minimal help ran into opposition, primarily from Southern congressmen, because it singled out New York's merchants for help that had never been given others in similar, though less spectacular, catastrophes. But the city gained

Might Live

· · ·

59

an eloquent champion in Congressman Stephen Clarendon Phillips of Massachusetts, who argued that although the assistance being contemplated was unprecedented, the city's merchants had in fact suffered an unprecedented disaster. "The city of New York is, far more distinctively than any other city, the commercial emporium of the United States," Phillips told his colleagues. "That city sustains a relation to the Government and the country which gives her a right at all times to claim from both the most-favorable consideration." Phillips's argument helped win the day, and the bill to refund duties was passed, but it was little more than a symbolic victory. New York had hoped for more direct assistance, and the citizens of Boston, Philadelphia and other cities supported their claim. In essence, and not for the last time, Washington told New York to drop dead.

Even as politicians and businessmen worked in harmony to rebuild a commercial district to suit the modern world of the nineteenth Century, recriminations concerning the Fire Department's performance on December 16–17 were surfacing. In fact, the second-guessing and finger-pointing started as early as December 18, when the Board of Assistant Aldermen considered a resolution that seemed to invite criticism of the volunteer firemen. One of the assistant aldermen complained that "there was no harmony existing amongst the several members of the fire department, no concert of action." The department was "in a state of disorganizaton and confusion." The board adopted a resolution that "the late conflagration should admonish us of the absolute necessity of establishing a more perfect and proper organization of the Fire Department." That admonition was directed at Chief Gulick.

Relations between the firemen and the aldermen had not been especially warm even before the Great Fire of December 16–17. The politicians had been complaining about the increasing number of young men and boys who loitered around firehouses, seeking some bit of reflected glory and admiration. These young men and boys tended to be street kids, poor and uneducated, and though they eagerly helped firemen in the hard work of pulling engines to fires, they also added to the chaos, confusion, and occasional criminality at fires. The firemen tolerated them, not only because they were, in fact, a help but also because so many of them eventually became full-fledged firemen. So when the aldermen criticized the young hangers-on, the firemen became defensive, taking criticism of the young men and boys as criticism of the Department itself. They asked citizens not to confuse "the acts of unruly boys with those of our department."

Whatever the actual intentions of the aldermen's criticism in the past, there was no mistaking their opinion of the Department in the Great Fire's aftermath. And soon there was no mistaking how some firemen felt about the politicians. At eleven o'clock on the night of January 1, 1836, Alderman Samuel Purdy heard the fire bells pealing, and he set out for the fire scene, as the law required. The fire was out by the time he got there, so he turned around and started back home via Chatham Street. When the men of Engine Co. 10 came roaring down the street, Purdy, carrying his staff, which identified him as a member of the Common Council, yelled, "Gentlemen, the fire is out."

One of the firemen yelled back, "Get out of the way with your staff," and amplified the remark with language that was deemed unsuitable for print in newspaper coverage of the incident. When Purdy asked his interlocutor to identify himself, another fireman, Luke Usher, told him it was none of his business, and took the opportunity to complain that the Common Council treated firemen "like dogs." Usher then pushed Purdy with one hand and belted him with the other. Another fireman did likewise. Purdy backed off and reminded the firemen that he was an alderman, which, alas for him, was precisely the point. Several more firemen struck him and he fell to the ground, his face severely bruised. Purdy picked himself up, retreated, and then returned with help. Two firemen, Usher and the inaptly named John Lightbody, were arrested and brought to the city's watch house. Later on that night, a group of twenty to twenty-five firemen tried to storm the watch house to rescue Usher and Lightbody, but they were turned back by the city's watchmen.

Purdy's colleagues on the Common Council quite properly regarded an attack on one of their number as an attack on all. And they were quick to respond with a foray against the prevailing firehouse culture, asserting that the firemen were "no longer worthy of the trust reposed in them." A little more than three weeks after the assault, on January 25, the Board of Aldermen passed a resolution condemning the "young men who appear at fires. . . who, by their insubordination, their utter lawlessness, and the consequent confusion they cause, have been a continual source of annoyance." The aldermen resolved that "it shall be the duty of all members of the Fire Department. . . to prevent all persons not belonging to the department, and especially *boys,* from entering any house, or handling any apparatus belonging to the department." A special committee was impaneled to investigate the assault on Purdy, and ten members of Engine Co. 10 were suspended after they refused to testify before the panel. Even Chief Gulick, who made it a personal crusade to establish better discipline in the Department, nevertheless declined to cooperate in the investigation, displaying yet again his suspicion of the city's political class. Eventually, nine members of Engine Co. 10 were expelled because of their behavior on January 1.

Still, the aldermen knew just how much the city depended on the volunteer services of the firemen. So, even as they laid down the law, they offered what they thought was a goodwill gesture. The Council made plans to hire maintenance crews to relieve firemen of the chore of looking after some of their equipment. Firemen with the rank of assistant engineer—the modern equivalent of a battalion chief—would receive a salary of $500 a year to supervise the maintenance crews. It didn't occur to the honorable aldermen that the firemen, proud of their volunteer service, might resent the salaries paid to the assistant engineers, and would see in the move a political conspiracy to replace the all-volunteer force with a paid Fire Department.

On May 3, 1836, the Common Council's Fire and Water Committee held a hearing to discuss the Fire Department in general and Chief Gulick in particular. After listening to a particularly abusive denunciation of the way he ran the department, Gulick, who had been in the back of the hearing room, moved forward and shouted, "Alderman, you lie!" The chief then stormed out of the building, and committee members chose to conduct the rest of their business in a secret session. They decided they would recommend Gulick's ouster at a meeting of the full Board of Aldermen the following day.

That afternoon, Gulick was in command of a fire in two buildings at the corner of Houston and Second streets. A member of Engine Co. 13 got wind of the committee's intentions and told Gulick. It was not the most auspicious place or time for a fire chief, particularly a popular fire chief, to learn that his services were no longer wanted. As the fire continued to rage, Gulick assembled his men and told them he was about to be fired. Then he turned away and walked home. It was an outrageous act of insubordination on the part of an otherwise admirable, if headstrong, public servant. Gulick had reason to consider himself ill-used, but as he well knew, his first obligation was to the safety of the city and his men. Days later, in hindsight, even his supporters admitted that the chief had acted rashly. It was much worse than that—in a single act of stubborn defiance, Gulick not only played into the hands of his enemies, but soiled his reputation as a man who put the deadly serious business of firefighting ahead of crass political maneuvering.

After Gulick left, his stunned men reversed their caps as a sign of protest and gathered up their hose. The foreman of Engine Co. 10—the very company that had disgraced itself with the January 1 assault on Alderman Purdy—announced that the firemen wouldn't work without Gulick. The chief's men cheered. And the fire continued to burn.

It wasn't long before Mayor Lawrence heard about the dangerous standoff, and it's not hard to imagine what went through his mind. Chief Gulick, at a moment of great peril, had refused a direct mayoral order that terrible night in December when he refused to light the explosives on Exchange Place. And now he had left the scene of a fire. Lawrence hurried to the blaze and ordered the firemen to go back to their posts. They refused, and not very politely. Infuriated, Lawrence retreated back to City Hall. James Gulick had defied him for the last time.

The chief finally returned to the scene after hearing the pleas of an insurance executive, and great cheering greeted his arrival. The men resumed their trade, and the blaze was soon brought under control. That could not be said of Mayor Lawrence.

When he reached City Hall, Lawrence realized that the Common Council was in session. He seized the moment handed him: He told the aldermen that Gulick had walked off the job, that his men were prepared to do likewise. Something had to be done, and done right now. Lawrence asked the aldermen to fire Gulick on the spot. They did, by a vote of fifteen to five. An assistant engineer, John Riker, was promoted to chief.

From the city's firehouses came angry howls of protest. The department's foremen and assistant foremen drew up a petition of protest. Not only did they demand Riker's removal and Gulick's reinstatement, but they also denounced the council's plan to pay assistant engineers an annual salary. The assistants already received all the "privileges" entitled any "honorable public-spirited citizen," they said. The firemen went on what might be called a rule-book job action, infuriating even the usually sympathetic *New York Herald* of James Gordon Bennett. "In a city such as this, the refusal of the regular firemen to work during the burning down of valuable property, on account of some quarrel between portions of their body and a portion of the [city government], is too gross—too bad—too alarming an outrage to be tolerated," the paper wrote. New York, the paper warned, "is truly on the edge of a volcano." The disaster of December 1835 was fresh in the city's memory; the burnt district, even in recovery, bore witness to the dangers the city faced from fire.

The standoff between the city's civic leaders and the firemen dragged on through the summer, with the firemen accusing the mayor and aldermen of injecting politics into the department. Finally, on September 21, the firemen made good on a threatened mass resignation. Between 600 and 800 of them marched to City Hall and turned in their resignations, leaving the city with just over 750 firemen. It was, in fact, a strike, and it could hardly have come at a worse time. Even before the resignations, the complement of about 1,400 firemen was too low, as the Great Fire of 1835 had demonstrated. Gulick might have spoken out and asked his men to return to their posts for the sake of the city's safety, but he didn't. Meanwhile, equipment was vandalized, and an increase in suspicious fires led some to believe that some of the departed firemen were up to no good. When it became clear that the mayor and aldermen were not going to fire the new chief and reinstate Gulick, the departed firemen formed their own organization, the aptly named

Resigned Firemen's Association, and chose to play a game they said they abhorred—politics.

Elections to various municipal positions were scheduled for November 1835, and on October 10, Gulick's friends announced their intention of nominating the fallen chief for the post of city register, a minor office with little power. Two ex-firemen from each of the city's sixteen wards were appointed to build an organization. Sensing an opportunity, the Native American party—a fledgling third party spawned by the burgeoning anti-immigrant movement—offered its line to Gulick. The even more opportunistic Whigs, who were the main opposition to the reigning Tammany Democrats, likewise offered Gulick a line. Nobody knew what Gulick's politics were, or if he had any at all. It didn't matter. He had name recognition, a grievance, and what appeared to be a formidable, albeit untested, organization behind him.

The *New York Evening Post*, which advertised its support for the Democratic presidential candidate, Martin van Buren, on its editorial page every day, derided Gulick's candidacy. Its editors reminded readers that he "abandoned his duty as chief engineer" in May. "Such a nomination," the paper thundered, "is an insult to the publick feeling."

The public felt otherwise. When the votes were counted, James Gulick not only was victorious, but in the city he even outpolled the Democratic ticket leader van Buren. Gulick had 19,443 votes, to the 13,388 recorded by Tammany's man, William H. Bunn. Van Buren had 17,414 votes in the city. It was a stunning display of organization, and a mighty blow for Tammany, which lost loyal voters to the Whigs. One person who wrote a letter to the Post seeking to explain this amazing turn of events said Gulick's election was the work of "the Irish electors" who were grateful to Gulick for prodding his mostly Protestant firemen into putting out a fire in old St. Patrick's Cathedral several years earlier. "On this occasion, at least, [Gulick] did his duty," the letter writer noted archly.

The firemen were not finished. When the governor called a special election to fill a vacant General Assembly seat in December, the Whigs nominated Morris Franklin—the fireman Chief Gulick had rescued from a burning building on Park Place in 1832. Unchastened, the *Evening Post*'s pro-Democrat editors decided that it was "folly to suppose that the people of New York are going to elect [Franklin] merely because he was a fireman, or that they will take his having pulled the ropes and pointed the hose of a fire engine as sufficient qualification for the business of legislating." Clearly the *Evening Post*'s editors and the city's voters had different ideas of what constituted proper experience for a state assemblyman. Franklin won in another upset, although his margin of victory was a good deal narrower than Gulick's. The following spring, the resigned firemen once again made common cause with the Whigs, and Tammany was ousted from the mayor's office and lost its majority on the Common Council. John Riker was promptly fired; a Gulick ally, Cornelius Anderson, was hired as the new chief engineer; the assistant engineers saw their annual stipend repealed; and many of the firemen who had resigned became active firemen again.

There was no mistaking what had happened. New York's firemen had established themselves as a political force, independent of the city's power elites. Tammany Hall, which had been on the wrong end of the firemen's wrath, took careful notice, and would respond accordingly.

CHAPTER FOUR

GANGS, FEUDS,
AND POLITICS

Bᴵʟʟ Tᴡᴇᴇᴅ ᴡᴀꜱ ᴀ ʏᴏᴜɴɢ ᴍᴀɴ with big ambitions, look-
ing for a way out of the drudgery of clerking and chairmaking—jobs he
took up after dropping out of school at age eleven. Born in 1823 at 1
Cherry Street (now the site of the Manhattan-bound approaches to the
Brooklyn Bridge), Bill was a child of the age of Andrew Jackson, a time
of populist democracy when, as Jackson's starchy critics sniffed, it
seemed as though *anybody* could become president of the United States.

Bill Tweed wasn't just anybody. Even as a teenager in the late 1830s,
young Bill stood out in a crowd. He was six feet tall, and he was larger
than life, a high-spirited, gregarious street kid who was quick with his
fists. Not surprisingly, young Bill became the leader by conquest of a
neighborhood gang, the Cherry Hillers, and proved that he was no mere
time-serving status-quo hack. In short order he rallied the Cherry Hillers
to famous victories over the Hill Street Gang, a rival outfit. Bill Tweed
was a shrewd young man. He saw opportunities, and he took them.

At the age of sixteen, Bill Tweed seized another opportunity: He
became a volunteer fireman. With his red shirt, broad suspenders, and
fire cap, Bill Tweed was one of the city's most dashing characters, a role

SO OTHERS
MIGHT LIVE

· · ·

67

model for other young men, and an instant hero. The next twenty-five years of the Fire Department's history were embodied in the story of William M. Tweed—street brawler, gang leader, clubhouse politician.

In the years just before and immediately following James Gulick's ouster as chief engineer, the Fire Department was changing, or, more to the point, it was becoming an exaggerated version of itself. Long a favorite gathering place for young men and boys, in the 1840s the firehouses became magnets for hardened gang members from the city's rough and rowdy neighborhoods. The firemen themselves often were tradesmen—blacksmiths and carpenters, not bankers and insurance executives—but as the Department expanded, it attracted even tougher characters from the city's growing ranks of unskilled laborers. To be sure, hard-knuckle politics and the Fire Department were no strangers to each other—as the Gulick affair demonstrated—but the 1840s saw individual fire companies become virtual recruiting stations for Tammany Hall. The age of rough and tumble urban politics had its symbol in William M. Tweed—uneducated, pugnacious, and ambitious, a man who saw the Fire Department as a stepping stone to respectability and rewards.

Despite his notoriety as a politician, Bill Tweed was hardly the most famous fireman of his era. That title belonged to a man even taller than Tweed—in fact, taller by two feet. He was a giant of a man, with appetites that made Tweed, who weighed 270 pounds by his twenty-first birthday, seem like the picture of monastic self-denial. This great volunteer fireman's name was Old Mose, and he was the leading character in an 1848 play called *A Glance at New York*. Old Mose was one of the legends of pre-Civil War New York—a brawler, a drinker, a righter of wrongs, a leader of one of the city's most famous gangs, the Bowery B'hoys—in short, a nineteenth-century superhero. He swilled beer from a fifty-gallon keg attached to his belt, and he feasted on copious amounts of oysters and beef, leaving the rest of the city in short supply. The historian Lowell Limpus and others have called Old Mose New York's answer to the legend of Paul Bunyan. The fact that this character was a volunteer fireman indicates the place firemen held in the public's imagination, and not just in New York. *A Glance at New York* and its character Mose was a smash hit in theaters around the country, leading to a series of plays that became known as "Mosaics." The actor who played him was a real-life New York fireman named Frank Chanfrau, and he often rushed from theater to theater every day to satisfy the public's demand for more of Mose.

Old Mose was based on the life and times of Moses Humphreys, a New York fireman who won his fame and place in New York folk history not so much for his courage or his firefighting skill but because he was one of the great street fighters of the age. In the story of Moses Humphreys, as in that of Bill Tweed, the story of New York's Fire Department intersects with the story of the rambunctious, violent, chaotic, sinister, and highly politicized city it served.

Moses Humphreys was a printer with the *New York Sun,* and an Irish American. His profession didn't make him rare among his fellow firemen, but his ethnicity certainly did. The Fire Department was only about 7 percent Irish in 1830, shortly before Humphreys became a volunteer. The majority of firemen, nearly 60 percent, were of British ancestry, and slightly less than a quarter were listed as "Nordic."

Humphreys was a member of Engine Co. 40, which, like many other engine and ladder companies in the 1830s, gave itself a special name, making it more distinctive. Engine Co. 40 was known as Lady Washington's Company, for George Washington's wife. Some companies named themselves in honor of patriots or historical figures, while others chose more colorful names such as Live Oak Engine Co. 44, or Niagara Engine Co. 4. The company that Bill Tweed would help found and make famous, Engine Co. 6, was known as the Americus Engine Co. 6, or Big Six.

The men of Lady Washington's Company were among the Department's most formidable firefighters, although the fighting for which they became most famous was directed not at flames but at other firefighters. By the late 1830s, brawls between fire companies were becoming more commonplace, a reflection of the lost leadership of James Gulick, who cracked down on firehouse rowdies and who instilled a sense of professional pride among the volunteers.

Actually, it was pride of a sort that helped ignite the era's Fire Department feuds. The first company at the fire scene was accorded the honor of extinguishing the blaze. Trailing companies, if they were needed, were deployed to the drudge work of delivering water from a reservoir or cistern through a relay system of pumpers. So when an alarm sounded and firemen hitched themselves to their wagons, the race, a real race, was on. Many companies, when confronted with crowded streets, jumped curbs and hauled their engines along sidewalks, to the dismay and occasional horror of the general public. Some firemen, to get a jump on the competition, began sleeping at firehouses. Beating the competition to a fire became a competitive sport played by broad-shouldered men with a keen desire to win. Had they been born 100 years later, the volunteer firemen of pre–Civil War New York would have played for Vince Lombardi's Green Bay Packers. And they'd have loved every excruciating minute of it.

Eliminating rival firefighters became an increasingly common method of winning the race to the fire. Moses Humphreys, of Lady Washington's Engine Co. 40, was the kind of firefighter who lived to eliminate his rivals. Like his fictional namesake, he was big, and he was tough, and on a summer afternoon in 1838 he was looking for a fight. As was becoming the case before, after, and sometimes even during fires, he wouldn't have to search very hard to find one.

Engine Co. 40's and Peterson Engine Co. 15's men often got in each other's way responding to fires via Chatham Street, near present-day Chinatown. Such occasions did not inspire civic confidence in the firemen. As they hauled their engines side by side, the companies traded insults, loudly and in language that went beyond the occasional "damn" that had once led to one-dollar fines. On this summer Sunday in 1838, the bad blood between the two companies soon was flowing in the streets.

It started as Humphreys and his men were returning from a fire near Wall Street. The men of Engine Co. 15 had also been at the scene. The blaze had burned for several hours, which presumably left them exhausted. Most of the work at a fire in the era of the hand-pumper involved exactly that—pumping water by hand, with teams of men on either side of the engine, working the engine's pumps, or "brakes," to keep water flowing.

If the two companies were, in fact, tired after the fire, they soon discovered a reserve of energy. Humphreys and his men followed the men of Engine Co. 15 as they pulled their engine toward their firehouse on Mulberry Street. Engine Co. 15 and Lady Washington's Co. 40 both had their full complements at the fire, and they were preparing to settle their feud once and for all.

After some ritual hazing as the two engines came alongside each other, a one-on-one fistfight broke out. Before long, hundreds of firemen were brawling in the streets. A nineteenth-century historian of the Department, Augustine E. Costello, who knew some of the participants in the fight, wrote that the "shock of battle rolled down the line, and quicker than it takes to write these words, one thousand sturdy, stalwart fellows were fiercely grappling each other in a hand-to-hand fight. The din was frightful. . . . The fighters were so thick that there was scarcely room for one to fall. . . .[T]hose who were unlucky enough to find mother earth were nearly trampled to death by the feet of friend and foe before they could escape." Costello's estimate of the number of men involved probably is wrong. A thousand men would represent about two thirds of the Department's total manpower in the late 1830s, although possibly the figure includes the young boys who loitered around firehouses and accompanied firemen to their alarms. But even if the fight involved as many as several hundred firemen, it must have been an epic battle. Costello observed with approval that the company's elected leaders, their foremen, "did their very best to maintain their reputation for courage and personal prowess." In other words, they were banging rivals' heads alongside their men instead of trying to restore order and some semblance of professional decorum.

The brawl raged for half an hour. And somewhere in the chaos, Moses Humphreys found himself in the fight of his life. His opponent was a firefighter named Henry Chanfrau—brother of the man who would later go on to play Old Mose in the theater. Chanfrau dismantled Humphreys (as his brother the future actor looked on with delight) in a fight that had the shock value of Cassius Clay beating Sonny Liston.

Fighting for the honor of putting out a fire sometimes was more important than actually fighting the fire itself.

With their champion down, the men of Lady Washington's fled, leaving behind their apparatus and their hard-won reputation for toughness. More humiliation followed, when Engine Co. 15 exacted its revenge on Lady Washington's apparatus, which was cruel punishment indeed. Engine companies lovingly decorated their engines and looked after them with such care that observers often insisted that a New York fireman loved his engine with passions ordinarily reserved for female companions. So it was with horror that Lady Washington's men discovered that Engine Co. 15 had washed out Engine Co. 40's elaborate white and gold paint job with a cruel torrent of water.

Moses Humphreys never recovered from his terrible defeat. He soon fled the city and wound up in Honolulu, which, as sites of exile go, was not the worst fate ever to befall a fallen warrior. But when he was resurrected as a fictional character, his defeat was forgotten. As played by the brother of his conqueror, Moses Humphreys/Old Mose was a hero again.

The battle between Engine Companies 40 and 15 became part of New York legend. Though it was not the first brawl between feuding engine companies, its scale and severity foreshadowed a violent period in Fire Department history that lasted from the early 1840s into the late 1850s. Newspapers of the period are filled with reports of violent incidents between competing fire companies, along with editorials lamenting these dangerous disputes. Augustine E. Costello, who wrote so approvingly of firemen defending their reputation for "courage and personal prowess," devoted dozens of pages of *Our Firemen,* his gigantic history of the Department, to the fine details of these brawls. Like other observers of the volunteer Fire Department in the middle decades of the century, Costello regarded brawls among firemen as evidence of their big-chested manliness, not as a sign of disorder and chaos. This was the era of what Costello and others called "the fire laddies," raucous man-boys who'd drop their ladder for the sake of a fight—and occasionally did just that, at some cost to the burning real estate.

Not coincidentally, the violence in the Department reflected growing violence in the city at large. Gangs like the Bowery B'hoys, the Pug Uglies, the Dead Rabbits and others roamed the city's dark, narrow streets, claiming as their turf areas like the notoriously squalid, overcrowded Five Points slum in lower Manhattan (named for the proximity of five streets in the sixth ward). Many gangs or gang members developed loose affiliations with local firehouses, complicating the already violent feuds between companies. It was hardly a wonder, then, that when a group of nervous citizens, as well as representatives of the city's fire insurance companies, came together in 1840 to study the Fire Department and fire protection, they were less than impressed.

It wasn't just the feuds that worried political, civic, and business elites who organized the Committee of Safety on January 31, 1840, in the newly rebuilt Merchants' Exchange. Tammany Hall, now back in control of the mayoralty and Common Council, had just attempted an amazingly brazen power play, even by Tammany standards. Humiliated by the Gulick-led revolt in 1836, Tammany tried to impose its control on the Fire Department two years later by creating, through the Common Council, twenty new hose companies—units in charge of the Department's thousands of feet of hose—that were designed to complement the engine companies.

The new companies existed on paper only. But that was enough to justify the creation of twenty new company foremen and twenty new assistant foremen, each commanding a vote on the Fire Department's

Board of Foremen and Assistant Foremen. Created by the Whigs in 1838, this board administered the Department's and its annual budget of $59,000, and it elected the Department's chief engineer. The new foremen and assistant foremen owed their jobs to Tammany and could be counted on to act and vote as they were told. This packed board tried its first major gambit in 1839, when it voted to appoint a new Tammany-approved chief engineer to replace Cornelius Anderson, but the public and press screamed so loud that the politicians backed down, and Anderson remained chief engineer.

But Tammany had only retreated. It had not surrendered. Control of the Fire Department, its men, and its budget for equipment and other expenses were prizes too great to ignore.

"The existence of politics in the Fire Department. . . is no doubt one of the principal causes of the present disorganized and insubordinate state of the Department," stated a report delivered to the Committee of Safety's forty-nine members when they met on February 15, 1840. The committee had commissioned the report two weeks earlier, after one member proposed a resolution calling for nothing short of a revolution in the Fire Department: the creation of a paid corps of firemen and the dismantling of New York's volunteer companies. A few days after this bombshell, members of the Committee of Safety and representatives of the city's fire insurance companies met with Chief Engineer Anderson to discuss the Department's condition. It was an astonishing interview. The committee members' greatest concern was with what they considered inadequate fire protection in the commercial and financial areas downtown, where fire had shown its power in 1835.

This important piece of New York real estate was one of the city's five fire districts, which had been created in 1838 to help pinpoint the precise location of fires by a network of bell signals. Of the 140 fires that occurred in the city between October 1, 1839, and February 1, 1840, 84 were in this vital area. Anderson conceded that only one ladder company, with thirteen men, was deployed in the district. Worse yet, he said that "of the 13 men attached to the truck there are about four willing to do duty." He confessed, further, that only half of the 5,000 feet of hose in the district was in good working order and that he had no idea how many firemen lived in the district—no small point, because firemen had to get from their homes to their firehouses quickly.

Anderson deserved points for candor. His answers, however, provoked a report that could have been written by the excitable prophet Jeremiah. "[It] is a fact. . . that the department is not, at present, an effective one—that there are evils connected with it that destroy much of its usefullness," the report read. "Since this is the state of things, what is to be done to restore discipline and efficiency to the Department? We answer, pay the Department for their services and arduous labor." Addressing the Department, the committee wrote: "We the People, your constituents, are entitled to a better disciplined and more efficient organization of the Fire Department, and to more security than you furnish to our property. . . . It is not an uncommon thing to say, 'If you want the job done well, you must pay for it.' The Insurance Companies, practicing the truth of this saying, have for several months hired a company of 85 men to patrol the streets, and to save the property at fires. It is remarked that the Insurance Companies have already saved by this Company property sufficient to pay the expense for years." The Committee buttressed their arguments by taking note of developments in other metropolises across the Atlantic and at home: "London, Paris, Liverpool, Edinburgh, and all the cities of Europe pay their Fire Department, and in Boston, in our own country, they found it necessary."

The Committee of Safety concluded that a professional Fire Department of 400 members each paid $100 a year—double the salary paid to Boston firemen—could do the work of a volunteer force of 3,000 at less expense to the city's treasury. Those were fighting words, and Tammany, the Common Council, and the firemen themselves knew it. The Committee of Safety likewise knew its high-minded reforms were doomed to be buried in City Hall, so members took their case to Albany, the state capital, where they hoped to find a more receptive audience, one less concerned about the opinions and votes of firemen and their friends. Tammany Hall was a step ahead of the reformers, however: It took one of the committee's complaints—the expense of running a volunteer Fire Department of several thousand men—and used it to its side's advantage. The Common Council passed a resolution that played to its hometown audience, to wit: Echoing one of the young nation's founding principles, the council members resolved that the "people of the city of New York are compelled to endure the burdens imposed by the great cost at which the [Fire] Department is supported, and ought therefore to have the supervision of it through their immediate representatives in the Common Council." Any interference "on the part of the Legislature. . . is considered an infringement of the chartered rights guaranteed to the city of New York."

The changes proposed by the Committee of Safety went nowhere. But the suggested reforms and the opposition they inspired offered a glimpse at larger tensions in a city on the verge of becoming a test case for modern multicultural democratic politics. The men on the Committee of Safety represented the city's elites, whereas Tammany, the Common Council, and the Fire Department represented the city's growing population of lower-middle-class laborers and working poor. After Ireland's potato blight of 1845–51, this social sector included waves of Irish Catholic immigrants, and these immigrants would transform the city's culture and politics, not to mention its Fire Department. In the two decades from 1840 to 1860, the portion of Irish firemen in the Department went from about 12 to nearly 40 percent. Irish Catholics were viewed as unruly and loyal not to Washington but to Rome; coincidentally or not, the increase of Irish firefighters led not only to demands for reform, but to open disdain of the Fire Department.

George Templeton Strong, a nineteenth-century diarist and unwitting chronicler of ruling-class prejudice, complained that "a large part of the firemen do nothing but bustle around in their caps, swear at everybody and try to look tremendous, the engines are never worked for five minutes in succession, and everything in short is as badly conducted as possible." Perhaps Strong had forgotten that his uncle Benjamin had served as a member of Engine Co. 13 earlier in the century. Or perhaps Strong simply thought firefighters were a better class of people back when his uncle was pumping water. Nevertheless, his characterization of the Department in fact confirmed Chief Engineer Anderson's testimony to the Committee of Safety, when he admitted that only four of

This nineteenth-century engraving probably exaggerates the chaos that ensued when fire companies raced to an alarm. But the exaggeration may be only slight.

the thirteen members of a ladder company downtown were willing to perform their duties.

The firefighters themselves were not above playing at class warfare. In his study of nineteenth-century firefighting, "From Community to Metropolis," Richard Calhoun noted that correspondents to *America's Own and Fireman's Journal* touted firefighters as the "sons of honest labor," while condemning the "pampered sons of aristocracy" who were nowhere to be found when the fire bells rang. And they took Jackson-era pride in the staunch democracy of various fire company balls, which were models of "true gentility, modesty and reserve" and a fine contrast to the "haughty, proud and supercilious" aristocrats who attended the city's cotillions. As with Strong's complaints regarding the rough class of firemen, there was some truth in the firemen's criticism of the gentry. It had become rare to find a firefighter like Strong's uncle, the president of a sugar refining company and of a savings bank who served as a volunteer fireman. Historian Stephen Ginsberg, writing on fire protection in New York in the first half of the century, observed that being a firefighter no longer seemed to confer status on groups that most likely were status-conscious.

Of course, Ginsberg's observation leads to the question of how one defines a status seeker. Firefighting was not going to help a merchant or salesman join the ranks of the haughty, the proud and the supercilious. For the poor, disenfranchised, or otherwise disconnected in slums like the Five Points, however, firefighting offered plenty of status. Despite their flaws, firemen in the 1840s remained idols of the poor, not to mention the occasional literary observer. Walt Whitman compared New York's firemen to "Roman gladiators." Firemen were neighborhood heroes. They lived near their firehouse, so their neighbors often saw them running from their apartments, often late at night, to respond to the ringing of the city's fire bells, and saw them return exhausted, wet, cold, and covered with soot and ash and smoke. With public acclamation came celebrity, and with celebrity, even in the mid–nineteenth century, came power. As Tammany Hall looked for new recruits to their political organization in the city's immigrant neighborhoods, they beat a path to the firehouse. In his book, *Five Points,* Tyler Anbinder found that the firehouse was one certain locus to make political connections and perhaps even launch a political career. Anbinder traced the career of Matthew T. Brennan, the son of an Irish immigrant, who joined the Fire Department in the early 1840s, was elected his company's foreman, put his influence to work on behalf of Tammany, and soon was awarded a small patronage job. Not long afterward he was in command of a small political machine of his own, thanks to his firehouse and gang connections, and was elected a police justice—a minor judgeship that did not, amazingly, require a law degree.

Tammany's street-level approach to municipal government, especially its recruitment of the despised Irish Catholics, disturbed the city's reformers, whose goals were not the well-being of immigrants and the lower classes, but the elimination of political patronage. The same impulses that led the city's civic leaders to demand changes in the Fire Department inspired, in a distorted way, the election of a virulent anti-immigrant, anti-Catholic, reform-minded mayor in 1844. The publisher James Harper, who ran as the candidate of the nativist American Republican Party, was a member of the city's civic leadership and New York's largest employer. He spoke for the civic elite's concerns about the city's ongoing experiment in rough-house democracy and cultural tolerance. The party's newspaper, the *American Republican,* charged in 1843 that some 200,000 Catholics, most of them Irish, had moved to New York that year. The figure was exaggerated, but it certainly was correct in its implication that Irish Catholics were coming by the hundreds of thousands. And when Ireland's potato crop failed so disastrously in the mid–1840s and early 1850s, nearly 1 million Irish emigrated to the United States, so that by 1855 some 28 percent of New York's population was Irish-born, the vast majority of them Catholic. Even before the arrival of the Famine Irish, the *American Republican* had warned that "public morals have become degenerated, pauperism and crime unendurably abundant, and religion and morality little better than words." Those concerns, as it happened, were not the aristocracy's alone. During his mayoral campaign, Harper was cheered by mobs shouting, "No popery." Included among those mobs, if not literally then figuratively, was a significant representation of Protestant, native-born firefighters. A Catholic newspaper in New York, the *Freeman's Journal,* complained in 1844 that the "fire boys" were among the "original 'native Americans'" who eagerly supported Harper's anti-immigrant campaign.

A month after Harper's election, anti-Catholic mobs burned churches during riots in Philadelphia, fanning fears that New York nativists, with one of their own in City Hall, might do likewise. The *American Republican* charged that the Irish had trampled on the American flag in Philadelphia and warned that in New York, "blood will have blood." To help satisfy this bloodlust, nativists in New York invited representatives of the rioters in Philadelphia to a public meeting in New York in early May. New York's Catholics prepared for the worst.

After an exchange of letters later published in the *Freeman's Journal,* the leader of New York's Catholics, an Irish immigrant named John Hughes, offered to meet with the new mayor in an effort to relieve tensions. Harper accepted, and soon had a firsthand insight into Bishop John Hughes's formidable personality. When the mayor asked the bishop whether he was afraid for the safety of his churches, Hughes replied, "No, sir, but I am afraid that some of yours will be burned." In case the mayor didn't get the point, Hughes vowed that if so much as a single church in New York was set on fire, New York Catholics would turn the city into a "second Moscow." It was a chilling reference—Muscovites had burned their city in 1812 rather than allow it to fall into the hands of Napoleon. Now, not a decade removed from the Great Fire of 1835, Bishop Hughes was threatening New York with immolation at a time when the Fire Department seemed unprepared for conflagration.

The great public meeting of nativists from New York and Philadelphia was called off. And no churches were burned in New York in 1844.

Amid the chaos and the brawls and the politicking, there was good news for New York's Fire Department—indeed, for all New Yorkers. After years of discussion followed by years of study and hard work, New York welcomed a new and abundant supply of fresh water in 1842. Finally, the plan to draw water from the Croton River in Westchester had become a reality with the construction of the forty-one-mile Croton Aqueduct, and the great civic ceremonies on October 14 that marked the conduit's being put into service bespoke of the city's pride, and relief. The *New York Herald* described the Great Croton Celebration, as it was called, as "the proudest day for the city of New York. . . since the discovery of this part of the world by Hendrick Hudson." A hundred cannon fired salutes at daybreak. Several hours later, a great parade began marching uptown from the Battery. It was nearly seven miles long and took two and a half hours to pass any given point along the way. And the heart of the parade was a contingent of 4,000 active, retired, and visiting firemen. Decked out in their colorful best, marching with the discipline and rigor that belied their critics' jibes, the firemen took an hour and seventeen minutes to pass cheering spectators—although it must be noted that they marched two abreast, while other units such as the policemen marched twelve abreast. In an acknowledgment of the Croton project's importance for the Fire Department, the mayor and Common Council presented firemen with a special banner for the occasion as a sign of the city's "high regard and estimation."

New York now had a dependable water source for firefighting. In time, though not right away, the Croton Aqueduct also would bring safe, dependable water to the general public (though not before yet another cholera outbreak, in 1849, killed 5,000 people).

It wasn't long before the Croton River-fed fire hydrants were put to a mighty test, reminding New Yorkers that even a marvel like dams and aqueducts were no insurance against destruction by fire. A few hours before sunrise on Saturday, July 19, 1845, fire broke out in a sperm-oil store on New Street in downtown Manhattan. Chief Engineer Anderson and his men were on the scene quickly, but the fire spread even quicker, enveloping several adjoining buildings. Soon, some of the same streets that had burned so terribly in 1835 were on fire again, and once again the heart of New York's commercial and financial district was in mortal peril.

New York's volunteer firemen, so recently denounced for their lack of discipline and organization, responded quickly to the alarms. Every fireman's name and address was on file with the local police captain. In the unlikely event that a fireman didn't hear the alarm bells pealing from various bell towers, police officers raised the alarm at the homes of firemen who lived on their beat. On this July night, the city's bell towers rang incessantly.

When Engine Co. 22 arrived, its men were ordered to pump water on a large multistory warehouse on Broad Street that had just caught fire. With great effort, Engine Co. 22's foreman, Garrett B. Lane, and his men entered the building and dragged hose up a staircase to get water on a fire on the fourth floor. Within minutes, Lane noticed heavy black smoke coming up the stairway, indicated flames beneath as well as above him. He ordered his men to evacuate, but it was too late for Francis Hart, Jr., who was trying to collect the company's hose. With the stairway below him in flames, he climbed up to the roof, and escaped the burning warehouse by scampering from rooftop to rooftop.

Without warning, about five minutes after Engine Co. 22 evacuated the warehouse, it blew up. Somewhere inside the building were stored large quantities of saltpeter, a highly combustible material. The explosion shattered windows a mile away and reportedly was heard as far

TERRIFIC EXPLOSION AT THE GREAT FIRE IN NEW-YORK!
DREADFUL LOSS OF LIFE!!

The fire of 1845 destroyed three hundred buildings, and for the third time in seventy years, New York had to rebuild from a terrible conflagration.

away as Sandy Hook on the New Jersey shore. The blast blew Hart across a rooftop; amazingly, he suffered only a minor ankle injury. Two other firemen, Augustus L. Cowdrey of Engine Co. 42 and Dave Van Winkle of Engine Co. 5, were desperately throwing water on an adjacent building when a second explosion ripped through what was left of the warehouse. Van Winkle was thrown into the street. Two days later, the *Evening Post* reported that Cowdrey, a young lawyer, had been found alive in the rubble. Sadly, it wasn't true. No trace of him was ever found.

Overmatched, Anderson sent for help from the men who had preceded him in the post chief engineer, including James Gulick. The retired chiefs hurried to the scene, as did volunteers from Brooklyn and Newark. Rumors spread that the vaunted water supply from Croton was exhausted. The *Evening Post* dispatched a reporter to the scene hours after the explosion. In an hour-by-hour account published later that day, the newspaper described yet another scene of ruin: "The confusion that prevailed at this moment [about 10 o'clock] beggars description. It was thought that several firemen had been buried in the ruins and although every exertion was made to ascertain whether such was the case or not, it was impossible to tell. Engine Co. 22 was buried in the ruins and completely destroyed. Seven men are missing." The newspaper went on to praise the Fire Department's "almost superhuman exertions," while the firemen made a point of praising the Police Department for keeping civilians away from the disaster.

As the fire finally showed signs of weakening in the early afternoon, a lone woman walked through the smoke and debris, weeping as she went. She told passersby she was looking for her seven children. She had left them for a moment as flames approached her house, and she hadn't seen them since. Otherwise speechless, the woman's friends quietly assured her that the children surely had been rescued. She continued her search.

The fire claimed the lives of four firemen and twenty-six civilians, although that number apparently did not include the seven missing children. Three hundred buildings were in ruins, and property damage was estimated at $10 million. For several days afterward firemen dug through the debris, searching for the bodies of their fallen comrades. "They were unwearied in their attention to their duties," an *Evening Post* reporter wrote. At least the pessimistic rumors about the city's water supply proved groundless—unlike 1835, there was no shortage of water this time.

But, as an *Evening Post* editorial noted, "a new facility can never be a substitute for vigilance and prudence." Aside from the institution of rudimentary building codes and the organization of the city into fire districts, firefighting in New York continued to be a reactive business, with little emphasis on fire prevention. That, the *Evening Post* maintained, had to change. "Square miles of London consist of alleys lined with vast and lofty warehouses. . . Yet how few fires occur in London. They are no more frequent in crowded Paris. The prevention of fires is made a duty of the police in both cities." The Committee of Safety had cited the insurance company-funded Fire Patrol for its good work in its otherwise dismal study of fire prevention in 1840. Clearly, though, more steps were necessary, for the fire of July 1845 was only the latest in a series of destructive blazes in the mid–1840s. Just a few months before, in February, the *New York Tribune*'s building on Nassau Street had burned to the ground. Firemen managed to save an adjoining building—Tammany Hall.

The cries for reform did lead to changes, such as the creation of a new reserve unit of firefighters. It became known as the Exempt Firemen's Company, because it was made up of firemen who had served enough time to qualify for lifetime exemptions from militia and jury duty, but who were no longer active volunteers. The number of years of service required to earn an exemption changed over the decades, from ten in 1816 to seven in 1829 and finally to five in 1847. Of course, many firemen continued to serve long after they had earned their exemption.

The Exempt Company's leader was Zophar Mills, one of the era's best-known firemen for the courage he displayed in 1835, when he helped stop the fire from crossing Wall Street. Mills was among the hundreds of boys who grew up hanging out around firehouses and running with the engines to fires, hoping for a chance to help their heroes. He formally joined the Department in 1832 and was quickly elected foreman of Engine Co. 13. He was nearly killed in the 1834 fire on Pearl Street, which took the lives of Eugene Underhill and F. A. Ward. The collapse that killed the two men buried Mills in rubble but left him with just a few bruises.

He quit the Fire Department after ten years because, he later explained, "I was a bookkeeper, and it was exceedingly severe on me, after serving for hours at a fire, to be obliged to go back to the office and post up my books." But the alarm bells still held their charm, and beginning in 1845, he eagerly agreed to put aside business on occasion to serve as leader of the Department's reserves. In that capacity he would continued to serve the city for the next twenty years.

The Fire Department's courage and sacrifice in 1845 silenced critics and won praise from the city's press. Four firemen whose only rewards were public acclamation and the company of like-minded men had given their lives in service to the city, so complaints like those cited by the Committee of Safety seemed out of place. Before long, however, firemen like Bill Tweed had dishonored the Department's gallantry.

It's not that Bill Tweed was a bad firefighter, or, except for his size, that he was all that different from the city's other firemen. Like Tweed, all firemen had jobs and many had families, but their first love, it often seemed, was firefighting. But that love—for the job and for their fellow company members, though not for members of rival companies—truly was blind. The firehouse's excesses were described as colorful and manly, a variation on the "boys will be boys" defense. Augustine Costello, the bard of the volunteer Fire Department, tried to explain that brawls between fire companies were "not lacking in a certain rugged element of chivalry which promoted manhood," although, he admitted, this came "at the expense of public order." Little is known about Bill Tweed's chivalry; what is certain, however, is that he was among the firemen whose behavior undermined public order.

This intensely masculine culture took pride in traditional ways of doing things, especially if brute strength was demanded, and was suspicious of new-fangled labor-saving equipment. New York's firemen resisted the use of horsepower to draw engines from firehouse to fire scene well into the 1840s, dragging their engines through the streets long after other cities converted to horses.

Such machismo was reflected in the Department's social life as well. Individual companies sponsored target-shooting exercises and weekly chowder nights, usually on Saturdays. They were nearly always all-male events, although there is some evidence that women were invited on occasion. Thick, hot chowder, consisting of a mixture of various creatures from land and sea—from eels to chickens—was a staple of working-class gatherings in the mid–nineteenth century, and New York's firefighters were renowned for their elaborate concoctions and ceremonies. Writing in 1878 about his years as a volunteer in the 1840s, James Tyler waxed nostalgic for chowder night: "About once a week we would procure a chowder pot, and with a halibut's head and fixings get up a chowder. . . . We did not eat the chowder in the dark, but had the engine-house lighted on chowder nights, with candles purchased at a neighboring grocery—plates and spoons sufficient to go around; and I venture to assert that no game supper with brilliantly lighted balls and music, was ever enjoyed more than our 'chowder.' "

Tyler's defensive comparisons between firehouse culture and elite society reflect the firemen's keen sense of class resentment, which became even more conspicuous as more of the city's despised Irish Catholics became firemen. The people who ate game suppers at brilliantly lighted balls were the very people who complained about the Fire Department's rowdiness, inefficiency, and—eventually—its ethnicity, and who, by the way, were nowhere to be found when fire broke out.

Then again, some fire companies were no slouches in the brilliantly lighted ball department, either. The *New York Herald* covered one such firehouse dance, sponsored by the Oceanus Engine Co. 11 in 1852 and attended not only by firemen but also some well-to-do civilians. "On approaching the house we found the streets lined on both sides, for about a block, with carriages," the paper reported. Inside the firehouse, "[T]he walls were tastefully decorated with appropriate engravings, and in the back part of the room was the book case, well filled with a collection of useful and entertaining books." The reporter estimated that the firehouse's "appointments" cost about $1,200, which members had collected among themselves.

By the late 1840s, the Fire Department had nearly 2,000 volunteers serving in thirty-seven engine companies, eight ladder companies, thirty-eight hose companies, and two companies charged with maintaining the Department's hydrants. For all the fun and games of brawls and chowders, the companies had a strict set of bylaws. Every May, each company elected its officers—foreman, assistant foreman, treasurer, and secretary—each with specific duties. Just as important, the bylaws of the Fifteenth Ward Hose Company stated that the secretary "shall procure at the expense of the Company such refreshments as the Foreman shall think proper." The foreman often thought it proper to procure alcoholic refreshments, especially in winter, but not necessarily for drinking—gin, brandy, or whiskey often was poured into the firemen's boots to keep their feet from freezing. Firemen who were late getting to a fire were fined 50 cents, and those who showed up without their fire cap had to pay 25 cents. The use of "profane or indecent language" cost a fireman 50 cents, but "introducing religious or political subjects" was deemed a lesser offense, drawing a fine of 25 cents. The fines went a long way toward paying for those expensive appointments in some firehouses.

In late 1848, Cornelius Anderson resigned as chief engineer after leading the Department since 1837. The various company foremen and assistant foremen elected Alfred Carson as their new chief. He was a plain-speaking fireman who had no patience with anything but orderly firefighting. His favorite drink, it was said, was sarsaparilla. This eccentric habit, and other fastidious qualities that might accompany it, did not bode well for some of the Department's best-known fire laddies. Or, for the matter, for members of the Common Council who would excuse almost anything in return for the laddies' votes.

Through it all, Bill Tweed was having a fine old time as a volunteer fireman. He was making new friends and political contacts, and would soon make his debut as a Tammany candidate for the Common Council. He was very much a young man worth watching. He and several fellow firemen split off from their companies in 1849 to create a new company, Americus Engine Co. 6. As always, Tweed was a conspicuous figure at the new company's first big dance—its coming-out party on the firehouse social scene. A contemporary remembered Tweed as "young and good looking then, with dark brown hair and clear, gritty eyes. He was a tip-top dancer and never wanted [for] a partner." He was elected Engine 6's foreman in August 1850 and was presented with the company's speaking trumpet, which the foreman used to help clear the way as the engine rattled through the streets, and to shout commands to his men at fires.

Colorful as Tweed's life seemed, it was not without hazards, and they often had nothing to do with firefighting. Since the 1840s the city had been home to a growing complement of gangs, often organized by ethnic group or neighborhood. Many gangs developed loose affiliations

As foreman of Engine Co. 6, Bill Tweed was a well-known figure in pre–Civil War New York. The speaking trumpet under his arm was used to shout commands to firemen and civilians alike.

with local politicians, who deployed them on Election Day to intimidate foes. Just for the fun of it, the gangs occasionally attacked the volunteers and damaged their equipment. Tweed had been foreman for just a few weeks when Americus Engine Co. 6 and two other companies were assaulted by murderous thugs who not only beat the firemen but also robbed nearby civilians and raped several women. It was only the latest in several such outrages. Chief Carson was beside himself with anger as his men and innocent civilians came under attack at fires.

But Carson's anger was not directed only at the gangs and the politicians he believed were protecting them. Though he loved firefighters, he was unafraid to admit that the Fire Department had its share of brawlers and miscreants, epithets that he believed described burly Bill Tweed. When he received a report in late summer 1850 that Tweed had attacked members of Hose Co. 31 with "boxes, barrels and missiles of various kinds," Carson was ready to make an example of the famous foreman. He brought the case to the Common Council and was delighted to hear that members of its Committee on the Fire Department, which had control over personnel matters, agreed that Tweed should be "forever expelled" and other members of Engine Co. 6 suspended for six months.

"Forever" lasted several days. An enraged Carson learned that the committee had reconvened with no advance notice and rescinded Tweed's expulsion, recommending instead a three-month suspension for the foreman and a month's suspension for the other members of Engine Co. 6.

As luck would have it, Chief Carson was due to appear before the Common Council in early September to deliver the Department's annual report. Usually the annual report consisted of a dry discussion of prosaic issues like the condition of hoses and engines, the number of firemen available for duty, and the Department's wish list for new equipment. Carson, however, was in no mood for business as usual. Facing the politicians who undercut his authority and failed to protect his men from gangs, he delivered a stinging sermon that condemned the city's corrupt politics and his Department's excesses.

He complained about "certain clubs of desperate fighting men. . . [that] make deliberate and bloody attacks on our firemen while going to, and returning from fires. . . . I have had many of these villains arrested for upsetting our engines, cutting the hose, beating our firemen almost to death. . . but they were no sooner in prison than the captains of police, the aldermen and the judges. . . would discharge them to commit fresh attacks on the firemen the following night." Carson continued, "Indeed, these scamps"—here he is referring to the gangs, not the aldermen—"openly boast that they can bring influence enough to bear on the captains of police, Aldermen and police judges from their clubs and political associations to effect their liberation."

This was just the beginning. Carson then named names. He charged that in the sixth ward, the city's poorest and most dangerous (it included the Five Points area), a man named Garrett solicited a $25 bribe from a would-be police officer on behalf of Aldermen Patrick Kelly and Thomas Barr, who had the power of appointment to the police force in that ward. Kelly was a particularly well-known local politician, not for any famous legislation he had authored, but for the discharges he had written, while drunk, for a couple of prostitutes the police hauled in from his neighborhood. The incident led to his arrest, which may have played a role in his winning reelection as alderman in 1849.

Carson went on to denounce gangs that deliberately set fires to lure firemen into ambushes. But he made it clear that the firemen themselves were not always innocent victims. "If my own father, or my beloved children, were guilty of the charges I hereby prefer. . . charges that I believe to be true from the sincerity of my heart—before God I solemnly declare that I would not shield them from the public's scorn and retribution." And then he named another name—William Tweed. He charged that Tweed's friends had cut deals with several council members—Alderman Florence McCarthy had accepted "sundry golden trinkets," Carson said—to rescind his expulsion from the Department. A "black and infamous transaction" Carson called Tweed's reduced punishment.

Returning to the gangs and murderous "clubs" that preyed on the Fire Department, Carson delivered one last and emphatic pledge: "I say if you do not act like men—like magnanimous, patriotic and honest men—and at once begin the great work of reform. . . the New York firemen will as assuredly uprise and exterminate the clubs of this city as that all men must die. They will take the whole matter into their own hands."

His performance shocked the city and delighted the newspapers, particularly the *New York Herald,* one of the Fire Department's most dependable supporters. The newspaper noted that it regularly condemned the "imbecility" of the Common Council, and it was glad to see its own views confirmed.

Members of the Board of Aldermen were not nearly as pleased. At a meeting on September 7, aldermen could barely await their turn to denounce Carson and his report. Alderman Kelly took pains to condemn Carson's suggestion that he would sell his authority to appoint police officers for $25. Perhaps Carson had the price wrong.

Responding to the aldermen's outraged speeches, the *Herald* said, "Such a commotion was never before witnessed within the four walls of City Hall. The worthy Aldermen fretted and fumed like maniacs, and acted as eels do when caught on the angler's hook, by twisting and turning themselves in every imaginary contortion."

On September 9, Bill Tweed presented a petition asking that he be given a chance to defend himself against Carson's charges. Tweed, after all, had big plans, and could hardly stand idly by while his reputation was soiled. He needn't have worried. Within a year, he and his men in Engine Co. 6 were guests of President Millard Fillmore in the White House, and in the fall of 1851, Bill Tweed himself was elected to the Board of Aldermen. It was the beginning of his famous career in politics.

It should go without saying that Chief Carson was not a particularly popular man in and around City Hall. Augustine Costello dismissed Carson as a crank, a "reformer in a non-reforming age." Nobody, Costello said, "cared a straw about his charges." But that simply wasn't true. In early 1854, firemen at a mass meeting passed a resolution condemning the Council for allowing the Department to deteriorate. Individual companies passed resolutions of support for their chief through the early 1850s, when New York's political insiders circled the date on the calendar when Carson would deliver his icy and eloquent annual report. The entertainment provided by theaters along the Bowery wasn't half as good as Carson's yearly condemnation of the aldermen and, it must be noted, of misbehaving firemen. A new newspaper called the *New York Daily Times* placed some of Carson's colorful reports on page one.

Carson was no dilettante or critic in an ivy tower. He was a member of the Department who cared deeply about its men and its mission, and he didn't care if he made enemies in pursuit of positive change. He successfully modernized the city's alarm system, linking the network of bell towers—which were still very much in use—to the Department's headquarters by telegraph. A new bell system more precisely located fires in one of the city's eight fire districts. To keep hangers-on away from fires, Carson ordered badges for his firemen. Anybody not wearing one was barred from approaching a fire scene. Crotchety though he was, he successful worked with a newly created Board of Fire Commissioners, headed by Zophar Mills. The commissioners, chosen by the firemen themselves, took over some administrative functions previously the bailiwick of the micromanagers of the Common Council.

One change Carson was not eager to implement, although nearly every other large city had already done so, was the transition from hand-pumpers to steam-powered engines. Just as with their hand-drawn equipment, the city's firemen clung to their labor-intensive hand-pumpers and found as many excuses as they could to spurn steam-powered engines. Some of this reluctance was driven by pride and tradition,

Firefighters in the 19th Century were street-tough characters.

but it also was motivated by self-protection. The new engines used steam power instead of hand pumps to deliver water through hoses, which meant the crews of men pumping water by hand would no longer be necessary, and that meant a sharp reduction in the number of firefighters.

The independent insurance company-funded Fire Patrol used a steam engine, but Carson complained that it took "half an hour to get it in operation after reaching the fire." Nevertheless, the Common Council wanted the city to have them, and ordered two from Lee & Larned (the firm would go on to build fire engines for New York for decades).

All the while, Carson continued to lecture the city's politicians about the dangers firemen faced from gangs and other rowdies. After a while, he and the aldermen gave up listening to each other. When he delivered his 1852 annual report he told the aldermen: "[I]n consequence of the disrespectful manner with which you generally treat such suggestions that emanate from me, however beneficial to the Department. . . I shall make no recommendations in the report." There was no point in wasting his time. But, just for laughs, he might have recommended that the aldermen stop siphoning off money from the Fire Department's budget. Between 1835 and the start of the Civil War in 1861, nearly $250,000 was budgeted for new engines, hoses and other equipment. Of that figure only about $100,000 actually made its way to the firehouses. As a result, in 1853 five of the city's forty-five engine companies and three of the thirteen hook-and-ladder companies had no apparatus.

By now the aldermen had had enough of the prickly Carson, but although the Common Council had the power to remove a chief engineer, nobody wanted a repeat of the Gulick affair. Instead, the Tammany-controlled council devised a more subtle plan to rid themselves of the insolent fire chief. They changed the procedure by which chief engineers were elected, giving the vote to all firemen, not just company foremen and assistant foremen. They then packed the Department with new firemen whose allegiance would be not to their chief but to their boss—the local alderman. From 1850 to 1853, the council more than doubled the number of firefighters, from 1,898 in 1850 to 4,125 in 1853. From 1852 to 1853 alone, 1,395 new firemen joined the force. By contrast, the Department had added only 45 firefighters from 1849 to 1850. Petitions to create new companies were granted routinely, and over Carson's objections. The chief knew exactly what the aldermen were up to. In his annual report in 1853, he challenged them to fire him, rather than rely on proxies in the Department. "Inasmuch as you have the power to remove me at any moment, why do you resort to such disreputable means as to effect it, and thus keep the Department in continual excitement and broil," he said. "You have created contention in companies in order to afford you a pretext to remove my friends and fill their places with your own. . . . And you have even disbanded whole companies friendly to me, and filled their places with my enemies. . . . I might speak of twenty years' service as a Fireman, but I will not. You are a band of political scoundrels and you can do your worst."

And so they did. They were foiled at first, when Carson won reelection in 1854. But in 1857, the politicians lined up behind the candidacy of Harry Howard as chief engineer, and Carson lost. By then he had become an ineffective voice for reform, having alienated the city's political leadership and even some of his friends on the Fire Department. With Carson out of the way, the Tammany-controlled Common Council quickly folded the Fire Department's budget into the city's Street Department, a lucrative cog in the political machine. The street commissioner, always a dependable Tammany man, was given explicit control over the Fire Department's finances, and the chief engineer was made subordinate to him on all matters of administration and finance.

Though the Carson era was filled with fascinating political intrigue, rip-roaring epithets, and great amateur boxing, they were sad and tragic years, too. One of the city's most horrific tragedies, and one of the Department's most terrible days, took place early on in Carson's tenure. They must have made his quarrels with Tammany seem both more frustrating and less important.

The school day was nearing an end on Thursday, November 20, 1851, when a teacher in P.S. 26 in Greenwich Village suddenly felt faint and could barely speak. Several of her frightened students rushed from the classroom to an adjacent auditorium, pleading for water for their stricken teacher. There were several hundred students in the auditorium, and when they heard cries for water, they assumed the school was on fire. The children raced for the doors, screaming, "Fire!" A teacher who heard the cries from outside the auditorium rushed to a door and was nearly trampled. There were 1,851 students in the building, and within minutes, most were running toward a staircase leading to doors that would lead them out of the building.

The doors were locked. Screaming, frightened children pushed forward from the staircases and pressed against the banisters. The banisters gave way, and children fell into the suffocating crowd gathered in front of the locked doors. Other children left the stairs, went back to their classrooms, and leaped three stories to the street. A passerby watched in horror as a young boy held the hand of his little brother and urged him to jump, promising that he would jump with him. The passerby moved near the window and caught the two boys, and eighteen more who followed.

Meanwhile someone contacted the Fire Department. Firemen, responding to the false alarm, tried desperately to open the doors from

Major fires brought out not only firefighters, but citizens in top hats who enjoyed watching the Fire Department at work.

the outside as they heard the screams within. But the doors were made to open inward, and the firemen couldn't get them to open quickly because of the crush of children stacked up in front of them. The false rumor of fire was spreading through the neighborhood, and now parents were outside the school building, screaming and weeping. Finally, after several dreadful minutes, the firemen pushed open the doors. They found the bodies of forty children who had suffocated or been crushed to death. That's why today, doors in public buildings in New York and elsewhere open outwards.

A series of fires over the next few years, culminating in the fiery destruction of the Harper Brothers publishing offices and more than a dozen other buildings in December 1853, killed four firemen. Ever the firefighter's friend, the *New York Herald* offered an eloquent tribute to the Fire Department after the Harper Brothers disaster, which had threatened to become a repeat of the fires of 1835 and 1845. "Amid crackling timber and hissing flames they forced their way, regardless of every peril, in their efforts to roll back the billows of fire," the *Herald* said. "[For] three long hours, the heroic firemen worked at their engines, and yielded not until they were masters of the angry element."

Such tributes, however, could hardly soften the blow of a far-worse calamity four months later, on April 26, 1854.

The fire alarm bell atop City Hall began ringing at about eight o'clock that night as fire roared through the William T. Jennings & Co. tailoring establishment at 231 Broadway. The bell had hardly finished pealing when the entire building was engulfed in flames. A newspaper reporter at the scene noted that the flames reflected "beautifully upon the marble columns of the City Hall," which was just across the street. The conflagration's beauty was matched by its fury. Among the first firemen on the scene was John O'Donnell, twenty-one, who was the son of the city's chief coroner. O'Donnell was given the assignment of salvaging whatever property he could from the burning building.

Meanwhile, companies were deployed south of the building in an effort to save the American Hotel and other adjacent businesses. Several men were ordered to the rooftop of a five-story building to the north of the Jennings building, while Harry Howard, the future chief engineer who supplanted Carson, led his men in Engine Co. 21 into the second story of the tailor shop. They directed a steam of water toward a staircase on the third floor. Through the smoke, Howard spotted a skylight leading to a two-story extension of the building. He ordered his men to get out on the roof of the extension to throw water on another part of the Jennings building, but as they did so, the rear wall collapsed. More than two dozen firemen were buried in debris. Zophar Mills, leader of the Department's reserves, was climbing a ladder when the wall fell, and managed to crawl to safety. "I got out I know not how, minus my cap," he later recalled. John O'Donnell was not so lucky. He was alive, but was trapped by a heavy wooden beam, helpless as flames burned nearby.

Fighting the fire now became a second priority to a desperate and dangerous rescue operation. Even while the building's roof seemed about to collapse and as scalding water from hoses still in play fell on the firemen, they frantically picked through the ruins to look for their injured colleagues. From the wreckage came O'Donnell's voice, pleading for help. Firemen shouted back and, with only their bare hands, tossed aside debris and tried to claw their way to him. Firemen knocked on piece of timber. "Is that near you?" they shouted.

"No," O'Donnell replied.

They kept digging, for O'Donnell and for others. O'Donnell shouted: "I can't stand this much longer."

Outside the building, O'Donnell's father, the coroner, and his brother, also a firefighter, paced the sidewalk and waited.

Finally the firemen got to O'Donnell. He was alive, but terribly mangled. His father and brother watched as he was rushed to an ambulance and taken to City Hospital, where he later died, after much agony. Ten other firemen died, too. It was the worst disaster in New York firefighting history, a melancholy record that would hold for more than a century.

When Harry Howard became chief engineer in 1857, he inherited a Department that bore the scars of Tammany Hall's plunder and negligence, but at least had been purged of feuds and other embarrassments. Leases on firehouses were expiring or were allowed to expire, threatening fire protection in several neighborhoods. Howard complained that Ladder Co. 4, "one of the most efficient and energetic in the Department, [has] been out of service for some time, in consequence of there not being a location provided for them by the Common Council." Ladder Co. 4's previous quarters had become so rundown it was condemned and torn down, but not replaced. The job of bell-ringer, designed in theory to help spread the alarm of fire, had become a nineteenth-century no-show position, leading Carson to complain that the good ones were fired and the bad ones allowed to stay on. Tammany controlled these positions, and it was happy to ignore Howard's plea to turn over the hiring process to the Board of Fire Commissioners.

In 1859 Howard did have some good news to report, however, and it offered some evidence that Carson's years of preaching and lecturing had some good effect: "A previous cause of complaint during former years (that of rowdyism and disorder) has been effectually eliminated, and I am free to say that the Department has never been in such perfect discipline."

That may well have been true. The days of Moses Humphreys and his sort—the fire laddies—clearly were over, but the shadow of the Department's excesses lingered. In 1859, a former member of Congress from the city, William M. Tweed, was appointed to serve on the Department's Board of Fire Commissioners. It was hard to argue with Tweed's qualifications—he was, after all, a former fireman himself. As a commissioner, Tweed was obliged to report to the Department's headquarters on Elizabeth Street twice a week to rule on cases of insubordinate or unruly behavior and otherwise help administer the Department. But his presence on the board meant that politics had not been eliminated from the Department.

The most memorable fire of Howard's years destroyed one of the city's best-known landmarks, but—miraculously—it killed neither civilians nor firefighters. The Crystal Palace, a glass-enclosed auditorium on Forty-second Street and Sixth Avenue, opened with great hoopla in 1853, but it lasted only until 1858, when it burned to the ground in a spectacular blaze. Disciplined firefighting helped prevent the loss of life, and kept the fire contained.

It was a measure of how far the Department had come in the 1850s that one of its most persistent critics, the *New York Daily Times,* was reduced to mere carping by the decade's end. The paper complained that fire bells were ringing in the night, awakening citizens from deserved slumber. "The tolling of bells for every petty fire is [a] nuisance that ought to be stopped," the paper whined. "There is no object to be gained by disturbing the sleep of half the Metropolis."

Before long another kind of fire bell would disturb the sleep of the entire nation. New York's Fire Department responded to the alarm as eagerly as ever.

WAR AND REVOLUTION

IF NEW YORK'S FIREFIGHTERS believed in omens, they had reason to regard the night of February 2, 1860, as a foreshadowing of the conflagration that would soon engulf the country.

It was a chilly winter's evening, with clear skies and a bright moon that inspired many New Yorkers to take a take a stroll before bedtime. Those with a little more energy grabbed their ice skates and happily descended upon Central Park, where the ponds were frozen and hundreds of skaters were frolicking.

In the city's salons and parlors that night, serious conversation would have focused on increasing tensions between North and South over an issue that had been described as a fire bell in the night—slavery. New York's civic elites were anticipating the arrival of Abraham Lincoln, the Illinois politician who had spoken about the grim prospects for a "house divided" two years before. He was scheduled to give a major address at Cooper Union in three weeks. There was talk that Lincoln would run for president in 1860 on the Republican party ticket, so his speech in New York took on special significance. As the renowned abolitionist Arthur Tappan had discovered thirty years earlier, New York

City did not share Boston's antislavery fervor. Run by merchants and financiers, New York worried that a disruption of the cotton trade would further depress an economy that had fallen into recession in the late 1850s. In the event, Lincoln's Cooper Union speech become part of his canon and in fact was a turning point in the year's political developments, but it didn't impress New York. Months later, on Election Day, Lincoln lost the city by 2 to 1.

The city's politics reflected hard times and the nation's acrimonious debate. In the fall of 1859, New Yorkers took part in a particularly bitter mayoral election, which saw a combination of Wall Street bankers, nativists, reformers and members of the fledgling antislavery party, the Republicans, oust Fernando Wood, who campaigned as a champion of immigrants, the poor, and working people. The election was over, but the city's divisions—between rich and poor, immigrant and native-born, management and labor—were particularly acute on this moonlit February evening. Civic leaders like Charles Loring Brace, founder of the Children's Aid Society, had been screaming that "emigration" was the only alternative for the city's small army of unemployed. Brace and his sort looked with growing hatred at the city's immigrants and the poor in general. Of the city's 813,000 people, more than half were immigrants, and of these, slightly more than 200,000 were Irish. They lived in the city's worst neighborhoods and competed with the city's 10,000 African Americans for the lowest-paid jobs. Brace soon had a solution to rid New York of this pestilence of impoverished immigrants. In the interests of humanity, the Children's Aid Society began taking children from indigent parents, most of them Irish Catholics, and sending them to live with families in the Midwest.

Housing conditions for the immigrant poor in New York were appalling, a circumstance people like Loring tended to regard as a reflection of the tenants, not of the landlords or, indeed, the social order. Many thousands lived in basement rooms, and even in such dismal quarters they had to share such facilities as there were with similarly disadvantaged families. Others, only somewhat luckier, lived in a comparatively new type of dwelling, the tenant, or tenement, house. These buildings started appearing in the mid–1830s, and became much more commonplace as the city became home to so many poor immigrants beginning in the mid–1840s. The usefulness of the tenement house was hardly a secret. Meeting minimum standards of safety and comfort, they were designed to warehouse the poor as cheaply as possible: Typically the rooms had few or no windows and the only sanitary facilities and source of water were an outside pump and a privy. A writer in *Harper's Weekly* observed that a New Yorker who strolled along Broadway near Madison Square could take pride in the city's beauty, wealth, and power. But in neighborhoods like the Five Points, there was another New York: "Of this population, 78,000 live in damp, dark, dreary cellar, often under water. . . . Of this population, 500,000 live in tenant-houses. . . . Every hideous form of misery and vice, hunger, murder, lust, and despair, are found in every corner. There is nothing that makes human nature repulsive or human life intolerable that does not abound in these tenant-houses."

In 1856, the state legislature appointed a committee to investigate the crowded, dangerous conditions in tenement houses and to make a series of recommendations. Committee members returned with four proposals, including one calling for regulations "as to the building of halls and stairways in houses occupied by more than three families, so as to insure egress in case of fire." Legislators nodded, but saw no reason to act. Though visitors continued to comment on the frequency of fires in New York, amazingly, few led to loss of civilian life. Politicians were content to extend the city's fire limits to Forty-second Street, meaning that new buildings to the south had to conform to rudimentary regulations over building materials.

At around the same time, a developer named Edmund Waring built a new tenement house at 142 Elm Street, on the Lower East Side. At six stories, it towered above adjacent buildings. The building was designed to house twenty-one families in three-room apartments consisting of a kitchen, bedroom, and parlor. On the night of February 2, twenty families—more than 100 people—were living there. One apartment was vacant.

Ferdinand Festoniere was a baker who used a portion of the building's first floor as his bakery. At about 7:30 that night, Festoniere's stepfather went down to the cellar to get some coal. He found two of the building's wooden coal bins on fire, and shouted for help. Festoniere raced down the stairs, but by then the flames had become so intense he and his stepfather could do nothing but retreat and raise an alarm.

It took only minutes for the fire to spread up the staircase to the second, third, and fourth stories. Caspar Storch, a married father of three small children, was eating his dinner when he heard noises outside their tiny apartment. He opened the apartment door and saw flames leaping up the stairs. He shouted to his wife to gather up the children.

Eyewitness accounts of the fire remarked on the speed with which the flames moved. Solomon Scheibier lived on the second floor, above the bakery, with his wife and two children. By the time they realized something was wrong, flames blocked their escape down the stairs. Tenants from upper floors, seeing the fire reaching for them, raced through Scheibiers' apartment and leaped out a window. Scheibier's wife did likewise, while Scheibier himself, with one of his children in his arms, raced to another window to await rescue. But another panicked tenant accidentally pushed Scheibier, and he and the infant plunged out of the window. Neither was hurt, but the Scheibiers' other child was still in the apartment. Only about three minutes had passed between spotting the fire and falling out the window, Scheibier later recalled.

Back on the fifth floor, Caspar Storch shouted to his wife, "Hurry up with the children." With a baby in her arms, his wife told him to go ahead with their two other children. She disappeared to find and secure her jewelry box. Storch tried to get down the staircase, but the smoke and heat were too much, and he returned to the apartment to find his wife leaning against a wall. She and the baby were dead of smoke inhalation. Storch, too, was beginning to suffocate. With little time to spare, he forced his way through a door leading to a window. There, he grabbed hold of a clothes line and made a daring and desperate escape. Somewhere in the confusion he lost his two older children.

Tenants who climbed to the building's roof discovered that they had nowhere to go. Since the building was three or four stories higher than those adjoining it, a rooftop-to-rooftop escape was impossible. The Parrott family—a mother and five children, the father out of the house and at work when the fire broke out—was trapped in their fifth-floor apartment. Alfred, the youngest boy, summoned the courage to leap from a window to the roof of an adjacent building, a fall of about twenty-five feet. Mrs. Parrott gently tossed three of Alfred's siblings out the window to the roof, and then tied some sheets together and tried to lower her ten-month-old infant to Alfred. The child fell out of the makeshift harness, but landed unharmed in a pile of snow. Mrs. Parrott then leaped to safety. Others did the same, including a thirteen-year-old French girl named Veronica Marchant, who survived.

When firefighters arrived at this scene of panic and desperation, they quickly deployed their ladders, only to discover that the equipment wasn't long enough to reach beyond the fourth floor. The *New York Times* reported the next day that because of the short ladders, the firemen "were obliged to abandon all hope of saving the poor creatures in the two upper stories." There were no fire escapes; no law-making body had thought to require them. Just as horrifying, the paper reported, was that "as the firemen stood on the ladders, they could see many women and children lying prostrated on the floor, surrounded by the flames, which rendered all attempts to approach them ineffectual."

Firefighters from Engine Co. 40, Moses Humphrey's unit, and Hose Co. 15 fought valiantly to save some of the screaming men, women, and children shouting for help from windows in the lower floors. James Mount, foreman of Hose Co. 15, pulled two people out of the building, and Daniel Scully of Engine Co. 40 rescued six more. Among the saved was the missing Scheibier child. But Caspar Storch lost his entire family: his wife and their three children. Their charred remains were found on February 5.

Twenty people perished in the fire. Among the dead were a widow named Mrs. McBride and her two children. Though the number of fatalities in 1845 was higher—twenty-six civilians and four firemen— the toll on Elm Street was more shocking. The victims did not die in several locations, as in 1845, but were all tenants in a single building. The Elm Street fire was not a citywide conflagration, nor was it a particularly spectacular blaze, like the fire that destroyed the Crystal Palace. It was a fire confined to one building, and it killed twenty people. A survivor contended, rightly, that had the fire broken out several hours later, when the tenants were asleep, the toll would have been far worse.

The city was stunned, and outraged. Not for the last time, New York realized that building practices had outpaced government regulation as well as the Fire Department's equipment. A *New York Times* editorial thundered: "We are our own masters. . . . And what is the result? Twenty-four families of American citizens are crowded, on this sixtieth year of the nineteenth century, into a building so constructed that when a fire breaks out in one of its lower floors, not all the zeal and all the apparatus of the Fire Department. . . can save one third of them from perishing." The paper slightly exaggerated how many families lived at 142 Elm Street, and it very likely was wrong about the tenants' all being American citizens. Certainly the tenants' names do suggest a surprising ethnic mix under one roof: Mrs. McBride, Solomon Scheibier, Ferdinand Festoniere, Caspar Storch.

The *Times'* ringing denunciation of shoddy construction methods and the resultant terrible conditions in the tenement houses, and of the blind eye politicians turned to both, expressed sentiments held by the city in general. A coroner's jury found that the tenement's owner, Waring, was "responsible, to a great extent, for this serious loss of human life." The jury insisted that it was Waring's "duty, in the construction of the building, to have made provision for a contingency not at all unlikely to occur in buildings as overcrowded as we find this one to have been."

It might have been Waring's moral duty to provide for fire exits, but it was by no means his legal obligation. Even as more and more New Yorkers crowded into tenement houses that were rising higher than the highest Fire Department ladder, there were no laws requiring builders to construct fire escapes.

Recriminations abounded. A letter writer to the *Times* noted that there was no good reason for the city's firemen to have such short ladders. London, the correspondent pointed out, had "a sort of telescopic ladder. . . mounted on a single pair of wheels" which could be raised by "simply the turning of a crank after the machine is in position." New York's firemen, while brave and unstinting, were still only grudgingly

The crowded tenements of Orchard Street were a fireman's nightmare in the late nineteenth and early twentieth centuries.

accepting the idea of horses pulling their archaic hand-pumpers. And most firemen still resisted widespread use of the steam-fed pumper—the first steam engine was introduced in 1858. The firehouse culture prized brawny courage over technical innovation. Besides, even if the Fire Department wished to update its equipment, its budget of more than $500,000 a year remained in the hands of the Common Council. The aldermen had a weakness for approving exorbitant repair bills, but were a good deal less interested in outfitting the firemen with the latest in firefighting technology.

The council was not so slow in responding to the public's anger over the Elm Street tragedy. Within weeks, the aldermen passed a new law requiring that dwelling places housing more than eight families have "fireproof stairs. . . attached to the exterior walls" or "balconies on each story on the outside of a building, connected by fireproof stairs." There was little opposition; the building industry wisely chose not to complain too loudly about the additional cost and inconvenience, or about the incessant burdens of government regulation. The law took effect on

June 1, 1860, and would become a model for political reaction to fiery catastrophes. The requirement for fire escapes was good, it was necessary, and it once again made clear that government had a role in requiring public safety in private construction.

But for the residents of 142 Elm Street, as for dozens more fire victims in the future, social progress arrived too late.

Less than a week after the Elm Street fire, on February 7, 1860, New York's firemen elected John Decker as their new chief engineer. He was thirty-seven years old, with thinning hair, impressive sideburns, and a patch of beard under his lip. Though still young, he already was a twenty-year veteran of the Department, and had risen through the ranks to become an assistant engineer. Like many other firemen, Decker so loved the work that he made volunteer firefighting a second career, serving well beyond the time required to earn exemption from militia and jury service.

His connection to the Fire Department began long before he formally became a fireman in 1840. He was born next door to a firehouse in 1823, and was among the young boys who gathered in firehouses in the 1830s hoping to join in the excitement and tore out into the streets. Legend has it that he saw service as a runner during the Great Fire of 1835, when he was twelve years old.

Like another famous chief, James Gulick, Decker had a commanding physical presence. In his prime, he was a muscular 190 pounds and proclaimed, "I could hold my own with the best of them, and that was no mean boast." Although there is no evidence that Decker was among the firemen who seemed to prefer streetfighting to firefighting in the 1840s, he indicated in his old age that he was no stranger to brawls. "I never courted a fight and never shrank from one," he told Augustine Costello, chronicler of the volunteers. "Each and every member of the company felt about as I did, and we were hard men to down."

More to the point, though, Decker never shrank from a fire. In April 1848, he responded with other members of Engine Co. 14 to a fire in a sugar house on Duane Street. As one of the company's most capable and popular men (he was elected assistant foreman of the company that year), he was given the honor of working the pipe, or nozzle. He took up a position near another fireman, Henry Fargis, the assistant foreman of Engine Co. 38, who was working near one of the sugar house's walls. The fire appeared to be fairly routine, so much so that Decker and Fargis were talking with each other as they battled the blaze. Then the wall near Fargis collapsed, burying several firemen in a steaming, hissing pile of debris. Fargis ran toward Decker but was struck in the head by a falling cornice. He was killed instantly. The Fire Department's senior officer at the fire, Assistant Engineer George Kerr, was killed in the collapse, and another fireman, Charles Durant, died of his injuries several days later. Years later, as he reflected on the tragedy, Decker spoke of the men he served with at the sugar house fire and many others in later years. "Fire duty was their religion," he said. "They sacrificed to it health, wealth, strength, wife's society, everything."

In his first few months as chief of the Department's 4,227 men, Decker surveyed its manpower and equipment needs in preparation for his first annual report to the Common Council, and some curious circumstances came to his attention. Although the council had appropriated $15,000, no small sum in 1860, to buy new hoses, none had been ordered. He also found that individual companies routinely billed the council for repairs to their apparatus, and the council routinely approved them with no oversight from the chief engineer. Decker estimated that the city was paying from 25 to 40 percent more than it should on repairs, and that some repairs were not necessary.

Decker insisted that he be given greater oversight over the Department's budget, instead of keeping it a matter between the individual companies, many with ties to political clubhouses, and the members of the Common Council. "A great saving might be effected," he argued. He was well aware that critics were accusing the Department of becoming a drain on the city treasury. The most prominent such voice was, inevitably, that of the *New York Times*. Though the *Times* conceded that its constant complaints may have an "air of ungraciousness," considering that the firemen were volunteers, the paper took issue with some admittedly huge bills for repairs and new equipment. In a single session of the Common Council in December 1860, the aldermen approved expenses of at least $50,000. The total for the month was about $100,000, according to the *Times'* calculation. Many expenses were approved without contracts.

Decker shared the *Times'* concerns about wasted money and murky work orders, in part because he believed the public blamed the chief engineer for the Department's high expenses, "although he, in reality, has no power whatever over the disbursement of money appropriated for his own department," Decker wrote. In his view, money the council wasted on unnecessary or overcharged repairs was money taken from more pressing needs, including one that particularly worried him. The pipes that brought water from the Croton River were beginning to burst, although they were only twenty years old or so. The situation was so critical, Decker warned, that engines ought to be altered "so as to take water from the rivers." To do nothing was to keep the city "at the mercy of that most destructive element, fire."

But the problem of the bursting water pipes was soon overshadowed by greater events. The firing of Confederate forces on Fort Sumter in Charlston, South Carolina, on April 12, 1861, ignited a national conflagration, and John Decker and the firemen of New York responded to the call to duty.

President Lincoln called for volunteers to suppress the rebellion in the South, and in a matter of hours 1,100 of the city's 4,000-plus firemen obliged. Sworn in on April 20, they formed their own outfit, the Eleventh Regiment of the New York State Volunteers. Informally they were known as the New York Fire Zouaves, so-called because they adopted the colorful baggy breeches and uniforms of the French Zouaves, an infantry unit composed of Algerians. Their commander was a professional soldier and onetime law student from Chicago, Colonel Elmer Ellsworth, but all the subordinate officers were firemen. Colonel Ellsworth was a young man eager for the glories he associated with war, and quickly got his men weapons and equipment. They set out for battle on April 29, 1861, arriving in Washington in time to see their first action of the war—they put out a fire in the Willard Hotel.

In the heat of late July, New York's firemen-soldiers in their red and blue uniforms found themselves encamped between Washington and Richmond, near Manassas Junction and Bull Run. They were without their leader, the hot-blooded Ellsworth, who had been killed weeks earlier when he tore down a Confederate flag flying outside a hotel in Alexandria, Virginia. The hotel owner, a Confederate sympathizer, shot him on the spot, and the owner in turn was hacked to death by Ellsworth's firemen. President Lincoln, who had met Ellsworth in the late 1850s, sent a personal letter to Ellsworth's elderly parents, praising a man he called "my young friend, and your brave and early fallen child."

Without their leader, New York's firemen were hardly prepared for war. Barely four months out of New York's firehouses, these untrained though unquestionably brave men were about to face troops led by Pierre Beauregard, J. E. B. "Jeb" Stuart, and an intense, religious cavalry officer, Thomas Jonathan Jackson, who had yet to earn the nickname by which he would become famous: Stonewall.

At the height of the battle of Bull Run, the firemen–soldiers were ordered forward as part of a general Union advance, and soon came under fire from Confederate sharp-shooters. As he heard a ball whiz by his ear, one of the Zouaves' officers, John Widley of Engine Co. 11, was reminded of the excitement he felt during the great firefighting brawls of his younger years. But he would soon discover the difference between a fistfight and a war.

After exchanging heavy fire with the Confederates, the firemen came face to face with one of the Confederacy's finest soldiers, Jeb Stuart. He and his men thought the Zouaves were a similarly clad Confederate unit, and they realized their mistake too late. They spurred their horses

Young, idealistic Elmer Ellsworth commanded New York's Fire Zouaves in 1861, but was murdered before he could lead them into battle.

and charged the firemen, sabers drawn. The Fire Zouaves were no match for the men on horseback, and they soon fled, leaving behind 100 dead, 200 wounded, and 125 prisoners. Confederates under Jackson, who had already held his ground like a stone wall that day, cheered as they watched Stuart's men hack away at New York's firemen.

Despite the disaster, another regiment of eager Fire Zouaves was soon on its way south, after training in a facility on Staten Island they called Fort Decker, named for their chief engineer. Decker remained at home, confronted with the enormous task of replacing all these enthusiastic young men who marched off the war. His annual report for 1862 reported 3,814 firemen in service, 413 fewer than a year before. His recruiting efforts clearly had had some impact, though, since nearly 2,000 firemen had left the fire service for the army in 1861.

New York's Fire Zouaves went on to fight in some of the war's bloodiest battles over the next two years. Some companies lost as many as 20 men to the Union cause, at a time when company strength ranged from 50 men in engine companies, 40 in ladder companies, and 25 in hose companies. About 325 Zouaves were deployed in the Peach Orchard at Gettysburg in July 1863. They suffered horrendous casualties: 51 killed, 100 wounded, and 8 taken prisoner.

Just days after Gettysburg, the firemen who remained in New York were engaged in combat, too.

CHIEF DECKER was fighting a losing battle over steam engines. Despite his independence and determination to reform Department finances, Decker was conservative in some respects, insisting that steam-fed pumpers, now commonplace in large cities in Europe and America, could "never take the place of the hand apparatus." But in fact, firefighters were getting accustomed to the new equipment, and even demanding more. Their frequent petitions to the council for steam engines were routinely granted, and Decker could do nothing to stop it. But in some cases the steam engines were actually a means, not an end. It worked like this: The state legislature, in one of its periodic efforts to tell the city how it should be governed, had limited the size of hose

New York's firefighters, visible on the left, join the ranks of soldiers marching through Manhattan on their way to war.

companies to twenty-five men, while allowing engine companies to have fifty members. Hose companies that successfully petitioned for steam engines, and many did, then asked to become engine companies, and were allowed to recruit twenty-five more members. Decker saw what was going on, and raised public objections, saying that this practice was "fraught with a great deal of evil" because it invariably led to an increase in expenses.

Meanwhile, the parades and bands that saluted the Fire Zouaves and all the other regiments as they went off to war had given way to the horrors of mass slaughter in places like Fredericksburg, Chancellorsville, and Antietam. Some of New York's political and civic leaders, who were not nearly as enthusiastic about the war as were the Zouaves, were openly advocating a settlement with the South. Throughout the country, recruitment had fallen dramatically, so much so that Lincoln demanded a draft, and Congress passed a conscription act. The first draft lottery was to take place in New York on Saturday, July 11, 1863.

The divided house of New York was about to collapse.

The draft was unpopular for any number of reasons. For starters, rich men could avoid service by paying $300 to hire a subsitute. Males of draft age—and their mothers and wives—saw the plain unfairness of the conscription law. Furthermore, many of the laboring classes no longer believed they had a stake in the North's victory: Free blacks in the city were being used as strike breakers to foil embryonic union movements and to drive down wages, and after Lincoln's Emancipation Proclamation, their numbers could only increase. Was that worth fighting for? To many the war seemed to have become a meaningless abattoir. The city's firemen were also unhappy with the draft, because it meant that they lost their traditional exemption from military service.

The conscription process got under way with little incident. Just over 1,200 names were drawn by lot in the provost marshal's office for the Ninth Congressional District at Third Avenue and Forty-sixth Street; more names would be drawn on Monday. The draft's opponents, including some firemen whose names had been drawn, took advantage of the pause to formulate plans for mass demonstrations when military officials reassembled.

On the morning of July 13, thousands of demonstrators gathered at Cooper Union and marched uptown to the provost marshal's office where the draft lottery would resume. They carried signs reading "No Draft," and harassed passersby. Police were deployed to keep the protesters—and at this point, that's all they were—away from the official proceedings. But into the midst of this tense but peaceful standoff, members of Black Joke Engine Co. 33 burst on the scene dressed in their red fire shirts. Several members of the company had been among the names drawn on Friday. Wielding stones, the firemen disrupted the proceedings and set fire to an adjacent building. It quickly spread to the provost marshal's office. The worst riot in American history was under way. Poor people attacked the rich; white people lynched blacks. Irish names were prominent among the rioters; they also were among the heroes.

Alarm bells in the city's bell towers began ringing incessantly as rioters began torching public buildings, newspaper offices, and the homes of rich people. Many of the city's firemen were newcomers who had replaced the men gone off to war, and now they found themselves quite literally on the front lines of an insurrection. Rioters threatened firemen with death at several fires, while other crowds, eager to let the mayhem continue, destroyed fire apparatus and killed horses pulling the engines. Members of Lafayette Engine Co. 19 defied rioters armed with stones who set fire to a building at the corner of Second Avenue and Twenty-first Street. The company foreman, James Brinkman, ordered his men to ignore the threats, but as the firemen stretched their hoses, rioters cut them and attacked the engine. Furious, the firemen turned on the rioters, who soon retreated. Meanwhile, the fire burned.

Later in the afternoon, a mob gathered outside the Orphan Asylum for Colored Children on Fifth Avenue between Forty-third and Forty-fourth streets. Chief Engineer Decker, who already had been at the scene of several fires that day, arrived as the mobs were ransacking the place and demanding it be put to the torch. "Here it was that Chief-Engineer Decker showed himself one of the bravest of the brave," the *Times* reported the next day. With several of his men, he foiled repeated attempts to start a fire inside the orphanage. All the while, men from Engine Co. 18 and a stage driver named Paddy McCarthy helped the institution's superintendent, William E. Davis, shepherd more than 200 frightened children out a backdoor to safety. After Decker extinguished yet another fire, the mob put aside their incendiaries and went after the chief engineer.

Fire Department legend has it that after giving Decker a terrible pummeling, the rioters pulled him away, semiconcious. He was brought near a tree, and one of the rioters produced a rope. "What good will it do to hang me?" Decker is supposed to have said. "You'll only stop my draft, not the government's." According to Lowell Limpus's history of the period, Decker's subtle bon mot drew an appreciative chuckle from the enraged and bloodthirsty crowd, and they decided that any man with such a quick wit didn't deserve to end his days at the wrong end of the rope. News accounts the following day made no mention of Decker's pun (though newspapers were not always reliable), but they do report that he intervened heroically to extinguish several attempts to burn the orphanage. They also reported that the mob threatened to kill him and go on to say that Decker mounted the building's steps and pleaded with the crowd, numbering some 2,000 and many of them drunk or halfway there, not to bring disgrace on the city. The *Times* account said this argu-

ment seemed to dampen the crowd's bloodlust. If so, it was only temporary. Regardless of whether Decker actually talked his way out of being
lynched or not, one thing is certain: His effort to turn back the crowd
was in vain. The building was burned to the ground, indicating that he
and his men were overwhelmed in some way. Still, his efforts at stalling
the marauders no doubt helped save the orphans who lived there.

The carnage, looting, and burning continued into the night. At 3:30
on the morning of July 14, a gang set fire to a shed attached to a hotel at
the corner of Third Avenue and 127th Street, an area of the city where
fire hydrants were in short supply (as Chief Decker had noted with
growing frustration in his annual reports). Tragedy was averted by
chance, for a member of Hose Co. 21, John Rosker, lived across the
street from the hotel, and he single-handedly put out the blaze before it
did much damage. Later that morning the same mob set fire to other
buildings in Harlem, but the exhausted fire companies uptown managed
to contain the destruction to a few buildings.

The riot was only just beginning. Relentlessly, murderously, and without rest, rioters killed, maimed, and burned, even when confronted with
artillery. Smoke filled the skies from fires burning to the north, south,
east, and west. By Wednesday, July 15, Union troops fresh from their
victory at Gettysburg had been ordered into the streets of New York to
restore order. Two weeks before, they had held off Pickett's Charge;
now, they were doing the charging, marching against the rioters' barri-

cades and ducking sniper fire from tenement rooftops. Among the soldiers redeployed to New York was a member of the Fire Zouaves, an Irish immigrant named Edmon Moncasey.

Peace finally was restored on Friday, July 17. As many as 1,000 people may have died, although the bodies of only 119 were ever found. Through it all, New York's firemen worked around the clock to contain, successfully, the mob's arson campaign. A hundred buildings burned, but contemporary observers believed the toll from fire could have been far worse.

The *New York Times* and the *New York Herald,* usually at odds over the merits and administration of the volunteers, agreed that the firemen were among the heroes of the dreadful riot. As order gradually was restored late in the week, the *Times* said "the firemen of this City deserve the heartiest thanks and gratitude. . . of the citizens of our metropolis. Notwithstanding the fact that they have run great risks in attempting to extinguish the conflagrations kindled by the mob, they have been fearless and prompt in the execution of their duties." The *Herald,* which generally didn't need an occasion to praise the firemen, singled out Decker's heroism, saying: "Chief John Decker is especially entitled to the gratitude of the owners and occupants of real estate in the upper sections of the city. That he absolutely saved for them their homes and contents is conceded by everybody. Never since the days of Gulick and Anderson has the Fire Department been managed with so much signal ability."

FEARLESS THOUGH the firemen were, able as Decker was, the days of New York's volunteer Fire Department already were numbered. The need for a paid Fire Department had been raised in 1840, a time and place that seemed separated from the New York of 1863 not by decades but by centuries. The reformers and high-minded critics of that time seemed to long for days that never really existed, when firefighting was a public service performed by gentlemen like themselves, and not by tough laboring men eager for excitement, a chance at public acclaim, and perhaps even an opportunity to improve their lot in life.

A quarter century later, the Department had restored a sense of pro-fessionalism, despite the egregious behavior of the Black Joke Company during the draft riots. But discipline over spending remained almost nonexistent. Not only was the Common Council eager as ever to approve spending requested by individual companies, but the overall budget of the Department remained in the hands of the Street Commissioner, and the Street Commissioner took his orders from his deputy, William M. Tweed. At the same time the city's insurance indus-try, which had been funding a paid Fire Insurance Patrol for years to sal-vage property, was chafing at the losses it was paying for year after year. Although the annual number of fires actually had decreased since the 1850s, the Board of Fire Underwriters believed fire remained too com-mon. So did the police. The Police Department's commissioners assert-ed that "New York ought to be better guarded against fire than any other city, but it is not." Insurance rates, the police commissioners noted, were higher than in other cities, a sure sign that "New York ranks low in the scale of safety."

On March 17, 1864, the insurance underwriters formed a committee to study ways of "promoting the greater efficiency of the Fire Department." As is generally the case with special committees, the out-come was not in question: Committee members discovered that there was only one way to promote "greater efficiency" among firemen, and that was to rid the Department of volunteers and pay a force of profes-sionals, just as Boston, Baltimore, St. Louis and Cincinnati—smaller cities with much less to lose in a fire—had done. The insurance compa-nies quietly began working with Republican lawmakers in Albany, always eager to impose order on the unruly, Democratic-run city. They had done so in 1857, when they seized control of the city-run police force and created a new department. At the insurance industry's urging, they appeared ready to do likewise with the Fire Department. Chief Decker soon complained that the legislature had stepped in and cut the Department's budget by $45,000 in 1864.

The chief engineer was determined to save the Department, from itself as well as from the reformers in Albany. He summoned its officers and the Board of Fire Commissioners to a meeting in Firemen's Hall, a building on Mercer Street run by and for the volunteers. He spared his colleagues nothing, saying that they had to change or have change imposed upon them. They had to cut expenses, they had to disband unnecessary companies, they had to enforce more discipline, and they could no longer expect the city to pay the cost of the Department's elections for chief engineer and assistant engineer. Months later, as momentum built in Albany to disband the volunteers, Decker again complained that the Department could not be held responsible for lavish spending, and attacked the politicians who had used the Department to enrich friends and allies. "The Common Council and Street Commissioners' Department. . . disbursed almost all the moneys charged to the Fire Department, its officers having little or no control of it. Costly houses, beautiful apparatus and extravagant furniture and supplies were granted to fire companies without consulting the Chief Engineer."

For all the respect Decker had earned during the draft riots, again he was fighting a losing battle against necessary change. The press had begun to turn against his men. The *Times* said, "[I]t is absurd, in a city like New-York, to gather a mob to extinguish a fire. Yet, every one who has ever attended one of these incidents in our city life knows that this is precisely what takes place." The Department, which the *Times* so recently had found brave and able, it now found to be nothing but a "hot-bed of profligacy and crime."

The end of the volunteer Fire Department was in sight, but before the volunteers faded into history, they had one more moment of glory.

In late 1864, the Confederacy was hurtling toward collapse. Abraham Lincoln, who had seemed certain to be a one-term president, was headed for reelection after a series of Union victories. Sullen, embittered Southerners sought some way of repaying the North for the ruthless warmaking of Generals Ulysses S. Grant and William T. Sherman. If victory was to be denied them, they would at least take a measure of vengeance.

They set in motion a plan to burn down New York and, if their luck held, to inspire an insurrection along the lines of the draft riots. If they failed to foment an uprising, however, they would at least give New York a glimpse of the South's suffering.

A group of saboteurs infiltrated the city in the fall. They did not necessarily have the element of surprise, as the Southern newspapers had been speculating about plans to burn Northern cities, and William Seward, the secretary of state, had advised officials in New York and elsewhere to prepare for rebel-inspired arsons on Election Day. Chief Decker put his men in the firehouses and the bell towers on special alert, but the election came and went without incident.

But on the evening of November 25, a suspicious fire broke out in the St. James Hotel. It was the first of many that night as the Confederate plotters moved from hotel to hotel, using phosphorus to start what they hoped would be catastrophic fires. In addition to the hotels, the conspirators set fire to Barnum's Museum, one of the city's most popular attractions, and the Winter Garden Theater, where the three Booth brothers, Edwin, Junius, and John Wilkes, were starring in Shakespeare's *Julius Caesar*.

Throughout the night fires continued to break out. None, however, proved serious. Thanks to the quick and efficient work of Decker's men, no lives were lost, despite the late hour and the possibility of panic in the hotels, the museum, and the theater.

A month later, in an attempt to outmaneuver the insurance industry and its allies in Albany, the Common Council adopted legislation that incorporated the reforms Decker outlined in his meeting with the Fire Department's Board of Commissioners in September. It was no use. Regardless of the actual pros and cons of disbanding the volunteers and instituting a paid Fire Department, the firemen were pawns in an ongoing political turf war between New York City's business interests, who put their trust in Albany, and its machine politicians. In January, lawmakers began debate over legislation calling for a paid Fire Department that would answer not to City Hall but to Albany and the governor. A new board of state commissioners would govern a metropolitan fire district that would consist of New York and Brooklyn. Each city would, however, have its own Fire Department. One lawmaker said of the proposed change, "It is a revolution."

Decker fought bitterly against the bill, publicly accusing the insurance industry of handing out $50,000 in bribes to lawmakers to make sure the legislature did its job. Though Decker provided no evidence, only a fool would assume that the charge was entirely baseless.

The bill passed the senate and assembly in late March, and the governor signed it immediately. On March 31, the gallant Decker sent a sad letter addressed to the "honorable" Common Council. "The Legislature has passed an act creating a 'Metropolitan Paid Fire Department' in the city and county of New York," he wrote. "[The] act authorizes the Governor to appoint four Commissioners, who shall take possession of all property, tools, implements, etc., now in possession of the present Department. All property, apparatus, etc., being under the sole control of your Honorable Body, I await your instructions." One could hardly imagine a more revealing comment: In the final hours of the volunteer Fire Department, its chief engineer had no power to dispose of its assets, no control of its equipment.

The Board of Aldermen rose to the occasion, replying to Decker the next day and praising the volunteers for their years of "preventing thousands of helpless women and children from being rendered homeless and destitute." The alderman bitterly complained about "the abuse that was heaped upon the firemen,"—by this they surely meant by the *New York Times,* which was crowing about the turn of events—and assured the firemen that their "self-sacrificing actions" would be remembered, and not the newspaper criticisms.

A series of court actions brought by the volunteers only postponed the inevitable. In the meantime, the new fire commissioners published plans to hire a Department of just under 600 men, with a budget of $564,000 for equipment and salaries for the rest of the year. In building a new paid force of firemen, the commissioners said, preference would be given to the volunteers. Nevertheless, the volunteers made their dissent known in characteristically forceful, and typically democratic, fashion. While the creation of the new Department was being litigated, the volunteer companies took a vote on whether to support the old Department or a new one. Seventy companies supported the volunteer system; one voted for a paid department.

The state Court of Appeals, however, ruled in favor of the new on June 22. Five days later, Chief Engineer John Decker submitted his resignation, and on June 30 he made public his final annual report. He remained bitter about the change, insisting that it had been undertaken at the behest of the city's "moneyed power," which was arguably true. The "moneyed power" had much to lose, and indeed had lost a great deal, through fire, and had been candid for years about its preference for a paid Fire Department.

Decker's message rang truer on the subject of his beloved volunteer force, now officially an anachronism. "[When] we consider that all their labor and thought for the public good was without recompense for their services," he wrote, "we can at least say, at the close of their work, 'well done, good and faithful servants.'"

On August 1, 1865, the new Metropolitan Fire Department took over from the volunteers, and a new chief engineer, Elisha Kingsland, was appointed by the new commissioners. The old Department sadly turned over its equipment to the professionals, some of whom were veteran volunteers. Each company accounted for all its equipment, from its apparatus to tables, scrub brushes, brooms, and mops. The Department had 2,247 chairs in good order and 218 broken ones, not to mention ten bars of soap and seven spittoons.

The change surely had to come. Charming and colorful though the volunteer system often was, the critics were not wrong when they asserted that a city of New York's stature could no longer rely on an eighteenth-century idea of republican civic spirit when it came to firefighting. Still, despite the criticisms leveled by the *New York Times* editorial writers, New Yorkers had formed a special and abiding affection for the men who so willingly risked their lives on behalf of property and strangers. They hated to see them go.

The volunteers were flawed, as the *Times* had continued to point out, and they were often their own worst enemies. But they offered their service with no strings attached, no demands for rewards other than public recognition. They sought excitement, yes, and sometimes took advantage of their celebrity, but they remained, in their public image, selfless men who dared to face and defeat a relentless foe.

The new Department would have to live up to that legacy.

CHAPTER SIX

"A DUTY,
NOT A PASTIME"

The transition from a volunteer to a professional department took place firehouse by firehouse through the summer and fall of 1865, as a sorrowful, war-weary city adjusted to peace and mourned the murder of Abraham Lincoln. The city surrendered control of the volunteers' equipment to the state-appointed fire commissioners beginning on June 24, 1865, in a directive signed by the city comptroller, Matthew Brennan, a onetime volunteer fireman who had used his connections in the firehouse and the Tammany Hall clubhouse to rise to political power.

The new fire service would consist of thirty-four engine companies and twelve ladder companies to protect Manhattan as far north as Eighty-seventh Street. One by one the old companies were disbanded: Hudson Engine Co. 1, which could trace its lineage to that day in 1731 when the Newsham engines were hauled uptown from the waterfront, ended its service on July 13; the new Engine Co. 1 of the Metropolitan Fire Department opened for business on July 31. Most of the melancholy conversions took place from September to November, amid reports of tension between the old and new men. Few of the volunteers saw any reason to hide their bitterness, and while most grudgingly cooperated in turning over their equipment, there were reports of slashed hoses and vandalized apparatus. And there was a more spectacular display of resentment: The quarters of Black Joke Engine Co. 33 mysteriously went up in flames in late November. As a protest the action failed miserably, for the fire reminded the public not only of the company's disgraceful behavior at the beginning of the draft riots but of the worst excesses of the volunteers generally. A spike in the number of suspicious fires in late 1865 and early 1866 only confirmed the reformers' view that the city would be better off without the volunteers.

During and just after the transition, the new firemen often drew derisive jeers at fires from former volunteers and their friends, who took to calling the new men "the Mets." It was hardly a term of endearment. The volunteers' bitterness went beyond that felt when the old must give way to the new and became the bitterness of rejection. Of the 4,000 or so disbanded volunteers, more than half applied to the new fire commissioners for appointment to the paid force. According to protocol and common sense, the volunteers were given preference over other applicants to the paid department. But the new firefighting force required fewer than 600 people, so most volunteer applicants did not get the call. That only added to their resentment of the new department.

High-ranking veterans who made the transition from one era to the next found the process very simple. For example, on September 6, 1865, more than a dozen assistant engineers in the old department turned in their resignations, with several making it clear that they were retiring permanently from fire service. Of the eighteen who quit, five were hired that same day to serve in the Metropolitan Fire Department.

Also among the volunteers selected for the paid department were two young Irish immigrants named John Bresnan and Hugh Bonner—a fortunate turn of events for New York. With their courage and utter professionalism—and their handlebar mustaches—Bresnan and Bonner would go on to become two of the great firefighters of the nineteenth century, and role models for the new professional force. They expanded the Department's efforts to prevent as well as fight fires.

They tinkered with equipment, and invented devices that would still be in use in 125 years later. And they were passionate advocates for those who invariably suffered the most grievous losses of life in fires—the impoverished tenement dwellers in the city's most deprived neighborhoods.

Hugh Bonner, an Irish immigrant and child of the Five Points, rose to become one of the Fire Department's greatest chiefs.

Bonner's family fled famine-cursed Ireland in 1847, the year the Irish would remember as Black '47. The suffering, the starving, and the dying that year were horrendous. Starting with the first appearance of the potato blight in 1845, hundreds of thousands perished because the potato crop failed, leaving them with nothing to eat. More hundreds of thousands fled to New York and Boston, where they faced a different kind of oppression in the unfriendly cities of antebellum Protestant America. By the time the Famine had run its course, more than a million Irish people were dead, and another million had fled, mostly to America. The Famine Irish, uneducated and unskilled, were the first huddled masses to arrive in America without the chains of slavery. Their memories of starvation, of eviction, and of oppression would be passed along to their children and grandchildren, who would eagerly seek the security of a government uniform and salary.

Hugh Bonner was eight years old when he came to New York, and within just six years, he was running with the firemen of Lady Washington's Engine Co. 40. By the time the volunteers were disbanded, he was the company's foreman, working at his day job as a tinsmith and living on Mott Street, part of the Five Points neighborhood in the raucous Sixth Ward.

Bresnan, too, lived in the Sixth Ward, a teeming, poverty-stricken district of tenement houses, theaters, and saloons that nativists and reformers regarded as their worst nightmares come to pass. Here, immigrants considered eternally alien—people with last names like Bonner and Bresnan, and later Italians and Jews, along with native-born blacks and poor whites—wallowed in what was regarded as their self-imposed misery, incapable of democratic thought, unwilling to better themselves through hard work and clean living. The canon of Five Points literature is large, and it is heavy with condemnation and moralizing, even today. When Charles Dickens, a writer already famous for his sympathetic portrayals of those on society's margins in London, came to New York in 1842, he made sure to tour the Five Points, between engagements arranged by Philip Hone and other civic leaders. There he found "narrow ways. . . reeking everywhere with dirt and filth." He was appalled by the neighborhood's "hideous tenements," where "vapors issue forth that blind and suffocate. . . . All that is loathsome, drooping and decayed is here," he asserted. Less charitable observers were much harsher in their judgments of the people who lived there. Protestant aid groups tried to proselytize in Catholic neighborhoods, explicitly linking their religion to their poverty. One Protestant clergyman compared the poor Catholics of the Five Points to "the most degraded heathen."

John Bresnan's family had left Ireland just before the mass starvation and emigration. They arrived in the Sixth Ward in 1844, when he was three years old, and like his future close friend and colleague, Hugh Bonner, young John Bresnan came to worship the red-shirted volunteer firemen in his neighborhood. He attached himself to Engine Co. 21 on Leonard Street in the Five Points. According to James L. Ford, a writer who became a friend of Bresnan's in the late nineteenth century, young John built a miniature fire engine which he dragged behind him as he raced to fires with the volunteers. He formally joined Engine Co. 21 as a volunteer in 1861, and soon thereafter joined the Union Army. His military career was brief and apparently uneventful, and he was soon back in the firehouse, serving with Engine Co. 21 until he was appointed to the new Metropolitan Fire Department in late October 1865.

The state commissioners who governed the new Department clearly were determined to make a permanent break with the excesses of the volunteers, a point that was driven home in the agency's rules and regulations. Not surprisingly, "racing to and from fires" was prohibited, as were "spirituous or intoxicating liquors" and "any game of chance." And no officer or fireman "shall use profane, immoral or indecent language" inside the firehouse or on his way to a fire. Except for the chief engineer, who was allowed to stand out from the crowd, the red shirts of the old days gave way to dark blue flannel. No fireman was allowed to be "a member of any political or partisan nominating convention." Politics was to go the way of races and brawls.

The sumptuous life of some firehouses during the Tweed era gave way to a spartan, quasi-military discipline. The firehouse roll was called every morning at eight o'clock; by that hour, the firemen were to have swept out their bunk rooms—they were all sleeping in quarters now, with their boots at their bedsides—and fed the horses. The firehouse doors, once open to all manner of visitors, were to remain closed. Each company was to have two firemen patrolling the neighborhood at all times, and they checked in every hour with a third fireman on house-watch duty. Daily patrol duty was split into four shifts to allow for a rotation.

For their annual salary of $700 (more for officers, and $3,000 for the chief engineer), firemen essentially lived in their firehouse and so were constantly on duty except when they were granted not so much a day off, but a twenty-four-hour leave. Such absences were limited to no more than three a month for firemen, slightly more for officers. Their families generally lived nearby, so the firemen were allowed to eat their meals at "home." Meal leaves were staggered so that the firehouse wasn't deserted if an alarm came in. And there would be no more feasts in the firehouses—chowder parties were very specifically banned, as were "other social assemblages."

The discipline was exacting, the work dangerous, and the pay no more than adequate, but the Metropolitan Fire Department was overrun with applicants. Even after the initial rush of volunteers seeking jobs, the commissioners reported that they had more than 2,300 applicants for just a handful of openings. In another drastic change from the old days, each candidate was required to undergo a medical examination to determine his "soundness of body, intelligence and good habits." In 1867, 156 candidates for appointment passed the test, while 145 were rejected because, in the words of the department's medical officer, Charles McMillan, "they exhibited evidence of defect of either mind or body."

All of this—the discipline, the uniforms, the testing, the very existence of a medical officer—was meant to imbue with professionalism a job that had been a hobby for decades. "Under the present system," wrote the department's commissioners, "the extinguishment of a fire is a duty and not a pastime."

Duty called on May 21, 1866, in what was to be the first real test of the Metropolitan Fire Department.

The Academy of Music, at the corner of Fourteenth Street and Irving Place, was one of New York's grandest theaters—in fact, when it opened in 1854 no opera house in the world was larger. It could seat as many as 4,000 people, and although it was lavishly appointed, its productions offered seats cheap enough for the public at large.

A performance of *La Juive* had just ended, the curtain was down, and crowds were streaming out of the theater, when, a little before midnight, fire broke out in the basement. As engine and ladder companies responded, the fire appeared to be fierce, but not spectacular. The steam engines, which by now were the department's standard-issue engine, took about ten minutes to work up enough pressure to get water on the building. One of the first firemen on the scene, James Timoney, the foreman of Ladder Co. 3, entered the building and spotted flames shooting up from the basement near the stage. John Denin and Hugh Kitson of Engine Co. 13 got inside the building with a hose, and were joined by several other engine companies. Two members of Engine Co. 5, Foreman David B. Waters and Fireman Peter H. Walsh, moved inside, looking to relieve their colleagues who were working the pipe, or nozzle. They were a good combination: Walsh was a rookie fireman with no experience as a volunteer, whereas Waters had been a volunteer for several years before giving up his trade as a printer to become a professional fireman. Somehow, as they made their way through the smoke and fire under the stage area, they lost their way.

Meanwhile, the fire's advance seemed to be checked, and some firemen joined theater staff in hauling out furniture and other property. Gas, however, was accumulating in the theater, and it exploded, turning the building into an inferno. Kitson and Denin of Engine Co. 13 were knocked down by the blast and were burned. Both crawled on their hands and knees, looking for an exit. Kitson got out, but Denin found himself trapped, with flames between him and the theater's front entrance. He had no choice but to leap through the flames and was severely burned. But he was safe.

There was to be no escape for Foreman Waters and Fireman Walsh. Kitson later recalled that as he crawled his way to safety, he passed a small opening in the floor and saw a man's clenched hand. He heard a voice shout "For God's sake, bring an ax and cut me out."

Firemen tried desperately to search for the missing men and to battle a blaze that was now out of control, but they were overmatched. Flames spread to adjoining buildings along Fourteenth Street, including a piano factory and a medical college. In the following days, estimates of the damage ranged from the *New York Times'* $1 million to the *New York Herald*'s $2 million. The Academy of Music was a smoking ruin. The first great fire of the new era was a terrible, fatal disaster.

The bodies of David Waters, twenty-six, and Peter Walsh, twenty-three, would not be discovered until the following afternoon, after hours of frantic searching. Walsh was found first, his arms and legs burned away. He was identified by a protective rubber coat. Waters was found hours later, his upper body charred. His firemen friends identified him by a pocketknife found in his trousers.

The disaster played into the hands of embittered volunteers and their friends, who charged that the new firemen were incompetent. Tammany-aligned politicians, smarting over the state's control over the Department and its annual budget of $1 million, soon were demanding an investigation of Chief Engineer Kingsland and the resignation of the four state-appointed fire commissioners. Those politically motivated recriminations were not easily dismissed, and they provoked a new round of wrangling between state and city that went on for the next several years. Far more relevant to public safety were the lessons the *New York Herald* salvaged from the ashes of one of New York's great entertainment palaces. Noting that the disaster could have been far more terrible had the fire broken out during a performance, the newspaper criticized safety measures in the city's theaters. "We trust that the very narrow escape of the public upon this occasion will lead to the passage of a law compelling all places of amusement to be made perfectly fireproof," the paper said. "There are theatres in this city which are mere shells and invite the flames. We hope that the Fire Marshal will investigate the matter, and if he can do nothing more let him at least prevent the aisles of our theatres from being blocked up with chairs. . . rendering sudden egress in case of fire impossible."

The *Herald*'s warnings would soon read like prophesy in the neighboring city of Brooklyn, where regulations were equally lax in the great age of nineteenth-century laissez-faire capitalism. For the time being, however, the only investigation ordered after the Academy of Music fire was that of the Metropolitan Fire Department. The state legislature, bowing to an orchestrated campaign of complaints—some said the firemen were slow in responding to alarms; others insisted that they were too reckless—ordered hearings, and the commissioners themselves reviewed the department's performance. The commissioners found little cause for complaint, but several lawmakers and insurance executives did, so the commissioners resigned. Taking their place was a new management team made up of several Civil War veterans, the most prominent of whom was Alexander Shaler, a retired general. He had no experience fighting fires, but he was tough, well organized, and ruthless if the occasion demanded it. He was given the title of president of the Board of Commissioners in 1867, and in just three years he recast the Department in his own image.

It turned out that there was something to the charge of inexperience and inefficiency in the Metropolitan Fire Department, at least in its first year or so. In 1867, there were 873 fires in New York, which caused $5.7 million in damages. These statistics infuriated the insurance executives who had campaigned so energetically (and, if Chief Decker was to be

believed, paid out so much money in bribes) to bring about a professional firefighting force in New York. By the time General Shaler was
through, the number of fires was somewhat lower, and damage to property had been cut dramatically, to just over $2 million, indicating that a
better-trained, better-disciplined department was learning how to contain, and not simply extinguish, fires. The Department's upgraded alarm
system also helped, as Shaler phased out bell ringers and expanded the
use of the telegraph.

Not surprisingly, given his army background, Shaler sought to organize the Department as a quasi-military force, to the point of grouping
companies into battalions and changing the traditional titles of officers
and men. Company foremen were given the title of captain, and assistant foremen were to be known as lieutenants. Assistant engineers,
whose area of responsibility was a piece of geography rather than an
individual firehouse, were dubbed battalion chiefs, and the chief engineer became chief of department. Shaler's military-style titles and divisions of authority survive into the twenty-first century, although their
use was suspended for many years after he left the Department. (Other
title innovations were short-lived, such as giving firemen the rank of
private.)

Shaler paid astonishing attention to the smallest details. In June 1867,
he recommended that his men make greater use of the firehouse
bathing tubs, "not only as a sanitary measure, but because cleanliness is
essential to public respect." Furthermore, he wrote, pillow cases and
bedspreads in the firehouse bunk room should "be used in the daytime
and removed at night. . . in order to ensure uniformity and neatness."
And he demanded that companies pay special attention to the "sleek-
ness of their horses' coats."

Not everybody was happy with the general's approach, including
the last man who would bear the title of chief engineer, Elisha
Kingsland, who resigned in 1869. By then, however, Shaler's military
approach to the Fire Department had silenced critics and banished
laments for the old volunteer department. The fire laddies finally were
finished. The professionals—proud, disciplined, and really clean—
had won the city over.

James Gordon Bennett, founding publisher of the *New York Herald* and an eyewitness to the Great Fire of 1835, always had been one of the Fire Department's most dependable champions. When his competitors at the *New York Times* found cause for complaint, which was often, Bennett's *Herald* fired back in the Fire Department's defense. Through the years, both newspapers had their moments of revelation, and their blind spots.

In 1869, after watching firemen put out a blaze in his summer residence, Bennett made a decision that would preserve his name in the Department's traditions long after his *New York Herald* published its final edition. He had his son, James Gordon Bennett, Jr., send the fire commissioners a note and a $1,500 donation to endow an annual gold medal to be bestowed "upon such members of the Fire Department as you may. . . consider best entitled to the reward." The delighted commissioners did just that, beginning yet another tradition that would last into the twenty-first century. The James Gordon Bennett Medal was first awarded in 1870, to Minithorne Tompkins, for his dramatic 1868 ladder rescue of a woman trapped by flames on an upper floor, and to Benjamin Gicquel for saving the lives of four children in an apartment house fire in 1869. The Bennett Medal remains the department's highest award for heroism, and is presented every year at Medal Day ceremonies.

Like Bennett, William M. Tweed never lost his interest in the Fire Department, although Tweed's motives were a good deal less pure. He was now the Grand Sachem, the boss of bosses, of Tammany Hall, the ruler of an empire of graft that magnified the lesser-known corruptions and excesses of Gilded Age New York. This was the era when people like the financiers Jay Gould and Jim Fisk hatched a nearly successful plot to corner the nation's gold market, and used a reputable private entity, the Erie Railroad, to fleece stockholders. Tweed was the public-sector version of these equally corrupt but, oddly, more obscure private-sector bandits. And as his power grew, he became increasingly frustrated with the various state commissions put in place to protect city agencies like the Fire Department from his control.

With its seven-figure budget and its constant need for equipment repairs and purchases, the Fire Department was a prize worth fighting for. Now a state senator and chairman of the senate's Committee on Cities, Tweed needed only a cooperative governor to return the Fire Department and other state-run agencies to the city's—his—control. Cooperation arrived in 1868, with the election of a Tammany man, John T. Hoffman, as the state's new chief executive. With allies in place in Albany and the city, and new friends flocking to him as he handed out more than a half million dollars in bribes, Tweed made his move. In early 1870 he proposed a new charter for the city which would disband the state commissions that had usurped the city's power over the Fire Department and other agencies. Tweed had invested wisely: In April, the legislature passed, and Governor Hoffman dutifully signed, what became known as the Tweed Charter. The Metropolitan Fire Department ceased to exist, as did the larger Metropolitan Fire District covering the cities of New York and Brooklyn. The charter called for the creation of a new administrative entity, the Fire Department of the City of New York, over whose commissioners the mayor would be given power. And so the initials FDNY replaced MFD in firehouses around the city. The firemen themselves, however, continued on as they had in the past. Tweed's power grab was not about personnel or procedures; it was about administration and finances.

The Tweed Charter and consequent reorganization of the Fire Department were among William Tweed's final displays of power. He was arrested in October 1871 (by another former fireman, Matthew Brennan, who was now a city sheriff), after a series of stunning stories in the *New York Times* detailing his thievery. Soon afterward, the city discovered that it was broke. The fire insurance industry had to lend the city nearly $200,000 in late 1871 to cover the Fire Department's payroll expenses.

After yet another administrative reorganization, this one designed to oust Tweed's allies as commissioners, the Department was fairly insulated from the political chaos of the early 1870s. A veteran from the volunteer days, Joseph Perley, the chief of department, was elevated to the post of president of the reorganized Board of Fire Commissioners, and another survivor of the volunteer force, Eli Bates, was named to succeed Perley as the new chief of department. At long last, Tweed was gone and a reform administration was in City Hall—and the Fire Department of the City of New York was free to further its experiment in turning firefighting into a science.

New York was now a city of a million people, most of them concentrated in what are now downtown and midtown. But the uptown neighborhood of Harlem was flourishing, and City Hall soon had its sights on some of the growing villages across the Harlem River in the southern portion of Westchester County, in what is now the South Bronx. The city annexed the towns of Kingsbridge, Morrisania, and West Farms in 1873.

To serve such a city, the Fire Department required not just hoses, hydrants, and heroes, but specialized equipment and training, and, inevitably, a bureaucracy. A special brigade of firemen known as the Corps of Sappers and Miners was founded in 1873. The Sappers and Miners received intense training in explosives and in the ancient art of blowing up buildings to help arrest the spread of fire. Considered an elite unit within the Department, the Sappers and Miners were, in essence, the forerunners of the Department's famous rescue companies, not to mention the descendants of the men who exploded barrels of gunpowder to try to stop the Great Fire of 1885. And the christening, in 1875, of the fireboat *William F. Havemeyer,* named for an early nineteenth-century mayor and volunteer fireman, extended the Department's reach to the waters around Manhattan Island.

With new tasks and challenges came a new layer of management, as the Department created a Bureau of Combustibles to regulate the storage of explosives, a Bureau of Inspection of Buildings to enforce fire-prevention regulations, and a Bureau of the Fire Marshal to investigate suspicious fires.

The city was growing not only north, but also higher, and the Department had to keep pace with that growth or face the possibility of another Elm Street tenement fire. Never quick to adopt new technology, whether the horse-drawn apparatus or the steam engine, the Department acted with dispatch when it saw the possibilities of a new eight-section aerial ladder that could be raised to ninety-seven feet. The commissioners ordered four, and planned a great demonstration of the ladders on September 14, 1875, in a public space at Canal Street and East Broadway known at the time as Tweed Plaza—even though the plaza's namesake was by then an involuntary guest of the very government he once plundered.

Battalion Chief William Nash was chosen to lead the demonstration, along with six other firemen, including Philip Maus and William Hughes. Nash was a natural choice to be the first one up the new ladder. A Civil War veteran and winner of the James Gordon Bennett Medal in 1873, he was fearless and experienced. He had won the Bennett Medal for his daring rescue of two children in an apartment fire on Division Street the day before New Year's Eve, 1872. He was a departmental legend—just the man to inaugurate the Department's new era of high-tech aerial ladders.

The ladder was hauled to Tweed Plaza early that morning, and was extended to its full length. A large crowd gathered to see not only the equipment, but the competence of these well-trained firemen, all of whom worked in ladder companies. Nash was the first one up, followed by Maus and Hughes, and then the others. The chief was near the top, about 100 feet off the ground, when the ladder cracked, and then broke apart. Horrified civilians looked on as Nash, Maus, and Hughes fell to the pavement. Nash and Maus were killed; Hughes was severely injured, and died several days later.

An investigation of the tragedy found that the ladders were poorly made and ought to have been subjected to more scrutiny and thoroughly tested before they were demonstrated. The new aerials were put away and never used again, and the department's search for bigger and better ladders was placed on hold, with tragic consequences. Firemen responding to a raging blaze in the offices of the *World* on a cold, snowy January night in 1882 discovered once again that the city's vertical growth had outpaced their equipment. Twelve civilians died as firemen tried in vain to find a way to get their seventy-foot ladders in position to save people on the upper floors. The city's tangle of telegraph wires hampered the ladder effort as well.

The toll at the *World* fire would have been worse had it not been for the quick actions of several firemen, especially James Rooney of Ladder

A fire in the offices of the New York *World* in 1882 made a hero of James Rooney, whose rescue of Ida Small won him the James Gordon Bennett Medal.

Co. 10. The young fireman climbed to the top of a ladder to rescue a woman named Ida Small, who was screaming for help from the fifth floor. The ladder was too short, but just barely. Rooney held on as firemen on the street took hold of the ladder and hoisted it with their arms. Paul Hashagen, a firefighter turned historian, in his book *A Distant Fire,* wrote that Rooney, atop the swaying ladder, reached for the frightened, endangered woman, grabbed her by the waist, and managed to get down to safety. Rooney won the James Gordon Bennett medal for his rescue.

After the *World* fire, the Department's commissioners took note of the gap between the city's construction practices and the length of its ladders. "Great numbers" of the city's residential and industrial buildings were being built "to a height exceeding 100 feet," the Commissioners noted, while fire ladders did not "exceed 70 feet." While the Department searched for alternatives to the disastrous aerial that collapsed in Tweed Plaza, it introduced a modest-looking innovation that became a symbol of the FDNY's daring and courage. The scaling ladder, already in use in other departments, looked like a homely cousin to the FDNY's larger and sturdier equipment. Firemen could extend their vertical reach by carrying this small ladder, which varied in height from 15 to 20 feet, to the top of their regular ladders. Consisting of a series of small rungs attached to a single central upright, its modest size and weight made it mobile, and that was the genius of it. The fireman positioned the scaling ladder so that it attached by a hook to a higher windowsill. It required a straight climb up and a straight descent—the scaling ladder wasn't fixed at an angle like regular ladders.

The humble tool showed its value in 1884, when a large, modern, and allegedly fireproof apartment house called the Saint George Flats on East Seventeenth Street caught fire. As the inevitable crowd gathered in the streets to watch the firemen at work, John Binns of Hook and Ladder Co. 3 climbed up a conventional ladder and then deployed the flimsy-looking scaling ladder to reach a young boy trapped on the seventh floor. As firemen and civilians alike watched this potentially horrific drama unfold, Binns carefully brought the boy down, using the skills he had learned as part of the Department's specialized training in the use of the new equipment. The scaling ladder had saved a life, and earned Binns deserved fame. Soon, after numerous such rescues, when the Department took part in one of the city's many parades, the men marching with scaling ladders won the heartiest cheers.

Among the firefighters who watched Binns's dramatic rescue was the chief of Battalion 6, John J. Bresnan. The immigrant child of the Sixth Ward and veteran of the volunteer days had made slow but steady progress in the Department's ranks, winning appointment as a battalion chief in 1880, the year he turned thirty-nine. Four years earlier, in 1876, a fire that became a melancholy part of Brooklyn's history had helped draw attention to John Bresnan's persistence, dedication, and innovative spirit.

In 1876, Brooklyn was a separate city, the third largest in the country, and was attached to Manhattan by neither political nor physical infrastructure. (The opening of the Brooklyn Bridge in 1883 made a merger with New York inevitable.) Its fire department was much smaller than New York's, and its firemen occasionally were somewhat jealous of the more famous men across the East River. A Brooklyn fire commissioner in 1869 accused his counterparts in New York of running an "extravagant and corrupt organization."

On the evening of December 5, 1876, hundreds of theater-goers made their way to Washington Street in Brooklyn to see the actress Kate Claxton starring as a blind girl named Louise in a play called *The Two Orphans*. The theater was just five years old, and, despite the large turnout on December 5, it was struggling financially. Even then, before subway trains and the bridge, the lure of Manhattan nightlife was irresistible. "[The] people of Brooklyn prefer to come to New York for their amusements rather than to take what they can get at home," the *New York Times* noted—an observation that might have been made a century later.

It must have been with some satisfaction that the cast of *The Two Orphans* looked out on the audience on December 5. It wasn't a full house, but more than 1,000 of the theater's 1,800 seats were filled. A crowd of enthusiastic boys and young men watched the play from the cheap seats in the gallery upstairs, which held 500 people.

At around 11:30 P.M., the curtain went up for the final act. Kate Claxton, the show's star, was lying on a bed of straw, surrounded by three other actors, including J. B. Studley, who was sitting on a stool, facing the crowd, and waiting for his cues. He heard a noise backstage and assumed it was a stagehand moving equipment. But somebody offstage whispered that a small fire had broken out behind the stage. The show went on. There was no smell of smoke, no crackling of burning wood. Still seated on a stool facing the audience, Studley watched the facial expression of another actor, Mary Ann Farren, change as she began to panic. He turned around and saw the drapery behind and above him on fire. Studley got up, moved to the edge of the stage, and asked the crowd to begin leaving the theater. There was no need to hurry, he said. Kate Claxton joined him, telling the audience, "We are between you and the fire. The front door is open and the passages are clear." A janitor named Sweeny was pointing people to safety, telling them, "For God's sake. . . don't hurry, and you will all get out in plenty of time."

Then flaming cinders began to fall on the stage. The actors quickly fled, and the quiet procession to the doors became a full-fledged rush. Claxton leaped over several people in her rush to the doors. Studley went to his dressing room and found himself surrounded by flames. With a coat covering his face, he made his way to a large window, broke it, and scrambled to safety.

In addition to the main entrance behind the audience, which was twenty feet wide, there were just five doors leading to the street, two behind the stage and three to the crowd's right. The doorways were narrow, allowing just two or three people to push through at a time. Stairways leading to the side doors were packed with people trying to escape the gallery.

Within twenty minutes of the alarm, as members of Brooklyn's Fire Department directed water from the outside and heard screams from inside, the theater's roof collapsed. Then walls began caving in.

Two hundred and ninety-six civilians died in the fire. It was the greatest calamity in modern Brooklyn's history. Many of the victims died of suffocation in the narrow stairway leading to the narrow doors even before the walls collapsed. Dozens of bodies could not be identified, and were buried in a common grave after a mass funeral service.

The effect of the Brooklyn fire was profound. Across the East River, New York immediately ordered a survey of all its theaters and large public accommodations, and discovered that only luck had prevented a similar catastrophe. In the famous old Bowery Theater, city officials found that the upper gallery, "the place patronized by newsboys and bootblacks," often held far more than the 700 people it could accommodate with seats. Only one exit led from the gallery to the street.

John Bresnan was horrified. A foreman in Engine Co. 33 at the time, Bresnan was a frequent theatergoer himself, although it was said of him that he rarely sat down for a performance, preferring to watch such shows as *Shenandoah*—one of his favorites—while standing in the back or on the side.

His love of theater and his devotion to fire safety drove him to pester the city's fire commissioners with demands that they order greater protections for theatergoers and the city's actors, many of whom he had gotten to know personally. Bresnan had only force of personality and public opinion going for him, because he was not a high-ranking officer who could command the attention of commissioners and politicians. But he did succeed in getting the commissioners to accompany him on a tour of the theaters he knew so well, and he pointed out the dangers in each. Among his suggested improvements was a requirement that a portion of theater roofs be made of glass, to allow for quicker ventilation in case of fire.

Not all of his proposals were adopted, but it is worth noting that although New York had its share of theater fires, the city never suffered a calamity like Brooklyn's. And Bresnan's obvious competence and leadership abilities led his promotion to chief of Battalion 6 on February 1, 1880. As was the custom for battalion chiefs at the time, Bresnan, his wife, Catherine, and their children moved into Battalion 6 headquarters, located in the quarters of Ladder Co. 3. The Bresnans' second son, John Jr., was born in the firehouse in 1883. The two other Bresnan children were Catherine, named for Mrs. Bresnan, and Hugh, named for John's old friend from the Sixth Ward, Hugh Bonner.

Bonner was making a name for himself, too. By the time Bresnan made battalion chief in 1880, Bonner had been chief of the Battalion 2 for seven years. He successfully operated the FDNY's first water tower, a device that could be raised to pump water on fires in upper stories, and he had two noteworthy rescues to his credit, having saved a half dozen people trapped on the sixth floor of a burning hotel in 1874 and, a year later, a woman who was hanging from the gutter of a burning building

In 1883, Bonner was named second assistant chief, making him one of the FDNY's top leaders, and was given a precedent-setting assignment. He was asked to plan, and then to preside over, a training school for new firefighters. It was yet another sign of the FDNY's leading role in turning firefighting into fire science, as men like Bonner and Bresnan showed the way not only with physical strength and courage, but with technical genius and imagination as well.

The School of Instruction started out as the equivalent of freshman orientation for new firefighters, but very quickly evolved into a training service for rookies and veterans alike. Firefighting was becoming more sophisticated and more dangerous, and the department's leaders believed it was no longer possible to simply rely on raw courage and

The first water tower is put on display outside the quarters of Ladder Co. 3.

rudimentary tactics. Or, for that matter, on just any eager male. In a general order published on April 23, 1879, the Department's commissioners declared that applicants had to be thirty years of age or less, and had to be at least five feet, seven inches tall. Specific weights and chest sizes accompanied height specifications—a man standing five feet, ten inches tall had to be at least 150 pounds and have a chest size of 35.5 inches.

The commissioners hired a life-saving specialist from St. Louis, Chris Hoell, to offer instruction in the deployment of scaling ladders, conventional ladders, and other devices used for rescue operations. To complement Hoell's tutorial, Assistant Chief Bonner offered instruction in what the department called "the practical duties of a fireman in quarters and at fires," including instruction in the department's equipment and apparatus.

The school was a modest affair at first, quartered on the third floor of Engine Co. 47's firehouse on Amsterdam Avenue. But it was the

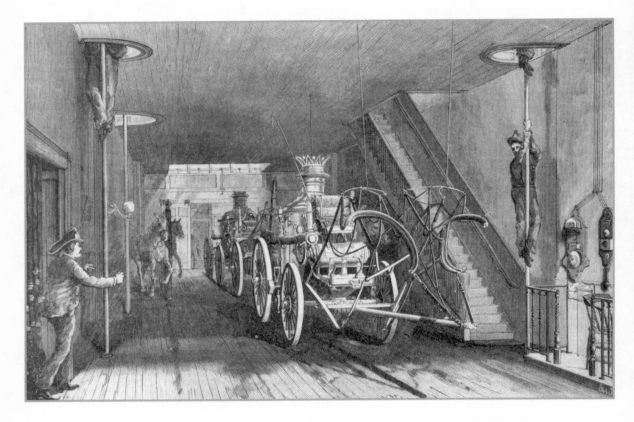

The sliding pole came into use in the late nineteenth century, speeding the trip from the bunk room to the apparatus floor.

beginning of what would become a model for firefighter instruction schools, and was the precursor to today's sprawling training and instruction facility on Randall's Island. Would-be firemen who passed the medical exam were expected to spend ten days at the School of Instruction without pay, after which their fate was in the hands of their instructor, who was told that "inability to learn the proper handling and use of the life-saving implements, or indifference to the instructions given" were grounds for disqualification.

Instruction soon was made compulsory for firemen seeking promotion, and although attendance was not mandatory for the 895 firemen already on the job in 1883, they were encouraged to "volunteer." They clearly could take a hint—by 1886, 604 veteran firemen had gone through the school. By 1888, all firemen under the age of forty who hadn't already received training in life-saving equipment were ordered to report to Assistant Chief Bonner, who by then had moved the school to the Department's splendid new headquarters on East Sixty-seventh Street. There, in a courtyard, rookies and veterans alike practiced with the Department's growing stock of life-saving equipment. Bonner, ever the innovator, bought a special dummy to be used for drilling firemen in the use of life-saving nets and other rescue devices. The Department also unveiled another piece of equipment that was to become one of the fire service's signatures: the sliding pole, which allowed firefighters to descend more quickly from sleeping quarters to the apparatus floor. Apparently New York's firemen embraced this particular piece of innovation with a bit too much enthusiasm. Included among the Department's general orders on June 13, 1888, was a reminder that "the body will be permitted to descend only at a moderate rate of speed." As the firemen approached to "within about four feet from the floor, a still-slower rate must be taken." This measure, the order noted, was to "prevent accidents in the future."

This push for greater professionalism coincided with New York's leading role in civil service reform in the aftermath of Boss Tweed's disgrace. Reformers (and nativists, although sometimes they were one and the same) had been arguing in favor of a merit-based government workforce since the 1860s, and the Tweed scandals seemed to prove their point. As Mike Wallace and Edwin G. Burrows point out in their history of New York, *Gotham,* these reformers adopted as their model the British civil service system, which allowed educated Victorians to pursue a respectable professional career in government without having to soil themselves with mere politics. One of the most prominent voices of reform, E. L. Godkin, the founder of *The Nation,* argued that government ought to be in the hands of "thoughtful, educated, high-minded men." This was the age of expertise, Godkin and his fellow reformers asserted. Fire Department professionals like Hugh Bonner and John Bresnan agreed with the reformers' insistence on high standards and meritocratic hiring. Curiously, though, Bonner and Bresnan came from the very class of people—poor immigrants from the Tammany recruiting ground of the Five Points—that reformers associated with the era's worst kind of abuses. It may not have occurred to Godkin and his fellow elites, in their zeal to stock City Hall with the right kind of people, that government service could, and would, offer the poor and poorly educated a chance to better themselves, and their city.

New York established a Civil Service Commission in 1883, the first in the nation, to begin shielding certain jobs from favor-dispensing politicians. In 1894, the city introduced a system of testing for civil service jobs, and Hugh Bonner was appointed as the chief examiner of testing for the Fire, Police, and Parks departments.

The civil service exam became a detached and nonpolitical test for young people who wished to become firefighters. If you met the Department's physical guidelines on height and weight, and if you passed the test and the medical examination, you were placed on a list of candidates. If you failed the test, you either tried again or looked elsewhere for employment. That single, unyielding standard, combined with the later addition of a physical test of agility and strength, became holy writ for generations of young New York men. When it was challenged—ironically enough, in the name of reform—almost a century later, a backlash of frustration and bewilderment ensued.

The Fire Department's increased emphasis on training, combined with an aggressive fire-prevention campaign in theaters and hotels, had tangible and spectacular results. In 1866, the average property loss per fire was $8,075.38; in 1888, the figure was $1,705.29, a 79 percent reduction.

Containment of a fire once started, however, was not the same as prevention. The number of fires was on the upswing, increasing from 796 in 1866 to 3,217 in 1888. The 317 percent increase easily outpaced the city's 110 percent population growth, from 796,000 to 1.6 million, in the same period. One of the most fire-prone sections of New York was the dry-goods district in lower Manhattan. Bounded to the west by West Broadway, to the east by Broadway, and running just to the north and south of Canal Street, the tinderbox neighborhood was home to warehouses, stores such as Lord & Taylor, and factories specializing in clothing, linens, and fabric. Making matters worse, water pressure in the neighborhood was notoriously poor because the pipes in the area were old and small. One nineteenth-century observer, taking note of the "buildings from 60 to 100 feet in height full of [inflammable] material," wrote that if a fire broke out and the wind was fierce, "everything would be against the Fire Department." In later years, as the garment industry grew, firemen gave the dry-goods district another, telling name: Hell's Hundred Acres. Insurance companies viewed the district with equal fear and dismay. They refused to fully insure many of the businesses in the area.

Augustine Costello estimated that fires in the dry-goods district from 1877 to 1882 resulted in losses of nearly $6.5 million, but merchants were insured for only about $2.3 million worth of their destroyed merchandise. Protection and prevention in the dry-goods district became a much-discussed issue in civic debate and in the press in the 1880s. In March 1884 a journal called *Van Nostrand's Magazine* devoted a long article to the plan of a New York civilian, Francis B. Stevens, to improve firefighting resources in the area. Stevens proposed a new water system that depended on both gravity and steam pumps to feed water directly from the Hudson River to the FDNY's engines when they came to the lower West Side.

Several other proposals, including one relying on underground cisterns, were put forward, to little avail. Fires continued to burn in the garment factories, shops, and warehouses, and great energy was expended in trying to better supply the area with water, while few voices suggested that stricter regulation of building heights, materials, and storage capacities might help, too.

On May 22, 1889, Hugh Bonner—survivor of the Irish Famine, child of the Five Points—was promoted to the FDNY's highest uniformed position, Chief of Department. (The commissioners to whom he reported were civilians, and their roles were administrative.) His appointment was a milestone, because he was the first Irish immigrant to occupy that post, and because by 1889 the story of the FDNY and the story of the Irish in New York were interwoven. It was impossible to explain one in isolation from the other, and this would remain the case for more than a century.

Of the approximately 1,000 firemen whose names are listed in a dusty departmental roster from January 1, 1888, 284 were born in Ireland. If American-born firemen with Irish names were included, the Department was more than 75 percent Irish. Many entered the fire service after holding skilled private-sector jobs such as machinist, plumber, or blacksmith. There was even one former undertaker, Thomas Connolly. Ireland was not the only source of immigrant firefighters—there were men from Germany, England, Prussia, and Italy—but no other group approached the Irish in numbers, and in influence. In the mid–1880s, just before Bonner became chief of department, the names of five of the Department's twelve battalion chiefs were Reilly, Bresnan, Mahedy, Lally, and McGill. A grimmer list was similarly weighted: Three of the four firefighters who died of consumption, or tuberculosis, in 1888 were Joseph Manning, James Meehan, and Michael Flynn.

In these formative years of professional firefighting, the Irish—a group reformers most associated with political chicanery and social pathology—were implementing meritocratic testing, insisting on high performance standards, and transforming fire service into fire science. One example of the latter is evident in the Department's annual reports beginning in the 1880s, which feature innovative statistical analyses of fires: what times of the day, or month, or year, were most dangerous; what kinds of buildings were most susceptible to fire, and what districts were most fire-prone. This was a nineteenth-century equivalent of the computerized statistical reports, called Compstat, that revolutionized police work in New York in the 1990s. The Fire Department reports noted the number of gallons of water used (25 million in 1886), the number of fires (3,479 in 1890), and the leading causes of fire (carelessness was usually at the top, but the 1880 annual report noted that six fires had been caused by hams falling into a fireplace). This was precisely the kind of professionalism reformers wished for in government service; that it was taking place in a branch of service dominated by the very group the reformers despised, the Irish, seems to have escaped their notice.

From its days as a volunteer force, when it defied (and occasionally beat up) the city's political leaders, New York's Fire Department had a long tradition of what amounted to self-segregation—a mirror image of elitism. Unlike other branches of government, the volunteer firemen elected their own leaders, from company foreman to chief engineer. They were considered, rightly or wrongly, a voting bloc of immense power. And they regarded each other as family—indeed, dating back to the Stoutenburghs, firefighting often was a family tradition, with a family's suspicion of outsiders.

Firefighting culture, then, was a good fit for the Irish Catholics who became the Fire Department's signature ethnic group. They lived in parishes that defied political or administrative boundaries, they often looked to their priests and bishops for leadership, and they viewed Protestant elites with a suspicion born of the certain knowledge that the Protestant elites held them in contempt. With their own school system, social organizations, hospitals, and other social service agencies, Irish Catholics already lived in a separate world of sorts, born of necessity at a time when public schools used Protestant Bibles, and when Protestant social reformers took Catholic children away from their parents and shipped them to Protestant households in the Midwest. Irish Americans understood why there was a scarred wall around old Saint Patrick's Cathedral on Mott Street: It was a barrier raised to protect the building from Protestant mobs in the 1840s. The mobs were gone, at least in their most flagrant form, but the wall remained, a wall of protection, a wall of separation.

The Fire Department's sense of separateness predated the arrival of Irish Catholics, as any number of early New York mayors and civic leaders could attest. Firefighting, even before the days when firefighters literally lived with each other, formed those kinds of special bonds, the kind that develop when people face danger together, the kind that regard all others as simply not part of the group. The Irish Catholics who came to dominate the Department understood that tradition of separation, and they built on it, even as the Irish won control of city politics, and even as the city became ever more green. Before long, their traditions and the Department's traditions were virtually indistinguishable.

With civil service reform came the promise of economic stability, which often was the deciding incentive for young Irish men who grew up hearing tales of the terrible insecurity of working rented farmland in Ireland, of being at the mercy of a capricious landlord. Generations of young Irish Americans would be raised to revere the civil service test as the gateway to a secure job and, eventually, a pension. (First proposed in 1894, this perk guaranteed half-pay pension after twenty years of service.)

That security, in the case of the Fire Department, had an ironic twist: Your job was secure all right, but it was among the most dangerous jobs in the world. Security was great—but you had to survive fire and smoke to enjoy it.

IN THE early-morning hours of June 13, 1888, a fire broke out in a four-story building at 34 Second Avenue, on the Lower East Side. Chief John Bresnan responded, and arrived to find the building in flames from the cellar to the roof, and every room filled with either smoke or fire. Nine people, including three children, were trapped on the third and fourth floors. Bresnan raced into the building and made his way through the smoke and fire to the third floor, where he found thirty-five-year-old Mamie Miller lying on the floor, overcome by smoke. He got her out of the building, as other firemen pulled out the remaining adults and children before it was too late.

It was a fairly routine rescue, the kind that the Fire Department regularly made, thanks to their training in life-saving techniques and fire-fighting tactics. Bresnan, close to fifty now, remained one of the Department's most valuable veterans. He had several innovations to his credit, including a hose roller and a revolving nozzle that was especially useful in cellars and other places where a firefighter's movement was restricted. It became known as the Bresnan distributor, and it remains part of the FDNY's repertoire. Knowing the importance of response time, he also pushed for such innovations as the sliding pole and a quick-harnessing device for fire horses.

Bresnan's personal life had been touched by grief. His wife had died in 1885, leaving him with three children to rear on his own. Not long afterward, Bresnan and the children moved out of Battalion 6 head-quarters on East Thirteenth Street and into an apartment at 60 Third Avenue. Catherine, Bresnan's oldest child, took charge of her two younger brothers when the chief went to work. Then as now, chiefs had drivers to take them to fire scenes, but Bresnan's longtime chauffeur once recalled that when an alarm sounded in the district where his children lived, the chief didn't wait for his wagon. He raced to the fire on foot. "When the fire was over," the driver recalled, "and I started to drive him home, he always turned to me and said, as if apologizing, 'Well, they ain't got any mother, you know.'"

Accounts from the time suggest that except when he was at the theater, and even then, Chief Bresnan's thoughts never strayed far from firefighting and fire prevention. That obsession added to his growing legend as one of the era's great firefighters. One time when he was off duty and at the theater, he leaped to the stage to help an actor whose costume had caught fire; another time, again while off duty, he spotted fire in the Union Square Theater, raced to the scene in his civilian clothes, and took charge of the operation. Chief Bresnan seemed to regard every fire as a personal challenge, which made him, in the early 1890s, an extremely busy man, as the number of annual fires climbed above 4,000.

Two calamities claimed the lives of nearly 100 civilians in 1891 and 1892. The first disaster took place on August 22, 1891, when the Taylor Building on Park Row collapsed and burned. Sixty-one people died.

Five and a half months later, at about three o'clock in the morning on February 7, 1892, a fire broke out at the bottom of an elevator shaft in the Hotel Royal on Sixth Avenue and Fortieth Street. As part of the Fire Department's stepped-up efforts at fire prevention, hotels were singled out for regular inspections to make sure the building had safety ropes and other means of escape. But even such measures were no match for a fast-moving fire in a structure the *New York Times* would describe as "a veritable tinder box" because the "external walls. . . were of such wretched construction" and "were bound in a forest of timbers and woodwork that had been rendered as combustible as paper or hay by years of drying and steam."

The flames shot up the elevator shaft, and within ten minutes the building's five stories were engulfed. Many of the guests were sleeping, although perhaps not all of them—the *Times* reported that the hotel "was patronized extensively by men and women who registered under fictitious names." Elevated railroad tracks ran alongside the Sixth Avenue side of the building, and when a train approached the burning building, its engineer stopped the train and blew the whistle, stirring guests from their slumber. Many quickly clambered down fire escapes, which proved their worth, or used rope ladders. But others were trapped—all they could do was shout from the windows for help. Ladder companies were racing to the scene, but the fire burned so quickly that people simply disappeared from the windows before they could be saved. A *New York Times* reporter witnessed a "fine-looking woman, apparently not more than thirty years old" pleading for help. "A fireman started for her. She was about to jump from the window, when somebody in the crowd below told her not to. She seemed to be completely out of her mind through fear. The fireman had nearly reached the woman when, with a shriek, she darted back from the window and did not again appear. . . . Her body was afterward found in the ruins and taken to the Morgue. There was nothing about it which would lead to identification except some jewelry."

Five guests, four of them identified simply as "unknown," were found dead in the debris. Chief Bonner told reporters at the scene that he didn't expect to find many more bodies, but he was too optimistic.

The search went on for several days, and when it was over, firefighters had found twenty-eight burned corpses.

Horrendous as the Taylor Building and Hotel Royal fires were, it was a more routine calamity that inspired the Fire Department, in the formidable persons of Hugh Bonner and John Bresnan, to become a passionate voice for social reform. Tenement fires in the late 1880s and early 1890s had killed 177 poor New Yorkers trapped in housing stock as susceptible to fire as the Hotel Royal. Nearly 600 others were injured in such fires, which accounted for more than half of the city's 4,000-plus blazes per year. Many of the fires were started by kerosene oil lamps and stoves in the perpetually dark, overcrowded apartments, but the Department's analysis of tenement fires also found fault with "the construction of buildings as dwellings for families with so-called light and air shafts." These flaws were the unintended consequences of tenement legislation in 1879 requiring landlords to provide more air and light in their buildings. These became known as "dumbbell apartments" (for the resultant shape of the floor plan), and the light and air passages "might properly be called fire shafts," which acted like chimneys to lead flames upward, according to the FDNY's annual report in 1893. With no other place to throw their garbage, tenants dumped it in these wooden shafts, making them all the more fire-prone. "Such shafts in case of fire become immediately an inflammable flue," Hugh Bonner wrote, "and make it almost impossible to save the building from total destruction."

The Fire Department's concerns about tenements coincided with a reform movement inspired by Jacob Riis's classic study of poverty in New York, *How the Other Half Lives*. These new reformers sought not to root out political favoritism, but to use government and politics to improve the lives of the poor. Chiefs Bonner and Bresnan knew about poverty from their childhoods in Ireland and in the Five Points. When, in 1893, the Charity Aid Organization established the groundbreaking Tenement House Committee to investigate conditions in the tenements, Bonner and Bresnan eagerly joined forces with the civic elites and philanthropists who made up the organization's membership.

Both chiefs testified about the fire hazards in tenement buildings, but their involvement, especially Bresnan's, went far beyond public statements. Richard Gilder, one of the Tenement House Committee's leaders, said that Bresnan "made it his business to take me to almost every serious tenement fire, so that I could study that phase of our subject to the very best advantage." Gilder was impressed not only with Bresnan's passion about tenement conditions, a passion they shared, but his scientific approach to firefighting. "He knew the botany of a fire," Gilder said. "He knew its seed and stalk and flower, the effects of different methods of construction upon it."

As well as Bresnan understood fire, he also understood that preventing it, and not simply reacting to it, was the surest way to save lives and property. So he brought Gilder and other members of the Tenement House Committee to the crowded apartments he knew well, from his childhood and from his years running into burning buildings. He showed them the faulty, blocked, or nonexistent fire escapes, the overcrowded apartments, the dangerous stairways that led directly from the cellar to the top floor despite laws forbidding the practice, and the weaknesses in building code regulations—like the failure to hold building owners or agents accountable for blocked fire escapes.

There was no shortage of fires for the committee members and Bresnan to investigate. In the first six months of 1894 there were 2,415 tenement fires, which killed fifteen people and injured seventy-two. One such blaze broke out at 12 Suffolk Street, a five-story tenement, in mid–1894. It was a dumbbell tenement, and inspectors later found "tubs and rubbish" in the shaft. The fire started in a first-floor saloon and moved rapidly up the shaft. Peter Rutz, a thirty-eight-year-old married father of six, hurried his family to the fire escape, but the way to it was blocked. He lost several minutes frantically removing the obstructions, then led his wife and children to safety. Lost in the confusion was his niece, four-year-old Lizzie Jaerger, who was in the rear bedroom. With the apartment filled with smoke, Rutz tried to make his way to the bedroom, but was driven back. The girl burned to death.

Horrified by what John Bresnan had shown them, the committee was finishing up a preliminary report about these wretched, dangerous

Battalion Chief John Bresnan was an innovator and a voice for social change before his death in 1894. His family's ties to the Fire Department would continue into the twenty-first century.

conditions in the last, freezing days of 1894. A meeting was scheduled for the evening of December 30 to discuss the findings and make some last-minutes changes.

Late in the evening of December 28, Battalion Chief Bresnan learned that he was about to be promoted to deputy chief, a higher post that he had long sought and one that would undoubtedly allow him to work even more closely with his friend Hugh Bonner. But he had little time to dwell on the future. The early-morning hours of December 29 were busy: He responded to a fire in a four-story tenement, which was easily extinguished, and a blaze in a bakery that took two hours to put out.

Conditions that night were horrendous. A snow and ice storm the day before made the streets almost impassable, slowing response time. Temperatures were well below zero, and pedestrians found themselves in snowdrifts up to their waists. At some point during the night, a young mother left her two children, a boy of twenty-one months and a four-year-old girl, in the care of their grandmother and an aunt. The children later were found frozen to death in a snow bank near First Avenue and Seventieth Street; the grandmother and aunt were found drunk, and were arrested.

Bresnan had barely returned from the bakery fire when duty called yet again. A large factory, Cassidy & Sons, between West Twenty-third and West Twenty-fourth streets near Sixth Avenue, was ablaze. Bresnan jumped in his wagon and set out for what would be at least his third fire in less than six hours.

The fire in Cassidy & Son's factory started on the fourth floor. When Bresnan arrived through the snow and ice, he sized up the blaze and ordered a second, and then a third, alarm, which summoned more help. He waited outside the building while laddermen with axes forced open an entry on West Twenty-fourth Street. He and another firemen, forty-six-year-old John Rooney of Ladder Co. 12—whose daring rescue of Ida Small at the *World* fire in 1882 had won him the Bennett Medal— trudged up a stairway to the fire floor, followed by firemen carrying hoses. Outside, Chief of Department Hugh Bonner arrived to take direct control of the three-alarm blaze.

Once the fourth floor seemed under control, Bresnan ordered the firemen to climb one more flight to the endangered fifth floor. Bresnan and Rooney were together on the fourth floor when the firemen on the stairway heard a huge crash. A three-thousand gallon water tower on the building's roof, its supporting beams weakened by the fire, collapsed through the roof and the fifth floor, landing near the spot where Bresnan and Rooney were standing.

The two firemen were alive, but trapped under the debris. Bresnan called for help, but rescue was hopeless; the tank was too heavy to move. An ambulance and a priest were summoned to the building, as was Richard Gilder of the Tenement House Committee. They waited outside, grieving with Bonner, while firemen continued their desperate, though futile, rescue efforts.

Chief John Bresnan's partially frozen body was found at about eleven o'clock the next morning. Rooney's was found a short time later. Gilder, in tears, hurried from the site and went to Bresnan's home to comfort the chief's three children, now orphans. The *New York Times* noted that Chief Bonner "exhibited acute distress" when the bodies were brought out in blankets and placed in hearses.

Chief Bresnan had made many friends in New York, and one of them, the publisher Simon Brentano, arranged a huge benefit for the Bresnan children in New York's Grand Opera House. The children were split up among friends and relatives who could take them in. The chief's namesake, John Bresnan Jr., went to live with his godfather, Captain Michael McAvoy of Engine Co. 60. Young John went on to join the Fire Department's telegraph service and rose to the rank of chief dispatcher of the Bronx. In his retirement in the late 1950s, he kept a Fire Department radio near his bedside in his apartment in the Bronx, so he could listen to alarms and dispatches. His grandson, Bill, would retain vivid memories of the old man lying in bed with the radio squawking next to him.

Members of the Tenement House Committee grieved for John Bresnan with the rest of the city, and when they met as scheduled the night after his death, they passed a resolution declaring: "[No] one connected with the committee has devoted more time and industry [than John Bresnan] in the collection of information in its behalf."

Hugh Bonner continued his friend's work with the committee, eventually teaming up with the secretary of the Charity Aid Organization, Lawrence Veiller, to coauthor the panel's special report on fire hazards in tenement buildings. Filled with tables and statistical analyses, the Bonner-Veiller report was a model of the FDNY's scientific, analytical approach to firefighting and fire prevention. It broke down the causes of 320 tenement fires that occurred in a single month, June 1900; it offered case studies of a range of tenement fires presented by several battalion chiefs; and it showed that 52 percent of all of the city's fires took place in tenements. Among Bonner's recommendations was a prohibition against new tenement buildings that were not fireproofed, and the mandatory fireproofing of all air and light shafts.

The Tenement House Committee's work led, in 1901, to sweeping new regulations that turned the work of Hugh Bonner and John Bresnan into law. Real estate interests in the city bitterly opposed the legislation, arguing that it would discourage construction of new housing and would add to landlords' costs. The law, however, was not the disaster the landlords foresaw, and it permanently divided the city's housing stock into two categories. Even a century later, firefighters and other municipal officials casually used the phrase "old-law tenements" to refer to buildings that predated the regulations of 1901.

The Tenement House Act did not cure poverty, overcrowding, or disease. Neither did it banish fire from the city's poorest neighborhoods. But the combined efforts of well-born philanthropists and two Five Points natives named Hugh Bonner and John Bresnan succeeded in making life in New York a good deal safer.

CHAPTER SEVEN

VERTICAL CITY

ON NEW YEAR'S EVE, 1897, crowds flocked to Union Square in a cold rain to watch a spectacular parade and fireworks show commemorating the birth of a modern metropolis, the city of Greater New York. Meanwhile, several miles uptown, the three members of the FDNY's Board of Commissioners quietly gathered in Department headquarters on East Sixty-seventh Street, adjacent to the Seventh Regiment Armory and just off fashionable Park Avenue. There were no fireworks, no parades, no great civic displays of power and might at headquarters. The commissioners were simply doing their duty, and doing it for the last time. Just after midnight, the three men turned over the FDNY to a new, single commissioner, John J. Scannell. He and the incumbent chief of department, Hugh Bonner, instantly became the leaders of a mega–Fire Department charged with protecting a sprawling entity of 3.4 million people and more than 300 square miles.

The creation of modern New York required a collective act of political suicide by Brooklyn and some 40 other towns and villages from the southernmost tip of Staten Island to the westernmost reaches of Queens County. These independent entities went to their graves at the moment Greater New York was born. No longer would there be a mayor of Brooklyn, or a Long Island City Fire Department. Now, all power flowed from City Hall in downtown Manhattan, and fire protection for the five boroughs of New York—Manhattan, the Bronx, Queens, Brooklyn and Staten Island—would be planned and executed from the red-brick headquarters on East Sixty-seventh Street.

The notion of a bigger and better New York had been kicking around since the end of the Civil War, and gained momentum when the city began absorbing towns in lower Westchester County as early as 1874. It seemed not only inevitable but proper that the nation's center of commerce should be allowed to defy the capricious will of mere geography. The sliver of Manhattan island was too tiny and too confining for New York's ambitions. Besides, rivals like Chicago were annexing new territory in outlying districts, threatening New York's dominance. New York had finished its conquest of Manhattan, and, to the chagrin of Chief Bonner and other Fire Department officials, the real estate and construction industries now were defying the sky. In leaping across the East River, the Harlem River, and the Lower Bay, New York would match its vertical growth with territorial expansion.

When the FDNY took over Brooklyn's professional fire service as well as the volunteer companies still thriving in the far reaches of Queens and Staten Island, Commissioner Scannell and Chief Bonner found themselves dealing with an administrative and operational nightmare. As recently as 1896, the Department's commissioners had pointed out the difficulties of providing fire protection to "sections of the city lying beyond the Harlem River, having an approximate area of 44 square miles," meaning the Bronx, which was still semirural in character. "Distances are so great, so many streets and roads are unpaved, and grades are so steep as to greatly delay and hinder the response of the apparatus," the commissioners wrote.

But expansion into the Bronx was nothing, or almost nothing, compared with the challenge of protecting a metropolis of five boroughs, at least two of which—Queens and Staten Island—were equally inaccessible from Manhattan. In terms of manpower and equipment, the overnight expansion of the FDNY was spectacular. On December 31,

1897, the last day of old New York, the Department consisted of sixty-three engine companies and twenty-two ladder companies, staffed by 1,223 firefighters. On January 1, the FDNY became an empire of 121 engine companies, 46 ladder companies, a hose company and a water-tower company. The Department inherited 989 firefighters from the paid departments of Brooklyn and Long Island City, which is in present-day Queens, and 3,687 volunteers in Queens and Staten Island. Apparatus and equipment varied from firehouse to firehouse in the newly annexed counties. Civil service regulations and fire codes were not uniform; neither, for that matter, were uniforms. Rank-and-file firefighters in New York were better paid than officers in the Long Island City Fire Department. The volunteer firefighters in Queens and Staten Island had to be disbanded and then incorporated into the FDNY. The sheer vastness of the new Department meant that command structures eventually were organized for each borough.

Challenging though the problems of geographic expansion were, they were not Hugh Bonner's biggest concern. Horizontal expansion was one thing; vertical growth was something quite different—something a good deal more frightening. In fact, there had been a vertical building boom in lower Manhattan in the 1890s. More than 300 buildings in Manhattan rose nine stories or more at the time of consolidation. In the Department's report for 1896, the commissioners warned that the "modern high building. . . is a menace to life and property," and noted that the "height to which engines can throw water effectively is about 125 feet," or about twelve stories. Any stories above that were out of range, and there was no shortage of buildings over 125 feet tall. The *World's* new building, which opened on Park Row in 1890, was 309 feet, inspiring the first use of the word "skyscraper."

These gigantic buildings had water tanks on their roofs—the kind that killed John Bresnan and John Rooney in 1894 when it fell through a factory roof—to feed water into primitive sprinkler systems, but it quickly became clear that such measures weren't enough.

The first great fire of the city's new era broke out late in the evening on December 4, 1898, as Greater New York prepared to celebrate its first anniversary. The blaze started in a building at Broadway and

Warren Street, and before long spread to an adjacent building, the sixteen-story headquarters of Home Life Insurance.

The Home Life building was just four years old, and was very much a part of the vertical building boom. It was advertised as fireproof, for, in addition to other modern touches, the building had a self-contained standpipe system, which allowed firefighters to hook up their hoses to an internal water supply.

As steam engines in the street worked furiously, belching smoke into the air, and hoses lined the streets in long, criss-crossing columns, firefighters made their way up the skyscraper's stairway, even as flames moved quickly to the building's top stories. Firemen inside the building retreated to the street, and took up the battle from the building next door, the Postal Telegraph Building. Once again they carried their hose up endless stairs to throw water on the blazing top stories of the Home Life Building, which burned almost all night. Although there were no serious casualties that time, FDNY leaders, including Chief Bonner, who was in command at the fire scene, knew that they were witnessing the fires of tomorrow, and that they were unprepared for them.

Years later, one of the firefighters at the scene, John Kenlon, recalled the impact of the Home Life fire on men like him. He had joined the Department in 1887, a time when firemen "were trained to fight fire and control it in a five-story city." But by the turn of the century, New York was no longer a five-story city. It was a twenty-story, even a thirty-story, city. Kenlon—a future chief of department—noted, "It was not until several disastrous fires. . . in high buildings, such as that in the Home Insurance Building. . . that Fire Department officials awoke to the necessity of addition protection for such structures. I well remember the great difficulty under which the firemen attempted to stretch hose lines up through the Postal Telegraph Building next door." That experience, he said, made it clear that all high-rises had to have standpipe equipment.

Even buildings that harked back to the days of low-rise New York were still capable of causing enormous problems and, tragically, appalling casualties. At three o'clock on the afternoon of March 17, 1899—the last St. Patrick's Day of the nineteenth century—a guest at the seven-story Hotel Windsor was standing in front of an open sec-ond-story window lighting a cigarette or cigar. The guest then flung the match, which was still blazing, out the window. At that moment, a sudden gust of wind blew the window's lace curtains, and they made contact with the match. They burst into flames.

As New York's Irish marched by the hotel's Fifth Avenue entrance, and hundreds of hotel guests watched the proceedings from upper-story windows, flames quickly engulfed the second-story parlor. Smoke began pouring out the window. The parade came to a halt as marchers and spectators pointed to the smoke and shouted for the Fire Department. Within minutes, the fire had spread down a second-story hallway and started its inexorable journey toward the hotel's top floors. The hotel's woodwork fueled the fire, and the building's elevator shafts offered quick passage from story to story. Guests who had been waving to the parade marchers a few minutes before were now screaming for help. Abner McKinley, the brother of President William McKinley, was strolling just outside the hotel when the alarm was raised. His wife and his handicapped daughter were in the building. He raced inside and was able to help them out through the fire, smoke, and chaos. Once outside, they hired a carriage to take them to the nearby Buckingham Hotel, where they sent a telegraph to the White House, informing the President that they were safe.

Police who had been given the pleasant assignment of parade duty now were ordered to begin pushing the crowd away from the burning building. A *New York Times* reporter watching the impending catastrophe noted how terrible it was to witness the crowd's mood change from gaiety to horror. "Women turned pale and screamed, little ones shrank back sobbing, and men felt the sweat break upon their brows as the heads of panic-stricken people protruded from the hotel windows, turning now toward the flames and now toward the sidewalk, and calling for help in tones that made the hearers sick."

Soon the pleas for help were joined by the sound of terrible thuds, as guests began jumping from windows even as other guests, including children, were lowering themselves from their rooms by safety ropes, which hotels were required to have for just such an emergency. One leaper landed on top of a man standing on the sidewalk. Both died. A woman and her baby screamed for help from an upper-story window, but as the flames closed in on her and there was no help in sight, she dropped the child, "dashing it to pieces," the *Times* reported, and then leaped to her own death. There were several exterior fire escapes, but they became so hot that they were rendered useless.

Among the first firefighters on the scene were men who had been marching in the parade in their dress uniforms. They joined the first-responding companies and grabbed emergency hoses inside the building and did their best to keep the lobby area free of fire as guests from lower floors made their escape. Meanwhile, ladder companies deployed conventional ladders to the third and fourth floors, and then, with speed so urgent, they pieced together a relay system of scaling ladders to reach guests trapped on the upper floors. Among the chiefs at the scene was John Binns, who had won the James Gordon Bennett Medal in 1884 when he used one of the first scaling ladders to rescue a young man from the St. George Flats fire.

It was not height that would prove tragic on this St. Patrick's Day, but another danger all too familiar to veteran firefighters—building collapse. After burning for less than an hour, the hotel's walls buckled and caved in, burying dozens of civilians in a fiery rubble. By nightfall, the *Times* noted, "not a stone" was left standing.

Forty-five hotel guests died in the fire, including those who jumped to their deaths before the Fire Department arrived. Chief Bonner had taken personal command of the fire at an early stage, and was in little doubt about how a single match could lead to such terrible destruction, as he later recounted: "There was not a fire-proof thing in the place, and absolutely nothing to check the spread of the flames all over the building once they gained a certain amount of headway," he said. "The building was not separated by cross walls, as required under the present laws. Had these walls existed, the fire would at least have been kept from spreading all through the place at once." Bonner noted that the hotel's owner had been very strict about maintaining a fire watch over the corridors during the overnight hours, but relaxed those precautions during the safer daytime hours.

Ultimately, though, Bonner blamed outdated construction for the tragedy. His complaint, as he surely knew, was depressingly familiar.

Of the many changes that accompanied the Department's unprecedented expansion, one factor remained a constant: politics, or at least the appearance of political influence. The new metropolis resembled the city of old in its push-and-pull struggle between reformers and the Tammany machine. Even with the gradual expansion of civil service testing, the Fire Department often found itself held hostage to the ambitions of civilians in and around City Hall.

Richard Croker was the most important boss of Tammany Hall since the Tweed era, and, like his famous predecessor, Croker saw the Fire Department as an opportunity to magnify his power, and he took it. The son of an Irish immigrant and veterinarian from Manhattan's West Side, Croker got his start in politics in a time-honored fashion—as a gang leader. His Fourth Avenue Tunnel Gang took its name from a streetcar tunnel that ran underneath Fourth Avenue. The tunnel is still there, although the avenue is now called Park Avenue South, and automobiles, not streetcars, use it.

Croker's apprenticeship on, or under, the streets of New York prepared him well for a career in politics, as became evident the very first time he cast a vote. Actually, as Edward Burrows and Mike Wallace point out in *Gotham,* Croker was so fond of the democratic process that he voted seventeen times on Election Day, 1864. Clearly he was headed for bigger things. He was elected an alderman in 1868, and five years later he ran for and won the post of city coroner. Croker had hardly any formal education and no professional training, but given his ability to deliver votes, the post of coroner seemed well suited to his talents.

In 1884 Croker made what seemed like the mandatory stop at the Fire Department, becoming one of the Department's commissioners. Within two years he was at the helm of Tammany Hall, taking over from "Honest John" Kelly, a man whose nickname showed that the machine did not lack a fine sense of irony.

Croker was the bane of the city's reformers, the most prominent among them being a certain barrel-chested Republican named Theodore

Roosevelt. Croker had gone into self-imposed exile in Europe in 1895, just as reformers were revealing how deeply the Tammany machine had become involved in vice rings and various other rackets. But he returned on the eve of consolidation, in time to engineer the election of the first mayor of Greater New York, Robert A. Van Wyck, whose campaign slogan pretty much summed up Croker's worldview: "To Hell with Reform." With his ally securely ensconced in City Hall, Richard Croker took control over the vast expanse of Greater New York, presiding over an empire of corruption that Boss Tweed would have envied.

He had not only his friends on the public payroll, he had a nephew, too. Young Edward Croker had spent most of his working life as a firefighter, and had risen on merit to become a deputy chief. He was a hard worker and was uninterested in the power and spoils that his uncle spent a lifetime collecting. All Edward Croker wanted to be was a fireman, and he was a very good one.

And not long after Uncle Richard reassumed command of Tammany Hall, young Edward received the promotion of his life, at the tender age of thirty-six. He was named to succeed Hugh Bonner as chief of department.

It was a measure of Bonner's place in the hearts of his fellow firefighters and all New Yorkers that in 1897, while he was still chief of deparment, the city struck a new prize for firefighting heroism and called it the Hugh Bonner Medal. After a forty-six-year career that spanned service in the volunteer days, leading the FDNY into the era of scientific firefighting, and then supervising its expansion into a five-borough force, Hugh Bonner retired as chief on May 1, 1899. Hugh Bonner had risen from the blackened potato fields of Ireland and the despised streets of the Five Points to become one of the great firefighters, one of the great heroes, of late-nineteenth-century New York. And his retirement as chief did not end his firefighting career. In 1902, Theodore Roosevelt, now President of the United States and eagerly building what he hoped would be an American overseas empire, appointed Bonner to organize a fire department in one of the country's new possessions, the Philippines. Bonner carried out his assignment and returned to New York, but would be called out of retirement one more

Chief Croker
sets out for a
fire in a
self-propelled
vehicle.

time, in 1906, to become deputy fire commissioner. Then, in 1908, he assumed the department's highest command, becoming fire commissioner. His was a short tenure—he died of pneumonia in March 1908, two months into his last duty.

The day before Bonner left his post as chief, Fire Commissioner Scannell made the eagerly awaited announcement that the great chief's successor would be Deputy Chief Edward Croker, a fifteen-year veteran of the FDNY who had made two notable rescues with a scaling ladder. He had the heart and soul of a turn-of-the-century firefighter, and would express his love for the job in words the Department would revisit in decades to come at medal ceremonies, retirements, and memorials: "I have no ambition in this world but one, and that is to be a fireman," young Croker said. "[Our] proudest endeavor is to save the lives of people—the work of God Himself. Under the impulse of such thoughts, the nobility of the occupation thrills us and stimulates us to deeds of daring, even at the supreme sacrifice."

Despite his impressive record and eloquence, Croker could not escape his last name. Scannell had a sharp exchange with reporters over the motivation behind the appointment of the young new chief. "There was no politics in it at all," he told a skeptical press corps after announcing Croker's promotion. "I made the selection. . . because I wanted to get the best man. . . . And let me say that Mr. Croker has won his promotion by sheer merit."

Not everybody agreed, and Hugh Bonner himself certainly didn't extinguish the flames of resentment when he declined a chance to endorse his successor. Asked about Croker's appointment, Bonner said simply, "Oh, I have not a word to say." Ironically enough, given its reputation as an antimachine crusader, the *New York Times* helped put an end to questions about the new chief's qualifications, saying it could not "see the justice of the criticism."

Neither, as time went on, could the firefighters themselves. They came to admire their chief for his respect for their work, and his willingness to put himself on the line, and in danger, on their behalf.

In late 1899, when he had been chief for only about six months, Croker was called to a blaze in a basement warehouse near the corner of Hubert and West streets in downtown Manhattan. The fire and smoke were intense, beating back firefighters under the command of Captain Joseph Martin of Engine Co. 31. The captain himself led a renewed charge into the basement, telling his men to take turns operating the nozzle, which was the most exhausting (and therefore, in Fire Department culture, the most sought after) work on an engine company. Martin himself remained with the nozzleman, directing the attack.

One by one, Martin's exhausted men retreated from the basement coughing up black mucus. It was the same with their replacements, and then with *theirs*. All the while, Joe Martin remained inside, until Croker took a head count and realized that everybody was outside the building except the captain. Was he dead, or injured? The chief assigned himself the job of finding the captain, or his body. He entered the basement, got on his hand and knees, felt for the hose line, and followed it, blindly. He later recalled that he "never took such punishment in my life" as he searched for the missing captain. He found Martin, finally, lying on the ground between two furniture crates and manning a nozzle by himself. The chief personally ordered the captain out of the building.

The two men crawled outside to safety, and when they emerged, Chief Croker spotted a gaggle of newspaper reporters covering the fire. He brought Martin over to meet them: "Gentlemen," he said, "this is Smoky Joe Martin, and by the gods, he certainly does love it."

Smoky Joe certainly did love firefighting. He nearly died in a fire in 1903, three years after he became a battalion chief. He and several other firefighters entered a burning building on Walker Street to search for a missing watchman. They fought their way to the fourth floor, where Martin kicked open a door to continue his search. "That floor won't hold you, Cap," one of the firemen shouted.

It didn't. The floor collapsed, and Martin plunged all the way to the basement. He was found unconscious, and was given last rites. But although he was burned and badly beaten up, Smoky Joe survived. He walked out of a hospital four months later under his own power.

Chief Croker was no less persistent than Martin, though in a very different sort of way. He was effective enough to make some people, especially firefighters, forget that he shared family ties with an increasingly discredited political boss. And he was respected enough that he could, and did, crack down on his men when the occasion warranted. In one of his special orders, he ordered officers to stop "the habit of different members of the Department wandering around the streets or in buildings while operating at fires." It made the Department look less professional. Like James Gulick, John Decker, and Hugh Bonner before him, Edward Croker demanded that his firefighters adhere to military-like discipline at fires. They were, after all, in battle.

Despite his effectiveness, however, Croker found himself caught up in New York's endless cycle of "machine out, reformer in" politics. After his uncle beat yet another hasty retreat to Europe, this time for good, and a reform administration under Mayor Seth Low was installed in City Hall in 1902, Edward Croker was fired on trumped-up charges of professional negligence. Another Fire Department legend, Charles Krueger, took his place, but not for long. Croker sued to get his beloved job back, and prevailed after a two-year legal struggle, much to the

The remains
of the *General
Slocum.*

embarrassment of the reformers. He went on to serve as chief until 1911, becoming one of the Department's greatest leaders and one of the city's most important, and most often ignored, voices for greater government regulation of housing and workplaces. He made a name for himself, and upheld his family name long after Uncle Richard was in exile in Ireland, racing horses and dreaming—successfully, as it turned out—of winning Britain's most prestigious race, the Derby.

THE FIRST decade and a half of the twentieth century would produce some of New York's most awful conflagrations, filled with tales of horror and heroism. One of the worst fires of the century, not just in New York but throughout the world, broke out on June 15, 1904, and it was beyond the reach of the FDNY. The 250-foot excursion boat *General Slocum,* with 1,300 men, women, and children aboard from St. Mark's German Lutheran Church who were going on a picnic outing to Long Island, caught fire while sailing north on the East River. Passersby along the East River waterfront in Harlem saw the fire on the paddle wheel steamer and summoned firefighters, who responded to the foot of East 138th Street, where they assumed the captain, William Van Schaick, would try to bring in the burning vessel. They could only watch as the *Slocum* continued to sail northward in midstream, on a course east of Randall's and Ward's islands. The captain didn't realize the ship was on fire for nearly ten minutes, and by the time he did, the *Slocum* had been caught by the powerful currents of Hell Gate, a narrow channel off the Astoria section of Queens, and could not buck the current to steer for shore.

Passengers, most of whom couldn't swim, scrambled for life jackets, but they were nearly fifteen years old, rotten and useless. By now, the wooden vessel was engulfed—it took only fifteen minutes to reduce the *General Slocum* to ruins. It was a terrible sight, and for the firefighters, horribly frustrating. Finally, the *Slocum*'s fiery journey came to an end, but not along the Manhattan waterfront, where engines and trucks awaited, but on North Brother Island in midriver, out of reach of any rescue apparatus. More than 1,000 people died, either by fire or by drowning. Some jumped from the ship only to get caught in the boat's paddle wheel. Most of the victims were German immigrants or first-generation Germans who lived in an ethnic neighborhood known as Kleindeutschland, or Little Germany, on the Lower East Side. After the Slocum horror, survivors and their families could no longer bear to live in the old neighborhood, with its searing memories. The community moved away almost to a person, trying to find solace in new surroundings uptown, in today's Yorkville section of the Upper East Side.

Among all the fire catastrophes of the early century, at least one blaze produced nothing short of a miracle, too, and it became part of firehouse lore. On January 6, 1907, just before 8 P.M., a six-story warehouse filled with cotton and paper on Roosevelt Street on the Lower East Side went up in flames. The fire trap was surrounded by tenement houses (suggesting how far application of New York's zoning laws had yet to come), so the ubiquitous John Binns, hero of the first scaling-ladder rescue, summoned extra help in the form of a second and then a third alarm. Sensing trouble, Binns ordered firefighters to withdraw from the burning building, but before the evacuation was complete, the building collapsed. Three firefighters from Engine Co. 32 were missing in the flaming debris, Thomas Lennon, Daniel Campbell, and Jack Seufert. There was little hope for them, and shortly after midnight, Fire Department officials sent word to their families that the men had been killed in the line of duty.

Jack Seufert's wife came to the scene, and when she was asked about funeral arrangements, she said matter-of-factly that they would not be necessary. She had had a premonition earlier in the evening that her husband was in danger but alive, and, she said, she believed he was somewhere under the smoking ruins.

The search continued, and hours later the charred bodies of the two other firemen were found. Mrs. Seufert remained at the scene, confident that her husband had survived. And Seufert *was* alive. He had fallen between bales of paper, and his arms and legs were trapped, but he was, amazingly, alive. Unable to move, and with water from the firemen's hoses running by his face and smoke gagging him, Seufert shouted as loudly as he could, but nobody heard him. Maddeningly, he could hear voices, one in particular, the voice of Harry Archer. Archer, thirty-nine, was a physician from an affluent New York family who, like street kids before him, idolized firefighters as a child. He worked for an insurance company, but his true love was firefighting, and by 1907, he had become a fixture at major fires, offering his services to injured firemen free of charge. He was, in a sense, the last volunteer.

Seufert was trapped in a crouched position, with his head bent forward, but he eventually worked his right hand free and began tapping on a gas pipe. Three taps, followed by two taps—3–2, for his engine company. The men working in the debris heard the signal, and followed the line of the gas pipe. Thirty hours after the building fell on him, Jack Seufert was pulled from the wreckage, taken to a hospital, and released after two days to the company of his wife, who never doubted that she would see him again.

. . .

NOT ALL the problems faced by the turn-of-the-century Fire Department were new. Obtaining sufficient water for firefighting and the technology to deliver it had been an ongoing problem for Manhattan. Now, Greater New York had its own water problems. Although the mid–century construction of the Croton Aqueduct and the reservoirs had ensured there was plenty to go around for drinking and bathing, it was becoming clear that there wasn't enough water pressure for the demands of modern, high-rise firefighting. Hoses could not be connected directly to hydrants because of pressure problems; instead, the hoses were connected to pumpers, which were in turn connected to hydrants. That inefficient process limited the number of lines that could be brought to bear at a major fire.

The problem dated back to the 1880s, when low water pressure in the dry-goods district was a constant concern. Throughout the first decade of the twentieth century, the city finally took action, building four pumping stations that delivered high-pressure water through special pipes to hydrants in parts of lower Manhattan where pressure had been a consistent problem, and where buildings were taller than elsewhere. When the new system was finished in 1908, one overenthusiastic editorial writer declared that large fires "would now become a thing of the past because they could no longer happen. The volume of water, and the power of the huge pressure system will overcome any fire in short order."

The FDNY, of course, knew better. High-pressure hydrants would help firefighters direct stronger and more efficient streams of water higher, but they would hardly begin to banish fire from New York. Firefighting was, remained, and would always be an art of reaction. Fire prevention, on the other hand, was proactive, vital and, in a city the size of New York, absolutely essential to prevent repeats of nineteenth-century horrors.

With that in mind, the FDNY in 1910 asked the city to fund a bureau dedicated to fire prevention, and Chief Croker himself argued repeatedly that building owners and businessmen ought to be forced to take more aggressive measures to protect employees from workplace fires, including the installation of automatic sprinklers and alarms. He contended that high-rise office and factory buildings did not have enough exterior fire escapes, that many were far too crowded, and that more modern structures that proudly bore the label "fireproof" were nothing of the sort. "They are fireproof, yes, when the builders get through and before the tenants move in," Croker said. "But after the tenants are in they are only slow-burning buildings. They are safe so far as property damage is concerned, but not so far as human life is concerned. There are more fire traps in the loft and office buildings. . . than you can realize." Just as John Bresnan and Hugh Bonner had seen firsthand the effects of private and public neglect in the city's tenements, Edward Croker saw, from the unique perspective of a firefighter, the dangers workers faced from callous employers, an aloof civic elite, and a negligent city government.

Croker and his colleagues also argued that they ought to have authority over the regulation of fire escapes, which were monitored either by the Buildings Department or the Tenement House Department. The Fire Department asserted that because "fire escapes are used not only for the purpose of escape in the case of fire, but also for fire fighting," it should have ultimate authority over the structures. The complaint was duly noted, and not acted upon. Croker also advocated the installation of sprinkler systems in all commercial buildings. Meanwhile, the business community held a meeting on Wall Street to condemn the chief. The business leaders whispered that Chief Croker, nephew of the now-disgraced Tammany chieftain, was pushing sprinklers because he was doing a favor for a sprinkler company.

As the political maneuvering continued, the century's worst fire stunned and shamed the city and silenced the critics of reform. The ten-story Asch Building at 23 Washington Place, just a few steps from the tranquillity of Washington Square Park, was the sort of structure that worried Chief Croker. It was considered fireproof—the walls and floors were built to the highest safety specifications. But then came tenants, and hundreds of workers and stock. They were not fireproof. And the building had no exterior fire escapes, and only one inside.

The Triangle Shirtwaist Company took up the top three stories of the Asch Building. There, about 600 workers, most of them young women, hunched over sewing machines to make clothing for other young women. Conditions on the shop floors were crowded and dangerous, a point that did not escape insurance inspectors who visited the factory in 1909. They asked the factory's owners whether they ever conducted fire drills. No, the owners said. One inspector, P. J. McKeon, who lectured in fire safety at Columbia University, said that "the place looked dangerous to me.

"There was a fire escape in the back and all that," he said, "and the regulations seemed to be complied with all right, but I could see that there would be a serious panic if the girls were not instructed how to handle themselves in case of a fire. I even found that the door to the main stairway was usually kept locked. I was told this was done because it was so difficult to keep track of so many girls." McKeon's fellow inspector, H. F. J. Porter, wrote a letter to the Triangle Shirtwaist Company's owners, telling them that he was available to help them devise a system of fire drills. He offered to meet with them "at any time that would suit your convenience." But he received no reply.

The fire in the Triangle Shirtwaist factory started on the eighth floor at around 4:40 P.M. on March 25, 1911. It lasted about thirty minutes, and it was confined to the building's top three stories. After it was over and Chief Croker's firefighters were mopping up, observers noted that the walls and floors in other parts of the building bore no trace of the fire. The walls and floors were, in fact, fireproof. But the fabric and other materials on the factory floor were not. And the door from the ninth floor to the stairway was locked, just as the inspectors had noted during their visit in 1909. And the young women working the machines were not instructed "in how to handle themselves in case of a fire." As ravenous flames, fed by a diet of combustible fabrics, and acrid smoke enveloped the shop floors, young women moved toward windows overlooking Greene Street. And they jumped 100 feet to their deaths. Or they fell down an elevator shaft. Or they were overcome by smoke while sitting at their sewing machines, dead or unconscious before flames burned their flesh to the bone.

Firefighters, including that veteran pioneer of the scaling ladder, John Binns, arrived within six or seven minutes of the fire's outbreak,

Firefighters attempt
to douse the blaze in
the Triangle Shirtwaist
factory. Somewhere in
the crowd, looking on,
Chief Croker raged
against building owners
who considered fire
safety too expensive.

but the fire spread with such speed and intensity that several victims already had jumped to their deaths as a growing crowd of horrified passersby looked on helplessly. Firefighters found their mangled bodies lying on the sidewalk. Above them, young women and a few men pleaded for help from windows and ledges.

The firemen scrambled to attach their hoses to several of the new high-pressure hydrants that were near the building. Others deployed life nets, designed to catch jumpers. But the nets were not made for leaps from eight or nine stories. Bodies hurtled down from the fire floors and ripped through the nets, landing on the sidewalk. Sometimes they came down together, holding on to each other in groups of three or four. A young firefighter with Engine Co. 18 recalled that the first thing he saw, as his engine pulled up to the scene, "was a man's body come crashing down. . . . We turned into Greene Street and began to stretch in our hoses. The bodies were hitting all around us."

Ladders were deployed quickly, but they reached only to the sixth floor. A young woman in a ninth-floor window, her skirt on fire, leaped for one of the ladders. She missed, and she fell to her death. Scaling ladders were brought out to reach to the upper floors, but by the time they were in place, the carnage was over. Those who dared had already leaped to their deaths. Those who couldn't were dead inside the building. Only about fifteen minutes passed between the death of the first jumper and the end of hope, when no more faces appeared in the windows.

The high-pressure hydrants at least allowed firefighters to direct water to the highest part of the building. But, as Battalion Chief Edward Worth later lamented, there was "no apparatus in the department to cope with this kind of fire."

The fire claimed the lives of 146 people, most of them young women, some as young as thirteen. The city's coroner, not unfamiliar with scenes of terrible catastrophe, wept as he examined the corpses, one of which was no more than a trunk. Chief Croker was at the scene, watching the appalling scenes with a mixture of fury and horror. Just a few feet from where he stood in the street, firefighters were gently dragging the broken bodies of young women from a hole in the asphalt that had been created by the force of human beings hurtling 100 feet to the street.

For years Croker had been warning of just such a catastrophe, in just such a building, but his words had gone unheeded, and landlords had slandered him and questioned his motives. Angrily, he lashed out at the real estate interests and other powerful groups that resisted elementary fire protection for workers. "Look around everywhere," he said, gesturing to the smoking building, "nowhere will you find fire escapes. They say they don't look sightly. I have tried to force their installation, and only last Friday a manufacturers' association met in Wall Street to oppose my plan. . . . The large loss of life is due to this neglect." When the flames were extinguished, he made his way to the fire floors to see the carnage for himself, and then reported back to the Manhattan district attorney, who was in the street, already planning a criminal investigation. "The floors up there are a frightful sight," Croker told the prosecutor. "Bones are there that have been burned to a crisp, the flesh having been burned away."

The public's outrage over the Triangle fire matched Chief Croker's, inspiring a citizens' movement against criminally negligent employers and building owners and launching the careers of three of New York's greatest political leaders, Alfred E. Smith, Robert Wagner, and Frances Perkins. As members of the state Factory Investigating Commission, they were charged with investigating the fire and the conditions of factory workers throughout the state. Once again, as with the Tenement House Committee of the late nineteenth century, an outraged Fire Department, which saw conditions on the ground as few other agencies could, aligned itself with reformers in the name of social justice.

The work of Smith, Wagner, and Perkins would go far beyond Chief Croker's understandably limited, though important, goals. From the ashes of the Triangle victims rose a movement that led to demands for a more activist government, to Smith's election as governor, to Wagner's election as one of New York's greatest U.S. senators, and to Perkins's appointment as the first woman cabinet member when she was named Franklin Roosevelt's secretary of labor in 1933. In a very real sense, the Triangle Shirtwaist fire gave rise to modern government regulation and the weaving together of the mid–century social welfare safety net. It is hard to imagine Al Smith's success in turning New York in the 1920s

Fire escapes were considered unsightly, but they were life-savers in crowded tenement buildings. This picture shows a fire escape in Chinatown.

into a laboratory for the New Deal without the terrible fire to spur him on, and to inspire public opinion. The fire came to symbolize the evil of passive government turning a blind eye to ruthless exploitation and criminal neglect in the workplace, which is why the Triangle Shirtwaist fire became far more than a local tragedy.

The outcry and the work of the Factory Investigating Commission led to the passage of some, though not all, of the reforms Croker had been seeking. The Department was given permission to create a powerful centralized Bureau of Fire Prevention, the first of its kind in the country, and it immediately launched an aggressive campaign of inspections—more than 100,000 in its first year of operation, 1912. Croker's demands for mandatory sprinklers in factory buildings became law with passage of the city's Fire Prevention Act of 1911. The law also gave the fire commissioner power to condemn commercial buildings regarded as inadequately protected against fire. The new law had one significant loophole, which the FDNY bitterly opposed: Oversight of tenement houses continued to fall under the jurisdiction of city housing agencies, rather than the Bureau of Fire Prevention.

NOT LONG after the Triangle Shirtwaist fire, Edward Croker retired as chief of department. But this time the appointment of a new chief of department would not be subject to charges of cronyism or nepotism. The age of civil service reform reached a climax when the city administered a special civil service test to fill the vacancy. Political considerations no longer could play a role in the selection of New York's fire chief. The test was the final arbiter. The highest score was achieved by John Kenlon, an assistant chief who had become the first person to head the FDNY's new marine division in 1909, and he got the job in August 1911.

Just under six months later, on January 9, 1912, another fire with far-reaching consequences broke out in the Equitable Life Assurance Building. It was about five o'clock on a bitterly cold and windy winter morning when employees working early or overnight shifts in the Equitable building at 120 Pine Street discovered flames in the basement. Grabbing firehoses, they attempted to extinguish the fire themselves using standpipe equipment in the building. After about twenty minutes they realized they needed help, and quickly. The fire had moved into elevator shafts and was climbing out of the basement. Among the first firemen at the scene was Deputy Chief John Binns, who seemed to show up early at every major fire. He immediately ordered second and third alarms. The second alarm summoned Chief Kenlon, who had been to a fire in Brooklyn several hours earlier, to take personal command of his first big fire as chief of department.

The Equitable Life Assurance Building, which had an ornate clock visible throughout much of the financial district, was not so much a single structure as it was several buildings linked together through years of renovations and improvements. The building, or patchwork of buildings, occupied a full city block, housed several companies and small businesses, and had one section that was ten stories high. Fortunately, because of the early hour few people were in their offices. But three people who worked in a café in the building found their escape route to the street blocked, so they took an elevator to the top floor and shouted for help from the roof. Firemen and a growing crowd of onlookers saw them in the predawn light of six o'clock, as flames began to penetrate the roof.

Kenlon ordered extension ladders deployed to save the workers, but, in a familiar variation on a constant theme, the ladders were short by three stories, or about thirty feet. "All the time," a *New York Times* reporter at the scene noted, "the men were yelling in a tongue which no one seemed to understand." The unfamiliar tongue was Italian; the workers were immigrants who rose before sunup to work in the Café Savarin.

Scaling ladders, the usual solution when extension ladders were too short, proved difficult to deploy because the building's ornate copings extended out four feet from the facade. Kenlon dispatched firemen armed with another new tool, a cable life line, to the tenth floor of an adjacent building across the narrow lane of Cedar Street. The firemen shot the lifeline from an open window across to the trapped men. Sensing salvation, they eagerly grasped the line and were securing it to a steam funnel when flames burst out a window, burning the lifeline and making it unusable. At the same time, the Equitable roof began to collapse, forcing the three men out on a ledge. As firemen prepared to fire another lifeline, one of the workers slipped and fell into the fire below. The other two men decided to jump together into the street. They landed with the kind of sickening thud many of the firemen remembered from the Triangle fire.

Conditions on the street were horrendous. As he directed the battle from the street, Kenlon's equipment, helmet, and mustache were coated in ice, and the streets around the inferno were turned into skating rinks as water drained off the building and then froze. Steam engines pumped furiously, belching black smoke into the air, as huge icicles formed on the apparatus. At six-thirty, FDNY institutional history was made when

Chief Kenlon issued the first-ever borough call, meaning that he summoned help from Brooklyn. Standing nearby, the police commissioner ordered his men to keep the Brooklyn Bridge free of all traffic except Fire Department apparatus.

Rumors spread that eight people were asleep somewhere in the building. William Walsh, chief of Battalion 2, asked for volunteers to accompany him inside the building to look for the eight missing workers. Fourteen firemen followed Chief Walsh up an extension ladder to the fourth floor, where they began their search. After finding nobody on the fourth floor, Walsh ordered his men downstairs to the third floor. He remained behind for a moment, saying, "Go ahead, boys, I can take care of myself." His men heard an ominous rumbling sound, then the inevitable crash of a collapse. Walsh and another firemen, Captain Charles Bass, were buried in debris. Kenlon ordered a search, and Deputy Chief Binns volunteered to climb to what remained of the fourth floor to look for Walsh and Bass there. Heat and smoke, however, drove Binns and other firemen away.

The collapse trapped William Giblin, a bank president who entered the building to salvage what he could from his office, and another civilian in the basement. A fireman named Seneca Larke, who had been an ironworker before joining the FDNY, offered to crawl to a basement window secured by iron bars and cut an escape route for the victims. Surrounded by cold, freezing water and ice on one hand and smoke and fire on the other, Larke cut through the window and finally, with help from other firemen, pulled Giblin and a companion to safety.

Walsh and Bass still were missing, but by late morning word spread that Walsh at least had been found, taken to a hospital and admitted under a wrong name. Walsh's wife and eighteen-year-old daughter, Catherine, rushed to the fire site and were there when the afternoon newspapers were distributed, with news of Walsh's miraculous survival. He was said to be in Gouverneur Hospital. Mrs. Walsh, weeping with joy, and her daughter left for the hospital.

But Walsh was still under the debris. He was dead, and his body was not to be recovered for several days. Bass suffered a skull fracture, but lived. The rumor of eight missing civilians turned out to be false.

Six people died in the Equitable fire. The casualty toll was not of the magnitude of the Triangle fire, but the recriminations were almost as loud, almost as angry. The newspapers published pictures that could not help but inspire the public's sympathy and admiration for their firemen: They were covered in ice as they battled fire. They looked miserable and heroic at the same time.

The following Sunday, January 14, the *New York Times* magazine section devoted several pages to the Fire Department's continued calls for reform of building codes and fire-safety practices. A headline asked: "Is New York City in Danger of Being Fire Swept?" The answer, according to the experts the newspaper quoted, was yes. Former Chief Croker delivered some of the most damning quotes. Calling Chief Walsh's death "a direct sacrifice to. . . the national carelessness and the national spirit of great haste," Croker said, "We build to burn and keep our buildings so it is easy for them to burn." If the Equitable building had had automatic sprinklers and alarm systems, Croker said, Chief Walsh and the five civilians would still be alive, and the building itself would not have been reduced to four charred walls. "[The] reason I am not a fireman now," he continued, "is that this matter of fire prevention weighed upon my mind and came to fill it so completely that the job of fighting fires from the firehouse end came to seem inconsequential compared to the possibilities of fighting them from the other end— from the end of stopping them from ever getting a start."

Croker's successor, Chief Kenlon, demanded a series of elementary steps that, shockingly, still were not required of builders and building managers: fire walls in factories, enclosed interior fire escapes, automatic sprinklers, wider staircases in tall buildings, tough regulations for the storage and disposal of rubbish, and, ironically, the banning of slate and metal fireproof roofs (they tended to crash through floors during a fire). The Equitable building had such a roof, and Walsh's body was found under it.

There had been 13,868 fires in 1911. The principal cause of fire, carelessness with lighted matches, was blamed for 1,366 fires. Carelessness with cigarettes or cigars ignited nearly 1,000 more fires, and carelessness with candles caused over 400. So it was not just employer neglect or wretched tenement housing that caused fires. In any case, however, after the Triangle and Equitable fires, the FDNY had had enough—of neglect, of carelessness, of unnecessary deaths. Crackdowns on arson, tough enforcement of building regulations, modern equipment, and new tactics were to be brought to bear on fire. "Fools must no longer be allowed to cause 3,000 fires a year," said Fire Commissioner Joseph Johnson. The commissioner, the chief, and the FDNY's 5,000 firefighters moved quickly against the fools, whether they were tenement house dwellers who were careless with matches or insurance company executives and landlords who were just discovering a crime that would become known in the 1970s as arson-for-profit.

On New Year's Eve, 1912, Commissioner Johnson dispatched a thick report to Mayor William Gaynor, complete with photographs and charts, that identified this startling new development in the FDNY's war against fire. "Without exaggeration," Johnson wrote, "our City is face to face with a grave public danger." The danger, Johnson wrote, was "incendiarism for the purpose of obtaining insurance money. . . . The murderous trade of fire-making," the commissioner noted, knew no sociological boundaries, for it was practiced by "the tenement dweller on the East Side" and "the wholesale merchant in the downtown business district." Such arsons, he said, were "frequently the readiest way to realize a quick return on a slow-moving stock of over-insured goods; it is also, at times, the only available method of averting impending financial ruin." Johnson calculated that arson-for-profit accounted for a quarter of the city's fires, for $4 million in damage every year, and had led to the deaths of several civilians.

In a piece of investigation and analysis that demonstrated yet again that firefighting in New York had become a science as well as a brutal physical struggle, Johnson's report offered a block-by-block, building-by-building breakdown of arsons in what he called the city's worst "firebug district," what is now East Harlem. The FDNY calculated that the south side of a single city block, East 100th Street between First and Second avenues, had been the site of fifty-two fires in fewer than three years, a figure so astonishing that Johnson spelled it out in capital letters.

Arson-for-profit, Johnson wrote, would continue to endanger fire-fighters and civilians alike as long as insurance companies failed to inspect insured properties. To demonstrate the carelessness and apathy of the city's insurance industry, the FDNY set up a sting operation in which it used its own staff to apply for insurance policies. They were able to buy 135 policies, covering $127,000 in potential losses on property worth $3.96. One such policy covered a virtually bare apartment at 208 East Seventy-third Street with property worth 12 cents. The FDNY's undercover team bought an $8,000 policy on the apartment's "furnishings."

Johnson's report embarrassed the insurance industry, and led to some reforms, but the FDNY's campaign against "fools" was just beginning. Another team of investigators, including a woman undercover inspector, visited more than 500 sweatshops employing about 500,000 people. They found a "large number of employees" who smoked cigarettes on the sweatshop factory floor, in the presence of highly combustible fabrics and in defiance of city laws. Those findings led to the distribution of thousands of "no smoking" signs printed in English, Yiddish, and Italian, "so that occupants of a building could not by any chance mistake the meaning of the Commissioner's order."

The fire-prevention crusade was brought to the city's public schools, too, as a matter of safety and education. FDNY inspectors found that "it is not a fact, as charged, that every public school building in the city is a firetrap," but there was no shortage of dangerous conditions in many, such as old wooden furniture and other rubbish in school basements, poorly maintained electrical wiring, and steampipes covered in wooden casings. The department began an annual fire prevention day in city schools, and members of the city's Boy Scout troops were recruited to hand out placards with fire-prevention tips.

In keeping with the legacy of John Bresnan, the FDNY also brought its fire-prevention campaign to the city's theaters. The Department built a small model of a perfectly fireproofed theater, with cutaways showing the preferred locations of fire escapes, sprinklers, standpipes, fire axes, and other equipment. And the Department ordered that a uniformed member of the FDNY had to be on hand at every theatrical perform-

A horse-drawn
rig makes one last
run outside City
Hall, marking the
end of an era.

ance involving a stage and scenery, a practice that was to delight many a firefighter throughout the ensuing decades.

Along with these revolutionary changes in fire prevention came a revolution in the FDNY's response time. Horses were giving way to the internal combustion engine.

Like so many other equipment changes in New York's fire service, the transition from horse-drawn to self-propelled apparatus took longer than expected, and did not receive a particularly warm embrace. Just as their professional ancestors had clung to the hand-drawn engine for as long as possible, and then a bit longer, New York's firefighters in the early years of the twentieth century treasured their horses. Like the firefighters themselves, fire horses received special training at a school of instruction, and the sight of a team of two or three horses charging through the streets with steam engine in tow was very much a part of the FDNY's well-tended public image.

One measure of the affection firefighters held for their horses was a picture on the cover of the Department's annual report in 1911. It

shows Mayor William Gaynor in a top hat and a formal morning coat gently stroking a fire horse's nose. It was meant as a gesture of farewell, for the report itself noted that the "motorization of the Fire Department is well underway." When the Department turned out for an annual parade in 1914, motorized engines, trucks, and chief's buggies led the way. In a parade held just ten years before, the only motorized apparatus had been an ambulance.

The FDNY's leaders planned to phase out horses by 1917, a process that presented no small number of headaches. Buildings that housed the FDNY's 295 companies had to be extensively renovated—horse stalls removed, gasoline storage tanks installed, apparatus floors strengthened—without interrupting a neighborhood's fire protection. This complication, along with the firefighters' tradition of clinging to tradition, led to a completely predictable delay in moving beyond horse-flesh to horsepower.

Inevitably, though, the change was made, and the last horse-drawn engine was put out of service in December, 1922. The motorized age had arrived. It would allow firefighters to respond quicker, and to a larger geographical area.

Eventually, too, the age would produce highways that would rip through old neighborhoods and beckon firefighters to a place beyond the city's limits, a paradise of green grass and inexpensive homes far away from the alarms and the sirens and the firehouse.

CHAPTER EIGHT

AMERICAN COLOSSUS

IT WAS AN UNSPECTACULAR, workaday blaze that brought Assistant Chief Joseph B. Martin to midtown in the early afternoon hours of April 14, 1930, a surprisingly hot spring day. The building on fire was an old brownstone near the corner of East Thirty-third Street and Fifth Avenue that had been converted from a residence to a business. It was a piece of old New York, a five-story remnant of the old Astor family estate, surrounded by modern high-rise office buildings and apartment houses.

Smoky Joe Martin, now sixty-eight years old and the FDNY's second-in-command, arrived soon after the first-due units and took personal command. He had more than a professional interest in this particular blaze, for on the building's roof, in charge of ladder companies trying to ventilate the fire, was his son, Captain Joseph B. Martin, Jr.

So routine was this blaze that authorities' major concern was the huge traffic jam the fire and engines created on Fifth Avenue, then a two-way street. Equally pressing was the number of pedestrians who were trying to get a glimpse of the fire. Next-day accounts estimated that 10,000 people watched Smoky Joe's men in action. Police on horseback patrolled the sidewalks to keep the spectators out of the Fire Department's way.

Things took a slightly more serious turn when a second-floor ceiling collapsed on six firefighters, injuring them slightly. At about the same time, a young girl in the crowd fainted. She and the six firefighters were brought for medical attention to the ever-present Dr. Harry Archer, now an official FDNY legend and an honorary chief medical officer— though still a volunteer. Six years earlier he had become the only civilian ever to win the Department's highest citation for valor, the James Gordon Bennett Medal. On his own initiative he had crawled into the cellar of a collapsed building undergoing repairs on Eldridge Street to rescue two workers trapped under rubble. After the workers were freed, Archer himself became trapped in the basement as more of the building collapsed. The firefighters he served so well scrambled down and got him out.

Smoky Joe took a glimpse at the roof, peering through his round eyeglasses to see where his son was working, and then chatted with some police officers who were helping with crowd and traffic control. In mid-conversation, the chief staggered forward. Two firefighters caught him before he fell to the street. He had suffered a massive heart attack. Doctor Archer quickly came to his side and began administering oxygen. Somebody called for a priest. Two responded, and they administered the last rites of the Catholic church to Smoky Joe Martin.

Word of the chief's condition reached the roof of the fire building, and Captain Martin climbed down to the street. Very much his father's son, Captain Martin personally supervised the transfer of the gravely ill chief to an ambulance, which took him not to a hospital, but to his home on East Fifteenth Street. Doctor Archer told reporters that the chief was in "pretty bad shape."

By nightfall, word made its way from Smoky Joe's bedside to the press corps that the chief expected to be back at the job in a few days. Though Martin did try to return a few months later, the FDNY's chief medical officer, Dr. Joseph Smith (that is, its official, paid chief medical officer, as opposed to Dr. Archer, whose title was strictly honorary), would have none of it. He declared that Smoky Joe Martin—born in a

The firemen of Engine Co. 93 proudly pose with their modern engine outside their firehouse.

house adjacent to Engine Co. 5's headquarters; who as a kid idolized the firefighters of his youth and as a young man went to college at his father's insistence but followed his heart to the FDNY; a fearless veteran who never slept between midnight and 3 A.M. because, he said, that's when most serious fires start—was no longer fit for duty.

Smoky Joe presented himself at Fire Department headquarters on East Sixty-seventh Street on October 2, 1930. He was wearing the unfamiliar attire of civilian clothes. He had an appointment with Fire Commissioner John Dorman, he explained to reporters who covered the Fire Department, but the commissioner was out to lunch. While Smoky Joe waited, a reporter asked the chief if a rumor of his impending retirement was true. "There's nothing to that story," Martin replied.

Some time later, when he emerged from his meeting with the commissioner, reporters noticed that Smoky Joe's eyes were red and watery.

An hour later, Commissioner Dorman announced that Assistant Chief Martin would retire effective November 1. "When the doctors decide, I guess it's time to move the boat," Martin said. Later, in talking about the nickname that had made him famous, Martin said, "No man's got a corner on the smoke department. There's thousands of men in the Fire Department who are just as much entitled to that name as I am. And they're named everything from Ike to Aloysius."

That night they told Smoky Joe stories in the firehouse kitchens. They recalled his eight words of instruction to junior fire officers: "Catch your fire early, and hit it hard." They told stories that sounded too good to be true, and maybe they were, like the time Smoky Joe smelled smoke while talking to a visitor in the firehouse. Nobody else picked up the scent, but within a few minutes, a report came in that a furniture store in an old wooden building—a fine combination—was on fire near the firehouse. Needless to say, that fire didn't get very far, thanks to Smoky Joe's nose for smoke.

Then there were the undeniable firsthand accounts of Smoky Joe's courage and persistence. There was the time on June 15, 1922, when a dropped cigarette started a fire in the Alverne section of the inaccessible Rockaways peninsula in southern Queens. Four hundred homes were destroyed, 10,000 people were left homeless, and property damage was estimated at $4 million. Miraculously, nobody was killed, but newspaper headlines reported that Smoky Joe—by then readers knew him by that name—was among the injured. When the raging fire seemed on the verge of becoming completely out of control, at untold cost of lives and property, Martin led a stand against an advancing wall of flames with a single hose line. The chief's face was burned and his eyes singed, leaving him temporarily sightless. When he recovered his vision, he disregarded a doctor's orders and returned to the fight, pausing only to issue a warning to reporters: "Some day this same thing is going to happen at Coney and then there's going to be the worst loss of life we ever had," he said. "Get that before the public." And then he went off to fight the fire again. He was right, or at least half right, about Coney Island, in southwest Brooklyn. A decade later, on June 13, 1932, a fire that broke out under the resort's boardwalk burned several blocks and left 5,000 people homeless. Martin's prediction about loss of life did not, fortunately, come true.

A month after the Rockaways fire, on the morning of July 18, 1922, an explosion and fire ripped through a warehouse on Jane Street in Manhattan. Martin was at the scene again, and was thrown backward when fire set off a second explosion. Again, he suffered burns on his face, and his eyebrows and eyelashes were damaged. He got back on his feet, and then climbed to an adjacent rooftop to try to fight the fire from there. But that didn't work either, so Martin retreated to the street, where he ran across Mayor John Hylan. Hylan asked the chief how he was feeling.

"I feel fine," he said, just before he passed out.

They carried him to a cot and bandaged his burns, and Dr. Archer told him to go home. "You're past sixty," said Archer, ignoring the fact that he wasn't much younger himself.

"I've got work to do," Martin replied, and he continued his command from his cot.

When this great old firefighter retired in 1930, and then his seventy-year-old friend and colleague, John Kenlon, stepped down as chief of department less than a year later, there was a sense that an era had ended. These were firefighters who had been children in the earliest years of the paid Fire Department, had been reared on romanticized stories about the volunteer days and had actually worked with ex-volunteers. They were young firefighters in the days of horse-drawn apparatus, and served until the last horse was retired from service. And now Martin and Kenlon were part of FDNY history, too.

Twenty-three deputy chiefs took a civil service test to determine who would be the next chief of department. It seemed appropriate that the winner was John J. McElligott—very much the model of twentieth-century firefighting and the man who had succeeded Smoky Joe as assistant chief. He had joined the Department in 1906 and in 1915 was given command of the first fire rescue unit in the nation. As captain of Rescue Co. 1, McElligott built an elite corps of firefighters who were trained not simply in fighting fires, but in using the latest technology and tools to assist civilians or other firefighters in life-threatening emergencies. The men of the rescue company were selected on the basis of physical strength and size, as well as previous experience as electricians or ironworkers or in other trades where their skills could and would prove useful in emergencies.

The notion of an elite corps of firefighters had been under discussion for several years, but it gained urgency when 200 civilians were overcome by smoke, and one died, in a subway fire in early 1915. The fire was nearly a catastrophe, prompting the FDNY to expedite its plan to train and equip a special force for special emergencies, including chemical fires and industrial accidents.

McElligott and a team consisting of one lieutenant and eight firefighters were outfitted with special smoke helmets that McElligott himself tested under extreme conditions at the FDNY's Fire College (founded in 1911 under Chief Croker to further firefighters' training and education). The helmet looked like something a deep-sea diver might wear—it covered the entire head and provided about an hour's worth of oxygen. The men of Rescue Co. 1 could now operate for an hour without worrying about smoke inhalation.

McElligott and his unit received special training, a special truck, and special equipment—like a torch designed to cut through iron quickly—and were sent into the most perilous situations. Their pioneering work eventually led to the formation of rescue companies in all five boroughs, each equipped and trained to act as the FDNY's special operations units.

Another new institution further defined the modern era of firefighting. In 1917, after decades of performing continuous duty and living at the firehouse rather than with their families, the FDNY's rank-and-file firefighters organized a union, the Uniformed Firemen's Association. Its members were firefighters with the rank of fireman first grade—the most senior rank-and-file title—and below. Almost immediately, the UFA won a salary increase from $1,500 to $1,900 per year, and in 1922, the city agreed to divide fire duty into two shifts, or platoons. Instead of working continuously except for three one-hour meal breaks and an occasional day off, New York's firefighters would work eighty-four hours a week. That may not seem like much of a victory, but it surely was a good deal better than being on duty 147 hours a week, as had been expected of firefighters since the beginning of the paid Department. And it had been a long time coming, for other cities had begun switching from continuous duty to a platoon system more than a decade earlier. New York was, in fact, the last large American city to do away with continuous duty.

By the late 1920s and early 1930s, the UFA had become an aggressive and highly successful advocate for its members. The union refused to go along with Mayor Jimmy Walker's demand for unpaid furloughs during the early years of the Great Depression, and when Walker's successor, Fiorello La Guardia, tried to cut salaries of unionized city workers, the UFA successfully challenged the popular mayor.

The UFA encapsulated several traditions within the FDNY—the sense of fraternity and exclusivity, the eagerness to challenge authority, the insistence on benefits for survivors in case of death or disability in the line of duty, and, ironically, the self-consciously Irish-American yearning for job security and a guaranteed pension. By the early 1930s, it was clear that few decisions about Fire Department personnel or finances could be made without considering the opinion of the UFA.

ON AUGUST 1, 1932, Fireman William L. Pratt returned to duty for the first time since hurting his back while fighting the huge blaze in Coney Island in July. Rather than report to his usual unit, Ladder Co. 7 on East Twenty-eighth Street, he was detailed—in civilian parlance, temporarily assigned—to Ladder Co. 2 on the Upper East Side. Pratt, thirty, had served in the Army during World War I while still a teenager and was a four-year veteran of the FDNY.

Just after 10:30 that morning, Ladder Co. 2 was called to respond to a fire in the sub-basement of the Ritz Tower Hotel at the corner of Park Avenue and East Fifty-seventh Street. It was a small fire that started in a sub-basement vault where paint, varnish, paint remover, and ammonia were stored. Hotel employees who spotted the fire had tried unsuccessfully to extinguish it before giving up and calling the FDNY.

When first-due companies arrived, nothing seemed out of the ordinary, leading some firemen to suspect a false alarm. There was no smoke pouring from the forty-one-story building's lower floors. But they soon realized that there was, in fact, a blaze near the paint storeroom in the sub-basement, and down they went. Smoke they couldn't see from the outside filled the sub-basement area. The men of the engine companies dragged their hoses down two flights of stairs, while the ladder companies opened iron sidewalk shutters that covered a shaft leading to the sub-basement. Members of Rescue Co. 1, outfitted with smoke masks for just such a fire, were called in to assist.

Lieutenant James Harnett of Hook and Ladder Co. 16 led several firemen down a ladder placed in the exterior shaft. They would attack the fire from another vantage point, while about thirty other firemen fought their way through the smoke from an interior stairway. The sub-basement, filled with fumes from the paint storeroom, exploded as Harnett and the men with him forced open a door. Harnett and another fireman, Thomas Finn of Engine 65, were killed instantly. Harnett was a widower who had two children, ages twelve and ten.

The blast cut off power to the building, plunging the sub-basement into darkness. Dazed firefighters regrouped and searched for their missing and injured colleagues. Then another blast, even more violent, rocked the smoky, dark area. More than a dozen firemen were injured, some of them burned terribly. Ropes were lowered into the basement, and the victims were extricated from the horror and evacuated to hospitals. Lost in the debris was Fireman Pratt.

He was unconscious, lying in a pool of water and invisible in the darkness and confusion. The dead, the maimed, and the walking wounded all had been evacuated before firemen found Pratt, two hours after the explosions. Though he was taken immediately to Bellevue Hospital and placed on an artificial respirator, he died without regaining consciousness.

Fireman Pratt was one of eight firemen who were killed in the Ritz Tower fire or who later died of their injuries. It was the Department's worst loss of life since 1920, when six firefighters had died when burning oil fell on them while they were fighting a fire in Brooklyn. Among the Ritz Tower dead was Lieutenant John Cosgrove, a twenty-eight-year-veteran of the Department who succumbed to second-degree burns after hours of suffering in Flower Hospital. Like Lieutenant Harnett, Cosgrove was a widower. He had eight children.

Casualty lists published in the next day's newspapers gave the names of thirty people—firefighters, police officers, and civilians—who were injured in the blaze. Most were identified either by their engine company, or precinct house, or their address. But one of them, Henry Burkoff, was described simply as "a civilian fire 'buff' with Engine 22."

Buffs—civilians who took an almost professional interest in firefighting—had long been a part of firehouse culture in New York. The civilians who turned out to cheer the arrival of the Newsham hand pumpers in 1731; the young boys who ran behind fire engines in the 1840s; and the distinguished physician, Dr. Archer, who turned up at every major fire to minister to the injured—all fit the description of fire buffs. Although not firefighters themselves, they studied tactics and strategy, knew the precise locations of individual companies and the area they covered, understood the Department's complex system of alarm bell signals, and relished their friendships with firefighters. Not all buffs put themselves in harm's way as Henry Burkoff did at the Ritz Tower explosion, but they were ubiquitous at fires large and small. As time went on, the buffs showed that they were a good deal more than mere hangers-on. Like the runners during the volunteer days, the buffs of the twentieth century offered useful service—in 1939 they founded an organization called the Fire Bell Club to raise money for favorite FDNY charities, including and especially the department's widows' and children's funds.

Buffs came from all walks of life, sometimes motivated by not much more than an admiration for the Department's courage and an appreciation of its traditions. One of the city's most legendary fire buffs was a short, stocky middle-aged man with a feisty temper and a colorful personality. His name was Fiorello La Guardia, and in 1933 he was elected mayor as a reform-minded Republican.

Of course, La Guardia's relationship with the FDNY was a good deal more complicated than the average buff's. In taking over City Hall in the midst of the Great Depression, and in the aftermath of the scandals associated with the Roaring Twenties mayor Jimmy Walker, La Guardia had an extraordinarily difficult assignment. He had to restore public confidence in municipal government; find a way to assist the city's pitiful army of unemployed, homeless, and hungry; root out the waste and corruption that Tammany had planted years before; and prop up the city's weakened finances. This historic assignment was bound to have a profound effect on the Fire Department. And it did.

Before the Depression and the retirement of Smoky Joe Martin and John Kenlon, the Fire Department had continued its seemingly inexorable expansion. The number of firefighters rose from 6,767 in 1920 to 7,587 in 1930, and beginning in the prosperous days of 1924, the city launched a new construction program that resulted in fifty-four new firehouses over the next sixteen years. (Those houses would become known within the FDNY as "Mayor Walker houses," in tribute to the somewhat disgraced mayor who resigned while under investigation in 1932.) Budget constraints forced La Guardia not just to slow the Department's growth but actually to reduce FDNY manpower for the first time since the conversion from volunteers to paid service. By 1936, the Department had 6,717 firefighters, about 800 fewer than in 1930. That decrease in personnel coincided with a three-year decline in fire damage to property, leading La Guardia to speak of a time when modern construction and superior tactics would allow the FDNY to shrink by half with no loss of fire protection.

The UFA foiled the mayor's plan to reduce the salaries of firefighters and other city workers, but La Guardia found other ways of lowering costs, prompted by his closest aide and confidante, C. C. Burlingham, a stalwart reformer. In a memo to the mayor, Burlingham had written that if he were in charge of the city's finances, he would "quietly begin to investigate the Fire Department." As Thomas Kessner points out in his biography of La Guardia, *Fiorello H. La Guardia and the Making of Modern New York,* the mayor was not particularly quiet when he discovered that a cartel of thirteen hose manufacturers had submitted identical bids to deliver hoses to the FDNY—having colluded to split the business at inflated prices. He launched a campaign against what he called the "Fire

Helmet in hand, Mayor
La Guardia looks as though
he has been to battle after helping firefighters in January 1939.

Hose Trust," leading to a federal investigation that found rampant price-fixing in the fire-hose business. Later on in his remarkable tenure, La Guardia personally blocked the early retirement of eight top Fire Department officials who feared that they would lose some pension benefits under cost-cutting changes the mayor sought if they waited for their proper retirement dates. The fire commissioner already had approved the retirements, but a furious La Guardia overrode that decision and ordered the men back to work.

The Fire Department's institutional suspicion of politicians in general and reformers in particular would have led to the confident prediction that relations between firefighters and the mayor would be less than cordial. La Guardia, after all, had tried to cut their pay, had succeeded in reducing manpower, had questioned the department's financial arrangements, and had even overruled the commissioner. But there was another side of La Guardia, one that many firefighters couldn't help but like. He was a genuine buff, a helmet-wearing, hero-worshipping buff.

Any collection of pictures from La Guardia's years as mayor includes several shots that defined the era and the man himself: La Guardia reading the comics over the radio during a newspaper strike; La Guardia smashing illegal slot machines with a sledgehammer; La Guardia in a double-breasted suit, delivering a municipal sermon. Just as iconic, just as enduring, is the image of the "Little Flower" in a rubber jacket and a white helmet, watching firefighters battle a late-night blaze. Sometimes he did more than just watch: In January 1939, La Guardia responded to a fire on Cherry Street and wound up assisting firefighters as they rescued a colleague trapped under a fallen beam. Photographers took a picture of a weary mayor as he left the scene: head down, white fire helmet in hand, his rubber jacket drenched and soiled. But he had been unprepared for his role of rescuer—he was wearing dress shoes rather than boots, so the lower portion of his pants suffered as badly as his jacket did.

He didn't claim to know much about firefighting. When he appointed Chief of Department McElligott to shoulder the additional job of fire commissioner in 1934, he wrote, "You know all about fire fighting. I know nothing about it. There will be no interference, no favoritism and I don't need to tell you there will be no politics." But, in the course of his twelve years in City Hall, La Guardia had plenty of opportunities to learn the business. He turned up so often at fires that critics wondered if he was more a fire buff than mayor. He replied, somewhat testily, that he considered fire duty part of the job. What, he asked, "would the men think if I didn't have the guts to go where they went, especially if there was danger?"

It was that kind of respect which earned him the Fire Department's goodwill. It didn't hurt that in the late 1930s, the city embarked on a new hiring campaign that not only replenished the manpower losses of La Guardia's first term but resumed the Department's expansion of personnel, always an important priority of the firemen's union. As La Guardia ran for a second term in 1937, the city hired 1,945 firefighters, one of the largest one-year increases in manpower ever. And plans called for the force to expand from 8,662 firefighters on January 1, 1938, to 12,500 by the fall of 1939, in anticipation of a three-platoon, or three-shift, staffing system. The manpower goal proved elusive, and the three-platoon system was implemented briefly, suspended, and never resumed, but still, by 1940 the city employed 11,631 firefighters. Their workweek was cut from eighty-four hours to fifty, although it reverted back to eighty-four when three-platoon staffing became a victim of the World War II manpower shortage.

La Guardia's hiring binge would yield unintended, but not entirely unpredictable, consequences for the Department in the late 1950s, when thousands of firefighters qualified for pensions after twenty years of service. They would retire in record numbers, forcing the city to hire replacements so quickly that many brand-new firefighters were ordered to report to firehouses without being trained.

After war broke out in Europe in 1939, Mayor La Guardia revisited a bit of firefighting history as President Franklin Roosevelt began preparations for the nation's first peacetime draft. Firefighters and police officers, the mayor argued, ought to be exempt from conscription not only because they provided an essential service but also because when war came—and La Guardia never doubted it would—they would be critical to civil defense. La Guardia's proposition had an echo of bygone years, when the city offered volunteer firefighters exemptions from military service. He became a national leader on behalf of draft exemptions for police and firefighters, coordinating the efforts of other mayors and governors who shared his view that police and fire work were essential to national defense.

In a letter to a skeptical draft board official on December 13, 1940, La Guardia argued, with characteristic candor, that "anyone having the slightest information could have informed you that fire fighting on coastal and strategic points is as necessary to national defense as the army itself. The City will suffer if firemen are now drafted." La Guardia's efforts won him the support of the city's Board of Fire Underwriters—the fire insurance industry—which passed a resolution on January 15, 1941, that firefighters shouldn't be drafted because "it

Mayor La Guardia was a genuine fire buff who seemed at home with his firefighters.

would not be possible to replace these highly trained experts."

After Pearl Harbor La Guardia was appointed to head the nation's civil defense effort. He continued his campaign to exempt firefighters from military duty, but he did refine it somewhat. He told other mayors who turned to him for guidance that he sought deferments only for firefighters and police with more than two years experience. In a letter he sent to Governor Richard Blood of New Hampshire on March 20, 1943, La Guardia claimed that his arguments had won over local draft boards in New York.

Even as the war neared its climax in early 1945, with President Roosevelt demanding nearly a million more men in uniform by the end of June, La Guardia was lobbying Washington to defer cops and firefighters. The director of the Selective Service's New York office, Colonel Arthur V. McDermott, told the mayor on January 26, 1945, that he agreed "that every possible effort should be made to obtain occupational deferments for all firemen over the age of 26."

But even as La Guardia fought for FDNY deferments, many firefighters were not waiting to find out whether or not they'd been drafted.

By April 1941, seven months before Pearl Harbor, more than forty fire-fighters had resigned to join the military. After the Japanese attack hundreds more signed up, and by war's end, nearly 2,000 New York firefighters were in uniformed service of a very different kind. To make up for the loss in manpower, the mayor and his new fire commissioner, Patrick Walsh, established an auxiliary fire service made up, at its peak, of 54,000 civilians trained in rudimentary firefighting and emergency response.

The FDNY regarded these amateurs with a professional's skepticism and a New York firefighter's suspicion. The civilians were not especially well trained, and of course they were not members of the union. Nevertheless, the national interest outweighed resentment, and the auxiliaries worked side by side with the professionals throughout the war years. On one occasion, an auxiliary was assigned the task of monitoring alarm boxes for false alarms during a wartime blackout. He noticed a short, stocky man stalking the neighborhood and shared his suspicions with FDNY officers. It must have been a dark night, and the auxiliary's vision may not have been up to Fire Department standards. The suspicious character was Mayor La Guardia.

Patrick Walsh was La Guardia's second fire commissioner, an Irish immigrant who had worked his way through the ranks, like his predecessor, McElligott. He was a throwback of sorts, seventy-two years old when he was sworn in as commissioner. He had joined the FDNY in 1901, shaving five years off his actual age of thirty-three to sneak in under the legal limit of thirty. If it seemed a desperate act, he was a man who had seen desperate times. In six terrible years, from 1897 to 1901, he and his wife, Mary Ann, had buried four children, all of them three years old or younger, two of them dying within five days of each other. All suffered from dysentery, and very likely received inept attention from the local doctor, a known drunk.

Walsh seemed well on his way to retirement—although he still was living by his fictional age—when La Guardia appointed him commissioner. McElligott had left abruptly and unexpectedly, having resigned under mayoral pressure in 1941 when six firefighters were charged with taking bribes while inspecting oil burners. La Guardia would accept no excuses from his commissioners, not even from a legendary firefighter like McElligott, the pioneer of Rescue Co. 1.

As America went to war, La Guardia and his new commissioner, Walsh, broadened the Fire Department's responsibilities to include training and drilling in civil defense, in case New York, like the great cities of Europe, came under attack. Broadly speaking, fire service—the number of fires—declined dramatically during the war, falling by 6,000 in 1942 alone. Yet the city's waterfront, filled with warships, troopships, and merchant ships loaded down with goods and material, was a new front line for the Fire Department. So numerous were ship fires, and so unfamiliar to most firefighters were shipboard conditions, that the editors of the department's official magazine, *With New York Firemen* (or *WNYF*), devoted a long article to "explaining the general anatomy of ships that any landlubber can understand." The most dramatic fire was the burning of the luxury liner *Normandie,* which was being converted for war use when it went up in flames at its pier and capsized in February 1942.

To make up for manpower lost not only to the military but to retirements, La Guardia and Walsh suspended the Department's three platoons. It was back to the heavier work load of the old two-shift, eighty-four-hour week, a move that infuriated the UFA. The union's fury in turn infuriated La Guardia, who considered himself the firefighter's friend. After all, noted Commissioner Walsh's biographer, Kathleen Walsh Packard, when Selective Service Administration officials continued to press for the drafting of firefighters, the mayor called them "fatheads."

Citing the state law that had mandated three-platoon manning and a shorter workweek, the UFA went to court to block La Guardia and Walsh from unilaterally imposing the old system and its longer hours on the Department rank and file. The union lost, with a judge ruling that the war emergency took precedence over work rules. The two-platoon shifts and eighty-four-hour workweeks were reinstated on June 1, 1944, five days before D-Day. When the war ended a year later, City Hall did not return to the three-platoon work schedule. But firefighters did see a substantial reduction in their workweek, down to forty-five hours in 1947, and finally to a standard forty-hour week in the early 1960s. The two-platoon system remains intact; one shift covers the firehouses from nine o'clock in the morning until six o'clock at night; the overnight platoon reports at six and works until nine the following morning.

THE FIRST large fire of postwar New York was one of the worst of the century. In the fading light of a late-autumn afternoon, just after five o'clock on December 11, 1946, two young boys were loitering on the roof of an ice house on West 184th Street in Washington Heights. The older boy, thirteen, ignited a pile of newspapers on the roof with a candle. He did it, he said, "for fun."

Firefighters were called, and they extinguished the small blaze with little problem. Seven hours later, a resident of a six-story tenement house adjacent to the ice house smelled smoke and saw sparks falling from the ice-house roof. She called the Fire Department again. About ninety-five people, including nearly three dozen children, were in the tenement, located at 2515 Amsterdam Avenue, at the time. It was midnight, and most of the building's residents were sleeping.

Fifteen minutes after firefighters arrived, they noticed a hissing noise coming from inside the ice house. Suddenly the building's concrete roof collapsed, its wooden beams weakened by a fire that had already been burning for hours. Fireman Frank Moorehead of Engine Co. 93, working the fire from an extension of the roof, vanished into the inferno. As the roof fell in, one of the ice-house walls collapsed into the tenement building on Amsterdam Avenue. News accounts later compared the scene to an image fresh in the minds of New Yorkers—the destruction was "reminiscent of London, Coventry or other war-bombed cities of Europe." Dozens of men, women, and children were trapped, and the stunned firefighters soon heard terrible screams for help from underneath the debris. Somewhere in the smoke, fire, and ruins, Edith De Rico and her young daughter, Margaret, were trapped with a neighbor, Betty Brancotti. They prayed together, until a weeping Mrs. Brancotti said, "I'm dying." She said nothing more.

Firefighters worked through the night with picks, shovels, axes, and their bare hands, trying to respond to the weakening voices begging for help. They built tunnels through the debris to rescue several people, but they had no idea how many remained. Initial reports indicated that one person was dead and four missing, but as the hours dragged on, the number of dead rose to seventeen, then to thirty-two, and finally, after three days of searching, the number of crushed, burned corpses reached thirty-seven. Ten children died in the collapse. The newspapers published a list of the dead whose bare alphabetical details told horrible stories: Biancardi, Anthony, 12; Biancardi, Elizabeth, 37; Biancardi, Joyce, 12; Biancardi, Lucille, 8; Biancardi, Monica, 7. Farther down: Sloan, Judith, 4; Sloan, Louise, 7; Sloan, Madeline, 36; Sloan, Peter, 36; Sloan, Rita, 11.

The Popper family—father, mother, and two children—was nearly wiped out. Eleven-year-old Adolph Joseph Popper somehow survived, pulled from the carnage by a firefighter named Neil Kinnick. Years later Adolph Joseph Popper joined the Fire Department, and as a young firefighter in Engine Co. 7, was reintroduced to the man who had saved him, Battalion Chief Neil Kinnick.

It was never determined whether the fire that the boys ignited on the icehouse roof wasn't completely extinguished or whether there was a second separate fire hours later. But two days after the collapse, December 13, the newspapers were filled with suggestions of an arson epidemic in the city. A nine-year-old boy in the Bronx confessed to setting fire to P.S. 12. The blaze went to five alarms and caused widespread damage. The fire marshal's office was investigating two suspicious fires in tenements on Madison Avenue. And police arrested a twenty-nine-year-old suspect in a string of five tenement fires in Harlem. The suspect immediately confessed, saying that he had set the fires because he was "sick and disgusted."

It would not be the last time New York's firefighters put their lives on the line because a "sick and disgusted" civilian decided to burn a building.

The social and demographic changes in postwar New York were to have a profound effect on Fire Department culture. The growth of the suburbs, the benefits of the GI bill, the construction of interstate highways, and the general prosperity of the 1950s changed many of the traditional patterns of firehouse life. Firefighters became home owners; they became commuters; they became part-time college students.

Nothing, however, promised more dramatic change than the burgeoning civil rights movement. As the minority population of New York grew, so too would pressure to integrate a Department that had only a small minority presence in the immediate postwar years.

One veteran firefighter set the tone for the coming battle over inclusion. His name was Wesley Williams. He was not the first black firefighter in New York—two other blacks had served on the paid Department before Williams was appointed. And legend has it that a female slave named Molly fought fires with the volunteers of Oceanus Engine Company during the winter of 1818. Williams, however, became the first black firefighter to break down other barriers in New York's fire service, and became a leader in exposing and rooting out racism from the city's firehouses.

After earning high marks on his civil service written exam and a perfect score on the Department's physical test, Williams was assigned to Engine Co. 55 in lower Manhattan. The white firefighters requested transfers—they were denied—and the captain retired the very day Williams showed up for work. Williams was told to sleep in the cellar instead of the bunkroom. When he refused, the white firemen moved their beds to the cellar, leaving Williams alone in the bunkroom. It was a foreshadowing of the treatment other black firefighters would receive when their numbers increased during Mayor La Guardia's hiring binge in the late 1930s. They were assigned to a designated "black bed," which whites refused to use even when no black firefighters were on duty.

A bodybuilder and future FDNY boxing champion, Williams literally fought off challenges from white firefighters in the 1920s. He later recalled that he "couldn't have stayed on the job if I'd lost" any of those brawls. "They would have thought I was a weakling and I would have been trampled on. There was no Human Rights Commission to complain to."

Enduring the less violent confrontations of silence and ostracism required another kind of strength. Williams withdrew to a world of his own, working out in a small gym he built in the firehouse and preparing

Firefighter Wesley Williams was the third African American to join the FDNY, and its first African American officer.

for the lieutenant's test, which he passed in 1927 to become the first black officer in FDNY history. This posed something of a dilemma: No white fireman had ever taken orders from a black man before, and some suggested that Williams should be assigned as an officer in headquarters, where he could perform staff work. Williams would have none of it. "I took orders from white officers," he said. "White firemen will have to learn to take orders from a colored officer."

Fortunately for Williams and the Department itself, the Fire Department's single-minded reliance on testing for promotion meant that no bigoted officers or politicians could stand in the way of Williams's success. He became the FDNY's first black captain in 1934, and four years later, just forty-one, he won promotion to battalion chief. With the prestige and power of his new title, in 1940 Chief Williams founded the Vulcan Society to act as a lobbying and support network for New York's fifty black firefighters. The Vulcans called public attention to practices like the black bed, and testified at a City Council hearing in 1944 about racial harassment in the city's firehouses.

The black bed, however, persisted into the immediate postwar years, as a future commissioner, Augustus Beekman, discovered when he returned from the war, became a firefighter, and was assigned to Engine Co. 58 in Harlem. There, two beds were set aside for blacks. Other forms of harassment continued into the 1950s, when two brothers named Reginald and Vincent Julius joined the Department for the same reason the Irish joined: to obtain a decent salary and job security. They had been raised in the South Bronx of the 1930s, when blacks lived in small pockets surrounded by Irish, Italian, and Jewish neighborhoods. Their father had reared them with a philosophy that they would remember into the twenty-first century: "You are better than no man," he said. "And no man is better than you."

One morning not long after Reggie Julius was hired in 1949, a white firefighter at Engine Co. 46 in the Bronx smashed a coffee cup that Julius had used at breakfast. Julius, a broad-shouldered Navy veteran of World War II who had been wounded when his ship took enemy fire during the Battle of Guadalcanal, started laughing. "Boy, you just gave me the chance," he said. He got up from his chair in the kitchen, walked over to a cabinet, and addressed his colleagues. "Let me tell you something," he said. "I ain't leaving this job because it's all I got. I will break every dish in this house. I will bend every knife, fork, and spoon, and we will eat off the table with our fingers. Don't fuck with me. I got shrapnel in my head, and I ain't too correct anyway."

For the record, the shrapnel went through Julius's upper arm, and he has the entry and exit scars to prove it. But his colleagues didn't know that. He had a few problems after that morning, but they were settled in the firehouse cellar, to Julius's satisfaction.

Vincent Julius followed in his older brother's footsteps three years later, and found similar attitudes in all-white firehouses. When he was detailed briefly to Ladder Co. 18, he had a days-long argument with his white colleagues that became so tense Julius was warned that nobody would speak to him for the remainder of his tenure in the company. "Ostracize me if you want," he said. "I didn't come here to make friends. I came here to make a living."

In organizing the FDNY's Vulcan Society, Wesley Williams paved the way for future black firefighters, like this one.

The breaking point came when the white firefighters threatened to cut Julius out of the firehouse meals, the worst possible breach of firehouse etiquette. "The day you cut me out of the meal, I will overturn that table and fight every one of you," Julius said. He would recall decades later that for the rest of his detail in Truck 18, about three more weeks, all he heard was, "Vinnie, dinner is served."

Reggie Julius went on to become a battalion chief. Vinnie Julius became a captain.

Another part of the story of postwar New York City is the story of highways that cut through the old neighborhoods of Brooklyn and the Bronx—the kind of neighborhoods were firefighters lived—and led to a green place called suburbia. Like hundreds of thousands of other

New Yorkers during the prosperity of the Eisenhower years, firefighters found they couldn't resist the lure of a home to call their own. A firefighter appointed in 1952 earned $3,725 a year without overtime, with an increase to $4,400 a year after three years. Around the mid-fifties, middle-class life became more than just a dream for New York's firefighters as they scanned the classified pages of the Long Island newspaper *Newsday* and discovered that they could afford to buy a three-bedroom Levittown house on a 40 x 100 lot for less than $10,000.

Before World War II, firefighters and other city employees were required to live within the five boroughs. But the changes brought about by highway construction, suburban development, a severe postwar housing shortage in the city, and the home finance opportunities that were part of the GI Bill led the UFW to demand for a loosening of residency restrictions. Firefighters sought their piece of the new American dream of suburban home ownership. With an understandable lack of enthusiasm, starting in the 1950s the city allowed firefighters to live in Nassau and Suffolk counties on Long Island and then, in the early 1960s, extended permitted residency to several adjacent upstate counties.

The transformation of firefighters into commuters, living far away from their firehouses and in communities quite unlike those in which they served, was something of a cultural revolution within the Department. During the volunteer era and for decades afterward, firefighters tended to live close to their firehouse for obvious reasons—in those days before mass transit and the automobile, it was imperative that firefighters waste as little time as possible getting to their firehouses and then to the fire. In the early decades of the twentieth century firefighters still lived in the boroughs, and often the very communities, they served. Company rosters show some movement in the 1920s, as subway lines to the Bronx and Queens allowed firefighters to move out of old neighborhoods in Manhattan. But they still were within the city limits, as the law required.

Once the city eased its restrictions, however, the exodus from the urban boroughs of Manhattan, Brooklyn, and the Bronx was dramatic. The names of Long Island towns like Massapequa, New Hyde Park, and Westbury began appearing on company rosters in the early 1950s, especially among newly hired firefighters. Suburban areas of Queens and Staten Island, the least-populated boroughs, also were becoming popular.

Into the old neighborhoods of the Bronx and Brooklyn moved new New Yorkers who were poorer, and blacker, and browner than the populace of 1945. As firefighters and their families piled into station wagons for their one-way journeys east along the Long Island Expressway or north along the Major Deegan, the new New York they were leaving behind seemed increasingly like a city of strangers, especially as second-generation commuter firefighters joined the Department in the late 1960s.

Thus, the automobile and modern highways did more than speed up Fire Department response time. It changed the relationship between many firefighters and the city they served. For thousands of firefighters, New York was no longer home, the streets were no longer their streets. With their flexible work chart, commuter firefighters often rearranged their schedules by swapping shifts—or, in FDNY lingo, "working mutuals"—to cut down on their increasingly longer commutes. Mutuals had long been a part of FDNY culture, part of the notion of comradeship and solidarity: You could depend on your brother firemen to help you out if you needed to switch shifts for any reason. And as many firefighters moved east and north, mutuals became even more important. By working their own shift and then a mutual partner's, firefighters were able to work twenty-four consecutive hours, which, under work rules, allowed them three full days off before they had to make the drive back to the firehouse, back to the city.

For New York's firefighters, the postwar years brought the good life of suburban home ownership, backyard swimming pools and family barbecues. While they were by no means affluent—in fact, most worked second jobs to help pay the bills—the gains in salary and benefits allowed them to enjoy a life their parents and grandparents could not have imagined. A gossipy column called "All Hands" in *WNYF* chronicled the fun and games of family picnics in new suburban paradises like Heckscher State Park, Jones Beach, and Lake Ronkonkama, and fishing

An engine
company
fights its way
into a burning
building.

trips in the Adirondacks. Equally telling, "All Hands" periodically took note of company golf tournaments. In fact, the July 1953 edition noted that Ladder Co. 125 was looking to sell its "golf machine. . . equipped with a yardage, slice and hook indicator." A firefighter's life was not, after all, just rescues and drills.

In the mid–1960s, a young firefighter named Dennis Smith, the product of tenement-house life in Manhattan, was commuting sixty miles from his home in upstate Washingtonville to the quarters of Engine Co. 82 in the heart of the South Bronx. He had a four-bedroom house on half an acre of property and a wife and five children. Years later, he would describe his life in a breathtaking memoir called *Report from Engine Company 82:* "The house is built on top of a hill, overlooking distant mountains and my neighbor's backyard. It is peaceful and plain. I can't enjoy the solitude Thoreau wrote about, not with the kids playing noisily in the yard. . . but I can plant a bean row if I want to."

Sixty miles from that patch of grass and semisolitude was Dennis Smith's place of business, on Intervale Avenue and 169th Street in the South Bronx. There, the would-be bean planter from the suburbs became an eyewitness to the burning of a once-vibrant neighborhood, a neighborhood that was to become synonymous with urban decay.

If firefighters seemed to be enjoying a share of America's postwar prosperity, they also were sharing in its unprecedented dangers. As a provider not simply of fire suppression and prevention but an array of emergency services, the FDNY was asked to prepare for the unimaginable during the most terrifying years of the Cold War. A Fire Department Office of Civil Defense began drawing up nightmare scenarios and projecting how the FDNY might handle them. The office also was given the responsibility of recruiting civilians to serve, as they did during World War II, in an auxiliary corps of firefighters and rescue workers to help with the Department's civil defense responsibilities.

During three days in late September 1953, the FDNY rehearsed its response to a terrifying fictional scenario: Two atomic bombs had been exploded over New York, one over lower Manhattan and the other over Queens. What would New York's firefighters do? What could they do?

The Department's officers found themselves trying to imagine such a catastrophe and then devising a plan to counter it. Some of the Department's 11,150 firefighters were sent to a proving ground in Queens, where civil defense officials used fire, smoke, flares, and fireworks to replicate some small version of a nuclear attack's aftermath. Meanwhile, FDNY officers used maps and models to try to devise some manner of orderly response to the what-if scenario. Their first line of defense, they wrote, would consist of "more than 700 pieces of apparatus" to be deployed about two and a half miles from the point of the bomb's explosion, which scientists called "ground zero."

Drilling and war-game exercises in preparation for a nuclear attack became a regular part of the Fire Department's routine. Firefighting in New York, it became clear through Cold War years of the 1950s, had become an even more complex and more dangerous job even as the number of fires fell from 52,741 in 1952 to 46,098 in 1956. The Department's journal, *WNYF* offered advice on "how we can live with our newest menace," which it called "the atomic bugaboo." It advised firefighters that in responding to fires caused by an atomic bomb, they should be careful to remove radioactive dust from their clothing and hair, but the article ended with a cheery note: "In the years to come, when radioactivity is as common as electricity is now, we shall. . . look back and wonder what it was that scared us all."

Amazingly, had the nuclear-war exercises of 1953 been an actual emergency, the Department's last volunteer would have been expected to be on the scene. Now eighty-five, Dr. Harry Archer still was responding to fires in 1953, sometimes at the expense of his social life. He often was spotted in formal evening attire as he administered first aid to injured firefighters. He smoked, he drank, and he ate whatever he wished, and remained more than just sprightly for his age. On New Year's Eve, 1947, Dr. Archer, wearing only a tuxedo, climbed an ice-coated FDNY ladder to get to a gravely injured firefighter on the second floor of a burning building. The firefighter, Winfield Walsh, died. Several hours later, as the building continued to burn, the physician crawled through debris to give first aid to five firefighters trapped under a collapsed wall. He was at the fire for ten hours, furthering his legend as one of the FDNY's greatest heroes—and surely the greatest fire buff in New York history.

Archer had attended every fire of note, at least those in Manhattan, since the late 1890s. When he died on May 17, 1954, his casket was draped in a flag and placed on the back of a pumper to be borne to a departmental funeral service in St. Patrick's Cathedral.

In the late 1950s and early 1960s, the young firefighters who had been appointed during Mayor La Guardia's second term were middle-aged and eligible for retirement on half-pay after twenty years. Thousands turned in their papers—nearly 700 in 1960 alone, and slightly more than 500 in 1961—meaning that thousands of new hires were needed. Twelve hundred new firefighters were appointed in 1960, and nearly thirteen hundred in 1962. The new generation was made up of people like twenty-one-year-old Lawrence McCarthy, whose firefighter father had told

Fire escapes not
only allowed
people to flee
buildings, they
allowed fire-
fighters a means
to bring a hose
to a burning
apartment.

him to go to college and find some other line of work. He tried college, but it didn't suit him, so he took the firefighter's test. "I was newly married, jobs were tight, so civil service seemed to be the best thing," he would say many years later. He was appointed on April 15, 1957, and was sent immediately to Engine Co. 231 in the Brownsville section of Brooklyn. The only way the Department could keep up with the number of retirements was to throw the new men directly into service as probationary firefighters, because they couldn't send them all to the School of Instruction at once. McCarthy was one of the new men who started his service in the firehouse and had to wait for his formal training.

Although he eventually did go to probie school, as the School of Instruction was called, McCarthy was perfectly placed for on-the-job training. With about a hundred runs a month, Engine Co. 231 was one of the city's twenty-five busiest fire companies. It would not be so many years before the members of Engine Co. 231 would look back on the days of hundred-run months as laughably slow.

The terrible scenarios played out in the Fire Department's Office of Civil Defense didn't seem so unimaginable in late October 1962. The Cuban Missile Crisis, coming about a year after President John Kennedy delivered a grave speech about the possibility of nuclear war and the necessity of civil defense preparation, made the war games of 1953 seem prudent.

On October 26, 1962, as Kennedy and Soviet Premier Khrushchev retreated from Armageddon over missiles in Cuba, a construction worker with a defective acetylene torch was taking apart some equipment in a soap factory in Maspeth, Queens. The torch spat out sparks that ignited a small fire, but the worker extinguished the flames without calling the Fire Department. It happened a second time, with the same result. When quitting time arrived, the workers locked up the soap factory and headed home, giving little thought to the small fires that had broken out hours before. By 9:30 that night, the two-story factory near the Brooklyn-Queens Expressway was ablaze. Engine Co. 325 and Ladder Co. 115 were among the first units on the scene.

The fire was difficult enough to require four alarms and the personal command of George David, the chief of department. Nevertheless, the fire was declared under control after about an hour. Although the fire was not extinguished, the mop-up had begun. A group of firefighters was overhauling the building—checking for unseen remnants of the fire—when a twenty-foot section of a corrugated metal roof fell, collapsing a wall. It crashed down on twenty firefighters, trapping them under debris and the remnants of the metal roof.

Some managed to crawl out of the rubble and others were rescued when firefighters cut through the wrecked metal roof. But six firefighters—Captain William Russell, George Zahn, Richard Gifford, James Marino, Francis Egan, and Richard Andrews—were dead. Andrews was the company's junior man, still a "probie," or probationary firefighter. He had been on the job less than a year.

A funeral Mass for the six firefighters was held in St. Patrick's Cathedral. Thousands of firefighters turned out in their dress uniforms and white gloves, and as they lined Fifth Avenue and saluted the caskets of their fallen comrades, New York's firefighters had little reason to suspect they were on the verge of greater catastrophe. The city's fire fatality rate—the number of civilian deaths per million inhabitants—was well below the national average. Nationally, there were sixty deaths per million; in New York in 1962, the figure was nineteen per million. Although the FDNY was by far the nation's busiest fire department, responding to 69,991 fires in 1962, the city they protected seemed more secure than ever.

Even what became the busiest day in FDNY history up to that point offered little hint of what was to come. But it did serve as a reminder of yet another way in which the Fire Department of New York faced challenges like no other urban fire service in America. Already charged with protecting the world's tallest buildings, the nation's most populous communities, and an array of buildings ranging from old-law tenements to modern apartment complexes, New York's firefighters on April 20, 1963, were summoned to the largest brush fire in the city's history.

Before the opening of the Verrazano Narrows Bridge in 1964, Staten Island was not so much a part of New York City as it was a rural afterthought. The island was by far the city's least-populated borough, with just 150,000 people, and was connected to Manhattan and Brooklyn by ferry only. By contrast, three bridges linked the borough to New Jersey, a more than symbolic statement of Staten Island's place as a suburb that happened to fall within the boundaries of the nation's largest city.

The island's southernmost section was positively rural, with long stretches of woods separating small, almost bucolic villages. Staten Island had few apartment buildings and commercial areas, so young, eager firefighters came to regard the borough as a retirement home. Still, when conditions were right—dry weather and whipping winds— the borough's woodlands and meadows burned, and those brush fires inevitably claimed single-family homes. Injuries were few and deaths extremely rare, but every gutted home represented a family tragedy.

Conditions were exactly right—or wrong—on Saturday morning, April 20, 1963. The first few weeks of spring had been dry, with only about a quarter inch of rain. A wind from the west was gusting up to fifty miles an hour, turning two midmorning brush fires on the borough's southern shore into raging wild fires that leaped across major thoroughfares and reduced dozens of houses to ashes. By midafternoon, ten square miles of Staten Island were in flames, overwhelming the Twenty-third Battalion, which covered the island. The borough's off-duty firefighters were ordered to report to their firehouses as reinforcements.

Water pressure in some areas quickly was reduced to nothing, and in more remote areas, amazingly, there simply were no hydrants to tap, leaving firefighters as helpless as they had been in 1835 when Manhattan's hydrants froze. Firefighters could only watch as winds carried the flames toward more houses, businesses, a summer camp run by the Volunteers of America, and a Catholic orphanage in the Pleasant Plains section of the borough. An eyewitness told a reporter from the *Staten Island Advance* that "some firemen cried as the houses burned down. There wasn't any water. The firemen stood by and couldn't do a thing." Fifty booster tanks filled with water were rushed to hard-to-reach fires, which saved some homes but arrived too late for others. A gasoline station at the corner of Hylan Boulevard and Page Avenue was celebrating its grand opening, with colorful plastic bunting and a clown waving to passing children. By nightfall, the gas station was a charred ruin.

The Fire Department quickly redeployed nearly seventy of the Department's 215 engine companies to the borough, which in turn forced redeployment of other companies to fill in the gaps. Moving fire apparatus to Staten Island, however, was no easy matter; in fact, the operation had a nineteenth-century quality to it. Engine companies waited impatiently in lower Manhattan and at the foot of Sixty-ninth Street in Brooklyn for commuter ferries—the only link between Staten Island and the larger city. Some companies were forced to take a circuitous journey across the Hudson River into New Jersey, and then cross one of the three bridges linking that state with Staten Island.

Then, even as companies were moved from Brooklyn and Manhattan to Staten Island, and from Queens and the Bronx to

Brooklyn and Manhattan, a five-alarm fire broke out in the East New York section of Brooklyn, and a four-alarm blaze raged through an apartment house in Queens. Fire dispatchers, who performed the vital work of directing companies to their assignments and redeploying units to even out protection, had never faced a day like April 20, 1963.

More than fifteen hundred firefighters battled the Staten Island blaze for ten hours. At one point in the afternoon, an FDNY officer at a makeshift command post betrayed the Department's desperation. As fires burned nearby, the officer told some of his men, "We can't worry about isolated houses. We have to stop this fire at the main thorough-fares."

One hundred homes were destroyed and five hundred people were left homeless. The orphanage was spared, but the summer camp was destroyed and never rebuilt. Incredibly, there were few injuries—although thirty-six firefighters, emergency workers and civilians were hurt, only five required hospitalization.

Eight hundred and fifty alarms were reported on April 20, making it the busiest day in FDNY history. The fire commissioner, Edward Thompson, said the Staten Island fires were "possibly the greatest task in the history of the New York Fire Department." Edward Cavanaugh, a former fire commissioner who was now a deputy mayor, estimated that 55 percent of the FDNY's manpower and apparatus were fighting fires on that windy, dry Saturday. Cavanaugh toured the devastated sections of Staten Island by helicopter, and remarked, "If we have another fire in this city, we'll be in big trouble."

Or course, there would be another fire, there would be many of them. And there would be big trouble.

THE WAR YEARS

Every year New York's mayor and fire commissioner hand out awards at the Fire Department's Medal Day ceremony. It is an impressive sight as firefighters and officers in dress uniforms are brought before their friends, families, and colleagues to receive honors that bear the names of the Department's legends—Hugh Bonner, Smoky Joe Martin, and Wesley Williams, among others—as well as some of the FDNY's most famous supporters and buffs: Mayor La Guardia and, of course, James Gordon Bennett. The ceremonies usually have moments of heartbreak, too, for on this day the Department also recognizes firefighters who have died in the line of duty since the last Medal Day ceremony. Spouses and children, or parents and other relatives, are presented with posthumous medals for bravery or with the Department's medals for supreme sacrifice. Rare are the years when these medals are not awarded.

There is no award or campaign ribbon devoted exclusively to fire service in New York from the mid–1960s to the late 1970s, but there could be—and perhaps there should be. These were the most tumultuous years in the history of New York firefighting; not coincidentally,

Firefighters assigned to ladder companies, known in the trade as "truckies," are responsible for ventilating burning buildings. Here, a truckie operates on a rooftop, close to a pocket of fire.

they were among the most tumultuous years in the city's history. Few firefighters, whether they served in quiet areas of Staten Island or in the hell that became the South Bronx, were untouched by the era's civil disorder, labor strife, fiscal calamities, and social disintegration. Firefighters who were young at the time were still telling stories about the 1970s to the untested probies of the twenty-first century. When they spoke about "the war years," they were talking about fifteen years of false alarms, assaults, layoffs, budget cuts, riots, racial violence—the breaking apart of the old New York their parents had fled in the 1950s.

Mostly, though, they were talking about fires—fires in numbers they had never seen before, fires that reduced famous neighborhoods to ashes, fires set because a landlord wanted insurance money, fires set because an alienated youth wanted to send a message to the establishment.

The war years were a civic apocalypse. From 1960 to 1977, the annual number of fires more than doubled, from 60,941 to 129,619, and the number of serious fires rose from 1,630 to 4,880. Firefighters listened, bitterly, as the era's celebrated radicals glorified arson as a social state- ment, shouting, "Burn, baby, burn" to the poor and disenfranchised, some of whom were all too eager to oblige. Just as eager, in their own way, were the not-so-poor and not-so-disenfranchised—landlords and business owners who decided their property was worth more in ashes than as brick and mortar. "Burn, baby, burn" became their method of operation, too. Amid this chaos, a wounded Fire Department of New York—scarred by internal politics and budget cuts, bloodied by the very people it sought to protect—desperately sought to extinguish the flames.

Vincent Dunn was a Navy veteran who, like thousands of other pro- bies, joined the FDNY in the late 1950s. A high school dropout, Dunn discovered the value of education in the firehouse. Working in Harlem with Engine Co. 59, he met another rookie firefighter, Frank Lomuscio, the son of immigrants from Italy. Lomuscio wore a college-style sweater to the firehouse, and he had big dreams. As he and Dunn suf- fered through the firehouse hazing rituals that greeted all probies, they became fast friends. Both were veterans of the military. "Look," Lomuscio told Dunn, "we ought to go to school together on the GI Bill." "All right, Frank," Dunn said. "I'd like to get paid to go to school." The two young firefighters registered to take classes at Queens College, a division of the City University of New York.

Dunn enjoyed learning, especially his classes in psychology and art, as well as fire science—and soon he began studying for the lieutenant's test, the FDNY's first and most formidable hurdle to promotion. He passed the test and achieved the coveted promotion in 1964.

On October 17, 1966—it was a Tuesday—he was in the East Village working the overnight tour with Engine Co. 33. Several blocks to the west, in the quarters of Engine Co. 18 on West Tenth Street, another lieutenant, Joseph Priore, was settling into the evening's routine. Priore, a forty-two-year-old Navy veteran of World War II who had just been promoted, wasn't scheduled to work on this night; he had worked a mutual with Captain Karl Kortum, and tonight, October 19, he was fill- ing in for the captain. The unit he commanded that night included sev- eral veterans: Joseph Kelly, thirty-five, a pipe-smoker who spent his down time studying for the lieutenant's test; Bernard Tepper, forty-one, a firefighter since 1955; and James Galanaugh, twenty-seven, a guitar-playing four-year FDNY veteran. Galanaugh had married into a fire-fighting family, one that was all too familiar with the job's risks. His father-in-law, Vincent John Laurance, had died of smoke poisoning at a fire in Brooklyn in 1955. Joining these veterans on the night tour was a twenty-six-year-old probie, Daniel Rey, who had been appointed in June and gotten married in July. He had yet to work his first big fire and was looking forward to it. Rounding out the company were Manuel Fernandez, the engine's chauffeur (firemen's lingo for driver), whose job it would be to connect hoses to the pumper, and John Donovan, twenty-nine, fresh from vacation.

Early in the night tour, Donovan was assigned to follow up on a complaint that cars in the neighborhood were parked in front of fire hydrants. Donovan spent the next few hours writing summonses—just part of the everyday life of firefighters when they weren't fighting fires. Before leaving the firehouse, Donovan put his gear on the back step of Engine Co. 18's pumper.

In the top-floor apartment of a four-story brownstone at 7 East Twenty-second Street, the north side of the street, Herbert Brown, an artist and the father of four children, smelled something unfamiliar at about 9:30. He and his wife had often discussed their fear of fire, especially with the children's safety to consider. Now, Brown went downstairs and then outside to investigate the odor. He spotted smoke billowing from the roof of an adjoining building, an aging three-story commercial strip that fronted East Twenty-third Street and housed, among other businesses, a pharmacy called Wonder Drug & Cosmetics. Brown raced back upstairs to alert his family, and Mrs. Brown called the Fire Department. The blaze was spreading so quickly that by the time the Browns collected their kids and started downstairs, the staircase was filled with smoke and the lights inside the building were out. But they made it to the sidewalk.

The first companies on the scene waited little time to sound a second alarm. That summoned several more ladder and engine companies, including Engine 18. Fireman Donovan still was on his rounds when the second alarm came in, but he saw the pumper leaving quarters. He raced back to the firehouse and looked in the house journal to find out the fire's location. He grabbed his helmet, jacket, and boots—his friends had thrown them off the pumper—dumped them into his car, and drove himself to the fire.

Lieutenant Dunn and Engine Co. 33 also responded on the second alarm and reported to an assistant chief standing outside the brownstone from which the Brown family had fled. Dunn saw heavy smoke coming from the cellar. It was, he thought, a "real good fire." Members of Rescue Co. 1, specially trained and equipped for smoky basement fires, were trying to take a hose line into the building. Dunn and his company were told to report to Deputy Chief Thomas Reilly on the northwest side of the building, near the corner of Broadway and Twenty-third Street. Dunn led his men around the corner, where he spotted Reilly, a World War II veteran and father of six children.

"Engine Thirty-three reporting, Chief" he said.

"Stand fast, Thirty-three," the chief responded. As Dunn and his men waited on the street for further orders, Lieutenant Priore arrived with Engine Co. 18. He joined Dunn and Reilly. The two young lieutenants knew each other from past assignments.

As they observed the fire and calculated their next move, the chief and two lieutenants spotted a member of the insurance industry's Fire Patrol approaching. More than a century after insurance executives had decided to pay for an independent fire salvage force rather than rely on the old volunteer department, members of the Fire Patrol's three units still reported to major fires, equipped with canvas tarps to protect property, stock, and business equipment from smoke and water damage. Though the men of the Fire Patrol were destined to be overshadowed by the FDNY, they often ran the same risks as the firefighters, with the same sometimes tragic consequences.

The patrolman reported to Chief Reilly. "We have fire in the baseboards around the drug store," he told the chief. Reilly turned to Priore. "Eighteen," he said, "get a line into the drug store." Then Chief Reilly turned to Dunn. "Thirty-three, you get a line in the exposure on Broadway," he said. Priore and the men of Engine Co. 18 went off to fight the fire in the drug store; Dunn and the men of Engine Co. 33 were to cover the exposure—to set up a defensive operation to contain the fire before it spread to other businesses to the west of Wonder Drug on Twenty-third Street. As he moved out, Dunn saw a friend of his father-in-law's, Lieutenant John Finley of Ladder Co. 7, putting on a mask as he entered the drug store's street-level entrance. Dunn knew that around the firehouse they called the lieutenant "Black Jack," but he didn't know much more about his father-in-law's friend.

Finley and Ladder Co. 7 would join Priore and Engine Co. 18 in searching for, and then extinguishing, any fire on the main level. But there was very little smoke and few signs of fire in the drug store. Finley's men hacked away at a wall adjoining the brownstone, finally exposing pockets of fire for Priore's hose line. Below them, in the smoke-filled basement, other firefighters reached a cinder-block wall some sixty feet into the structure and reported very little fire. They didn't realize that the wall was not part of the foundation, that the basement continued for another forty feet. And beyond that wall, on the Twenty-second Street, the side of the building, a fire was raging.

Dunn and Engine Co. 33 got their hose line into the west side of the building and were trying to force open a bathroom door to give them better access to a pocket of fire. The door had a frosted window, and through it, Dunn noticed a sudden orange glow. A battalion chief yelled, "Everybody get out of the building!" Dunn and the rest of Engine Co. 33 withdrew.

A portion of the floor in the Wonder Drug store had collapsed. Out on the street, Manuel Fernandez of Engine Co. 18 was connecting hoses to the pumper. Just then John Donovan arrived, and asked Fernandez where the rest of the company was. "They're in there," Fernandez said, pointing to the drug store. Then they heard a crash and saw a fireball explode from the drug store basement. Fernandez ran to drug store entrance, yelling, "Eighteen! Eighteen!" There was no answer.

Ten firefighters in the rear of the store had fallen into the burning basement. The fireball that Dunn had seen through the bathroom window burned two more men. Hoses were repositioned to provide cover for a rescue attempt. Donovan and several other firefighters moved into the drug store with a hose line. The smoke was horrendous—Donovan went back and got a mask from the sidewalk. Donovan had the nozzle, and was treading carefully across the slippery floor. An officer behind him had a heavy-duty flashlight, but it was of little use. There was smoke, and there was an orange glow. That's all Donovan could see. But he knew his friends were trapped somewhere in this hell.

Donovan never saw the abyss. He simply took a step, and there was no more floor. He plunged towards the inferno. He had the nozzle, and as he fell forward, he held on to it with three fingers. His helmet fell into the burning basement as he dangled from the hose line. Flames were burning his legs. "I'm in the cellar," he yelled. "Get me out." The other firefighters reached through the smoke, grabbed him, and pulled him back up to safety.

Trapped in the inferno below were ten men: Chief Reilly, Battalion Chief Walter Higgins, the rest of Engine Co. 18, Lieutenant Finley of Ladder Co. 7 and one of Finley's firefighters, Carl Lee. They hadn't realized they were standing above a roaring fire in the basement. The floor's four inches of cement and one inch of masonry gave no hint that the fire was consuming the supporting beams and an old wooden floor beneath the cement. As the floor collapsed, flames exploded where Chief Reilly's aide, William McCarron, and another member of Ladder Co. 7, Rudolph Kaminsky, were working on the first floor.

The ten men who had fallen into the basement and the two men on the first floor were dead. Ten more firefighters, led by Lieutenant Royal Fox of Ladder Co. 3 and Captain Patrick Murphy of Engine Co. 5, managed to escape from a portion of the basement near the collapse. The fire intensified after the collapse, and Lieutenant Dunn and Engine Co. 33 kept working.

At around midnight, about ninety minutes after the collapse, Dunn heard that twelve firefighters were missing. Mayor John Lindsay was summoned to the scene at about one in the morning; he put on a helmet and other gear before entering the drug store. "It's terrible in there," he said after he returned to the street. He conferred with Fire Commissioner Robert Lowery. Lowery was in tears.

The first bodies, those of McCarron and Kaminsky, were pulled out just after the mayor arrived. With the fire still raging and other parts of the building in danger of collapse, it was impossible to enter the basement where the ten had fallen. The Fire Department dispatched officers and chaplains to the homes of the victims, but some family members already had heard about the fire and the missing men. Virginia Galanaugh, wife of Engine Co. 18's James Galanaugh, was among several wives who hurried to the scene. "He's all right, isn't he?" she asked. "I have to be with him; he's all right, isn't he? They got him out, didn't they?" The silence of other firefighters told her the terrible news. She had lost her father a dozen years before. Now, she had lost her husband; now her child, too, was fatherless.

Through the morning of October 18, after the fire was extinguished, firefighters by the hundreds gathered on the sidewalks and closed-off streets, waiting for the bodies. The last one, that of Engine Co. 18's probie, Daniel Rey, wasn't recovered until the afternoon. Chief of Department John O'Hagan assembled his firefighters in Madison Square Park across the street from the smoking ruins. O'Hagan had been on vacation when the fire broke out, but he returned when he heard about the disaster. He took off his white helmet and said, "This was the saddest day in the one-hundred-year history of the Fire Department. I know we all died a little." He paused, and then asked his men to pray for their fallen comrades.

Vincent Dunn went home that afternoon and went to sleep. Later that night, his two-year-old daughter came into the room and jumped on her daddy. He smiled, but his thoughts instantly returned to the horror he had left behind. Twelve women were widows; thirty-two children had lost their fathers. One of those children, Joseph Finley, would one day follow his father's footsteps, not just into the FDNY but into the very same ladder company.

Ten funeral services took place in midtown Manhattan on October 21. Eight flag-draped coffins rested in the center aisle of Saint Patrick's Cathedral, and two were carried into St. Thomas Episcopal Church two blocks to the north. After the services, as ten thousand firefighters from across the country stood at attention on Fifth Avenue, the coffins were

One of the saddest days in FDNY history: Flag-draped caskets containing the remains of eight of the twelve firefighters killed on October 17, 1966, leave Saint Patrick's Cathedral.

placed on pumpers for their final journey. The two other funerals were held on Long Island, where five of the twelve lived. Flags were ordered at half-staff in New York City and also in suburban Nassau County.

Lieutenant Dunn went on with his life after the Wonder Drug fire, for he had no choice. He was on the promotion list for captain, he and his wife had just bought a home in the Douglaston section of Queens, he was a father, and he still was a part-time college student. He didn't think about what had happened, about Chief Reilly's order that sent Engine Co. 18 into the drug store and Engine 33 to the exposure. Eleven years later, when he was a deputy chief and on his way to a master's degree in urban studies, he wrote an article for the departmental journal *WNYF* about the dangers of building collapses. Then he wrote another. And another. He would rise before dawn and write, churning out yet another story about building collapses for fire journals around the country. He'd write while he was on vacation at the Jersey Shore. Finally, in 1988, he turned his articles into a book about building collapses, *Collapse of Burning Buildings: A Guide to Fireground Safety,* and became a national authority and lecturer on the subject. Eventually, he acknowledged the connection between what he saw as a young lieutenant in 1966 and what drove him to write and to teach. "We didn't have stress debriefings back then," he said. "So I carried whatever it was with me from that collapse for the next eleven years, when I wrote my first article. They say writing exorcises your demons. That's what it did for me."

By the time the Department marked the one-year anniversary of the Wonder Drug fire, the city was fully involved in the social, political, and financial conflagration that would burn and smolder for the next decade and more. Although New York did not suffer ruinous riots in the summer of 1967, as did Newark, Detroit, and other urban areas, the city's firefighters knew that low-intensity unrest was simmering in poor neighborhoods in upper Manhattan, central Brooklyn, and the South Bronx. Every year of the 1960s saw dramatic increases in the number of fires, and even more dramatic increases in malicious false alarms, from 13,326 in 1960 to 48,106 in 1967. And by the mid–1970s, the 1967 false-alarm figure would look positively innocent.

Far more shocking, however, was a wave of assaults on firefighters in the summer and fall of 1967. Until then, firefighters rode to fires on the backs or sides of their apparatus. It was not the safest or most comfortable spot to be when speeding to a fire, but such was FDNY tradition. Besides, it did not occur to firefighters that riding the back step of their pumper would make them a target for a young man with a grievance and a brick, a bottle, or a gun. Bullets were fired at firefighters nine times in six weeks in 1967. Engines and ladder trucks were hastily altered to provide firefighters with covered seating, shielding them from assaults and ambushes that would continue for years to come. This new danger was bewildering—firefighters were not law enforcement officers; they were not the National Guard; they were not looking to arrest anybody. They came when they were needed, and they saved people

New York's fire-
fighters were
eyewitnesses to
the tragedies of
the 1960s. Here, a
portion of Harlem
burns after the
murder of Martin
Luther King, Jr., in
1968.

from burning buildings. And now they were ducking missiles and bullets. A job that always demanded solidarity became even more insular as
exhausted firefighters bitterly faced hostile communities. "Nobody was
going to look out for us except one another," said Larry McCarthy, who
in 1964 moved from Engine Co. 231 to Ladder Co. 120 in Brownsville,
one of Brooklyn's angry neighborhoods. "We had to be aware to take
care of one another." Occasionally McCarthy and his comrades were hit
with tiles thrown from roofs and windows when they pulled up to a fire.

On April 4, 1968, Martin Luther King, Jr., was murdered by a sniper
in Memphis, Tennessee. The King assassination unleashed an outbreak
of rioting in black ghettos across the country. In Chicago, seven blacks
were killed and hundreds arrested as fires and looting devastated huge
sections of the city. Other cities saw similar violence. New York, how-

ever, was spared the horror of Chicago, and much of the credit for that went to Mayor Lindsay, a popular figure with the city's black community who walked Harlem's streets the night of King's murder. Lindsay's presence defused much of the rage blacks felt over King's death. A headline in the *New York Times* two days afterward reported that "outbreaks" in the city were "relatively mild."

But "mild" was not the word used in the firehouse to describe the nights immediately following King's death. In New York's predominantly black neighborhoods like Brownsville, Harlem, Bedford-Stuyvesant, and East New York, firefighters—most of them white—battled both fire and enraged civilians, some of whom were prepared to exact revenge on anybody representing the white American establishment. And that included firefighters making $10,000 a year.

Larry McCarthy was on duty with Ladder Co. 120 in Brownsville the night of King's murder. Now a ten-year FDNY veteran, McCarthy was assigned to a neighborhood that hope had passed by. Four of five families in Brownsville were on public assistance, living in homes abandoned years before by the white, mostly Jewish, middle class. Landlords abandoned buildings, drugs took over entire blocks, and it was just a matter of time before arson was added to Brownsville's plagues.

Like so many other predominantly black communities, Brownsville erupted in violent protest after Martin Luther King, Jr., was killed. Ladder Co. 120 and the neighborhood's other companies were on constant duty on the night of April 4. After putting out a fire in a four-story commercial building that night, Ladder 120 responded to a tenement fire on Strauss Street near East New York Avenue. There already had been reports of gunfire in the neighborhood, so a police escort accompanied Ladder 120 to the fire. Gunshots rang out as the firefighters arrived, and a motorcycle cop returned fire. The men of Ladder Co. 120 stayed under cover as best they could as they fought the blaze.

Other parts of Brooklyn were burning as well, and so was Harlem, leading Fire Commissioner Lowery—the first African American to hold the post—to declare a fire emergency just before the day tour ended on April 5. Nobody left the city's firehouses until the emergency was over. Three days later, as firefighters continued to battle a wave of arson, the

In the 1970s the FDNY raced to thousands of fires in some of the city's poorest neighborhoods as radicals shouted, "Burn, baby, burn." Invariably, the chief victims of the arson plague were the tenants who were left homeless.

FDNY's black fraternal organization, the Vulcan Society, issued a strong statement of support for the Department and its efforts to protect lives and property. The Vulcans said they took "great pride in devotion to duty and the exemplary efforts of members of this Department in the protection of property and saving of lives, regardless of color, religion or political persuasion." It was a welcome message.

The angry fires of early April subsided, although attacks on firefighters continued through the late 1960s. One of the most shocking signs of the breakdown of civic order in New York was the firebombing of an engine on the night of June 18, 1970. Firefighters were battling a tough tenement house fire in the East Village when a Molotov cocktail hit Ladder Co. 11's apparatus and exploded. A firefighter suffered a heart attack, and another slipped as he attempted to extinguish the incendiary. Meanwhile, a dozen firefighters in the tenement were injured as they successfully led sixty people out of the building and to safety.

THREE HUNDRED and ten civilians died in fires in 1970, nearly triple the number in 1960. The year's statistics suggested a permanent state of fire emergency: nearly 130,000 fires, 3,500 of them considered serious, and a beefed-up uniformed force of more than 14,000, the largest headcount in FDNY history. And it was only the beginning of the war years.

A single day of anarchy and tragedy, March 6, 1970, brought home the new dangers that firefighters and civilians alike shared. At around noon that day, an explosion ripped through a landmark townhouse on West Eleventh Street in fashionable Greenwich Village. Firefighters arriving at the scene took cover when they heard two more explosions; they were not as intense as the first but set off a fire from basement to rooftop. After only a few minutes, the building's front wall collapsed.

Fire officials at the scene, including Chief of Department John O'Hagan, suspected a gas leak. They were partially right—the second and third blasts that greeted firefighters had in fact been set off by leaking gas. But the first explosion was the work of a more sinister force, one that already had become familiar to the FDNY. Young radicals, many of them college students from affluent families, had set off hundreds of explosions throughout the country since 1968. In New York, small bombs had set off fires in four department stores that year.

The explosion on West Eleventh Street was the work of a domestic terrorist group known as the Weather Underground. The townhouse basement served as a munitions dump for Manhattan-based members, who were in the planning stages of a more aggressive, and inevitably more lethal, onslaught. As part of their preparations, two Weathermen were building a bomb in the townhouse basement when the device detonated, killing them instantly and setting off the initial explosion.

There were no FDNY casualties that afternoon on West Eleventh

Street, although there might have been had Chief O'Hagan not ordered firefighters out of the rubble when he feared further collapses. Once the blaze was extinguished, firefighters spent several hours combing through the debris, looking for survivors. There were two, both of them members of the Weather Underground, but they had disappeared just after the first explosion.

The Village bomb factory was not a particularly noteworthy disaster, at least not in terms of pure firefighting. Firefighters at the scene had fought far more difficult jobs. But it was a memorable symbol of a frightening and deeply troubling age. The Village explosion may have ended the radical careers of the two bomb makers, but it was hardly the end of the radicals' bombing campaign. Five days later, on March 11, three office buildings in midtown Manhattan were bombed, and the following day 300 bomb scares forced the evacuation of 15,000 people in Manhattan. The president of New York's City Council, a former police officer named Sanford Garelik, declared that the city had become a target for homegrown terrorist organizations. "These are urban guerrillas, the outgrowth of an era of disrespect for law and the acceptance of a Maoist philosophy of guerrilla warfare," he said.

Firefighters who witnessed the burning of New York in the 1960s and '70s would come to despise the college-aged or college-educated radicals from homes far more comfortable than their own who preached violent revolution against something called "the establishment." Just as bad, in the firefighters' view, were the journalists and intellectuals who seemed to sympathize with those who set off bombs in department stores or who burned down tenement houses and called it revolution. Radicals and their apologists spoke of alienation, but as the 1960s gave way to an even worse decade, at least from the FDNY's perspective, New York's firefighters knew all about alienation. Those who worked in the busiest firehouses were responding to thirty, forty, even fifty alarms a night, and fighting two, three, or four major fires. They saw the effects of arson, of bombings, of social disorder. They were on the firing line of what seemed like nothing short of civil war. Their workload, measured by fires, emergencies, and false alarms, had risen from 94,000 total alarms in 1960 to 263,659 total alarms in 1970.

They were alienated, too. But they didn't set fires. They risked their lives to put them out.

On that Friday, March 6, firefighters still were examining the wreckage on West Eleventh Street when, across the East River, somebody, probably an alienated youth, pulled a fire-alarm box near the intersection of Hopkins Street and Sutter Avenue in Bedford-Stuyvesant. Two ladder companies responded to the alarm—but there was no fire. It was one of 89,432 malicious false alarms that would be recorded in 1970. Nevertheless, companies assigned to that box responded, as they always did—they couldn't know whether there was a fire or some other emergency until they got there. And, as they always did, firefighters checked the area to make sure that there was no sign of fire before declaring a false alarm. They were still doing that when another alarm came in minutes later, for a fire in a three-story residence several blocks away on Saint Mark's Avenue.

Five sisters, the oldest of whom was five and the youngest, seven months, were alone in a second-story apartment they shared with their mother at about nine o'clock on that Friday night. The children were playing with matches, and they started a fire that quickly swept through the apartment. In an adjacent apartment, the children's aunt smelled smoke and called the Fire Department. Because nearby companies were responding to the false alarm at Hopkins and Sutter, they were about ten minutes late in getting to the blaze. By the time they got there, all five children were dead, as were two other children who lived in the building. Chief O'Hagan, who already had spent hours supervising futile rescue operations in the Village, bitterly noted, "[I]f we had responded to the fire immediately, some of the children could have been saved."

If the chief thought the tragedy would lead the city's alienated young people, the primary perpetrators of false alarms, to consider another hobby, he was sadly mistaken. The number of false alarms would grow to 285,290 in 1978, more than double the number of fires. Firefighters found that they could track a single youth's progress through a neighborhood by the location of the alarm boxes he or she pulled. At the headquarters of Rescue Co. 2 in Brooklyn, Pete Hayden quickly learned the pattern. "It was three o'clock in the after-

In some New York neighborhoods, firefighters were such frequent visitors that children hardly paused from their games when the Fire Department arrived.

noon, and you'd get an alarm from the pull box outside the local school," he said. "Then you'd get one three blocks down the street, then another one a few more blocks away. Then you'd get another one, and you'd realize he or she had turned east, or west, and was going down another block."

There was nothing playful or charming about such behavior. False alarms killed, and the victims could be seven children in an apartment building in Brooklyn, or they could be firefighters. In the opening pages of his firefighting memoir, *Report from Engine Company 82,* Dennis Smith recalled the death of a close friend, Mike Carr. Fireman Carr, father of two young children, died when he fell off the pumper as it was speeding to an alarm on Southern Boulevard in the South Bronx. It was a false alarm, pulled by a nine-year-old boy. "Kids do this a lot in the South Bronx," Smith wrote. "His friends giggled, and they all ran up to the street to watch the fire engines come." Smith summed up the frustration of the entire Department when he noted that few people were punished for false alarms. "I understand the sad social conditions in which this child has been forced to live, but I have lost sympathy for the cry that poverty founded the crime, not the boy."

Although Smith and his colleagues lost sympathy for those who tried to excuse pathologies that killed firefighters and civilians alike, they were not without some understanding of the grinding poverty and atrocious conditions they witnessed with every tour of duty. Through the summer of 1970, the Fire Department held a series of twenty-four "youth dialogues" with groups of twenty-five to thirty young men from poor neighborhoods. The young men and ten firefighters who volunteered to help with the project lived together for forty-eight hours at a special facility on Hart's Island off the Bronx's eastern shoreline. In addition, Commissioner Lowery was encouraging firefighters to play a greater role in community relations programs throughout the city. The outreach was designed to reduce tensions between firefighters and some of the communities they served, but the rising numbers of arsons and false alarms suggested just how far apart the two sides were.

New York's firefighters were losing patience. Not with their job, but with a government and society they regarded as unappreciative and even hostile. In the fall of 1973, there was a new president of the Uniformed Firefighters Association, Richard Vizzini, and he made it clear that he was prepared to order his nearly 11,000 members out on strike if the city didn't agree to an annual pay raise of $2,000. At the time, senior firefighters below the rank of lieutenant were making $14,300 a year, plus overtime. Vizzini certainly had numbers on his side, for there was no denying the stunning increase in the FDNY's workload. Nevertheless, City Hall was looking to disband a handful of companies as a cost-saving measure. Though the public didn't realize it for several more years, New York was in the verge of financial ruin.

In its negotiations with the UFA, the Lindsay administration offered less than half what the UFA demanded. Public opinion, especially in the city's press, was turning against the city's unions after nearly a decade of disruptive work stoppages and what seemed like lavish raises along with generous increases in fringe benefits, vacation time, and health-care coverage. Lindsay administration officials charged that Vizzini's demands would cost the city $750 million a year.

After several contentious bargaining sessions in late October, Vizzini announced that he had "no qualms" over leading the city's firefighters on strike. This was not only illegal—state law prohibited strikes by public employees—it was unthinkable. Vizzini's argument on behalf of his members, that firefighters deserved a raise because of the huge increase in work, made the prospect of a strike all the more terrifying. Parts of the city already were burning down with a full complement of firefighters. What would happen if they were walking a picket line?

Firefighters hadn't walked off the job since 1836, when the volunteers turned around their caps and slowly walked away from a burning building when they heard that Chief James Gulick was about to be fired. The UFA and the officers' union, the Uniformed Fire Officers Association, had had its share of contentious negotiations with the city in the past, but nothing like this.

The union canvassed its members by mail in late October, asking them to either authorize or turn down a strike. With great fanfare, Vizzini announced that his members had voted "overwhelmingly" in favor of a strike. The news came as something of a surprise to the newly famous Dennis Smith, whose book about life in Engine Co. 82 had been published in 1972 and had sold two million copies. Smith voted against the strike, but more to the point, it seemed to him that nearly everybody who worked in the South Bronx voted the same way. But he was a fierce union man, and if the union decided there would be a strike, he had no choice but to stand with his brother firefighters. "You were either a part of these men, or you weren't," he would say years later. The solidarity of the firehouse, of the company, and of the union would come before everything else. It always did.

Vizzini set a strike deadline of nine o'clock, November 6, 1973, which happened to be the day New Yorkers went to the polls to elect a new mayor. The task of preparing for the unknown fell to John O'Hagan, the longtime chief of department who had just taken on the additional responsibility of fire commissioner (only two others—James Gulick and John McElligott—held both titles simultaneously). As the mayoral candidates debated each other for one last time, O'Hagan announced his contingency plans to use civilian volunteers to assist fire officers—their union was not involved in the strike threat—in stretching hose lines. The civilians would not be allowed to enter burning buildings, O'Hagan noted.

Most city residents found it hard to believe that their firefighters really would walk off the job, especially after a judge, a week before the deadline, had ordered them not to. A *New York Times* story noted that even if a walkout occurred, it was unlikely to be very effective, given "the firemen's traditional dedication to duty." The newspaper's editorial page was not so magnanimous in its assessment. "In all the long history of excesses inflicted on the city by its overstrong civil service unions, few compare in irresponsibility with the decision of the Uniformed Firefighters Association to set Election Day as the deadline for a strike," the paper editorialized. '

The night of November 5, Fireman Edmund Staines of Ladder Co. 147 was out with other firefighters and their wives at a dinner-dance sponsored by the FDNY's largest ethnic organization, the Emerald Society, an Irish American group. The talk in the dance hall, naturally, was about what would take place the next morning. A friend of Staines's, a former firefighter who had gotten his law degree and become a judge in Brooklyn, gave him a blunt warning: "Don't mess with the Taylor Law." The Taylor Law, passed in 1967 after a subway workers strike crippled the city for nearly two weeks, allowed public employees to organize, but prohibited them from going out on strike.

Staines and his wife returned home after midnight, but he couldn't sleep. Staines was on the lieutenants list, which meant he was on the verge of earning a promotion and a raise. O'Hagan had said that nobody on the lieutenant's list would dare risk going on strike. Staines, the grandson and uncle of firefighters, was scheduled to be off duty the next day, but that would become moot if the Department canceled all days off, as seemed likely.

Staines had a couple of beers in his living room, and then drifted off for a few hours. He woke up to an unusually cold morning, and he told his wife he was going to the firehouse. "Why?" she asked.

"I wouldn't want to be anyplace else if something happens," he said. He left for the firehouse, not sure what the next few hours would bring.

Before dawn, Al Washington, a probationary firefighter undergoing his first week of training, was on a subway train from his home in

Brooklyn to Manhattan. From there, he planned to catch a bus to the FDNY's training facility on Welfare Island (now called Roosevelt Island). Before leaving his training session the day before, he and his fellow probies had been instructed to report to Welfare Island early the following morning. They were part of the FDNY's plan to staff firehouses if the UFA walked off the job.

Washington had left a position as a professional arbitrator because firefighting offered the medical benefits his young family needed. He hadn't considered the Fire Department until he stepped out of a subway station one morning in 1971 and someone handed him a recruiting flyer from the Vulcan society, the FDNY's African American group. He'd been sworn in as a probie on September 29, 1973. And now he was in the middle of a strike. And probies had no job protection.

The UFA had tried to persuade probies to join the strike. But the officers at training school told them that if they didn't show up for work on November 6, they might as well turn in their badges.

At eight-thirty, half an hour before the day tour would begin, UFA President Vizzini announced over the all-news radio station WINS that the union was on strike. All across the city, firefighters on the overnight tour walked out of their firehouses, grabbed placards, and began walking picket lines. Inside the houses were chiefs, captains, and lieutenants grimly facing the prospect of answering calls with just two or three men—probies, or men who had crossed the picket line. The usual complement on an engine was one officer and five firefighters.

The newspapers the next day would observe that the firefighters seemed like reluctant class warriors. The picket lines were subdued, and some firefighters later would confess to uneasiness and feelings of guilt.

Larry McCarthy picketed outside his firehouse in Brownsville, and watched as several of the most respected firefighters in the house crossed the line and reported to work. His firehouse was bitterly split, with about half reporting for work, and the other half manning the picket line. It was the birth of tensions that would take years to dissipate, not only in McCarthy's firehouse, but in every firehouse where individual UFA members refused to join the strike. Firefighters who crossed the picket line were treated like pariahs. When they returned to

Firefighters walked the picket line for five and a half hours on November 6, 1973. Though the strike was short-lived, the divisions it caused in some firehouses lasted for years.

their cars at the end of the tour they found their tires slashed. Only decades later, with the tensions of that day a distant, though not completely faded, memory, would some strikers concede that those who worked that morning did what they thought was right.

A picket line greeted Al Washington when a bus took him and the other probies from Welfare Island to Queens Borough Command, near the huge apartment complex known as Lefrak City. There they were assigned to individual firehouses. They were so new they hadn't yet been given their custom-fitted helmets. Officers handed them old orange civil defense helmets instead. When Washington got to the firehouse—the first firehouse he had ever seen firsthand—picketers outside the building offered no harassment. They understood that the probies had no choice. The strikers were more concerned about those who did have a choice, and chose to work.

Among those who did were many members of the Vulcan Society. Though members of the union, the Vulcans had reservations about it, for they believed that the UFA had not fought hard enough against discrimination and racism on the job. Equally embittering, in their eyes, was the UFA's past support for relaxing residency requirements, which had the effect of expanding the pool of white applicants at a time when the city's black population was rapidly increasing. About 4.2 percent of the FDNY was black in the mid–1970s, when the city was about 30 percent black. Less than a decade earlier, the black population of the city had been 16 percent, and the percentage of blacks in the Department, slightly higher, about 4.5 percent. Black and Latino firefighters had sued the city to throw out the 1971 firefighters' written test on the grounds that the exam was biased against minorities. The UFA bitterly opposed the suit, but a federal judge sided with the blacks and Latinos, and ordered that one minority candidate from the 1971 list was to be selected for every three white probies.

For many Vulcans, however, the decision to work rather than go on strike that day was based on one simple reality: Most black firefighters lived in the city, in neighborhoods where fire was common and protection desperately needed. They, and some white firefighters who also lived in the city, believed they couldn't turn their back on their families and friends. The strike, then, revealed or exacerbated divisions within the department: labor versus management, black versus white, city versus suburban. For years afterward there would be a new line of division: striker versus nonstriker.

Tensions were not as high outside Ed Staines's firehouse in Flatbush. It was clear on that cold morning that few if any of the men on the picket line wanted to be there, or felt entirely justified in walking off the job. It was hard, after all, to personalize their conflict, because their immediate supervisors were not the mayor or fire commissioner, but lieutenants and captains who were brother firefighters and union members, although their union, the UFOA, was not on strike and was not expected to honor the UFA's picket line.

As the morning wore on and the city braced itself for a possible catastrophe, Staines and other members of his company carried their signs and did their best to keep warm. They began to take turns dropping out of the picket line for a coffee break on nearby Coney Island Avenue. As lunchtime approached, a lieutenant appeared and, remarkably, invited the strikers inside the firehouse. "Hey, this is your commissary," the lieutenant said. "If you want coffee, come inside." The commissary in every firehouse is stocked with food and supplies paid for and purchased by the firefighters themselves.

The strikers faced a dilemma: continue to picket, or join the lieutenant and other officers inside the firehouse for coffee. They didn't deliberate very long. They went inside, after agreeing to keep two picketers outside for appearance's sake, and they not only helped themselves to coffee, but whipped up a huge bowl of stew for lunch. The kitchen came alive with chatter and camaraderie.

About eighty fires broke out through the morning, and civilians teamed with fire officers and nonstriking firefighters to stretch hose lines and break the windows of burning buildings. The most serious fire broke out in a vacant three-story building in the Williamsburg section of Brooklyn. Fire companies arrived at the scene with a police escort, which had been requested by the firefighters to help get the apparatus past picket lines.

In a command post in lower Manhattan, Chief Augustus Beekman was monitoring telephone communications between headquarters staff and chiefs in the field. Chief Beekman was in charge of the FDNY's Division of Fire Control, making him the highest-ranking black fire officer in the Department's history. He was a World War II veteran who had spent twenty-seven years fighting fires in New York, but nothing prepared him for this morning's dangers. On the command post walls were huge maps of the five boroughs. As the morning wore on, the maps became pockmarked with red circles indicating the location of firehouses with no firefighters. The FDNY was trying to cover the city with only 20 percent of its usual strength. Every now and again, somebody printed a green *P* on the map. That told Beekman of firehouses staffed entirely by probies.

In the Queens firehouse where Al Washington was serving, the lieutenant on duty realized that none of the probies in the house was qualified to drive the apparatus. (In trying to balance their duties as officers with their obligations as fellow union members, lieutenants and captains that day generally declined to perform the duties of rank-and-file firefighters, like driving apparatus or stretching hoses.) The lieutenant called a battalion chief, and the chief said he was on his way to designate one of the trainees as a driver.

In the early afternoon, Commissioner O'Hagan called a news conference to announce that the city was in "imminent peril." Reporters noticed that O'Hagan's hands were shaking as he spoke. UFA President Vizzini and city negotiators were in an unheated courthouse in Manhattan, talking to each other through mediators.

Lunch at Engine Co. 147 broke up at about one o'clock when the chief assigned to the house came into the kitchen and said, "Okay, you guys have been here long enough." The strikers were ordered out of the house and back into the street. Ed Staines's uncle, a veteran firefighter named Connie Metzger, had gone upstairs to the bunk room and was sitting by himself in a corner. He was in tears.

Thirty minutes later, in a radio broadcast just after one-thirty in the afternoon, Vizzini ordered his men to report back to work. Earlier in the afternoon, Vizzini showed up as requested in the courtroom of State Supreme Court Justice Sidney Fine, who was acting as a mediator between the union and the city. Fine told Vizzini that the UFA could face a penalty of $1 million a day for the strike's duration. Not long afterward, the union and the city agreed to further outside mediation, and Vizzini declared the strike over. It had lasted five and a half hours. Al Washington and the probies in Queens never learned which one of them would be asked to drive a rig. The strike was over before the battalion chief arrived.

Firehouses were fully operational by three o'clock, and the night tour reported as scheduled at six o'clock. Later that night, a fire roared through a three-story home in the Bedford-Stuyvesant section of Brooklyn. Four people, two of them children, died. There was no shortage of manpower or equipment at the scene, but there was no saving the victims. They didn't have a chance. But the fire reminded the city of what might have happened during those five and a half hours when New York's firefighters walked a picket line.

Less than two weeks afterward, firefighters, politicians and the city in general were stunned to learn that the UFA's leaders had broken their trust with their members and with the city they were sworn to protect. Newspapers reported that the firefighters had not, after all, authorized a strike. In fact, they had voted against the strike motion by 4,119 to 3,827. An independent monitoring organization, the Honest Ballot Association, had reported the correct result to the UFA's leaders, but the ballots were destroyed after they were turned over to the union. Vizzini had decided to go ahead with the strike despite the negative vote. His lawyer later argued that Vizzini had no choice but to falsify the result. "If he lied, he lied for the benefit of the union to maintain his position in bargaining," the lawyer, Abraham Brodsky, said.

Vizzini and two other UFA leaders eventually were indicted on several charges, including obstruction of governmental administration. They entered guilty pleas on a reduced charge of reckless endangerment in July of 1974. Vizzini remained in charge of the union until losing a reelection bid in 1975, but he returned for another term in 1977.

The damage to the union's credibility was incalculable. Victor Gotbaum, head of the city's largest public employee union, condemned the UFA for "one of the most destructive acts in recent memory." The *New York Times* angrily asserted that "the whole episode provides frightening evidence of the hazards involved in reckless sloganeering by unionists seeking to gain power within their organizations by outdoing one another in militancy." But the falsified vote was more than a public relations disaster; it was also a body blow to the morale of many firefighters, who had been trained to believe that the mayor, the commissioner, the chiefs, the officers and the press all might betray them, all might lie to them, but they could always rely on their union. Years later, firefighters like Dennis Smith, Al Washington, Larry McCarthy, and many others would speak bitterly of being misled about an issue that went beyond union politics to the safety and lives of civilians, and led to unnecessary tensions in the city's divided firehouses.

The embarrassed union and the city signed a new contract in

December, as Mayor Lindsay prepared to turn over his office to Mayor-elect Abe Beame. Firefighters were awarded a $700 a year raise retroactive to July 1, 1974, and another $250 raise that would take effect on January 1, 1975. The union celebrated the pay increase as a hard-won victory. But a new struggle with City Hall already was under way, and it was destined to end with victories for nobody.

Tom Cashin was twenty seven-years old when he finally decided to follow his father's boot prints by joining the Fire Department. He had been working on Wall Street as a bond trader for several years after graduating from St. Francis College in Brooklyn with an economics degree, and then taking graduate classes at Pace University in Manhattan. He had become disenchanted with his career choice, and he began thinking about how happy his father, John, always seemed to be. As a child growing up in Brooklyn in the 1950s, Cashin played stickball in the street and listened carefully when he heard the bell alarm ringing in the firehouse around the corner. When the alarm called the local engine company to a fire, Cashin and his friends went to the firehouse—the doors were always open, he remembered—and slid down the poles leading from the bunk room to the apparatus floor.

Cashin's father retired from the Department in 1968, and gently suggested that Tom consider taking the test. "You'll never get rich," his father said. "But you'll have a lot of fun. And it's a secure job."

Cashin finally took his father's advice, and in 1973, after passing the written and physical exams, he was summoned to the FDNY's instructional school. His introduction to his new life came in the training school's smokehouse, where he and other probies learned why firefighters were called "smoke eaters." It was, he would recall, nothing short of torture. He had no oxygen mask, and really no clue. He couldn't see, he couldn't breathe, but he was expected to endure the punishment. As he coughed and stumbled and crawled his way though the smoke, he realized that the life of a firefighter was a little more complicated than he thought. "I thought being a fireman was all fun and camaraderie," he recalled. "I just wanted to get out of there." But he stayed, and endured it, and in a matter of weeks he had a secure job as a New York City firefighter, just like his dad.

As Tom Cashin adjusted to his new life, poor Abe Beame was realizing that life as mayor of the City of New York also was a bit more complicated than he thought it would be. Beame had won the mayoralty on the day of the firefighters strike in 1973 after selling himself as a fiscally conservative manager—as opposed to the charismatic, quixotic John Lindsay. "He knows the buck," his campaign literature said. The suggestion was that the other candidates did not know the buck, and that theme resonated with voters who had become wary of the city's free-spending ways. A surprisingly shy, diminutive accountant who had served a term as city comptroller from 1966 to 1970, Beame was a great New York story, an immigrant from England whose parents had fled pogroms in Poland. Young Abe grew up on the streets of Brooklyn and took advantage of the free education offered at the City College of New York, where he received his degree in accounting. On January 1, 1974, he became the first Jewish mayor of New York.

Before long, he too was gasping for breath and struggling blindly in an atmosphere unlike anything he or any other mayor had experienced. He inherited a city of cooked books and overdue bills, of accounting practices that would have shocked his professors at CCNY, and Tom Cashin's at St. Francis.

It meant, after more than a century of almost unbroken expansion, the Fire Department of New York would be forced to contract, not just in numbers, but in facilities as well. It was to be the fate of every other branch of government, but for the Fire Department, the city's fiscal crisis came at a particularly bad time. The hardest war years were yet to come. The poor neighborhoods of Manhattan, Brooklyn, and the Bronx were burning and would continue to burn, and so the Fire Department would have to do more with less.

The cutbacks began before Mayor Beame had been in office a full year. Faced with a budget deficit of $330 million—it would only get larger—the city laid off workers for the first time since the Depression. The Fire Department and other uniformed services were exempt from layoffs, but the mayor imposed a hiring freeze and ordered the disbanding of five engine companies and three ladder companies. Talk of eliminating companies had been around for years, but pressure from the union, City Council members, and outraged citizens prevented talk from becoming action. Times were different in 1974, and though the UFA and individual citizens and neighborhoods filed suit to block the closings, they failed. By the end of the year, the shrunken Fire Department had set several dubious records: most alarms in a single year, 353,458; most false alarms, 164,401; and most fires, 130,324. Those records were destined to be short-lived, even as the FDNY suffered more grievous cutbacks.

Seven months after the layoffs of November 1974, Mayor Beame had even worse news. With an acknowledged deficit of $700 million and a "hidden deficit"—the amount by which the city had overstated federal and state assistance to give the appearance of balanced books— estimated at another $2 billion, the mayor ordered catastrophic layoffs and service cutbacks. On July 1, 1974, the first day of the city's new fiscal year, 40,000 city workers were summarily fired, including 1,600 firefighters. Among them were Tom Cashin and Al Washington, both of whom had left the private sector for the economic security and benefits of civil service.

Another one was a Marine Corps veteran who had fought in Vietnam, John Fox. Fox had been on the job for twenty months, working in Engine Co. 290 in the East New York section of Brooklyn. He hadn't given much thought to the Fire Department when he was a kid growing up in the Flatbush section of Brooklyn. He took the test because his father had signed him up for it while he still in the Marines. He came home, passed the test, and was assigned to one of the city's busiest firehouses, averaging 5,000 alarms a year. And he loved every minute of it, loved knowing that every tour, day or night, would bring a major fire, maybe even two or three. But when he reported to his firehouse on July 1, 1975, he was told he no longer had a job.

About 700 firefighters were rehired within a matter of days as the city scrambled to find other revenue. But the remaining 800 were out of luck and out of a job they thought would protect them from the storms of the private sector.

Between layoffs and a hiring freeze, the number of firefighters fell from more than 14,000 in 1970 to slightly less than 11,000 in 1978.

The usual engine company complement of five firefighters was reduced, in many cases, to four. In early 1976 the city came up with a novel idea to cut the Department's annual overtime expenses of about $15 million. When firefighters reported for duty to relieve comrades who happened to be away from the firehouse fighting a fire, they were ordered to take a cab, or a subway, or walk to the fire's location in full gear and relieve the men immediately, rather than wait for them to return on the apparatus. The new system got under way on January 16, when three cabs brought a relief crew from a firehouse to a fire on Staten Island that had no respect for the FDNY's shift change. The men who had been fighting the fire left their posts and were ordered to pile into the waiting cabs for the return trip back to the firehouse. Tips for the cabbies, the *Daily News* reported, were restricted to ten percent of the fare.

All the while, parts of the city smoldered and burned.

By 1975, the South Bronx was a modern no man's land. The plagues of crime, drugs, unemployment, apathy, and fire reduced once-vibrant neighborhoods to desolate wastelands, and the burned-out shells of the borough's distinctive H-style tenement buildings invited comparisons with the bombed-out cities of 1945 Germany.

In 1974, fifteen of the city's twenty-five busiest engine companies and ten of the twenty-five busiest ladder companies were in the South Bronx. A Fire Department map of the area included five black blotches to the south of Fordham Road and to the east of the Grand Concourse. These, the map stated, were "severe burn-out areas." They included parts of East Tremont, Morrisania, Melrose, Hunts Point, and Fort Morris. Thanks in part to the astounding success of Dennis Smith's book about Engine Co. 82, writers and journalists from around the world came to the South Bronx to chronicle the death of a neighborhood, and what seemed like the impending death of a city.

Arson fires in the South Bronx generally broke out between 1 A.M. and dawn, and the buildings often were fully engaged by the time firefighters responded, evidence that accelerants were being used. The phenomenon was not attributable to mere vandalism—a more pernicious influence was at work.

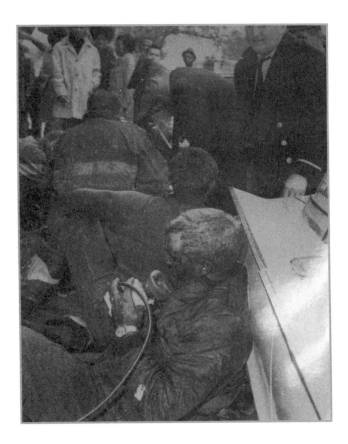

The 1970s left many New York firefighters exhausted and gasping for air.

As had occurred in the early twentieth century, many landlords con-cluded that their properties were worth more dead than alive and acted accordingly. Some of these blazes broke out in small shopping strips known to landlords and firefighters alike as "taxpayers." They were cheaply built structures put up on otherwise useless property for no reason other than to generate rent to pay the developer's property tax bill. When tenants left, rents dried up and landlords used their fire-insurance policies as a way to wring some more money out of the property.

But landlords were not the only people in the South Bronx playing with fire. Inspired by radicals who glorified arson as a political state-ment, misguided civilians torched their own buildings in what had the look of carefully planned actions. Firefighters often pulled up to apart-ment building fires to find tenants standing on the sidewalk next to their furniture and suitcases. They had been warned that their building was going to be set on fire. Many believed that the city would then build better housing in the community.

A special arson task force for the Bronx was established in the summer of 1974, but it quickly fell victim to the city's fiscal crisis. Commissioner O'Hagan and Bronx residents themselves pleaded for a change of heart, and the cash-strapped city launched a new task force a year later. More than a third of the city's fire marshals were deployed to the Bronx, and they worked hand in hand with the Police Department and the Bronx district attorney's office to investigate arsons and arrest arsonists. A police patrol car in each of the neighborhood's six police precincts was outfitted with a Fire Department radio. The task force's aggressive patrols led to hundreds of arrests in its first year of operation. Still, the odds seemed to be against them. On one day alone, June 2, 1975, arsonists set forty fires in three hours in the South Bronx.

The fires of the Bronx already were an international story on the night of October 12, 1977, when a barely recognizable vestige of old New York intersected with the new. The Yankees were playing the Dodgers in the World Series, a matchup that evoked memories of the legendary battles the two teams had fought before the Dodgers abandoned Brooklyn for Los Angeles twenty years earlier. The Yankees had, of course, remained in the South Bronx, and their ballpark had undergone an extensive renovation in the early 1970s, at the very time when the neighborhood itself was falling apart.

Early on during Game 2 of the Series, an abandoned primary school near Yankee Stadium caught fire. By ten o'clock, the entire building was ablaze, and the flames were visible in the distance beyond the ballpark's centerfield fence. The television crew covering the game for ABC knew a story when it saw one: Images of the fire were broadcast to millions of viewers throughout the game, as the announcer, Howard Cosell, intoned, "The Bronx is burning." The announcers mistakenly said the fire was in an apartment building, conjuring images of horror within sight of 55,000 spectators.

There were no deaths and only minor injuries from the fire. Nevertheless, the image and Cosell's words captured the moment.

Although the Yankees—the Bronx Bombers—went on to beat the Dodgers, and did so again the following year, there was little cheering in the abandoned, forsaken and burned-out streets of the South Bronx.

Howard Cosell would have been more on target on that night in October 1977 if he had said, simply, "New York is burning." Though the number of fires actually declined in 1977, to 129,619, compared with 153,263 in 1976, serious fires remained near all-time high levels (4,640) and the number of false alarms continued to climb, to 262,290 that year. Months before the World Series fire of 1977, a massive power blackout and the arson-murder of a firefighter in Manhattan reminded the city how far it had fallen, and how New York's firefighters were on the front lines of urban disorder and social chaos.

Shortly after three o'clock on the afternoon of July 2, 1977, a fire broke out on the fifth floor of an abandoned building on Eighth Street on the Lower East Side. Riding with Engine Co. 15 to the fire scene was twenty-five-year-old Marty Celic, who was assigned to Ladder Co. 18 but was working an overtime shift with the engine company. Celic was a popular fireman who became something of a legend at his very first fire. It was an arson fire at a synagogue, and when Celic's company pulled up, the young fireman spotted a young man with a pipe threatening an older man. Celic raced not to the fire, but to the older man's assistance. He wrestled the would-be assailant to the ground—it turned out the man with the pipe had started the fire. Afterward, Celic was reminded, gently, that he was a firefighter, not a police officer.

After a rough patch, Celic's young life was beginning to come together nicely in mid–1977: Six months earlier he had received a telephone call from the Fire Department inviting him back to the firehouse eighteen months after he had been laid off. Those months had been difficult, and Celic was out of work when he got the call to rejoin. With his prospects brighter, he proposed to his girlfriend, and they were preparing to be married in October.

With sixty pounds of equipment on their backs, Celic and the men of Engine Co. 15 made their way to the building's top floor. As they fought the blaze, they soon realized that another fire had broken out below them. Somehow, several teenage boys had entered the building, doused the second floor with an accelerant, probably diesel oil, and set the secondary fire. The firemen had not noticed fire on the lower stories on their way up to the fifth floor, so they were not expecting to be in one of firefighting's most dangerous positions—above a fire.

The flames below Engine 15 moved quickly. The smoke and heat were so intense that firefighters dragged themselves to open windows and shouted for help. A tower ladder was moved into place, and one of Engine 15's men stepped from the windowsill into the platform. Smoke was pouring out of the window, blinding Celic as he moved toward the window and the ladder. Years before, as a student at Monsignor Farrell High School on Staten Island, Celic had been a champion hurdler. He leaped for the tower ladder, but, weighed down with equipment and barely able to see, he missed the ladder and fell fifty feet to the street.

Celic lingered in Bellevue Hospital for eight days, his fiancée, parents, and siblings by his bedside day and night. He died on July 10. His funeral on July 14 in Our Lady Queen of Peace Church on Staten Island brought out not only firefighters, but neighbors and friends who were part of what had become a large and close-knit civil service community on the island. For years afterward, Celic's brother Tom kept the hero firefighter's memory alive by organizing an annual road race through the streets of their childhood home.

In late September 1977, fire marshals arrested a seventeen-year-old boy and charged him with murder for setting the fire that killed Marty Celic.

A day before the young firefighter's funeral, at about 9:30 on the hot summer night of July 13, the lights went out in New York. For a moment, the power outage brought back memories of another massive blackout, in 1965, fondly remembered as the inspiration for a mini–baby boom nine months later. This time, however, darkness inspired very few acts of love.

The lights were out for twenty-five hours in some neighborhoods. In that time, firefighters responded to more than 1,000 fires and nearly 2,000 false alarms. Fifty-nine firefighters were injured in the chaos. The worst of it came in the Brooklyn neighborhood of Bushwick, once

Fires in the South Bronx gained national attention in the 1970s, but neighborhoods like Bushwick in Brooklyn suffered terribly, too. The neighborhood looked like a war zone after the blackout of 1977.

known for its breweries and its strong German–American community. By 1977, the Germans were gone. So were the breweries, and the jobs. The neighborhood was poor and crime-ridden. And when the lights went out on July 13, the neighborhood went up in flames. A *Time* magazine correspondent noted that "as firemen fought blazes from [tower ladders], the looters went about their business virtually unmolested. Occasionally they would step over to one of the fire trucks and drink water from a running outlet."

Larry McCarthy had made lieutenant by 1977 and, as was the case when a firefighter was promoted, he had been transferred from his old company in Brownsville and reassigned to Ladder Co. 112 in Bushwick. After long hours at other fires that night, he was called to a blaze on the first floor of a commercial building near the neighborhood's burning business district. Padlocked metal gates covered and protected the building's storefront, but all ladder companies had large saws to cut their way through these security devices. However, the building's owners had taken the extra precaution of blocking up the building's back windows; this made ventilation from the rear impossible. Ventilation prevents a buildup of gases and a dangerous backdraft.

As the firefighters started cutting through the gates, the buildup of oxygen inside the building created a backdraft, an unexpected explosion of fire, which slightly burned several firemen working just outside. A rule of thumb in firefighting has it that once the backdraft has exploded, it's safe to proceed. McCarthy led men from Ladder Co. 112 under the gates and into the building. That's when he came face to face with a rare phenomenom known as a double backdraft. The explosion of fire burned his face, ears, and hands. McCarthy reversed course and tried to retrace his steps out of the building, but as he did so, he could hear the jagged humming of a saw as other members of Ladder 112 continued to cut through the gates at the front. McCarthy wasn't wearing an oxygen mask—many New York firefighters still went into buildings without them—so he was trying to hold his breath. He was burned, and he couldn't see because he was surrounded by fire and smoke. But all he was conscious of was the sound of the saw. If he ran out of the building, he was certain he'd run right into the saw and get cut in half. He didn't run into the saw, but he did spend the next two days in the hospital.

Bushwick never recovered from the fires. A third of the community's businesses closed; 20 percent of its housing stock was gone. Another firefighter, Pete Hayden, said that arson became so common in Bushwick that tenants in some buildings slept in shifts. That way, somebody was always awake and ready to sound the alarm. During the worst of the war years, 1975 to 1979, nearly 1,400 civilians died in fires citywide.

By 1978, the city's fiscal crisis had eased enough to allow the rehiring of all remaining laid-off firefighters. John Fox, Al Washington, and Tom Cashin were among the hundreds who returned to fire service eagerly, despite the workload and the dangers. They found that the private sector couldn't offer anything like the challenge of fire service and the opportunity to save and protect other people. Even with the exhausting tours, the mind-numbing routine of responding to false alarms, and the effects of budget cutbacks, they hurried to get to work early and relished the time they spent fighting fires. But they were never far removed from reminders of what might await them on their next tour of duty.

On the morning of Wednesday, August 3, 1978, just before the night tour ended at nine o'clock, firefighters in and near the Sheepshead Bay section of Brooklyn roused themselves from their coffee and kitchen chatter to respond to a fire in a Waldbaum's supermarket. Just after 8:30, construction workers inside the store noticed a fire in a men's room. About a dozen early-morning shoppers were inside the store; several who were on the checkout line demanded to be taken care of even as store employees ordered an evacuation.

Probationary Firefighter William O'Connor, the son of a Fire Department captain in Ladder Co. 168 and the grandson of a New York fireman who died in the line of duty, was looking forward to the end of his tour at nine and spending the day at the beach with his family. At the age of twenty-nine, he had achieved his dream of joining the Fire Department eight months earlier. The fiscal crisis and hiring freeze of the mid–1970s had delayed his appointment, but O'Connor had hardly put his life on hold. He was married, with three children under the age of five, and lived in the same Brooklyn neighborhood, Prospect Park, where he had grown up. His wife, Louise, and the children were on their way to the firehouse to pick him up.

When O'Connor's family arrived at the firehouse, they were told that William and the rest of Ladder 156 had been sent to the Sheepshead Bay Waldbaum's. Louise O'Connor got back into the family's car and, with the children in the back seat, drove to the fire.

As a member of a ladder company—a truck man, or truckie, in FDNY lingo—O'Connor's assignment at the fire was routine and familiar. He and the other truckies deployed their ladders, carried their saws, and climbed to the roof to ventilate the fire while the engine men stretched their hoses into the building. The ladder company's work of

The fire is out, and now this ladder company pokes through walls and ceilings, looking for hidden pockets of fire.

ventilating has to be coordinated closely with the engine companies' as they advance with their hoses into the building.

O'Connor climbed his ladder and glanced at the scene below him. He spotted his wife and children as they watched him. He waved to them, and then went about his business on the roof.

Moments later, a portion of the roof collapsed. O'Connor and five other firefighters were hurled into the fire's core. Frantically, hoses were repositioned to cover the collapse area, and firefighters and Police Department emergency services personnel hammered away at a wall, trying to reach the trapped men. It was all in vain. As word of the collapse made its way through the city's tight-knit firefighting community, a young man on crutches showed up at the firehouse where his father, George Rice worked. Rice was one of the men on the Waldbaum's roof. Firefighters took the young man aside and told him the terrible news.

Meanwhile, Carol Rice drove to the fire scene. A front-page picture in the following day's *New York Times* showed her anguish as Fire Commissioner Augustus Beekman told her that her husband was dead.

The life stories of the six men who died in the Waldbaum's fire revealed much about the kind of people whose work took them into burning buildings. William O'Connor had given up a fine job as a Transit Authority police officer to follow in the footsteps of his father and grandfather. Harold Hastings, a thirty-nine-year-old chief's aide, was about to go on vacation to Disney World with his wife and three children. James McManus, forty-five, was active in his Roman Catholic parish, St. Adalbert's on Staten Island, and the father of two girls. George Rice, thirty-eight, had two children and was a devout Catholic. Charles Boutan, the father of five, often took his family on canoe trips and was active in the local PTA. James Cutillo, thirty-nine, was a Little League coach and the father of two. Four of the men lived on Long Island.

The families turned down an offer to have a joint funeral in St. Patrick's Cathedral, explaining that they felt more at home in their local parish churches.

It was hard to believe, as flags flew at half-staff throughout the city for the six fallen firefighters, but the war years were nearly over. In the city's poor and devastated neighborhoods, there was, literally, very little left to burn. As the city's spirits—and finances—improved with the election of Ed Koch as mayor in 1977, the Fire Department got money to flood the streets of the South Bronx with fire marshals to stop arsonists even before they got their hands on a gasoline can and a book of matches. Called the Red Cap Program, the aggressive assault on arson worked, resulting in huge increases in arson arrests, fewer arsons, and fewer false alarms in six of the city's most troubled neighborhoods.

By 1983, the annual number of fires dipped below the 100,000 mark for the first time since 1967. False alarms were down to 139,083, a figure that had been unthinkable as recently as 1970, but a good deal better than the 285,290 false alarms of 1978. Serious fires were about half what they had been in the mid–1970s; civilian deaths had been cut from a high of 310 in 1970 to 228 in 1983, and for the most part they would continue to decrease.

It had been a terrible struggle, but New York's firefighters had prevailed during the war years. Even as they ended, though, another kind of war erupted within the Department. And just as surely as the fires of the 1970s reflected a chapter in the city's history, this war, too, was a product of changing times.

CHAPTER TEN

A BATTLE FOR INCLUSION

In 1977, with the city's fiscal crisis easing and all the laid-off firemen from 1975 back at work, it was time to replenish the depleted and exhausted ranks of the FDNY. On the morning of September 7, 1977, nearly 2,000 people lined up outside the city's Personnel Department office in lower Manhattan to sign up for the Fire Department's test, being given for the first time since the early seventies. The city anticipated hiring 5,000 new firefighters over the next several years.

At first glance the scene didn't look any different from earlier such occasions. A sprinkling of women were among the hundreds of men waiting to apply, but that wasn't unusual: Wives, girlfriends, and sisters often filled out applications on behalf of their loved ones who couldn't get the day off, or who were away at school or in the military.

But September 7, 1977, *was* different—in fact it was historic and precedent-shattering—because the intentions of a handful of those women were different. They weren't filling out applications on behalf of some male friend or relative. They were filling out the paperwork for themselves. For the first time in FDNY history, the city's rigorous two-part fireman's test was to be open to women.

By the late 1970s, millions of well-educated young women were transforming the practice of law, politics, medicine, journalism, and many other male-dominated white-collar professions. But women had yet to stake a claim on some of the ultimate male jobs, like firefighting. Even though many a would-be lieutenant could testify to the mental demands of firefighting—knowledge of building materials, for example—it still was considered a brawny job held by men with big shoulders. Firefighting, particularly New York firefighting, was indelibly linked to masculinity, in a way that no white-collar job was. There had been women politicians before 1977, and women doctors and women newspaper columnists. But there had never been a woman firefighter in New York.

The possibility of women invading the ultimate male preserve of the firehouse had been raised in 1974, when Commissioner John O'Hagan said that in light of a series of court decisions barring discrimination by gender, "[I]t isn't a case of 'if' we're going to have women, it's going to be 'when and how.' " O'Hagan also warned: "[I]t's going to be a traumatic adjustment."

Awaiting the women who sought a place in FDNY history in 1977 was a physical test that promised to be one of the toughest the Department had ever given. It was to be scored by grades, not, as was often though not always the case in the past, on a simple pass/fail basis. Candidates with the best scores would be higher on the eligibility list than candidates with lower passing scores. The test also placed enhanced emphasis on upper-body strength. Among other tasks, applicants would be required to pick up a dummy weighing 120 pounds, throw it over their shoulder, carry it up a flight of stairs, along a marked path, and back down downstairs. To the quickest went the highest scores.

Lorraine Cziko was a twenty-year-old college student looking for direction in her life when she took the subway from her family's home in the Middle Village section of Queens and joined the crowd at the Personnel Department in downtown Manhattan. As an adolescent growing up in the Middle Village section of Queens, she was the beneficiary of a quiet legacy of the feminist movement of the 1960s—well-funded scholastic sports programs for girls and young women. Cziko played volleyball, basketball, and softball at Newtown High School, and admired the work and dedication of her coaches, many of whom were pioneers in women's athletics. After graduating from high school in 1975, she enrolled in nearby Queens College and majored in physical education so she, too, might tutor young women in sports.

To her surprise, she soon learned that phys-ed teachers were expected to know a good deal more than the basics of a good jump shot, or how to set up a relay from the outfield. She struggled through chemistry classes, and then, facing the prospect of anatomy, she decided to change her major to Spanish, a language that came easily to her in high school. She would teach Spanish, then, rather than phys-ed.

During her college years she played softball with her church's team, and it was through a teammate's father, who worked for the city Sanitation Department, that she learned about the upcoming Fire Department test and its historic opening for women. Her teammate wasn't interested in the firemen's test, to her father's chagrin, but Cziko was, and for reasons she didn't quite understand. There were no fire-fighters in her family, and although she had dated firefighters, she'd never thought about being one, and knew very little about what the job entailed. She did know one thing, however, and it left a strong impression: A firefighter boyfriend of hers always left early for work. She often asked herself, "Who in the world gets to work an hour early?"

On September 7, she grabbed a clipboard and an application form, sat down on the floor outside the Personnel Department, and officially declared herself a candidate. A *New York Times* reporter at the scene picked her out from several other women who were playing the more traditional role of supportive spouse or mother or sister. She told the reporter that she had decided that "if men want to try this job, I might as well, too." The job sounded exciting, she said, with something new every day. She didn't anticipate any problems with male firefighters, she added.

She was not alone in her optimism. Few people foresaw problems between men and women firefighters because few believed women would make it to the firehouse, even though about 500 applied to take

Young firefighters are told to trust their scaling ladders and safety equipment. This is how that trust is learned.

the test. They might pass the written exam, but they were bound to fail the physical. Through the fall of 1977, as the city accepted thousands of applications from would-be firefighters, firehouse gossip hyped the rigors of the Department's new physical exam, suggesting that only a modern Hercules would dare attempt it.

The fireman's test was to New York's firehouses what the SAT was to the nation's elite colleges—it was accepted, and even revered, as an impartial and detached measure of ability. Those who made the grade were invited to join; those who failed were left out. The firehouse was a rough-and-ready meritocracy where neither brains nor brawn alone was good enough. To become a New York City fireman, a candidate had to pass a written test and have the strength to carry that dummy up and down a flight of stairs while a monitor stood by with a stopwatch. What separated the firehouse from, say, Harvard University, was that the FDNY was an absolute meritocracy. No endowment could buy a bed in the firehouse bunkroom. Reformers of another age had banished favoritism and corruption from the Department, and replaced it with the test.

In some neighborhoods in the outer boroughs and the nearby suburbs, civil service exams were as much a ritual of young adulthood as senior proms and flashy cars. The fireman's test determined whether a son would follow in his father's footsteps or be forced to look elsewhere—a dim prospect in the economically battered 1970s, as the New York region suffered not only from oil shocks but the beginnings of massive blue-collar job losses. The test could ensure a young man of a quarter century of protection from recession and unemployment—assuming, of course, that the fiscal crisis of the 1970s was never repeated. Engagements, weddings, and pregnancies often followed word that a would-be fireman had passed the test.

New York's fire service had adopted the test with the passion of an old-time reformer, and the Department was now far removed from its days as an arm of the city's political clubhouse. The test was scientific, it was apolitical, it was disinterested, and its results were quantifiable. The rules of civil service testing governed not only hiring, but promotion as well: Nobody became a lieutenant, a captain, a battalion chief, a deputy chief, or even, for a time, the Chief of Department without first passing the appropriate civil service test. In no other city agency, not even the Police Department, was the civil service test as all-determining as it was in the FDNY. Not unexpectedly, the strict rules linking promotion with testing frustrated mayors—which, of course, was precisely the point. Police commissioners appointed high-ranking officers above the rank of captain, but a fire commissioner had no say in the selection of battalion chiefs and deputy chiefs. Those titles were awarded on the basis of test scores alone. Firefighters were raised or trained to believe in the purity and fairness of the civil service test, and to accept its results as just and final. Those were the rules, and they abided by them.

The rules, however, were changing. It was to be one of history's ironies that the fireman's test, which was devised to protect the Fire Department from political influence and corruption, came under assault as a barrier to justice and progress. The first challenge came in 1971 from members of the Vulcan Society and the Department's Hispanic Society, who successfully argued in court that the content of the written test was biased against minorities. Many white firefighters deeply resented the implication that somehow they were the beneficiaries of a rigged system and that they themselves in fact were part of the problem. They had been brought up to believe something else, something a good deal simpler: The test was fair, and its results were beyond

Old and new methods of firefighting meet in this blaze. On the roof is a nineteenth-century water tank, which was used to douse the building fires of old. Surrounding the fire are three modern tower ladders.

reproach. The test decided who would become a firefighter. Not a judge, and not a politician, not even a chief with a couple of sons.

In fact, the dilemma was more complex than many firefighters realized. Most white firefighters had attended good schools, whether in the suburbs or within the city in places like Staten Island, south Brooklyn, and western Queens. Black and Latino firefighters often were reared in underserved, poor neighborhoods with failing public schools. The argument over the merits of the written test, about what it actually measured, would foreshadow by decades a national debate over IQ tests, college aptitude tests and other standardized measures of ability or potential.

Then, beginning in 1978, the other half of the firefighter's basic text came into question.

Lorraine Cziko passed the written portion of F.D. Exam 3040, as it was known, in December 1977, but she simply skipped the physical when it was administered in early 1978. She had gone to one of several practice sessions the Department sponsored before the actual exam, and found that she was the only woman in a gym filled with hundreds of men. She couldn't get the 120-pound dummy over her shoulder. She couldn't pull herself to the top of a twelve-foot wall. All the while, she would later recall, the men in the room were yelling at her, and their comments were not necessarily encouraging. Humiliated, she decided she would never pass the exam, and she gave up on the idea of firefighting. She graduated Queens College in 1980 with a degree in Spanish, applied for a job as a public school teacher, and found one—teaching general science to high school students.

Some months later, she received a letter from the law firm of Debevoise & Plimpton, telling her that she was to be included in a class-action sexual discrimination lawsuit filed on behalf of women who applied to the FDNY in 1977. The lawsuit was entitled *Berkman v. The City of New York, et al.*

Of the 389 women who passed the written exam, only 89 showed up to take the physical part of the test. Brenda Berkman, a twenty-seven-year-old lawyer, was one of them. A native of Asheville, North Carolina, who had been reared in a suburb of Minneapolis, Berkman's first challenge to a male-dominated society came in 1958, when she tried to join her local Little League baseball program and was turned down because it was boys-only. With a B.A. from St. Olaf College and a master's degree in history from Indiana University, she arrived in New York in the mid–1970s to study law at New York University. While still a student, she signed up to take the fireman's exam.

After passing the written exam, she showed up in an armory in Brooklyn on February 22, 1978, to take the physical. She was the only woman at this particular testing site, and all eyes were on her. Proctors administering the test urged candidates to cheer each other on as they performed each of the test's components: running up and down a staircase with the dummy; a standing broad jump; a hand-grip test; a ledge-balance exercise; an agility test requiring the scaling of a five-foot and an

So Others
Might Live

. . .

263

eight-foot wall; a flexed-arm hang; and a one-mile run. The men cheered for Berkman at first, but when she encountered problems—she didn't perform the dummy carry in the required amount of time, and she said she didn't get credit for scaling the walls—the cheering stopped. She failed the test, as did every other woman who took it (more than half the men also failed).

Working with Laura Sager of the Women's Rights Clinic at NYU and with Congresswoman Bella Abzug, a friend of her ex-husband's family, Berkman filed a complaint with the city Commission on Human Rights, saying that the physical test was biased against women. In documents filed with her complaint, she noted that no other women were present for her test, which she "found to be a psychological strain which impaired my physical performance." She asserted, too, that the dummy carry "put an emphasis on upper body strength and did not permit me to use the strength in my legs and lower back." The commission turned down her complaint.

Now she enlisted the support and resources of Debevoise & Plimpton, one of the city's most powerful law firms, and in 1981 she filed a class-action lawsuit on behalf of all of the nearly 400 women who had passed the written test in 1977. For the second time in a decade, a judge would decide whether the test—that supposedly equitable gatekeeper, that nearly sacred civil service text—was in fact fair.

ED KOCH was a reformer's reformer from bohemian Greenwich Village, but on many issues he spoke the language of the city's firefighters. As a mayoral candidate in 1977 and then as mayor in the late 1970s and early 1980s, he talked tough on crime and signaled his impatience with those who seemed to excuse social and civic disorder as the inevitable result of poverty and injustice.

History, however, seemed to demand that relations between the mayor and the Department be tense if not downright antagonistic. And such was the state of affairs between Koch and the Department—or, more particularly, the Uniformed Firemen's Association. As of 1977, Richard Vizzini was back for another term as union president, and seemed particularly hostile to Koch as early as the mayor's first week in office. When Koch proposed, almost immediately upon taking office, city legislation prohibiting discrimination against homosexuals in city employment, Vizzini warned that if obliged to hire homosexuals, the Fire Department would have to provide "separate bathrooms, showers and living facilities" for them. Those comments inspired the *New York Times* to wonder whether Vizzini imagined a "sudden epidemic" of "firemen in high heels."

A more substantive dispute, and one that would linger for years and through several administrations, concerned manning requirements on engine companies. To the union's everlasting enmity, the city had managed to reduce many engine companies to four firefighters (plus an officer) per shift during the fiscal crisis, and restoration of five-man engine companies became one of the union's highest priorities. Furthermore, in engine companies that had been exempt from manpower cuts, the union wanted the preservation of work rules that mandated filling out that five-man roster when somebody called in sick. Koch didn't object to five-man staffing as such, but he deplored the costs involved in the strict five-man rule, calling it a "bone in your throat." Absentees were replaced by firefighters from the previous shift, who then made time and a half. The costs, Koch said, added up to millions of dollars in overtime every year. He insisted that many companies could get by with four men for a day, or should be able to fill out the roster with a desk-duty firefighter. The union's skillful lobbyists, however, beat back any attempt to reduce staffing, arguing that there was no calculating the cost of five-man engines, because they saved lives.

Relations between the firefighters and Koch deteriorated to the point that by the summer of 1980, yet another UFA president, Nicholas Mancuso, was vowing to take his men out on strike beginning July 3. This time, however, the firefighters would be joined by police officers, corrections officers, and sanitation workers—in essence, there would be a general strike by the city's uniformed services. All of their contracts were up, and all the unions were demanding higher salaries. Firefighters at the time were making $19,341 without overtime.

On June 27, as the city and its unions contemplated yet another unthinkable scenario, a fire on the sixth floor of a tenement on West 151st Street required twenty FDNY units, including companies that shared a graffiti-scarred firehouse known as the Harlem Hilton. Gerard Frisby of Ladder Co. 28, a firefighter for eighteen months, was on the fire floor, and somehow became separated from other firefighters, some of whom had moved up to the seventh floor. He found his way to a window and shouted for help.

Lawrence Fitzpatrick of Rescue Co. 3 was on the roof when he heard Frisby's shouts. Fitzpatrick, thirty-eight, was a 14-year veteran and the father of eight children. Like Frisby, he was the son of a New York firefighter. With no time to get a tower ladder in position, Fitzpatrick quickly prepared to execute a rope rescue. Rope rescues are the most dramatic life-saving techniques in the FDNY's arsenal, and they need to be and are well rehearsed. Fitzpatrick put on a harness, and other firefighters secured one end of the 150-foot rope to a chimney. The rope was made of lightweight nylon, and had been handed out in 1976 to replace the department's older, heavier Manila ropes.

Four firefighters lowered Fitzpatrick down two stories to Frisby, who was at the sixth-floor window, as the rope, resting on a piece of tile coping along the building's facade, pulled taut. Fitzpatrick, a member of one of the FDNY's elite units, knew exactly what to do: He reached out for Frisby and grabbed him by the arms and legs. As he did, the coping along the roof cracked, and a piece of tile severed part of the rope. It snapped, and the two firefighters fell to their deaths.

At the funerals on July 1, Mayor Koch stood near some of the very union leaders who were threatening to leave the city without fire, police, or sanitation services in forty-eight hours. The drama, however, ended quietly, with no strike and more negotiations. For the Fire Department, talk of defective ropes replaced discussion of a new strike. In his last act as fire commissioner, Augustus Beekman ordered the ropes placed out of service pending further tests.

To replace Beekman, who had been the second African American to lead the Department, Koch went outside the Department and chose a lawyer with a reputation for fighting rackets and political corruption, Charles Hynes. The new fire commissioner, popularly known as Joe, was the first to admit that he knew very little about firefighting. But he had two advantages. He was part of what Koch called an "Irish mafia" of lawyers, City Hall advisers, and political insiders—including a young Tim Russert—which kept tabs on the historically Irish Fire Department. And one of his neighbors in the Brooklyn community of Flatbush was Lieutenant Gerry O'Donnell of Ladder Co. 147. As Hynes prepared to take over from Beekman, he sought O'Donnell for advice. "It's important that the brothers see you," O'Donnell said.

Two days before he was sworn in, on a Saturday afternoon in the Bronx, Hynes stopped by a firehouse near Van Cortlandt Park, where one of his children was competing in a road race. The company was out of the house, but one member remained inside on house-watch duty. Hynes mumbled something to the effect that he was the new commissioner, and then, in a louder voice, he asked for a cup of coffee—O'Donnell had told him to ask for coffee whenever he was in a firehouse. The firefighter on house watch brought Hynes into the kitchen and opened a cabinet. On the door was a vulgar comment about the commissioner's new boss, Ed Koch. Hynes realized that the house watchman had no idea he was serving coffee to Ed Koch's new fire commissioner. His education in firehouse culture had begun: Firefighters reflexively disliked authority figures, and firefighters poured coffee for any civilians who asked.

Charles "Joe" Hynes was one of the Fire Department's most popular commissioners with rank-and-file firefighters. Given the firehouse's traditional skepticism of authority, Hynes's popularity was, and remains, a rarity.

The next day, Hynes visited another firehouse, identified himself more clearly, and found himself learning more about the Department he was to lead. He met a firefighter who had been injured and was using crutches to get around. He was on sick leave, but was spending time in the firehouse with his friends. "That guy has to get on the subway and go to the medical office every god-damn Monday," one of the firemen told Hynes. Another insight: Firefighters despised the way the medical office treated them when they suffered line-of-duty injuries. Hynes took down the firefighter's name, and told him that he was under the commissioner's orders not to report to the medical office the following day.

The next day, Gerry O'Donnell asked his friend what was going on. "Everybody's asking me if you'll come visit their house," O'Donnell said.

"These guys," Hynes said, "have better communications than the Iroquois." Within a week, Hynes fired the medical office's head doctor and head nurse, and he hired replacements who were instructed to make sure every injured firefighter was greeted warmly and was immediately attended by a nurse who took the injured man's blood pressure, if only for the symbolic value of establishing a better bond between the office and the rank and file.

It was the beginning of one of the warmest commissioner–firefighter relationships in the FDNY's history. Hynes bought himself a turnout coat (a rubber jacket), a helmet and boots so he could respond to all four-alarm fires. (He tried responding to all three-alarm fires, but reality and exhaustion soon suggested a less energetic policy.) And he listened. A firefighter whom Hynes had seen being taken from a fire on a stretcher wept as he told the commissioner that he had been left at the hospital with no departmental support. Hynes checked with the police commissioner, Robert McGuire, to find out how the police department dealt with that situation, and was told that the NYPD essentially took over a hospital when a wounded cop was brought in. Hynes proceeded to found a team of firefighters on light duty—too injured to fight fires, but recovered enough to perform desk jobs—to be deployed to assist hospitalized firefighters and their families. He called it the HELP team.

Hynes's outreach had tangible results for his boss's bookkeepers: With an improved medical office, firefighter sick days declined, and so did overtime costs. But there was an intangible benefit, too. By listening to the rank and file and acting on complaints that seemed justified, Hynes improved morale at a time when tragedy and contract negotiations dominated conversation in the firehouse kitchens.

Though they found themselves named as defendants in Brenda

Berkman's sexual discrimination lawsuits, neither Hynes nor his boss, Mayor Koch, were opposed to hiring women as firefighters. Both men were progressive Democrats who supported the aspirations of women and minorities seeking to break down old barriers. Which is not to say they had no opinions about the controversy. Hynes believed that upper-body strength was a legitimate requirement for the job, and he made it clear that unless some way could be found to improve the upper-body strength of women candidates, the city should oppose their applications and the Berkman lawsuit. Koch said that he had one simple test for a would-be firefighter: He or she should be able to carry a 210-pound mayor out of a second-story window. That, he said, was the basic requirement.

As the city prepared to defend its position in federal court, Hynes urged the corporation counsel (its attorney general) to argue that there was no substitute for upper-body strength. And, in an effort to reach a compromise settlement before the case made its way into a courtroom, he proposed that the city set up a training course to help women build up their upper-body strength, or that the city hire women applicants as fire marshals who could then train for firefighting work. Both suggestions were rejected by the corporation counsel's office, and the case reached the federal courtroom of Judge Charles Sifton in 1981. On March 5, 1982, Sifton ruled in Berkman's favor, rejecting the city's contention that the fireman's physical was job-related. What was even more shocking, at least to veteran firemen, was the judge's assertion that the test should be used to identify "not those who are strongest and fastest, but instead those who, with the benefit of training in pacing or because of their native capacities of endurance, can perform the punishing tasks of fire-fighting as they are actually required to perform." He argued that the 120-pound dummy used in the carry, which was one of the main points of contention, "presented. . . a considerable technical problem to the uninitiated as to how to lift and hold it."

Not only did Sifton order the Department to develop a new physical exam, he demanded that forty-five women be appointed to the FDNY immediately if they passed the new test. "This is what we asked for and that is what we got," said a victorious Brenda Berkman.

In the new test the dummy's weight was increased to 145 pounds, but rather than carry the dummy up and down stairs, candidates were to drag it along a marked path. Other parts of the test were modified, but, as Berkman and other women would point out (often in vain) for the next twenty years, the Department used male firefighters to establish performance standards and rehearse the new exam before the women took it.

In addition to the dummy drag, the women were required to stretch an 80-pound hose 145 feet, carry a folded section of hose weighing 46 pounds up five flights of stairs, and raise a 20-foot ladder weighing 50 pounds from the ground to a vertical position. Then, to simulate forcible entry, the women were required to climb a ladder two stories, enter a window, grab a bar weighing 16 pounds, then climb three more stories to the fifth floor, enter another window, and use an 8-pound sledgehammer to hit a rolled-up hose weighing 60 pounds. Then came the dummy drag. Not counting a seven-and-a-half-minute rest period between the hose section and the ladder section, the series of tasks was to be performed in four minutes and nine seconds or less. The candidates performed these tasks while wearing a turnout coat, gloves, boots, a breathing device known as the Scott Air Pak, and a helmet. Gone from the first test were the standing broad jump, the hand-grip test, the ledge walk, the agility test, the flexed-arm hang, and the one-mile run—which was ironic, because it was one of marathon runner Brenda Berkman's particular strengths.

Along with a revised test came a revision in the title held by the FDNY's rank and file. No longer were they firemen. As of June 1, 1982, they were firefighters.

Seventy-one women took the new test in 1982; fifty-one passed, and forty-two accepted the ensuing offer of appointment, including Brenda Berkman and Lorraine Cziko, who along with 105 men were sworn in as probationary firefighters on September 22, 1982. Addressing the class, Mayor Koch said: "The City of New York formally acknowledges what all just and thinking men and women have known all along: the valor of the human spirit knows no sex." Commissioner Hynes, preparing to end his short but happy tenure and practice law, promised that all the probationary firefighters would be subjected to a rigorous six weeks of training at the FDNY's Bureau of Instruction facility on Randall's Island.

Rigorous it was, so much so that four women and two men dropped out during training. But on September 5, 1982, eleven women made history as they became the city's first female firefighters at a graduation ceremony on Randall's Island. Brenda Berkman and Lorraine Cziko were among the graduates; in fact, Cziko's picture appeared on page one of both the *New York Times* and *Newsday* as she was given the honor of carrying an ax during an honor guard procession. The ceremony certainly represented a social and cultural revolution in the Department, but not all traditions were shattered: The names of six of the new firefighters— Catherine Riordan, Judith Murphy, Marianne McCormack, Janet Horan, Maureen Hartnett, and Patricia Fitzpatrick—made it clear that the feminist movement had not altered the FDNY's conspicuously Irish presence.

The other women probies, along with six men, were held over for additional training. They eventually followed their sister firefighters through graduation and assignment to a firehouse.

In many ways, their trial had only just begun.

Brenda Berkman received a hint of what was to come even before her formal graduation, when she received a "Dear Member" letter dated September 28, 1982, from Nicholas Mancuso, president of the UFA— her union. Mancuso advised her that the union was planning to appeal *Berkman v. The City of New York et al.* "If the Union is successful on that appeal," Mancuso wrote, "in effect the Court will decide that your position as a female firefighter was improperly granted and that your appointment should not have taken place."

The court did not so decide. But the firehouse did. The treatment meted out to Berkman, Cziko, and many other women appointed in the early 1980s tarnished the Fire Department's reputation. Every probie firefighter was forced to endure months of hazing, not unlike a rookie football player or a newcomer to a frat-house, but they also were mentored in the science of firefighting. Many of the women received only the hazing part, and it was particularly cruel. Even though it was the work of a minority of male firefighters, the hazing and harassment reflected poorly on the Department as a whole. Little, if anything, was done to stop it.

Berkman became a particular target for harassment and ostracism. It was she, after all, who had initiated the lawsuit that, in the firehouse view, had led to a diminution of standards—not, as Berkman argued, to a test that better reflected job-related strengths. She was not a New Yorker, or even a Long Islander, she had a high public profile, and she was a lawyer. The chasm between Berkman and the rank-and-file Fire Department was wide. Some of the men she worked with made it unbridgeable.

She was assigned to Engine Co. 17 on Pitt Street on the Lower East Side, and, as was the case with all the women, she was the only female in the house. Within a few weeks, she handled the nozzle at a tenement fire, a rite of passage for any new member of an engine company, and on February 2, 1983, she was part of a unit that won a merit citation for its work at a five-story-building fire on Clinton Street. She found the work as satisfying as she had imagined. Her captain gave her a score of 6 for her three-month evaluation, meaning that her work was good. A score of 5 meant that the probie's work was satisfactory.

The work environment, however, was something else again. Her locker was broken into, her bed was left unmade (such household work was divided up among members on any given day), and none of her colleagues would work mutuals with her. She was barred from the firehouse tradition of communal meals, even though she paid the house tax—money firefighters paid for food and coffee. There were complaints that she didn't open the nozzle quickly enough.

She coped with this ostracism by turning inward, spending her free time at the firehouse in the workout room or, as months passed, reading *The Idiot* in the bunk room. She ate peanut butter and jelly sandwiches by herself while her male colleagues made lunch or dinner in the firehouse kitchen.

As part of a regular rotation of probies, she was detailed to Ladder Co. 11 on East Second Street for thirty days in the early summer of 1983. At mealtime during the day tour on June 28, she noticed that there weren't enough plates set on the table. She was told there wasn't enough food for her, which, if true, would have marked yet another historic precedent in firefighting history. Taking the hint, she left the kitchen and walked to the apparatus floor, trying very hard not to cry. A lieutenant who was filling in from another firehouse saw her and asked what the problem was. She explained, he disappeared, and then he returned and told her to go to the kitchen and eat. She did, but when she later asked if anybody wanted to play paddleball with her, the men refused.

Her place at the table was short-lived. Through the rest of her short detail at Ladder Co. 11, she was kept out of meals, was forced to endure pranks like eggs placed in her boots, and suffered the silence of her colleagues.

It was much the same story for Lorraine Cziko in Engine Co. 275 in South Jamaica, Queens. She was subjected to lewd gestures (somebody carved a penis out of honeydew and left it by her locker), firecrackers were thrown in her direction when she was on house watch, and when she was polishing the bottom of the sliding pole, a colleague dumped polish on her head from the second floor. Nobody answered her questions about basic firefighting tactics.

Rochelle Jones was among the groundbreaking women who joined the FDNY in the early 1980s. She went on to become the Department's first woman officer.

As with Brenda Berkman, Cziko's colleagues wouldn't work mutuals with her, until finally somebody asked her to work for him so that he could extend his vacation. She did so, and he then worked for her to complete the bargain. But when she asked the same man to work a mutual for her, he refused.

Tensions finally exploded at a company picnic. Cziko didn't want to go and didn't have a boyfriend to take to what was designed as a family outing, but she saw no point in further alienating the men by not going. Besides, the picnic would include a softball game, and Lorraine Cziko was a pretty good softball player. The first competition was a tug of war, pitting Engine Co. 275 against another company. Cziko huddled with her colleagues, until the very same firefighter who wouldn't work a mutual with her said, "Hey, who wants her in?" They took a vote; Cziko was asked to leave.

When it was time for softball, Cziko was ready to take the field until the same firefighter asked, "Who wants her in?" She lost the vote, again, and was told she could participate in an egg toss with the wives and children. She did, and she finished the game with an unbroken egg in her hands. That led to an idea, and the idea led to action fueled by a couple of drinks. Spotting her tormentor near the playing field, Cziko walked over to him and crushed the egg in his face.

She retreated to a gazebo where the drinks, oysters, and a watermelon spiked with vodka were being kept on ice. She was there only a few seconds when she was attacked from behind. The other firefighter hit her with two eggs, dumped a garbage can filled with oysters on her, and then finished the proceedings by hitting her with the watermelon. Wives were screaming, and the other firefighters pulled the man off Cziko. She left, never said a word, and to this day will not identify her attacker.

After her year's probation, Cziko's captain recommended that she be fired. Berkman was also fired—she learned about it when she showed up for work one day in September 1983 and was told that the *Daily News* was reporting her dismissal. She and another high-profile woman, Zaida Gonzalez, successfully sued to get their jobs back, survived intense retraining on Randall's Island, and resumed their duties. Cziko was not fired, but was sent for further training, and then was transferred to another company, Engine Co. 303, where the social conditions were better.

It was no secret in the Department that men in some firehouses were making life miserable for the women, with the express purpose of driving them out of the firehouse. Some officers tolerated it, some preferred not to know, and some took action against it. Reggie Julius, who knew about firehouse harassment firsthand from his days as a lonely black firefighter in the early 1950s, was now chief of Battalion 12 in upper Manhattan. He had heard that a woman in the battalion was having a hard time with the men in Engine Co. 59 and Ladder Co. 30 in Harlem. Julius decided to pay a personal visit to the firehouse. He assembled the men and told one of them to shut all the doors. "Now," he said, "I'm gonna tell you motherfuckers something. You guys are screwing with this woman. The law says she's allowed to be here, she's duly appointed here, and if you keep screwing with her, I'll transfer every one of you. Where do you live, Rockland County? How'd you like to work in Coney Island? You want to play games, I'll screw you."

There were no more harassment problems, but there were problems of another sort. Chief Julius found that another woman in the battalion was calling in sick from exhaustion after tough fires. He called her to battalion headquarters. "Listen," he said, "I'm sick and tired of these medical reports. The next time you go sick on me or anybody else, I'm gonna throw you off the roof, and you'll have a line-of-duty funeral."

Not all of the women from that first class suffered as Berkman and Cziko and others did. Cathy Riordan, a divorced mother of two sons, left her job as a daytime bartender for a chance to become a firefighter and never had reason to regret the choice. Assigned to Engine Co. 38 in the Bronx, she worked in a busy house, which may have worked to her advantage. There was little time for pranks. She also worked for a captain who made it clear to other officers and the rank and file that he would not permit harassment. That kind of strong leadership was absent from other houses.

Before long, Riordan was chatting in the kitchen with her colleagues just like any other firefighter. The change was gradual, but it was brought home one afternoon when she found herself talking about childbirth with a couple of male colleagues whose wives had just given birth. They had been in the delivery room, and they seemed delighted to discuss the blessed events in all their gory detail. An officer walked into the kitchen, caught part of the conversation, shook his head and said, "What in the world is going on here?"

Riordan got to know the wives and children of her male colleagues, they teased her about her lack of ability in the kitchen, and by the end of her career, she was working as a chief's aide, which meant she handed out assignments and orders from her boss. They never questioned her when, for example, she told an arriving company with a tower ladder to deploy the apparatus in the rear of a building.

Susan Byrne, a onetime swimming coach and lifeguard in the Rockaways hired just after the first class of women, had a similar experience when she was assigned to Engine Co. 93 in the Washington Heights section of Manhattan. She caught grief when she lost her helmet at her first fire, but anybody would have. And like any other firefighter, she put herself at risk: She was stretching hose outside a burning building in upper Manhattan at four o'clock in the morning when a backdraft blew through the building's windows, burning away her eyebrows and eyelashes and leaving her with second-degree burns.

By 1984 there were thirty-seven women in the Fire Department, and in subsequent years, the number remained about the same, a source of much frustration to Berkman in particular. In 1986 she sued the city again to block a new physical on grounds of sexual discrimination, but this time Judge Sifton sided with the city.

EQUALLY FRUSTRATED were the Department's racial minorities. (They had supported Berkman's lawsuit despite the union's staunch opposition.) Even as New York's population became blacker and browner, and events like the West Indian Day in Crown Heights replaced Saint Patrick's Day on Fifth Avenue as the city's biggest public spectacle, the Fire Department remained more than 90 percent white.

Dissatisfied with the Department's recruiting efforts in minority communities, throughout the 1980s the Vulcan Society stepped up its own outreach programs. Al Washington, who was a nervous probie when the UFA went on strike in 1973, was by 1987 the president of the Vulcan Society and a member of Rescue Co. 2. He had been introduced to the

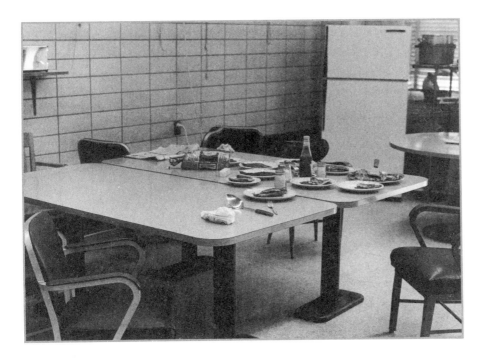

Snack, interrupted. When an alarm sounds, a company's afternoon or evening meal becomes just a fond memory.

legacy of the long-banished black bed on his first day after probie school, when he and a Puerto Rican firefighter, Dennis Mojica, showed up at the quarters of Engine Co. 290 in Brooklyn and saw racial epithets written on the firehouse blackboard. He would later say that his first few months on the job, from late 1973 to early 1974, were "like being in Archie Bunker's living room." Engine Co. 290 served the black neighborhoods of East New York and Brownsville, and Washington quickly gathered that some of his white colleagues were not particularly fond of the locals. He began to wonder about the career choice that had taken him from a white-collar office to a firehouse kitchen, where, he believed, some of his coworkers hated him because of his skin color. And yet, those very same men would put their lives on the line to save his, and did just that to save the men, women, and children in the neighborhood.

Any doubts Washington had about his transformation from a professional arbitrator to a firefighter were resolved on a December evening in 1974, when he climbed a ladder to rescue a little girl trapped in a burning building. Nearly three decades later, he still remembered how tightly the girl squeezed his neck as he brought her down to safety, and how she hugged him when the ordeal was over. Suddenly, everything else seemed less important.

Washington was laid off in 1975 and spent eighteen months off the job, but shortly after he returned he was selected to become a founding member of a reorganized Squad Co. 1 in Brooklyn. Squad companies were a new type of special unit that had been introduced in the 1970s; they were the FDNY's equivalent of an army's highly trained mobile reserves. Members were drawn from companies around the city and received advanced training in areas such as rescue operations, hazardous material response, and special emergencies, like building collapses. The squads' pumpers were equipped with some of the tools and equipment of a ladder or rescue company. Washington's new officer at Squad 1 was a captain named Ray Downey; already a legendary fire officer, he was destined to boost his reputation even higher as one of the Department's master tacticians.

Washington spent five years at Squad 1, a time he would describe as "great days" because they were busy, because he was serving under a great teacher in Ray Downey, and because of the bonds he formed with his colleagues in the squad. He no longer was sitting in Archie Bunker's living room. Instead, he was working with a group of highly motivated firefighters who had no time for nor interest in disparaging minority groups around the firehouse kitchen. They took their cue from Downey, who, unlike some officers, was not reluctant to assert his authority in the firehouse. "He was the captain, and he didn't let you forget it," Washington said.

Downey had personally selected the members of Squad 1. They bonded not only in quarters, but also when they were off duty, performing what Washington slyly called their "community outreach sessions" in the bars of Park Slope. The firefighters of Squad 1 took such pride in their unit that they soon were revisiting a piece of New York firefighting history, the competition between different companies: Their goal, they decided, was to beat Brooklyn's Rescue Co. 2 to fires requiring special units.

In 1981, however, Al Washington transferred to Squad 1's rival. He loved the work and the men of Squad 1, but there were larger considerations at work. The Vulcan Society had fought for years to make sure blacks were included in rescue companies, the FDNY's most elite units. The only black working in rescue in 1981 was Rescue 2's John Mitchell, and he was getting promoted and transferred. Washington felt obliged to request a transfer to fill Mitchell's spot, and Downey obliged.

When he took over the Vulcan Society in 1987, then, Al Washington had firsthand experience with the lingering racism of some white firefighters, as well as the color-blind camaraderie of Squad 1 and Captain Ray Downey. But even as Washington integrated black women into the Vulcans and reached out to minority youngsters through career days in local high schools, the Department's percentage of black firefighters was stuck in the low single digits. The same was true for Latinos. Combined, minority firefighters made up just 6 to 7 percent of the FDNY's rank and file.

Few Fire Department officials had been more frustrated with the stagnant number of blacks and Latinos than Fire Commissioner Augustus Beekman, who had experienced the humiliation of the firehouse black bed. As fire commissioner from 1978 to 1980, he ordered training classes for minority candidates in public schools and aggressively publicized the job's benefits in poor neighborhoods. But, he later told the *Newsday* columnist Dennis Duggan, "on the day of the exam very few people of color showed up. That was a big disappointment." Beekman's successor, Joe Hynes, was similarly frustrated.

The Vulcans blamed the low minority participation on the Department's inadequate recruiting effort, and in response to the criticism the Department developed its Cadet program, aimed at black and Latino youths. But little seemed to change. The overt racism that Wesley Williams, Augustus Beekman, and the Julius brothers faced was long gone. But as of 1990, when New York's first African American Mayor, David Dinkins, took office and introduced the phrase "gorgeous mosaic" to the city's lexicon, the Fire Department remained an anomaly among city agencies. Even the Police Department, despite well-publicized clashes with the city's minority community, was achieving unprecedented success in diversifying its personnel. The Fire Department, however, baffled the efforts of those who demanded change—and not, by any means, for the first time.

By the end of the 1980s, as society's culture wars were being played out in the city's firehouses, actual firefighting had decreased dramatically; in 1983 the number of fires fell below six figures for the first time since 1967. But even as firefighters began to complain that the era of big, memorable fires was over, they knew better than anyone that even a small fire was a potential tragedy. Through the 1980s, the annual civilian death toll never dipped below 200. In fact, the 245 civilian deaths in 1987 matched the figure for 1975, a year associated with large-scale arson and building fires in the South Bronx and central Brooklyn. Line-of-duty deaths did not stop, either. Nineteen firefighters died in the 1980s.

In the last half of the twentieth century, the makeup of New York's population changed, but the percentage of minority firefighters remained in the single digits. Mayors, commissioners, unions, and the rank and file grappled with issues of race and gender into the new century.

Bill Bresnan, the great-grandson of Chief John Bresnan, served in Ladder Co. 15 in downtown Manhattan for most of the decade of the eighties. Not surprisingly, given the locale, Bresnan became a veteran of high-rise fires. They were not spectacular—there were no towering infernos—and they rarely caused enough damage to merit a mention on the evening news, but Bresnan did notice a pattern to the fires. They often broke out in rooms where records and other vital documents were stored. Fire, even on a small scale, continued to serve the unscrupulous.

His work also took him to low-rise sections of lower Manhattan, and there he saw the casualties and tragedies that continued to occur, despite the improving fire statistics. As the new immigrants of the 1980s crammed into substandard housing in Manhattan's Chinatown section, fires inevitably followed. One such blaze brought Bresnan into a building that had been illegally subdivided into living cubicles for newly arrived Chinese families. He found the bodies of several children by a window.

He remembered how his firefighter father had struggled with the nightmare of finding the charred bodies of children in burned-out apartments and houses. "It tugged at his heart," Bresnan said. As a firefighter himself, Bill Bresnan learned to detach himself, as best he could, from the images that haunted all firefighters, especially during times they inevitably described as quiet.

In the early hours of Sunday morning, March 25, 1990—seventy-nine years to the day since the Triangle Shirtwaist fire—a man with a grudge and a jug filled with gasoline set fire to a social club in the Bronx. The club, called Happy Land, had no liquor license and had been ordered to shut down because of building-code violations more than a year earlier. It continued to operate as an after-hours spot, and in the predawn hours of Sunday morning, dozens of young people were drinking and socializing inside the graffiti-covered fire trap. Many were recent immigrants from Central America.

Julio Gonzalez, thirty-six, had been thrown out of the place hours earlier after arguing with a former girlfriend who worked at the club. He returned with a dollar's worth of gasoline in a plastic jug, dumped it through a door, tossed a couple of matches, and walked away.

The place was ablaze in minutes. Death came so quickly that some victims were found still clutching their drinks, their bodies burned only slightly but their lungs filled with smoke and poison. Eighty-seven people died, though Gonzalez's former girlfriend was one of a handful of people who survived. Gonzalez, who returned to the scene to watch firefighters put out the blaze he had started, was arrested and quickly confessed to the crime.

Unlike the Triangle fire, which touched off a social-reform movement that foreshadowed parts of the New Deal, the Happy Land fire inspired little outrage. The city cracked down on illegal social clubs in immigrant neighborhoods, but the city's worst fire since 1911 saw no modern Edward Croker pacing the sidewalk outside the charred building, condemning the owners who blithely ignored violations and a city that couldn't prevent such a danger from threatening the lives of a new generation of immigrants.

CHAPTER ELEVEN

A NEW WORLD

THE FUTURE ARRIVED just after noon on February 26, 1993. Lieutenant John Fox of Squad 1 was prowling the aisles of the Key Food supermarket on Seventh Avenue in the Park Slope section of Brooklyn, looking for the raw material for the day's meal in Squad 1's kitchen. It was an unusual assignment for Fox, but he went along with it because he saw a chance to get something for his dinner later that evening.

Firefighters take their apparatus and equipment to the grocery store when they're getting their meal, with the chauffeur designated to stay with the rig and monitor radio traffic. While Fox and other members of Squad 1 were sizing up the offerings on the supermarket's meat counter, the squad's chauffeur, Jim Brogan, got a call from Brooklyn borough command ordering the unit to the World Trade Center. Brogan called Fox on a handy-talkie—a small walkie-talkie firefighters wear on their chests—and told him that food shopping would have to wait. "We have to run into Manhattan," the chauffeur said. Squad 1 trotted out of the supermarket and climbed aboard the rig. Fox asked Brogan, "What do they have over there?" The chauffeur didn't know.

"Ah, we ain't gonna do nothing over there," Fox said. Squad 1 drove around the corner, picked up its second rig, and drove toward the Brooklyn–Battery Tunnel. As Brogan tried to steer the apparatus through Brooklyn traffic, a car collided with another car in front of the apparatus, and the second car hit the rig. Fox jumped out of the cab, wrote down his name, phone number, and his company on a piece of paper, handed it to the drivers, and said, "Look, we've got to go." He never heard from either motorist.

Back in the cab with Brogan at the wheel, Fox switched his radio to a Manhattan frequency and heard frenzied transmissions between firefighters heading toward the World Trade Center and dispatchers trying to make sense of the calls they were getting. Fox heard a call for a third alarm, then a fourth alarm, and then two fifth alarms. Fox still wasn't sure what was happening, except that there was a big job at the Twin Towers. He turned to Brogan. "I changed my opinion. We're going to be doing something over there."

When the rig reached the tunnel that would take Squad 1 to lower Manhattan, Fox saw that it was closed to all traffic except emergency vehicles. "Something's really up," he thought as police officers waved his rig through the toll plaza.

Though they had a clear view of the World Trade Center just before they ducked into the tunnel, the members of Squad 1 still had no idea what was going on. Only much later would they learn that Islamic terrorists had set off a huge car bomb in a garage underneath the complex. A new age—for the nation, for the city, and for the Fire Department of New York—had begun.

Engine Co. 6 reported a 10–76—Fire Department code for a high-rise fire—at Box 69 in downtown Manhattan at twenty minutes after noon. Initial reports from the field indicated a transformer explosion in the vicinity of 3 World Trade Center, which was the address of the Vista Hotel. Engine Co. 6 almost immediately dispatched signal 10–45, Code One—meaning they had found a dead civilian. It soon became clear that the explosion was endangering the lives of thousands of people in 1 World Trade Center, the north tower. Dispatchers received reports of intense smoke and trapped civilians as high as the forty-fifth floor. The FDNY's Division 1, which covered lower Manhattan, set up a command post to coordinate what was shaping up to be the largest rescue operation in the Department's history.

On Staten Island, in the quarters of Rescue Co. 5, Captain Edmund Staines was beginning to realize that today wasn't going to be the quiet day he had been expecting. Staines's regular assignment was with Squad 1 in Brooklyn, but he had been ordered to cover for Rescue 5's captain, Charlie Driscoll, who had the day off. Rescue 5 was the slowest of the city's five rescue companies, stationed as it was in the city's least-populated borough, Staten Island. Covering officers, who often were strangers to the firefighters under their temporary command, were expected to mind their own business, and Staines had every intention of upholding that tradition. But then a bomb went off at the World Trade Center, and the members of Rescue 5 approached their captain for a day. "Hey, Cap," one of them said, "call the dispatcher and tell them we'll go." The call went in, and Rescue 5 was ordered to lower Manhattan. As they raced over the Verrazano Narrows Bridge into Brooklyn, and then along the Gowanus Expressway to the Brooklyn–Battery Tunnel, the firefighters of Rescue 5 prepared the high-rise equipment they rarely had use for on suburban, low-rise Staten Island. From the radio reports they were monitoring, they knew there had been an explosion of some sort, and that they should expect a large number of casualties.

A dispatcher radioed Battalion 4 with news that 300 people were trying to evacuate the forty-third floor of 1 World Trade Center in heavy smoke conditions. "They're really getting loaded up with people," the dispatcher said. Rescue Co. 5, when it arrived, would be deployed to help with the evacuation, the dispatcher said.

While Squad Co. 1 and Rescue Co. 5 were on their way to Manhattan, Firefighter Kevin Shea of Rescue Co. 1 was making his way through the noise and smoke of the bombed-out garage. Shea never saw the crater the bomb had created, and he plunged thirty feet into the darkness. He survived the fall, but his leg was badly hurt, he was trapped under falling debris, and he had no idea where he was. "Mayday!" he hollered into his handy-talkie. Other firefighters spread the word: Somewhere in the darkness, Kevin Shea of Rescue 1 was trapped in a hole.

Squad Co. 1 pulled up in front of the Vista Hotel to what was, in John Fox's first glance, not a particularly memorable scene. Rigs were scattered all over West Street, and firefighters by the dozens were arriving from all over the city, but there was little sign of catastrophe. Fox could see some signs of fire, and some smoke drifting out from the garage levels. He and his company were ordered to report to Deputy Chief Steven DeRosa in the hotel lobby. DeRosa had been Fox's captain when Fox served in Ladder Co. 112.

"We're missing a man," DeRosa told Fox. "Go downstairs."

Fox and the squad found a staircase that took them from the lobby to the basement and garage levels. Through the noise of car alarms and water rampaging through broken pipes, he heard firefighters yelling, "This way! This way!" As they ventured farther into the garage and underneath 1 World Trade Center, conditions worsened dramatically. One of Squad 1's men, Peter Runfola, noticed through the smoke and destruction that many of the tower's steel supporting beams seemed untouched. "This thing is never coming down," he thought. A voice from somewhere in the chaos shouted, "There's a big hole down there!" Fox and his men crawled the next forty feet until they came to the edge of a gigantic crater.

They hardly knew it was there. One of Fox's men, Runfola, figured the hole was about three or four feet wide. In fact, it was about one hundred fifty feet in diameter. Smoke was pouring up from the blast site, covering the hole in an acrid shroud. But in the distance, in the hole itself, Squad 1 could see small fires. They were the blazing ruins of dozens of cars.

As Fox and firefighters from other companies at the crater's edge considered their next move, every now and then they could hear a voice from somewhere below: "I'm over here. I'm over here." It was Kevin Shea, and he sounded very far away. More prominent was the noise of water cascading from broken pipes above them.

One of Fox's men found a life-saving rope—it wasn't the squad's rope, it had been left there by another company. That discovery determined the next move: a rope rescue. Somebody would be lowered into the smoke and fires below, into a hole he knew was there but couldn't

really see. "All right," said Fox, "I'm
going in." It was a dangerous operation, and he was the lieutenant. It was
that simple.

There was no place to secure the
rope, so they looped it around a safety
belt worn by Squad 1's Willie Walker.
The other end was looped around John
Fox's belt. Walker positioned himself
near the edge of the crater, and firefighters from Squad 1 and Ladder
Companies 6 and 101 formed a dozen-
man daisy chain holding on to Walker
and to each other. Fox crawled backward to the edge, trying to find a spot
that wasn't too close to the fires burning below them. He found one, but
then he noticed the broken and bent
reinforcing rods that were sticking out
of the crater's edge. He crawled onto
one of them and said, "Okay, let's go."
He disappeared into the smoke.

Elsewhere on the crater's edge was
Ladder Co. 15's Bill Bresnan, who had
heard the mayday calls over his radio.
Somehow he had become separated
from the rest of his company, and soon
found himself staring down a hole that
made him think he was looking down

Armed with his pike-like hook, a firefighter
pauses before heading into the World Trade
Center after a bomb exploded in a basement
garage in 1993.

from the top of a baseball stadium. Cables and wires were hanging above
him, and the only light in the garage came from the fires of burning cars.
He heard a voice close by calling for help, but could see nobody. He
started to move closer to the crater, but then remembered that somebody already had fallen into the darkness. Meanwhile, burning cars were
starting to blow up nearby, and he caught glimpses of chunks of con-

crete falling around him and into the smoking pit. Bresnan was scared, scared enough to think about throwing his turnout coat on the ground and telling somebody, anybody, in authority, "Hey, this is crazy. Enough's enough. I'm done."

Thick pipes and a portion of a ramp jutted out beyond the crater's edge, toward the voice pleading for help. As Bresnan considered his next move, or considered whether he even had a next move, a captain came out of the smoke. "We've got this guy out here," Bresnan said, "but I'm not sure how we can go get him."

"Well, we gotta get him," the captain said.

"Oh great," Bresnan thought. "Who's going first?"

The captain did, followed by Bresnan. They made their way along a cluster of pipes and spotted a civilian wedged between two slabs of concrete, suspended on a horizontal piece of steel. Underneath was a fifty-foot drop to the concourse level of the Trade Center's basement. Above them, cars were beginning to fall into the crater. All the while, Bresnan couldn't shake the thought that the whole building might come down on him. He had no idea what was happening elsewhere; he was convinced that hundreds, and maybe thousands, were dead.

The two firefighters pushed and pulled the injured civilian onto the relative safety of the pipes, then dragged him back to the crater's edge. The civilian's ankle was smashed, but he was alive. He was crying and laughing at the same time.

WHEN RESCUE CO. 5 arrived at the command post, officers scrapped the plan to send the company to the upper stories to help with evacuations. As Staines reported to a deputy chief inside the Vista Hotel lobby, he saw somebody in a Port Authority uniform opening a staircase door. Out poured thick, suffocating smoke. The deputy chief told Staines, "Eddie, somebody's missing. I want you to take your company down there."

Staines looked back at the open door and said, to himself, "Why me?"

One of Kevin Shea's colleagues from Rescue Co. 1, Gary Geidel, was in the lobby, and he said he knew where Shea was. Geidel and one of

Staines's men, Jack Tighe, went off on their own. Staines and the rest of Rescue 5 started their descent into the smoky, noisy and burning basement. With their masks on but without the protection of a hose line, the firefighters descended a stairwell, feeling for a search line that the company's forward member was unfurling as he led the way. The search line would enable them to retrace their steps if they became lost or had to evacuate quickly.

By the time Rescue Co. 5 reached a second flight of stairs that would take them lower into the garage, the search line became entangled in the debris and was abandoned. Over the roar of explosions and car alarms, Rescue 5's Butch Foley could hear Kevin Shea's mayday calls over his handy-talkie. But there was no telling where he might be. Lacking the search line, Foley made mental notes of the surroundings in case a collapse or an explosion forced the company to retreat.

Ahead of Foley, Rescue 5's Louis Modafferi and Gus Tripoli forced open a door that was blocking their descent. They heard a woman moaning close by. Tripoli turned to Staines. "I hear something, Cap. You hear that?"

"I'm the oldest guy here," Staines said. "I don't hear as good as you guys."

Modafferi, Tripoli, and Staines searched through the smoke until they found a small office, where Linda Nash lay semiconscious. She was burned and bleeding, suffering from multiple injuries including a broken leg. She could hardly speak, but she managed to tell the firefighters that the last thing she remembered was closing the door of her car in the garage. The bomb went off at that moment, and she had been thrown about fifty feet into the office. She told the firefighters that somehow she had blown up the place. Modafferi, Tripoli, Foley, Staines, and Michael Connelly, another member of Rescue 5, brought her back up to the hotel lobby, then returned to the search.

Somewhere in the smoke, Jack Tighe had lost sight of Gary Geidel. Tighe was soaked from water pouring from burst water mains and pipes, and he had to negotiate huge chunks of concrete blocking his path to. . . somewhere. He was on his own. He couldn't hear his handy-talkie, he had no search line, and he had last seen Geidel several minutes earlier.

He was afraid. He wondered how much air he had left in his tank, but he couldn't read the gauge in the darkness. He kept crawling.

THEY WERE LOWERING John Fox too fast. He yelled up to his men, "Slow down!" He wasn't wearing his mask, but he had it with him on his back. The firefighters gathered around Willie Walker tightened their grip, and Fox came to an abrupt halt, dangling over the pit.

"Go slower," he yelled, and the descent continued, slowly. About forty feet later, John Fox touched down, landing on his back on a pile of jagged concrete. He rolled over on his stomach, looked around, and there was Kevin Shea, about fifty feet away toward the center of the crater. Fox took off the rope, climbed through the rubble, and made his way to the fallen firefighter. All around him, he heard huge crashes as pieces of concrete continued to fall from the upper levels.

"How you doing," Fox said when he got to Shea.

"Well, my leg's all screwed up," Shea said.

The plan had been to secure the rope around Shea and pull him to the top of the crater. But Fox now realized that was impossible. The retaining rods sticking out from the crater's edge would block any attempt to get the injured firefighter over the top.

There was no Plan B. And now the cars near Fox and Shea were beginning to explode, and debris kept falling. Water again was falling on them, this time from FDNY hoses trying to extinguish the car fires. The firefighters on the hose lines had no idea that Fox and Shea were in the crater. Communications between units was sporadic at best all day. "I don't know what we're gonna do," Fox said.

While Fox was attending to Shea, Runfola and O'Donnell spotted an injured civilian who was sprawled on what looked like a refrigerator perched perilously close to the crater's edge. Runfola and O'Donnell crawled over to the victim, dragged him to safety, and brought him upstairs.

After about five minutes, Fox caught a glimpse of a flashlight beam penetrating the darkness. Rescue 5's John Tighe had found a ramp leading down into the crater. Tighe had been a medic in Vietnam, and he cut off Shea's boot to examine his injuries. He called Staines on his handy-talkie—some radio communication was working—to report that the missing firefighter had been found, and that he would need a special stretcher and portable ladders to evacuate him. Before long, there were fifty firefighters in the hole, helping to get Kevin Shea to a hospital.

Once he got back to the top of the crater, John Fox sat on what remained of a garage ramp. He was wet, he was cold, he had taken a lot of smoke, and he was exhausted. Then he made his way back to street level. He found the rest of Squad 1—Joe O'Donnell, Peter Runfola, Jimmy Brogan, Ed Stoebe, and Willie Walker—and he shook hands with each one of them.

The job hardly was finished. Members of Rescue 5 continued to operate in the garage levels, searching cars for possible victims. When they found cars so demolished that entry was impossible, they listened for moaning or cries for help, and if they heard none, they moved on, crawling to the next car. After two hours, Rescue 5 returned to the street and was ordered to help another chief with evacuations. When they reported, the chief told them to stand fast. He had no assignment for them.

Finally, they were told to go home. They had done enough.

Bill Bresnan was carrying out car searches in another part of the garage. He returned to the street after four hours, expecting relief. Instead, he was sent to the thirty-seventh floor to assist a pregnant woman. Hours later, Bresnan was interviewed on television about the day's horror. The civilian he had helped rescue in the garage saw the broadcast from his hospital bed and tracked him down to say thanks.

Many hours after the explosion, after nearly 50,000 people had been evacuated from the two office towers, New York's firefighters learned that they had fought a front-line battle against international terrorism. Islamic militants, inspired in part by the anti-American rhetoric of a blind Egyptian cleric in Jersey City named Omar Abdel Rahman, had set out to topple the towers and kill thousands. They succeeded in killing six civilians, a figure the firefighters in and around the bomb crater considered miraculously low. The destruction they saw was so devastating they assumed that many more people were dead. Bill Bresnan had wondered how the Department would handle all the casualties.

For his courage in going to the aid of a fallen brother, Lieutenant John Fox won the James Gordon Bennett Medal. Rescue Co. 5 was among several companies that won a unit citation for its work at the World Trade Center. Captain Edmund Staines had the pleasure of writing citations for both Rescue 5, where he happened to be covering officer the day of the bombing, and for Fox, because Staines was Fox's captain at Rescue Co. 1.

Looking back on the bombing almost a decade later, Staines called it a "very telling moment in Fire Department history. . . . You think you're the best Fire Department in the world, and then you realize how much you can be out of control," he said. "Not that we were doing crazy things, but that we didn't have control. Thank God for our training and dedication, because that's what got us through it." When Staines filed an incident report analyzing Rescue Co. 5's actions at the Trade Center, he took special note of the communications problems his company and others had as they tried to retain some element of control, writing: "[T]he number of messages [and] the cutting in on messages. . . were innumerable, so as to render the whole system extremely flawed. . . almost to the point where accuracy had to be . . . doubted."

For the Fire Department, the bombing of the Twin Towers was less a firefighting job than it was a rescue mission—the most-successful rescue mission it had ever attempted. In that sense, it spoke to the Department's evolving role as a first responder to emergencies, whether or not they involved fire. Of course, the Department had always responded to any alarm, and traditionally New York's firefighters did what they could in nonfire emergencies, whether somebody required first aid or simply had locked himself out of his home. In the social chaos of the 1960s and '70s, New Yorkers learned that the quickest way to summon medical assistance was not by calling for an ambulance but by calling the Fire Department. The number of annual emergency responses—everything from car accidents to heart attacks—increased from 16,868 in 1960 to 72,243 by 1979 and to 143,489 by 1993.

Meanwhile, in the early nineties the annual number of fires continued its astonishing decline, decreasing to just over 60,000 in the late nineties, about the same number as in 1960. All the while, the number of firefighters held steady at about 11,000, several hundred more than the Department had when it battled 153,000 fires in 1976.

With their training in CPR and first aid, their rescue equipment, their specialized units, and their reduced fire work load, New York's firefighters seemed to be an underutilized asset, at least to the city's elected leaders and budget watchdogs. An editorial in the *New York Times* captured the argument of those who sought to redefine the FDNY's mission. "The Fire Department's basic function is, of course, putting out fires, but there is a lot of idle time," the *Times* wrote. "To make use of it, the department is already training fire fighters to give emergency treatment before the E.M.S. paramedics arrive. On average, fire engines can get there first, partly because city traffic gives way faster to big red fire trucks with menacing horns."

Throughout the country in the mid–1990s, public policy technocrats and a new generation of young political leaders were promising to reinvent government. By merging government agencies, eliminating duplicate services, streamlining paperwork, and, of course, promising to root

So Others
Might Live

· · ·

293

out patronage, these proudly postpartisan, nonideological Democrats and Republicans pledged to deliver better government at lower costs to the taxpayer. Rudolph Giuliani, a Democrat turned Republican, spoke the language of government reinvention as a candidate for mayor in 1993. He condemned not government itself—as Republicans since Ronald Reagan had often done—but inefficient, unnecessary, or corrupt delivery of services. When he took office in 1994, the city was suffering through its worst fiscal crisis since the mid–1970s. Giuliani, a veteran prosecutor and self-styled reformer who owed his election to very few of the city's traditional interest groups, made it clear that he sought nothing less than the reinvention of New York's government.

Early in his first term Giuliani proposed merging the city's Emergency Medical Service, which operated ambulances attached to city-run hospitals, with the Fire Department. Many other large cities had combined the two services years earlier, but New York's firefighters and paramedics had successfully fought off halfhearted talk about combining the nation's largest Fire Department with the nation's largest corps of EMS technicians. The Fire Department's rescue and emergency work already had led to a turf war with the Police Department's Emergency Services Unit that recalled the bitter fire company rivalries of the 1840s. Several ugly scenes between firefighters and cops in the early 1990s inspired memories of Bill Tweed's days—ESU cops stole a Fire Department banner at a NYPD-FDNY hockey match, photographed themselves setting it ablaze, and used the picture as a Christmas card. Tensions culminated in the arrest of a firefighter during a dispute with police over jurisdiction at an auto accident.

From both a technical and cultural point of view, EMS and the Fire Department were not the obvious match that budget makers envisioned. EMS workers earned less money than firefighters and were predominately minorities and women. They were more accustomed to dealing with police officers, their computer system was linked with the Police Department's, and they were dispatched to emergencies by the NYPD's 911 operators. Among the three emergency-response agencies—police, fire, and medical—the FDNY was considered the out-

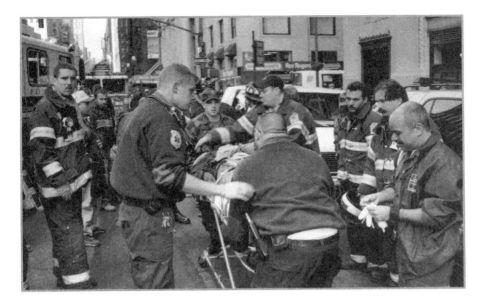

Throughout the
1990s, as fire
service
declined, fire-
fighters became
first responders
to an array of
emergencies.

sider, with its antiquated communications (firehouse fax machines,
never mind computer terminals, were rare until the mid–1990s) and its
historic embrace of the Irish motto "Ourselves alone."

The strong-willed Giuliani, however, had the advantage of running
City Hall at a time when New Yorkers were growing weary with old
arrangements and inefficient government. Known for years as the capital of the American welfare state, New York in the early 1990s was
impatient with old bromides and skeptical of those who insisted on the
status quo. Giuliani seized on the public's mood by proposing a series of
previously unthinkable reforms and efficiencies, including the merger of
the city's three police departments—the NYPD, the Transit Authority
Police, and the Housing Authority Police—and, in 1995, the Fire
Department's takeover of the EMS. Fire Commissioner Howard Safir
strongly supported the plan, promising that the result would be faster
response time to medical emergencies and lower administrative costs—
a formula taken directly from the reinventing government playbook.
Safir moved quickly to prepare the Department for a new mission;
among other steps he ordered Hurst tools, used to extricate trapped
passengers from autos (they are popularly known as "the jaws of life"),
for every ladder company.

In the midst of a debate that went to the heart of the FDNY's changing role, terrorism struck again. A bomb exploded in a federal office building in Oklahoma City in May 1995, killing 169 people. The Department's chief of operations, Ray Downey—by now known to the rank and file as "God"—swiftly put together a contingent of FDNY volunteers to fly to the site and assist in the rescue and recovery effort. The mission furthered the Department's reputation not just as a superior firefighting force, but as a highly trained corps of life-savers as well.

It took a year of wrangling among City Hall, the City Council, the unions, and the state Legislature, but on March 27, 1996, Daniel Nigro, a veteran firefighter and son of an FDNY captain, was sworn in as the Fire Department's chief of its newly affiliated Emergency Medical Service. The department's familiar FDNY brand was stamped on all city-run ambulances, the city's paramedics now reported to a fire chief, and firefighters received training as certified first responders, capable of using such life-saving equipment as defibrillators.

In the new, merged world of fire, emergency, and medical services, engine companies took over some of the work that had been the province of ladder companies, such as water leaks and electrical emergencies. And engine companies generally were first on the scene at medical emergencies, arriving ahead of the ambulance and given the task of stabilizing patients and victims. The informal arrangement of calling firefighters for all kinds of help was institutionalized.

Diminished fire service clearly did not mean diminished risk when firefighters entered burning buildings. Though the Giuliani administration was replacing the firefighters' traditional turnout coat and high rubber boots with more fire-resistant outerwear, even the most up-to-date protection couldn't guarantee safety from conditions such as the unforeseen backdraft, the sudden flashover, and the building collapse, which remained the FDNY's deadliest enemies. These enemies were always lying in wait—even when fires seemed routine.

Early in the evening of March 28, 1993, it looked as though a blaze in a first-floor apartment on Watt Street in the West Village had been vanquished. Firefighters allowed at least one resident of the three-story brick building to go back inside his apartment to retrieve some clothes.

Captain John Drennan of Ladder Co. 5 and two firefighters, James Young and Christopher Siedenburg, made their way up a stairway to a second-floor apartment to make sure no civilians were trapped inside. The apartment door was locked, and the team was preparing to force its way inside when the whole stairwell exploded in flames. Superheated gases and smoke had risen from the fire apartment into the staircase, and fed there by oxygen, they burst into a fireball called a flashover.

Firefighter Young was incinerated. He was thirty-one years old, one of three firefighting brothers. After beating back the flames, Young's comrades found him burned to the bone. They wrapped his remains in a blanket, placed his helmet on the blanket, and carried him out to a rainy Manhattan night. Firefighter Siedenburg and Captain Drennan both were burned terribly and were still conscious when firefighters found them. They were taken to the famous burn unit at New York Hospital–Cornell Medical Center, but Siedenburg died the next day. He was twenty-five.

Though burned over more than 50 percent of his body, Drennan held on. The forty-nine-year-old captain was a popular officer, and a well-known coach and athlete in his home borough of Staten Island. Nearly twenty years earlier, Drennan had coached Tottenville High School's football team to the borough's championship, defeating the perennial champion Monsignor Farrell High School, Firefighter Siedenburg's alma mater.

He hung on for a week, then two, then three, and then a month. His wife, Vina, the mother of their four children, maintained a vigil by his bedside. She spoke to him as he lay unconscious, his body grievously wounded. A columnist for the *New York Daily News,* Michael Daly, chronicled the Drennans' ordeal in a series of heart-rending columns that made this tragedy all the more poignant. After suffering for forty days, Captain John Drennan died on May 7, 1994.

Vina Drennan buried her husband and then became a public crusader for improved fire safety. After two high-rise fires within days of each other in December 1999 killed three firefighters and four civilians, she led a campaign to require automatic sprinklers in all existing high-rise buildings. As the widow of an FDNY hero, Mrs. Drennan had the instant respect of the city's politicians, and she used the power of her grief and suffering to shame the city's real estate developers who insisted that the proposal was too expensive. She and her husband's union, the Uniformed Fire Officers Association, threw their weight behind a City Council bill calling for sprinklers and a public address system in all high-rise residential buildings, regardless of when they were built. Speaking at a City Council hearing, she spoke directly to the bill's opponents in the real estate industry: "My husband lived for forty days. . . in a burn unit. I challenge anyone who says, 'We cannot afford a sprinkler system law' to visit the burn unit." To the Council members, she said: "I hope you have the courage to stand up to the forces that will block you."

Drennan and her allies were able to show that the city lagged behind other major urban areas in sprinkler enforcement, and eventually the city and the real estate industry agreed on a compromise requiring sprinklers in new high-rise residential buildings. The shock was that such a requirement was not already in place.

THROUGH THE last years of the twentieth century, as public and private employers learned to embrace the notion of workplace diversity and to celebrate the new civic religion of multiculturalism, the Fire Department of New York continued to resemble the last outpost of the middle-class white male. The percentage of African American and Latino firefighters seemed stuck between 6 and 8 percent, compared with 40 percent in San Francisco, 28 percent in Chicago, and 25 percent in Philadelphia. Lower still was the percentage of women—not much more than three dozen of the FDNY's eleven thousand members.

As president of the Vulcan Society in 2002, Captain Paul Washington, the son of a firefighter, said he usually was the only African American in his firehouse, and that was the typical black firehouse experience. When conversation in the kitchen turned to entry criteria used by the Department, white firefighters from the suburbs cited the firefighter's test as the best and only standard, whereas Washington and other blacks called the test's validity into question and talked about the gap between inner-city schools and suburban school districts. "You're not going to get much agreement" between black and white firefighters on the topic, Washington said. Still, he conceded that race relations clearly had improved since the days of the black bed.

For women, too, conditions were better, even if the number of woman firefighters remained minuscule. Resentment of women in the Department had in many cases given way to acceptance, some of it grudging and some of it sincere. Rochelle Jones, who had joined the Department in 1982, was promoted to lieutenant in 1994, thus becoming the first woman fire officer in FDNY history. She later became the first woman captain, and, if the most recent civil service test results are any indication, she very likely will become the first woman battalion chief.

As Jones was earning her first promotion, a young woman from Queens named Susan Blake reported to Engine Co. 58 for her first day as a firefighter. A graduate of Queens College with a degree in psychology, she had taken the firefighter's exam in 1989. Though she scored 95 on the physical portion, she was angry with herself for not getting a perfect score. While waiting for her number to be called on the appointment list, she worked on Wall Street and went back to graduate school.

Blake didn't come from a family of firefighters; her four brothers had become a doctor, a lawyer, a minister, and a teacher. The idea of becoming a firefighter had come up in a casual conversation. She was working as a trainer at a health club, and two male firefighter friends told her that if anybody, male or female, could pass the Fire Department physical, she could. They gave her an application, and she decided to try it. And they were right.

At Engine Co. 58, she found no cruel ostracism, no depraved high jinks, no leering innuendo. More than a decade had passed since Brenda Berkman walked into a firehouse for the first time, and now younger men in the bunkrooms and firehouse kitchens were used to seeing women in nontraditional careers. She went to her first fire on her second night on the job—a standard apartment fire in a high-rise housing project. With 60 pounds of equipment on her back—she weighed

125—she walked up ten stories to the fire. Even after the rigors of pro-bie school, she was amazed at how little she could see once inside the smoky apartment.

When it was over, when she helped put out the fire and then climbed back down the stairs and got back on the rig, she had just one thought: "Oh my God, this job is great!"

She was a New York City firefighter.

CHAPTER TWELVE

SEPTEMBER 11, 2001

NOTHING COULD HAVE PREPARED the Fire Department of New York for September 11, 2001.

There was nothing in FDNY's operations manual about airplanes flying into a pair of skyscrapers that held the population of a small city. There was nothing in the Sunday-morning drills with tower ladders and water appliances that anticipated two fireballs hundreds of feet above Manhattan's financial district. There were no questions on the lieutenant's test about the effects of thousands of gallons of burning jet fuel on the supporting beams of two of the world's largest buildings. There was no rehearsal in probie school for climbing forty, fifty, sixty, or seventy stories with hoses and equipment. When the alarm came in from Manhattan Box 8087 at 8:47 that morning, the firefighters of New York might as well have been holed up along the Maginot Line in May 1940, studying the tactics of trench warfare while a madman and his tanks outflanked them.

And yet, except for its flawed radios, the Fire Department of New York was well prepared for September 11, 2001. Years of service in the nation's busiest Fire Department had taught New York's firefighters to suppress their fear of flames and smoke. Drilling and training meant that they knew their duties, their equipment, and their capabilities. Company cohesion provided some semblance of order amid chaos. And the bonds of the firehouse kitchen assured them that even if the job were in hell itself, they would not work alone.

As pumpers and trucks and rescue rigs and chiefs' cars raced downtown or through tunnels and bridges from the outer boroughs, as off-duty firefighters commandeered buses or drove their own cars to the mortally wounded World Trade Center, they already knew the only piece of information they needed to know. Thousands of people were inside those smoking, burning towers, and they had to get out, quickly. New York's firefighters would go inside and get them. Everything else was just a detail to be worked out by the chiefs in their white helmets.

The mood in the firehouse kitchens before Box 8087 changed the world was no different than it might have been on a September morning in 1970, or 1930, or 1870. Authority figures were reviled over morning coffee and cigarettes; probies absorbed the time-honored lesson that outsiders—mayors, judges, even commissioners—couldn't be trusted to do right by the rank and file. They said all the right things at funerals, but those flowery tributes seemed hollow when committee work was handed out in the morning and some hero was given the assignment of cleaning the firehouse toilet bowls.

They were grumbling about one of their own who now wore a jacket and tie and stood by the mayor's side at big fires. Tom Von Essen, a veteran of Truck Co. 42 during the war years in the South Bronx, had been raised from firefighter first grade to the post of fire commissioner without first passing through the officers' ranks. But this story of swift and unprecedented promotion was not so simple, for on the day Von Essen was named commissioner, he was serving as president of the Uniformed Firefighters Association, the proud tormentor of mayors and commissioners. In the firehouse kitchen, Von Essen's overnight transformation from union leader to commissioner was seen as a betrayal of the firefighters' ethic; worse, it seemed like Von Essen's reward for not fighting Giuliani's merger of the Fire Department with Emergency Medical Services.

A veteran of the Bronx during the war years, Tom Von Essen, left, made the leap from president of the Uniformed Firefighters Association to Fire Commissioner under Mayor Giuliani, right.

The kitchen wouldn't be the kitchen without complaints and finely woven conspiracy theories. Not everybody was pleased with the union leadership's recent acceptance of a new contract and a 10 percent raise. First-grade firefighters were making about $60,000 a year, but, as many veterans were quick to point out, it took five years, as opposed to the old standard of three years, to become a first-grade firefighter. And the emergency runs still annoyed the veterans, most of whom dated their service back to the war years—as they often reminded probies. The firehouse elders hadn't taken the fireman's test so they could check the pulse of some old man with chest pains. They'd taken the test so they could fight fires.

The Department on this morning still was grieving for three brothers—Harry Ford, Brian Fahey, and John Downing—killed on Father's Day. They left behind eight children.

Still, as always, the reasons for the moaning and grumbling were nothing compared with the job's satisfactions. And on the morning of September 11, 2001, they were as innumerable as ever. The annual total of civilian deaths was plunging toward double figures, a historic achievement. The first year of the new century brought great promise, with the lowest death total—107—since 1946. Firefighter deaths were down, too: 22 had died in the 1990s, compared to more than 100 during the relatively tranquil 1950s. In the Department's annual report for 2000, Chief of Department Peter Ganci, Jr., had noted that New York's firefighters were "enjoying an almost unprecedented approval rating from the general public." The chief wasn't surprised. "We always respond," Ganci wrote. "Wherever needed, we go."

As a newly promoted officer, Lieutenant Bob Bohack moved around a lot, covering for other lieutenants who were out sick, injured, or on vacation. On the morning of September 11, Bohack was filling in for a lieutenant in Engine Co. 5 on East Fourteenth Street. He left his home, wife, and four young kids on Long Island early that morning so he could be at work at eight o'clock—an hour before he was due.

The older firefighters knew Bohack's name, though not because he was a particularly famous young lieutenant. His family had founded and run the Bohack's supermarket chain in and around the city until the stores closed for good in 1977. Bohack was sixteen years old at the time. He would not have the option of going into the family business. He had no blood connection to the Fire Department when he was growing up in the Woodhaven section of Queens, but he needed none: The sight and sounds of those FDNY rigs racing through the streets of Queens made any recruitment pep talk from an uncle or cousin unnecessary. Bohack tinkered briefly with the idea of being a doctor, but medicine would require years of school, and that was not nearly as exciting as the prospect of riding a red fire engine.

Bohack became a firefighter in 1986, at the age of twenty-five, and was assigned to Engine Co. 249 in the Crown Heights section of Brooklyn. It was a good assignment—not because it was slow and safe, but because it was busy. Fires still burned in the neighborhood's old apartment buildings, and young firefighters in a company like Engine 249 learned quickly what it took to be a member of the FDNY.

After he made lieutenant on January 1, 2000, he bounced from assignment to assignment, as all new lieutenants do. His duty at Engine Co. 5 in the late summer of 2001 offered him a rare glimpse of nearly every layer of Manhattan society, from the elegant townhouses surrounding Gramercy Park to the middle-class apartment complex of Stuyvesant Town–Peter Cooper Village to the ever-crowded tenements of the Lower East Side.

The first run of September 11 was a false alarm. The alarm came in from the Gramercy Park neighborhood, home to the city's only privately maintained park. While Bohack and Engine Co. 5 went through their false-alarm routine, checking to make sure there really was no fire in the vicinity, they heard a call over their radios from Battalion 1 in lower Manhattan to the FDNY's dispatcher: A plane had just hit the World Trade Center.

In his office in Division 1 headquarters on Lafayette Street in SoHo, Deputy Chief Pete Hayden heard the unfamiliar but unmistakable roar of a jetliner. He scrambled to a window, but saw nothing. Then came the explosion. "There's a plane crash somewhere," Hayden told his aide. Division 1 was made up of Manhattan's battalions south of midtown; Hayden, as the division's commander, would be in charge of organizing the FDNY's response on the ground and would be in command until a higher-ranking chief, Joe Callan, arrived. As Hayden prepared to turn out, he heard the same radio transmission as Bohack and Engine Co. 5: A plane had hit the World Trade Center. The First Battalion transmitted a third alarm while Hayden raced downtown. The attack took place at a time when many firehouses in the city had double their usual complement—firefighters on the overnight tour were getting ready to go home, and the day tour was on hand to relieve them as of nine o'clock. When the alarm came in, both tours jumped on the rigs.

Pete Hayden was one of the Department's most popular chiefs, a soft-spoken, matter-of-fact officer who preferred firefighting to administrative work. He joined the Department at the beginning of the war years, in 1968, and earned his reputation as a firefighter's firefighter as a member of Rescue Co. 2 in the battles of central Brooklyn during the 1970s. In his thirty-two years on the job, he had experienced nothing like the scene he was heading toward, but he knew the drill. He'd get to the command post, establish whether the building's infrastructure—the elevators, the standpipe system, the internal communications—was working, and then deploy units upstairs.

Smoke was pouring from the horrific hole in 1 World Trade Center when he arrived. Debris fell from the gash, and the sidewalk outside the lobby was littered with shards of glass from blown-out windows. Inside, office workers with ghastly burns from jet fuel were screaming for help. Hayden took over a command post already set up by the chief of Battalion 1, Joseph Pfiefer, the first chief on the scene. A podium with the FDNY logo on it had been placed in front of the building's long security desk, decorated with drooping greenery, and underneath a half-circle walkway one floor above. Hayden quickly learned that he could count on very little help from the building's equipment, including the elevators—they were not working. All the while, dispatchers were trans-mitting pleas for help called in from civilians trapped throughout the building, in offices and in the elevators.

Company after company filed into the lobby and lined up in front of the command post, awaiting orders. Ladder companies passed by carry-ing long hooks and huge axes; with their weapons, the protective hoods they wore under their helmets, and their long coats they looked like medieval warriors gathering on some contested field that time has since forgotten.

Bob Bohack and Engine Co. 5 reported for duty within ten minutes of the alarm; they were dispatched to the seventy-ninth floor and told to bring their equipment. They would fight the fire upstairs, if they could. They strapped on their oxygen tanks, threw a tightly bound section of hose over their shoulders, and trudged toward the A stairwell. Each fire-fighter was carrying about sixty pounds of equipment. To reach their assignment, they would be climbing up the stairs for at least an hour.

As they began their long walk up, civilians were streaming down, and several of them told Bohack and his men that they had little to fear. "I was here for the bomb in '93," said one civilian. "This is nothing." It seemed true—the building still had power, the stairwell lights were on, and there was very little smoke. Maybe this wouldn't be so bad. Bohack and his company moved on, and up.

Not long after Engine Co. 5 set out for the stairwell, the chiefs at the command post realized that the fireball in the sky was too intense to be extinguished. The FDNY's primary mission would be search, rescue, and evacuate. Hayden now told officers and their companies to leave their hoses behind when they were sent upstairs. Some held on to them anyway. They were like security blankets.

More distress calls came over the radio. There were dozens of reports of civilians trapped in elevators, of civilians in wheelchairs unable to use the stairs, of burned civilians above the fire floors pleading desperately for help. Hayden began handing out assignments based on specific distress calls, and then assigned other officers and companies to search a specific series of floors. The officers then took their companies up one of the building's several stairwells to the upper stories. Another officer tried to keep track of the assignments using a suitcase-like board. But some companies didn't stop and wait for orders. They went on ahead. Other companies had firefighters from both the day and night tour; still others rode with off-duty firefighters from other companies. Nobody really knew exactly how many firefighters were in the building.

In these early minutes of September 11, the officers gathered around the command post calmly talked over their assignments and their assessment of what was happening almost a quarter mile above them. Hayden was joined by the Department's top civilian and uniformed brass: Commissioner Von Essen, Chief of Department Peter Ganci, First Deputy Commissioner Bill Feehan, and, of course, God himself— Ray Downey, head of FDNY Special Operations. All around them were the sounds of chaos: incessant and garbled transmissions from the handy-talkies, sirens from arriving rigs, police vehicles and ambulances, and the occasional crash of falling debris. But, as video shot by a French film crew inside the lobby would later show, there was no panic at the command post, no sense that the situation was beyond the FDNY's control. As far as the firefighters knew, they were fighting a high-rise fire. It was the biggest high-rise fire they had ever fought, but it was a fire nevertheless. They were not actually suppressing the flames—that would have to come later, after the civilians were evacuated—but they were fighting the products of fire: panic, confusion, fear.

As chief of department, Peter Ganci, Jr. led his firefighters into battle on September 11, 2001, and was among the 343 members of the FDNY who died at the World Trade Center.

Then the second plane hit. Any doubts about what the FDNY was facing on this day were erased. This was not a twenty-first-century version of the plane that struck the Empire State Building in 1945. This was not an inexplicable accident. This was war, and the firefighters of New York, along with their colleagues in the New York Police Department, the Port Authority Police Department, and the Emergency Medical Services, were on the front lines.

Handy-talkies crackled with the cry of "Mayday! Mayday!" A firefighter near the command post said the south tower had just been hit. Huge chunks of debris from the second attack fell outside the lobby doors. Civilians on the walkway above the command post started running for doors, some hunched over as they reflexively covered their heads.

The conversations at the command post took on greater urgency. "Stay together, stay together," one chief told a ladder company. "You got a long way to go." Von Essen, Feehan, Ganci, and Downey left Hayden in the north tower while other officers set up a command post in the south tower. The department's chaplain, Father Mychal Judge, paced the lobby by himself, his arms and hands behind his back, his lips mouthing quiet prayers. Twenty-four hours earlier, the popular Franciscan had been celebrating Mass on the apparatus floor of Engine Co. 73 and Ladder Co. 42 in the South Bronx. "You get on the rig and. . . you have no idea what God's calling you to do," he had said in his homily.

Then the bodies started falling. Above the fire, just above where Bob Bohack and Engine Co. 5 were heading, men and women were leaping from windows eighty, ninety, or a hundred stories up. And they were landing with sickening crashes on the cement outside, or on the hoods and roofs of emergency vehicles, or blasting through windshields. Firefighters turned their heads in the direction of the crashes, but not for long. As minutes went by, the terrible sounds of lives ending became part of the background noise of hell.

Bohack and Engine Co. 5 took a short break on the thirteenth floor. The staircase was wide enough for two people to pass each other with ease, but it still was tough going. Through it all, the civilians heading for the exits remained surprisingly calm. Bohack thought they looked like they were simply heading downstairs for a quick bite to eat. Then again, as they reminded the firefighters, many of them had been through this routine before.

The calm belied the rumors that were sweeping the staircases, most of them spread by civilians who had called friends or relatives before leaving their offices. They told Bohack that the second tower had been hit not by an airplane but by a missile. Other people said they heard that thirteen planes were unaccounted for and were headed for New York.

Still, Engine Co. 5 had its assignment. After their rest, Bohack and his company of strangers—as a covering lieutenant who floated from firehouse to firehouse, Bohack hardly knew the men he was leading up the staircase—saddled up and resumed their climb. As they reached the nineteenth floor, Engine 5's Derek Brogan told Bohack he had pain in his chest. They rested for about ten minutes, and Brogan felt better. They started climbing again. But they were down one man. The company's youngest member, Manny Delvalle, was a faster climber than the rest of the company, and somewhere early in the climb he had become separated from Bohack and the others. Now, he was nowhere to be found.

Four stories later, on the twenty-third floor, Brogan said he had pain shooting down his arms, a classic symptom of a heart attack. "That's it,"

Bohack said. "You're done." They moved out of the staircase, and ran into two Port Authority police officers who gave Brogan some oxygen. A firefighter from another company who was a trained nurse examined Brogan and said that he didn't think it was a heart attack, although he couldn't rule it out.

Lieutenant Bob Bohack faced the dilemma of his career. He had his orders: He was to help extinguish the fire on the seventy-ninth floor. But those orders were given before he heard rumors of missiles, of more airplanes heading for New York. Communications were horrendous. One of his firefighters was missing, and another was having chest pains.

And he still had more than fifty floors to climb.

LIEUTENANT CHUCK MARGIOTTA was driving to his home on Staten Island after working an overnight mutual in Brooklyn when he heard about the attacks downtown. He got off a highway and drove to the nearest firehouse, the quarters of Rescue Co. 5 on Clove Road, less than five minutes from the Verrazano Narrows Bridge. Rescue 5 needed no introduction to mayhem at the World Trade Center, having played so valiant a role in the search for and rescue of Kevin Shea after the bombing in 1993.

The company was now under the command of Captain Louis Modafferi, one of the men who had crawled his way through the smoke and chaos in the World Trade Center garage that afternoon. Modafferi, a forty-five-year-old married father of three, was off duty on September 11, but he drove to his firehouse when he heard about the attacks.

Margiotta climbed aboard the rig as it left quarters for its second trip to the Twin Towers in less than a decade. In the small town that is Staten Island, population 450,000, Margiotta was a well-known character. In high school he had played football for Monsignor Farrell, and he went on to play for Brown University and was on the team that won the Ivy League championship in 1976. He weighed in at 240 pounds and wore fierce-looking tattoos—although even a picture of Winnie the Pooh would look fierce on Chuck Margiotta—and he was a hunter. He also had double-majored in English and sociology at Brown; was a passionate gardener; had a side job as a teacher; coached children's soccer and basketball; and was married with two kids.

As Rescue Co. 5 raced across the Verrazano Bridge into Brooklyn, Margiotta reached for his cell phone and called his mother. From the bridge he had a clear view of lower Manhattan, now covered in black smoke, and of the mutilated towers. "It's bad," he told her.

John Fox, one of the heroes of the World Trade Center bombing in 1993 and now a battalion chief, had planned to spend the morning taking care of some paperwork for headquarters. His stroll to his neighborhood firehouse, the quarters of Engine Co. 254 in the Marine Park section of Brooklyn, became a sprint when he saw huge clouds of smoke to the west. He didn't know what was going on until he reached the firehouse doors and saw a knot of firefighters standing by the house watch desk, eyes glued to the television.

"What's going on here?" Fox asked.

"Chief, a plane just hit the Trade Center," somebody said. Fox joined the group in front of the television, and thought, "I'm going to work today." His next thought was about his teenage son, who was in high school and who would be expecting his father to be home in the afternoon.

Fox climbed up to the firehouse roof, where he could see downtown Manhattan and the smoke pouring from 1 World Trade Center. He climbed back down and heard somebody yell, "Another one!" Until now, Fox assumed he was watching a terrible accident. Now he knew better. An announcement came over the firehouse public address system: "All off-duty members are ordered to report to work." Fox didn't need to be told.

He started walking, quickly, back down Avenue U to his house to get his gear. He passed a bar that was pouring drinks at 9:15 in the morning. The door was open, and Fox saw a familiar face inside. He walked in and saw a couple of men from the neighborhood drinking and watching the towers on television. Fox stood at the bar for a minute, then said, "I'm on my way to work."

"Be careful," one of the drinkers said. Fox nodded and left.

Fox kept his gear in the trunk of his car, because he was a covering chief who moved from assignment to assignment. He grabbed his stuff, went into the house, and got dressed. But before he did anything else, he had to figure out what to do about his son. He called his mother, who lived on Staten Island and sometimes took the bus over to Brooklyn to watch her grandson when her son worked a night tour.

"Ma, you know what's going on?" Fox said. She did, of course.

"Well, I've got to go to work." He asked her if she could help, but she said was trapped on the island. The bridges were closed. So Fox called his neighbors around the corner, Eddie Hughes, a firefighter in Engine Co. 281, and his wife, Eileen. Fox left a message asking Eileen Hughes to look after young John. He didn't say it, but he assumed he wouldn't be home for days.

OFFICERS IN the lobby of 1 World Trade Center were discovering, if they didn't know it already, that their radios were useless. Transmissions were garbled, messages were getting cut off by other messages, and chiefs who tried to summon companies in the stairwells received no reply. They paced the lobby with their handy-talkies, never shouting, but repeating themselves over and over again, calling battalions by number. They pressed the radio to their ears, hoping for a response. Often, there was only static or garble. They shook their heads. Eight years earlier, Captain Ed Staines complained about communications problems in his incident report of the World Trade Center bombing.

Hayden and the other chiefs talked about the possibility of a collapse. The intense heat, they knew, was certain to melt steel supports, which very likely would lead to a partial collapse of the upper floors. But they still had time, they thought, and thousands of civilians still were streaming down stairwells. The FDNY had to get them out. That, the chiefs agreed, was the first priority.

. . .

ON THE twenty-third floor of the north tower, Bob Bohack reviewed his options, which were limited: He could continue to up the stairs and maybe find his missing man, the young and eager Manny Delvalle, or he could reverse course to get Derek Brogan down to an ambulance at ground level. If they kept going up, would the standpipe equipment they'd need to fight the fire be working? Probably not. Meanwhile, he kept hearing stories about missiles, about more planes heading for New York. "I don't like this," he said. "We've got a guy with chest pains, we're getting hit with missiles, there's twenty floors of fire in this building, there's jet fuel burning. Let's get the hell out of here. This is a losing battle."

Bohack and Engine Co. 5 picked up their equipment and headed for the closest stairs, the C staircase, instead of the A staircase which they had climbed. The C staircase faced the south tower, and as they began filing downstairs, they felt a huge rumble. "We've got to get out of here now," Bohack said. "Right now." The stairs were not entirely clear, but they were much less crowded than an hour before. As Engine Co. 5 raced down the stairs, the building's emergency lights went out, and smoke and debris filled the stairwell. They had no idea that the south tower had just collapsed, but they knew they had to get out to the street.

They were almost there. Then, when they were down to the third floor, piles of debris blocked their path. "Stay here," Bohack told his men. "I'll look for another way out." He found the A staircase, in the core of the building, and called to the firefighters to follow him. Three of them did, but a fourth, Gerry Gorman, was unaccounted for. He had been with them minutes before in the stairwell, but now he was gone. Now two of Lieutenant Bohack's men were missing.

Twenty minutes after they started their descent, the four firefighters of Engine Co. 5 made their way to the north tower command post. Nobody was there, and the lobby was covered with white dust inches thick in some places. "This isn't a good thing," Bohack said. "We've got to get out of here." The others said they had to go back to find Gerry Gorman. Bohack was an outsider in this group—some of them had met him for the first time only hours earlier. The other men knew Gerry Gorman. He didn't. Of course they wanted to save their friend. But

With the skeleton of the World Trade Center in the background, firefighters
begin the grim search for bodies.

Bohack ordered them out. "Look," he said. "I have a bad feeling about this." Flaming pieces of debris were falling outside, and each piece seemed bigger than the last. That was the tip-off—the building was falling apart. "We've got to get out of here," Bohack repeated.

Jimmy Andruzzi wouldn't go. "We have to get Gorman," he said.

"We ain't getting Gorman," Bohack said. "We've got to cut our losses or we're going to get killed." Bohack said he'd wait a minute to see if Gorman would show up.

BEFORE THE south tower fell, the officers at the command post in the north tower had heard a version of the rumors Bohack had heard in the stairway. A civilian in a green helmet and a walkie-talkie had announced, "There's another plane coming." Hayden and the chiefs ordered an evacuation. The catastrophe was now outside the realm of the Fire Department of New York. The city was under attack, and New York's firefighters were in grave peril.

Some companies heard the order over their radios. Others, like Bohack and Engine Co. 5, did not. And those in the south tower never stood a chance. The command post and the lobby shook as the south tower crumbled. The air turned brown, and then black. Firefighters scattered for cover, diving on the floor, running up escalators. Chief Pfiefer got back on his feet and repeated the order to evacuate the north tower. Somebody in the darkness yelled, "Hey, Pete! Pete!" Father Judge was lying at the base of an escalator. He was dead. Pete Hayden and several other firefighters placed the priest on a board and brought him outside, where other rescue workers gently put him in a chair and carried him to the altar of St. Peter's Church, a few blocks away. The chief then searched for another command post near the FDNY staging area on West and Vesey streets.

Inside the blasted north tower lobby, firefighters were covered in pulverized concrete. Flashlights cut ineffective beams through the suffocating brown air. The command post was in ruins and had to be abandoned. Voices over the radio, now suddenly clear, shouted, "Mayday! Mayday!"

Gerry Gorman did not show up in the minute Bob Bohack had allotted. "Okay, let's get out of here," Bohack said. They heard a terrible groaning sound from the building, and that ended the argument. When they got outside, Bohack looked up to watch for falling debris or bodies. He heard somebody say, "Look at that." Bohack saw what looked like a crack in the tower about thirty floors up. "We got to get out of here," he said, again. He and his company of three walked north on West Street about two blocks, where they found their rig and two off-duty firefighters from Engine Co. 5. The two told Bohack that the south tower had collapsed. He had no idea.

Bohack ordered the company to get aboard the rig and drive it north toward Chambers Street, where, he figured, it would be safe if the north tower tipped over sideways. They found a place to pull over just as the north tower imploded. Five minutes had passed since they had given up on Gerry Gorman and evacuated the lobby.

With the collapse of the second tower, the top command structure of the Fire Department of New York ceased to exist. Chief of Department Peter Ganci, Jr., Chief Raymond Downey, and First Deputy Commissioner William Feehan died doing the job they loved, died with the people they loved, the firefighters of the city of New York. Centuries of experience, decades of promise, and the hopes and loves of thousands of parents and spouses and partners and children were gone—buried, crushed, or turned to dust in the unspeakable ruins. Bill Bresnan, just a few weeks into his retirement, was watching the horror on television. The great-grandson of Chief John Bresnan, who had died in a collapse more than a century earlier, burst into tears. "All my buddies," he sobbed, "are dead."

Susan Blake was at a firefighter friend's house in Queens, getting ready to cycle over the Triborough Bridge into her firehouse in Harlem. She, too, was watching as the towers turned to dust. She turned to her friend's daughter. "Jennifer," she said, "a hundred firefighters just died." She had called her firehouse earlier in the morning and had been told that Engine Co. 58 had been sent to the towers and, the last anybody knew, had been deployed in the Marriott Hotel, adjoining the Trade Center complex on West Street. Blake and her friend got on their bikes and rode to work.

Lieutenant Peter Runfola of Squad Co. 61 in the Bronx arrived at Chambers Street about ten minutes after the collapse. He and the squad were delayed getting into Manhattan, first by a hesitant dispatcher, then by traffic—otherwise they very likely would have been in or near the north tower when it fell. He got out of his rig and looked for somebody—a captain, a battalion chief, anybody—who could give him an assignment. As he saw soot-covered firefighters emerging from the smoke, he asked them if they saw any officers, or if they knew where he should go. They looked at him, and kept walking.

Runfola, who had been in the World Trade Center garage with John Fox in 1993, saw nothing but smoke where the towers had once stood. He walked the perimeter, looking for somebody in a white helmet. He found only the profound shock of a battlefield. Finally he found a chief who told him that a company of firefighters was still alive and trapped in the wreckage. "We know they're in a B staircase, but we don't know where they are," the chief said. Runfola and Squad Co. 61 were told to check the B staircase in 5 World Trade Center.

The middle portion of 5 World Trade Center already had collapsed, and was on fire. Runfola and the squad entered the building on the Vesey Street side, found their path blocked, went up a flight of stairs, and then searched for the B staircase. They found it, but there was no company of trapped firefighters. Instead of reporting what they found, or didn't find, and getting out as quickly as they could, Squad 61 searched as much of the building as they could before it completely collapsed. They stumbled on an unconscious police officer lying near the collapse area. He had been struck on the head and suffered broken bones in his arm and leg. They put a mask on him and carried him outside.

The missing firefighters, it turned out, were in the B stairway of the 1 World Trade Center, the north tower. Two hours after the collapse, more than a dozen firefighters and a civilian were brought to safety, the only miracle of September 11.

As Chief John Fox drove from his house to the headquarters of Battalion 33 in Brooklyn, he saw other cars running red lights—cautiously—and crossing double-lines to pass other cars. They were being driven by the off-duty firefighters of South Brooklyn, who were rushing to their local firehouses. He stopped off at the quarters of Engine Co. 321 on Gerritsen Avenue. "What do you wanna do, Chief?" one of the firefighters said. "Get all your men and report to the Battalion Thirty-three," Fox said.

When Fox showed up at battalion headquarters, he was told that he and the other firefighters would be bused not into Manhattan, but to the headquarters of Division 15 in Brownsville. "Ah, Jesus," he said. He called a friend who was a chief in Battalion 43 in Coney Island, hoping he could catch a lift with somebody who was going directly to the disaster, but they were pulling out, and Fox couldn't ask them to wait. "Good luck," Fox said, "and be careful."

There were papers to fill out at the Division 15. The chiefs wanted a record of everybody who was about to be bused into Manhattan. Fox could barely contain himself. Finally, when the paperwork was finished, he was on his way. The bus took him to the Brooklyn side of the Manhattan Bridge, where it slowed to a stop, and Fox and the other firefighters got out. Civilians were streaming over the bridge, many of them covered in soot, many of them sobbing. Fox saw a woman he knew, the wife of a firefighter. "Be careful," she said as she passed. Though Fox and the other firefighters wanted to walk over the bridge, chiefs with more brass than Fox forbade it. The firefighters milled around, plotting to defy the chiefs' orders, until the chiefs stopped them and ordered them back into the buses. Carefully, the buses started moving over the bridge, passing through the mass of shell-shocked, ash-covered civilians, refugees of a new and terrible kind of war.

As they approached the disaster site, Fox spoke on the bus's public address system: "We've got to stick together," he said. "This is going to be bad. Prepare yourselves." Fox thought the firefighters would be wading through thousands of bodies.

They got off the bus on Park Row near City Hall. There were no bodies. Only inches-high piles of dust, remnants of the World Trade Center. Somebody said, "There's eight hundred firemen dead." Fox saw no reason not to believe it.

From her home in the Park Slope section of Brooklyn, Lieutenant Brenda Berkman walked toward the smoke of lower Manhattan. She

An enduring image from September 11: New York's firefighters marching into the ruins.

stopped at a firehouse, borrowed some gear and tools, and joined other off-duty firefighters in a police van for a ride across the Brooklyn Bridge. Berkman anticipated a long climb inside the towers, so she brought regular work shoes rather than the clumsier, heavier bunker boots. As the van crossed the bridge, she realized the towers were gone.

Bob Bohack, Engine Co. 5, and the company's rig escaped the terrible debris cloud after the second tower fell. Bohack and the other men tried without success to call family members to tell them they were safe. He still believed missiles or other airplanes were heading for the city, so he ordered the company into the truck for what he called a reconnaissance mission. All he really wanted was to clear his head. They drove across the width of the island, all the way to South Street, and back again. They found a working fire hydrant on Broadway near Cedar Street, hooked up to it, and relayed water to another engine.

Later on in the afternoon, Engine Co. 5 learned that Gerry Gorman was alive. He didn't realize that Bohack and the others had retreated from the C stairwell and gone down the A stairs. Somehow, Gorman had gotten through the debris that was blocking the C stairs, and he made his way to an exit on the north tower's mezzanine level. When the tower began to fall, he found shelter behind 5 World Trade Center. But Manny Delvalle, who had gone on ahead of Bohack as they were struggling up the stairs, still was missing.

THE QUARTERS of Engine Co. 58 in Harlem had been turned into an assembly point for off-duty firefighters reporting in for assignment. Susan Blake kept herself busy with routine duties as she waited for news about her colleagues downtown. The house got a call at around four o'clock. The firefighters of Engine Co. 58 had been buried in the first collapse but had managed to dig their way out, except for Lieutenant Robert Nagel. He was trapped in a pocket, but his firefighters found him after a few minutes. He was unable to move in the rubble, and he told his men to get some tools from their rig. They left him, but as they did so they unwound a search rope so they could find their way back. Then the second tower fell, and when the firefighters of Engine 58 scrambled back to the collapse area, saw the rope, and retraced their steps, they found only a huge pile of debris. In the firehouse, it was said that Lieutenant Nagel had sent his firefighters away knowing the second tower was about to fall.

With the towers down, the FDNY turned its attention to 7 World Trade Center, a forty-story building on the northern perimeter of the complex. It was empty, and it was just a matter of time before it, too, collapsed. John Fox reported to a new command post on Park Row and was told that he and the men he had brought from Brooklyn would serve as runners. The chiefs now knew they couldn't rely on their radios. They would send their orders by messenger instead.

Fox was given a message to deliver to a deputy chief who was preparing a collapse zone for 7 World Trade Center. "Seven's coming down soon," the chiefs told him. "We want to expand the collapse zone. You deliver this one personally." He found the chief, gave him the message, then walked north to help clear the area. Near the corner of Chambers and Greenwich streets, just two blocks from 7 World Trade Center, Fox saw a flatbed truck parked in the middle of the street. There were about a hundred steel coffins on the truck, and workers were beginning to unload them. "This ain't no good," Fox said to himself. Fox told police officers on the scene that they'd have to move everybody back at least two blocks because 7 World Trade Center was about to come down. Workers put the coffins back on the truck. "Just go north," Fox told the driver. "I don't know where you can go, but just go north." The coffin truck moved out.

Fox heard noises to the south, and he turned toward the burning hulk of 7 World Trade Center. Glass windows began to explode, and then the building fell. Fox searched for victims caught in the debris field, then returned to the command post and waited, and waited, with other firefighters. They saw rigs from New Jersey fire departments getting waved through toward the ruins, which annoyed them. They were happy for the help, but they couldn't help wondering why they were standing around waiting for orders while New Jersey companies were getting in on the action. Finally, Fox and the firefighters with him were told to go home. They would be expected back at their firehouses in the morning.

They found a city bus, empty except for a driver. "We need to go home to Brooklyn," Fox said.

"No problem," said the driver. "Hop in." And the bus brought the firefighters back to their firehouses in Brooklyn. John Fox drove home and went to bed.

Bob Bohack and Engine Co. 5 returned to quarters on Fourteenth Street after 7 World Trade Center fell. There still was no word about Manny Delvalle—his remains would be found weeks later, just before his memorial service. Bohack couldn't help but second-guess himself. If only he had kept Delvalle on a tighter leash. If only. . . But Delvalle was young, and he was eager. And he was needed.

No firefighter had to be told that there was a chance, probably a good chance, that somebody was alive underneath the seven-story ruins of the towers. The rescue of the firefighters and lone civilian from the north tower's B stairway provided all the inspiration they needed. Firefighters continued to pour into lower Manhattan after the collapses to help with the frantic and dangerous work of picking through the smoking rubble, looking for colleagues and civilians alike. Paul Washington, president of the Department's Vulcan Society, arrived at the pile at two o'clock in the afternoon by a city bus he had commandeered. The devastation was overwhelming, but he was certain civilians and colleagues were alive somewhere underneath the horror. They would be pulled to safety, the one or two or dozens or scores who were trapped, through the afternoon and into the night. "Let's get as many as we can," he said.

Brenda Berkman was sifting through rubble near West Street, watching as fires continued to burn in buildings adjacent to the Trade Center site. Earlier in the afternoon, she had been fighting a fire in a building on Church and Liberty streets when word came of 7 World Trade Center's imminent collapse. She was ordered to help prepare a collapse zone. The enormity of the task was horrifying. They had very little equipment, dozens of rigs were smashed, hydrants were useless, and the Department's chain of command was in ruins. And three of Berkman's colleagues in Ladder Co. 12 were missing somewhere in this scene from hell itself.

Piece by piece, bit by bit, working with their hands or whatever tools they could find, firefighters and rescue workers tried to clear the debris and listen for voices they knew they would hear. They worked into the night, and many of them, like Paul Washington, were shocked to hear nothing, to see nobody. Like the citizens of New Amsterdam more than three centuries earlier, they were deployed in two lines: One line passed empty buckets toward the pile; the other line passed debris-filled buckets to a rubble field. They worked through the night, as the agony of September 11 yielded to the tears of September 12. They heard no cries for help.

Nearly three thousand people were dead. Three hundred and forty-three of them were members of the Fire Department of New York.

CHAPTER THIRTEEN

GOING HOME

SOME TIME IN THE LATE MORNING and early afternoon of September 12, firehouses across the city received a long fax from Fire Department headquarters in Brooklyn. John Fox was at the headquarters of the Battalion 58 in Canarsie when his aide brought him the fax. "See this, Chief?" he said.

A heading on the first page read "Confirmed Dead." There were about thirty names, and Fox saw the names of five or six firefighters he knew. Then, under the heading "Missing" were pages and pages, six, seven, eight, nine, ten pages, names by the dozens, by the hundreds. They were listed in alphabetical order, and after a while Fox was afraid to move on to the next letter, afraid of the horrors that awaited on the next page. Was his friend John McAvoy on the list? McAvoy, who would be turning forty-eight years old in just a few days, was last heard from the thirty-first floor of the north tower with the other members of his company, Ladder 3. A married father of two teenagers, McAvoy was renowned for whipping up huge meals for family, friends, and fellow firefighters. Fox looked under "M." McAvoy's name was there.

The same scene unfolded in firehouses around the city, from the slowest, on the southern tip of Staten Island to the busiest, in central Brooklyn. Firefighters with tears in their eyes studied the casualty list, checking first for the names of friends, then trying to grasp the enormity of the loss. Some firehouses didn't need a list to put names to the horror; these were the firehouses where an entire tour—or more—was gone, where firefighters went to their houses on September 12 and learned that everybody who had worked on September 11 was dead or missing.

On September 12, 2001, statistics were transformed into names, and names into faces, and faces into tragedies. As darkness fell hours after the attacks, the city, the nation, and the world had gone to sleep—if they slept at all—knowing that the casualty total would be, in Mayor Rudolph Giuliani's words, "more than we can bear." The next morning truly was unbearable.

The firefighters already knew they had lost Peter Ganci and Bill Feehan and Father Judge. Now they learned that among the missing were Fire Department legends like Chief Ray Downey, who had spent so much time in recent years studying the city's vulnerability to terrorism, and Captain Patrick (Paddy) Brown of Ladder Co. 3, who had a chest filled with medals from his service in the FDNY and in Vietnam, and Captain Terence Hatton of Rescue Co. 1, the son of a retired deputy chief and a father-to-be.

Lieutenant Dennis Mojica of Rescue Co. 1 was missing—he was the Puerto Rican probie who reported for duty with Al Washington in 1973. Rescue 1's Gary Giedel was missing—he was the firefighter who had led Rescue 5 into the World Trade Center garage in 1993 in search of Kevin Shea. Rescue 1 also lost one of the Department's great old buffaloes, sixty-three-year-old Joseph J. Angelini, a forty-year veteran. His son, Joseph Jr., had followed his father's footsteps and was a member of Ladder Co. 4. He, too, was missing.

Lieutenant Chuck Margiotta, who had gotten off a highway on his way home and rode to Manhattan with Rescue Co. 5, was missing; so was everybody else in Rescue 5, including Captain Louis Modaferri. All five rescue companies at the scene had been wiped out; so were entire squad, ladder, and engine companies. The list of missing by company was sickening: Nine missing in Ladder 4; nine missing in Ladder 3; seven in Ladder 15; seven in Engine 33. Of the 341 dead or missing firefighters (the two other missing members of the service were EMS workers), 214 were assigned to ladder, rescue, or squad companies, or served in other specialized emergency units, like special operations or hazardous materials. Ninety-two were from engine companies, and the rest were from headquarters staff or various battalion headquarters. One hundred forty-five were members of the Department's Irish American fraternal group, the Emerald Society. Forty-six lieutenants, twenty-three chiefs, and twenty-one captains—the core of the Fire Department's leaders—were dead or missing.

The sorrow went beyond the numbers to the Department's extended family. For nearly a quarter century, Thomas Celic had kept alive the name of his brother, Marty, in an annual cross-country race in their home borough of Staten Island. Marty Celic died in 1977 in an arson fire on the Lower East Side, falling five stories as he tried to leap into a tower ladder. Tom Celic was a senior vice president for the financial firm of Marsh & McLennan, and on September 11, he had a breakfast meeting in the firm's offices in the north tower. Now, he too was missing.

As always in times of tragedy and heartbreak, New York's firefighters turned their thoughts to those left behind, or those who were waiting, hoping and praying for a miracle under the rubble. From the earliest days of the volunteer department, the city's fire service had made special provisions for spouses and children of fallen firefighters. But no other personal tragedy, no other terrible day, could compare with this one. Retired officers volunteered to help the Department console hundreds of spouses, and hundreds more children.

Exhausted, shocked, angry, and heartsick, the firefighters of New York draped the facades of their firehouses in purple and black bunting, the colors of mourning. But there was no time to dwell on the loss, because there were people buried in the rubble downtown who had to be rescued, people who still needed the Fire Department of New York. There would be a time to grieve and weep and remember, but there was no time now, not while there still was hope at a place designated Ground Zero. Firefighters by the thousands reported for duty at the pile of debris that was the World Trade Center. Some were off duty, some were retired, some were from out of town, some were from out of state. There was a handful of veteran firefighters whose sons had grown up over dinner-table talk about the joys and security and laughter of the job and who had become firefighters themselves. Now those sons were buried somewhere underneath two of the world's biggest buildings, and their fathers were looking for them.

Throughout the day of September 12, as the world recoiled in horror and collapsed in grief, firefighters and other rescue workers—police officers, emergency medical workers, ironworkers, among others—picked their way through the rubble, looking for a pocket, a void, a miracle. The Twin Towers had been brought down by terrorists wielding plastic knives and box cutters, and now their ruins were being excavated by firefighters using their hands.

Hours passed, and then days. They dug, they listened, and then they dug some more. They crawled over piles of steel into narrow passages they hoped would lead to a rescue. They were risking their lives, and surely their health, but they were convinced that somewhere in this unimaginable scene of horror and destruction, somebody—a mother, a son, a husband, a sister, a lover, a friend—was alive. "Everybody was hoping we'd find a hole with a hundred and fifty people in it," said Chief John Fox, who would put in 400 hours at the site over the next few months.

Firefighter Susan Blake worked the pile two days after the attack. The images from television did not prepare her for the devastation, and for the surreal images: As huge floodlights were trained on the wreckage, she felt as though she were on the set of a Hollywood disaster film—but here, Bruce Willis wasn't going to appear out of the hole with 3,000 people following behind.

Retired Battalion Chief Reginald Julius, seventy-seven, threw his old turnout coat and his boots and his white chief's hat—gear he hadn't worn in battle since the mid–1980s—into the trunk of his car and drove from his home in Teaneck, New Jersey, to the headquarters of Battalion

12 on 124th Street and Third Avenue. From there, he boarded a commandeered city bus and joined dozens of firefighters for the trip to Ground Zero. He reported to a deputy chief, who looked at him and said: "Well, I guess they're calling in all the old buffaloes."

Julius smiled. "Screw you," he said. "Let me do my work."

He pulled four twelve-hour tours at the site, putting body parts in buckets and bodies, what was left of them, on stretchers. He found himself feeling sorry for some of the rescue dogs, whose paws bled as the animals searched through twisted steel. On Friday, the chief and a young police officer uncovered the mangled torso of a woman. The officer turned away, and was on the verge of throwing up. Julius caught his eye, and fell back on gallows humor. "Don't you get sick," he told the cop. "Otherwise, we'll have to clean up that, too."

They continued to find bodies and parts of bodies. But by Friday, when President George W. Bush visited the ruins and threw his arms around firefighters bearing the marks of exhaustion and grief, it was becoming clear that this desperate search was over. The missing firefighters were dead. Now, and for the next eight months, the Fire Department of New York would be part not of a rescue mission but of a recovery effort, looking not for the living but for traces of the dead. Twenty-four hours a day, seven days a week, firefighters in the southeast corner of the site combed through piles of debris with rakes, searching for remains.

They looked for everyone—firefighters, police officers, and civilians. But there was no mistaking their priorities: They would not leave, they would not stop digging, they would not stop crawling into holes until they recovered the remains of their fallen comrades. When Mayor Giuliani tried to reduce Fire Department staffing at the site seven weeks after the attacks, he found himself staring at the angry ghosts of Chief James Gulick and his volunteers. New York's firefighters marched on City Hall, scuffled with the police, and carried signs reading, "Let us bring our brothers home." The strong-willed mayor relented. He had no choice. He was arguing against centuries of New York firefighting tradition, and it was an argument even he could not win.

Firefighters worked the pile for thirty-day tours, after which they received a stress debriefing. That kind of treatment would have been disdained as unnecessary as recently as the 1970s, when New York's firefighters still were running into burning buildings without their masks on. Now, however, in the face of a catastrophe that overwhelmed even the tragedies of the FDNY's war years, nobody who went to the pile left it without getting counseling. All the while, New York's firefighters buried the bodies they found, and memorialized those who left behind only their love.

The Fire Department's general orders for September 13, 2001, announced the deaths and pending funerals of Chief of Department Peter Ganci, Jr., First Deputy Commissioner William Feehan, and Chaplain Mychal Judge. They died, in the dry language of the department's bureaucracy, "as [a] result of injuries sustained while operating at Manhattan Box 8087, transmitted at 0847 hours on September 11, 2001." The funerals of all three were held on September 15. Hundreds more would follow.

The firefighters whose bodies were recovered were buried first, as the families of the missing waited not for a miracle, but simply for something to wake, something to bless, something to bury. By late September and early October, each day brought a fresh round of funerals and memorial services in the civil service towns of Long Island and the nearby upstate counties, in the old churches of Queens, Brooklyn, and the Bronx, in the sprawling parishes of Staten Island, and in the grandeur of St. Patrick's Cathedral in midtown Manhattan. The city's newspapers printed pictures of the fallen firefighters and short obituaries as they were buried or remembered, providing New Yorkers and the world with a glimpse of a culture they had taken for granted, or simply ignored. The obituaries spoke of men—all of the dead firefighters were male—who coached sports teams and tutored children, who took advantage of their odd working hours to spend time with their kids, who held college degrees in the arts and sciences, who reported for work early because they loved their jobs and each other. Working in the planet's most glamorous city, a world consumed with fame, they were content to live obscure lives in unfashionable neighborhoods. They lived in or near a city defined by commerce and money making, but they

Lieutenant
Brenda Berkman
comforts a friend
at Father Mychal
Judge's funeral.

happily worked for a civil servant's middle-class salary. They were sur-rounded by a culture of irony and self-indulgence, but they were pre-pared to risk injury and death to save a stranger. The culture asserted that nothing of substance mattered. The portraits of dead firefighters insisted otherwise.

On the sunny, summerlike morning of October 5, the inexorable waves of grief and ritual crashed through even the sturdiest barriers of detachment and denial as fifteen firefighters were buried or memorial-ized, the most tearful day yet. The depleted Fire Department of New York could not perform the time-honored final salute on its own. Firefighters in dress uniforms from Boston, New Jersey, Long Island, and other cities and towns filled gaps in the long blue line of mourning.

Thomas Cullen III of Squad Co. 41 was among the firefighters remembered on this day. His memorial service took place on the Upper East Side, in the Jesuit church of St. Ignatius Loyola on Park Avenue. A graduate of Fordham University with a degree in political science, he had just turned thirty-one, was married and had a two-year-old son. Inside the church, mourners held a memorial card bearing his picture—he was dressed in his bunker gear—and his wife Susan's farewell: "When I was young, I dreamed of finding someone really special who would come into my life. . . . When I grew older, I found that person." They had met at Fordham and had been married for five years.

Outside, in the sunshine, firefighters prepared for the rituals that would be repeated fourteen times that day, and hundreds more over the next few months. A small corps of bagpipers, reminders of the Department's Irish traditions, sat in the shade of the Park Avenue median, smoking cigarettes and waiting for the moment when they would play their lament. A captain with a piece of chalk drew a line in the traffic-free street: When the mourners emerged, firefighters would line up to the left of the mark. A firefighter with a bugle paced the street by himself, blowing an occasional note. On-duty firefighters in work clothes stood near their rigs, waiting, but they left early and discreetly when a dispatcher sent them to an alarm. Some civilians mingled with the firefighters, asking about September 11, but others seemed blithely unaware, strolling past the church while chatting on cell phones. A child pointed to a rig from Englewood, New Jersey, and asked why it was decorated with flags. "It's for the people who died," the child's nanny replied.

Applause from inside the church signaled an end to the small talk, the smoking, and the pacing. Firefighters in white gloves and dress uniforms who were inside the church streamed down the building's stairs and lined up in the street. Nobody had to direct them—they knew this awful and moving drill, and they knew it was taking place outside fourteen other houses of worship or funeral homes on this morning.

As Thomas Cullen's family emerged, the double row of blue came to attention and saluted. Bagpipers played the hymn they often played at precisely this moment: "Going Home."

"Going home,
Going home,
I'm just going home.
It's not far,

Just close by,
Through an open door."

The last note cued the bugler, who played "Taps," the final high note cracking with grief. The pipers played again, this time with "America the Beautiful." It was not always part of the Fire Department funeral repertoire, but after September 11, it seemed not only appropriate but necessary.

Thomas Cullen's body hadn't been found, so there would be no flag-draped casket to hoist aboard a pumper. His friends and relatives walked slowly past the row of saluting firefighters, and then disappeared. An officer shouted, "Dismissed!" and the firefighters broke ranks, and held on to each other.

Over and again through the fall and winter, firefighters lined up and saluted, buglers played "Taps," and bagpipers sounded the notes of "Going Home." The Fire Department had known grief before, but never like this. It was unrelenting.

Thomas Cullen III was one of nearly eighty dead firefighters who lived on Staten Island, five miles across New York Harbor from downtown Manhattan, a world away from both the affluence of the Upper East Side and the poverty of central Brooklyn and the South Bronx. The city's least-populated borough was among the region's hardest-hit communities on September 11, because it was a place where firefighters and cops lived next door to traders and brokers who worked in the Twin Towers at firms like Sandler O'Neill, Cantor Fitzgerald, and Marsh & McLennan.

The toll of dead on September 11 was so large, the suffering so intense, that it would be hard to designate any one place as grief's Ground Zero. But Staten Island's loss of so many firefighters was magnified by the borough's close-knit culture, a culture very much like the FDNY's. It was an island, after all, and proudly and stubbornly and often maddeningly so. It was not always as welcoming as it could be. It was predominately white and Catholic. It was defiantly middle class in outlook, appearance, and accent.

And in the weeks and months after September 11, it was a place where neighbors embraced each other and mourned their friends, their parents, their children, their classmates, and their spouses. If the hero-ism of the Fire Department and other rescue workers on September 11 marked the beginning of a cultural shift away from shallow fame and cheap achievement, Staten Island was at the epicenter of the quake.

Obituaries for Staten Island's fallen firefighters were filled with simple details that spoke to the essence of the Fire Department of New York:

✦ Assistant Deputy Chief Gerard Barbara, fifty-three years old, worked with stained glass, listened to opera, built a pond in the family backyard, and took his wife and two children on fabulous vacations around the world. He was last seen in the south tower, with Chief of Department Peter Ganci.

✦ Firefighter Brian Cannizzaro of Ladder Co. 101, thirty years old, not only followed his father into the Department but took his father's badge number. When he and his wife had their first child fifteen months before September 11, he wasn't holding her hand in the delivery room—he delivered the baby himself.

✦ Firefighter Francis "Frankie" Esposito of Engine Co. 235, thirty-two years old, was sailing with his wife in New York Harbor the week before September 11 when the boat start to take on water. Esposito went below decks and fixed the problem himself. The cruise went on.

✦ Lieutenant Paul Mitchell of Ladder Co. 110, forty-six years old, was driving home after a twenty-four-hour shift when the planes hit the towers. He drove to a nearby firehouse, got on a rig, and died. He was a golf coach at his daughter's Catholic high school and a girls' basketball and soccer coach for his parish school, Our Lady Star of the Sea. He was married with two children.

✦ Firefighter Sean Hanley of Ladder Co. 20, thirty-five years old, grew up with stories about his firefighter grandfather, who died in the line of duty in 1939. Hanley's father was a firefighter. Hanley's brother was a firefighter. "He really wanted to help people," his father told the *Staten Island Advance*. "That is our family tradition."

✦ Mark Whitford of Engine Co. 23, thirty-one years old, had a degree in business management from Seton Hall University in South Orange, New Jersey. He was working at Chase Manhattan Bank in 1997 when the Fire Department offered him an appointment. He took it, eagerly. He was married with twin sons, thirteen months old.

◆ Thomas Sabella of Ladder Co. 13, forty-four years old, had won a departmental medal for a daring rope rescue he made in 1999, saving a man on the sixth floor of a burning apartment building. He was a one-time welder and self-trained carpenter and woodwooker whose skills were invaluable at home and in the firehouse. He was a softball and baseball coach, the married father of two children.

◆ Joseph Ogren of Ladder Co. 3, thirty years old, followed his father, Robert, and his twin brother, Lance, into the Fire Department after quitting a job in the office of the Manhattan district attorney. He and his brother were studying for the lieutenant's exam, and he was engaged to be married.

Eleven firefighters, including the captain of Rescue Co. 5, Louis Modaferri, were members of Saint Clare's Roman Catholic church in the Great Kills section of Staten Island. All told, the small parish lost thirty people on September 11, and through the fall of 2001, each was remembered at a funeral or memorial Mass. Most of the victims were young, with young families. The church's pastor, Monsignor Joseph Murphy, presided over the services for the parish's firefighters, and he took some comfort in the courage he saw in the pews. "It is a privilege to see how much these men wish to honor their brothers," he said. "Sometimes tears come to my eyes to see the sorrow." At the memorial service for Rescue 5's captain, Commissioner Von Essen announced that Louis Modaferri had been promoted posthumously to battalion chief. The congregation rose and applauded.

On a fine fall weekend in late October, some thirty firefighters descended on a century-old house in the Staten Island neighborhood of West Brighton, where the aging parents of Firefighter John Santore lived. The house needed a new roof, and Santore, who grew up in the house and lived nearby with his wife and children, had been planning to replace it in the fall of 2001. He didn't intend to do it alone—Santore was assigned to Ladder 5, which shared quarters in Greenwich Village with Engine 24, and he planned to recruit some of his handy firefighter friends to help with the job.

On September 11, Santore and seven other firefighters from Ladder 5 were in the north tower, evacuating workers from the thirty-seventh floor when the building fell. Chief Hayden and others already had given the order to evacuate the tower; the men of Ladder 5 may not have heard the order, or they may have decided they couldn't leave while civilians still needed their help. Santore's body was found four days after the attacks.

Santore's buddies knew their friend's grieving parents still needed a roof before winter. So, a few weeks after Santore's funeral, somebody posted a sign on the firehouse bulletin board asking for volunteers. They bought what they needed—shingles and plywood and nails and hammers—loaded ladders onto pickup trucks and spent a weekend reroofing the house.

Santore's friends didn't think much of the gesture, because they knew he would have done the same for them. One of Santore's friends from Engine 24, Cosmo DiOrio, called it "the firehouse way." When DiOrio was remodeling his house several years earlier, Santore came by and helped him put up sheetrock. And when, late into the pregnancy of DiOrio's wife, Gerri, there was a heavy snowfall, Santore showed up unannounced and shoveled the sidewalk in front of the DiOrio home.

Like firefighters in other companies and other firehouses around the city, Santore and his friends from Engine 24 and Ladder 5 all socialized together, and their children all knew each other. They celebrated each other's birthdays, and shared each other's heartbreaks. "All my friends are the wives of firefighters," Gerri DiOrio said. "We all do everything together."

Dennis Taaffe and Santore came on the job together on July 11, 1981, and they had planned to retire together in a few years. Taaffe was among those who organized the roofing party for Santore's parents.

"This is not an ordinary coworker relationship," Taaffe said of Santore and all the other firefighters with whom he served. "The nature of the job is to save lives, and to look out for the life of your coworker. It's not a nine-to-five job where everybody goes his separate way at the end of a shift. At the firehouse, it's more personal. We call each other brother, and that's not an accident, and it's not just a union thing. It's heartfelt."

Firehouses were turned into shrines as New Yorkers paid tribute to their firefighters in the weeks after September 11.

Gerri DiOrio turned forty years old two days after the World Trade Center attacks. The week before, she had been making plans to celebrate her birthday with her husband, whom she calls "Mister Fireman."

When the day arrived, Mister Fireman was digging through the rubble, looking for John Santore, his friend, his brother.

"I wouldn't have expected him to be anywhere else," she said.

Epilogue

We cannot finally understand firemen; they have risen to
some place among the inexplicable beauties of life.
—Murray Kempton,
New York Post, August 3, 1978

A QUARTER CENTURY after the *New York Times* photographed
her eagerly filling out an application to join the Fire Department of
New York, retired Firefighter Lorraine Cziko is a regular visitor at her
local firehouse on Metropolitan Avenue in the Ridgewood section of
Queens. Cziko ripped up her left knee twice while on the job, developed
arthritis in her right knee, and then put in her papers in 2001 after working nearly twenty years. The knees still hurt; so do the psychological
wounds inflicted two decades ago, when she suffered through inexcus-
able hazing and harassment. But these days, it's the knee, not the bad
memories, that she finds disabling.

The walk to the firehouse, which serves as quarters for Engine Co.
291 and Ladder Co. 140, isn't long, but Cziko takes her car because she
may never take a painless step again. She brings along some Entemann's
cakes or Italian pastries, respecting firehouse tradition that demands
such offerings from firefighters reporting for the day tour. She gets hugs

and kisses when she visits, and not just because she comes bearing gifts. She worked at Engine Co. 291 for the last two and a half years of her career, and she developed warm friendships with the men in her company and in Ladder Co. 140.

Even before September 11, she had been noticing new faces, younger faces, faces of probies who weren't born when she confidently told the *New York Times*, "[I]f men want to try this job, I might as well, too." As the Department rebuilt after its losses on September 11, there seemed to be no end of fresh-faced firefighters right out of the training academy. She counted seven or eight of them at one time, in a house with a full complement of about forty-eight officers and rank-and-file firefighters.

She made a point of introducing herself to each probie, explaining that she had once worked in the house. They shook her hand, asked her about the job, about fire service, about what it's like to go into a building and see nothing but smoke and fire—they treated her no differently than they would treat any other retiree who stopped by for a cup of coffee and a rekindling of the camaraderie of the firehouse kitchen. One afternoon in the spring of 2002, Cziko was leaving a neighborhood drug store as Engine 291's rig came barreling down the street. The chauffeur spotted her and blasted the pumper's horn, and the young men in the cab waved and yelled, "Hey, Lorraine!"

"You have no idea," she said, "how good that made me feel."

The next time she stopped by to say hello and raise the firehouse's collective cholesterol level, she was invited to the company's annual summer picnic. That long-ago day of humiliation and physical assault—on and by her—was part of another era.

The post-9/11 rebuilding started on September 16, when Daniel Nigro was promoted to chief of department, replacing Peter Ganci, and 170 other firefighters received the equivalent of battlefield commissions to replace the lieutenants, captains, and chiefs who died at the World Trade Center. (Five of those promotions were awarded to firefighters who were missing in the ruins.) Nigro's appointment had special significance because he had overseen the merger of the city's emergency medical services with the FDNY before becoming Chief

Ganci's chief of operations. The integration of the two services, which had very different cultures and workforces, had become even more pressing as the city prepared for several years of austerity and budget cuts. In November 2001, construction began on a combined firehouse–EMS station on the west shore of Staten Island, offering a glimpse of the firehouse of the future. Several months later, the new administration of Mayor Michael Bloomberg announced plans for another firehouse–EMS station in the Far Rockaway section of Queens.

Eighty firefighters were recruited to rebuild the FDNY's devastated rescue and squad companies. They were given forty-five hours of hazmat training and eighty hours of special rescue training, but it would take years to develop the experience and expertise lost on September 11. In March 2002, Captain Philip Ruvolo of Brooklyn's Rescue Co. 2 told the *Wall Street Journal* that he "could never bring back or equal the talent that I lost." Seven members of Rescue 2 died at the World Trade Center.

The Department lost not only irreplaceable lives and knowledge on September 11 but also millions of dollars in rigs and equipment. Eighteen pumpers, fifteen ladder trucks, and two rescue company vehicles were destroyed, along with several specialized units. Rescue companies lost their Halligan tools and their scuba gear, ladder companies lost their Hurst tools. The city's two specialized high-rise units were out of service. Cities, towns, and civic organizations across the country raised money to buy new equipment for the Fire Department of New York, the nation's symbol of sorrow and of courage in an age without precedent.

Less than two months after the attacks, on November 1, 2001, 240 probies graduated from the training academy and were assigned to the first firehouses. During an emotional ceremony in an auditorium at Brooklyn College, Mayor Rudolph Giuliani told them, "You've grown up faster than firefighters have had to grow up in the past." As the mayor looked out at the young faces in dress uniforms, he could see a row of six chairs, vacant except for a covering of purple and black bunting. Six members of the probie class, Richard Allen, Calixto Anaya, Andrew Brunn, Michael Cammarata, Michael D'Auria, and Anthony

Rodriguez, had been ordered to report for duty on September 11. It was their first and last fire.

Hundreds more probies would be on their way in the next nine months as the Department sought to replace head count, if not the centuries of experience it lost on September 11. A new probie class began training at the end of October, and two more classes had started by spring 2002. To help with recruitment, the Department reduced its requirement of thirty college credits to fifteen. In the eyes of one of the Department's most-revered veterans, retired Deputy Chief Vincent Dunn, the turnover was certain to have at least one good effect: no longer could a company's old buffalo—the veteran of thirty or forty years who often set the tone in individual firehouses—talk down to FDNY's new generation about the war years of the 1970s. "I got sick of the old guys saying that the kids don't remember the war years," said Dunn, who retired on August 12, 1999. "These kids today have more technical skills than they ever had. The only good thing that will come out of September 11 is that the old guys have to stop talking about the war years. If a firefighter was at the World Trade Center and saw that six-teen-acre rubble field, no old-timer can talk to him about the old days."

Even though he is retired, Dunn is still the FDNY's expert in building collapses, and he contributed to the Department's intense evaluation of what happened and why on September 11. Even before the release of a government study analyzing the effect of intense heat on the Twin Towers' steel beams and trusses, Dunn wrote a report on the larger issue: the high-rise builder's cost-driven preference for lightweight, steel-supported towers over heavier, more expensive concrete. The concrete-supported Empire State Building, Dunn said, is a firefighter's idea of a skyscraper, not the World Trade Center. But rarely is a fire chief asked for an opinion when master architects plan their great works of art.

Vincent Dunn was a survivor of the FDNY's worst disaster until September 11, the Wonder Drugs fire and collapse in 1966 that killed twelve firefighters. As an officer, he became known around the country as an authority on collapses. In retirement, he has his own Web site, where firefighters can order his training videos. The Fire Department of

New York has been a part of his life since the day he reported for work on February 1, 1957.

But the years, and September 11, have led him to wonder whether he should have done something else with his life. He was a part of an organization called "The Bravest," but he insists that he was not particularly brave at all. "I probably should have been an accountant," he said several months after September 11. "Maybe I shouldn't have been a firefighter. I think about that a lot. I'm in good shape, I run all the time, but I'm not a man of action. I'm not a brave guy. I worked with some tremendously brave risk takers. They didn't think about themselves. I thought about myself. That's why I'm not a risk taker. That's why I write about safety."

On May 11, 2002, Chief Dunn wrote a letter to Tom Ridge, President Bush's director of homeland security, explaining the safety needs of the Fire Department of New York in the new age of terrorism and noting that the FDNY received no federal money for its enhanced role in civil defense. The Department needed fire boats, firefighting robots, early-warning systems for building collapses, better breathing apparatus, minimum manning of five firefighters and one officer in high-rise engine companies, and better radios. "We can no longer ask our firefighters to be the 'miner's canary,' that is, the first to take casualties at fires, haz-mat emergencies and acts of terrorism," he wrote. "We can do better for the fire service of America."

Even as a cash-strapped City Hall prepared firefighters for a new round of spending cuts to help close a $5 billion budget gap, it couldn't ignore at least a part of Chief Dunn's list of urgent needs. After years of warnings and complaints about the Fire Department's balky, unreliable radios, the city allocated $14 million in the spring of 2002 to replace the system that failed so miserably not only on September 11, but at the World Trade Center bombing in 1993.

ON THE morning of May 2, 2002, a wet and miserable spring day, the Fire Department of New York's family gathered in a small auditorium in the FDNY's headquarters building in downtown Brooklyn. The hall filled up quickly as civilians and firefighters alike scrambled for good seats to watch their children, their parents, their friends, and their comrades receive a salute from Chief Nigro and a promotion from Fire Commissioner Nicholas Scoppetta, who replaced Tom Von Essen in January.

It was the second scheduled promotion ceremony since the battlefield commissions awarded on September 16. The earlier event had been held in a bigger hall in New York Technical College, just around the corner from FDNY headquarters. As late-arriving family members were forced to stand in the aisles—nobody dared mention anything about fire-code violations—a firefighter pressed against a back wall grumbled, "Why didn't we have this ceremony in the college? I'll tell you why: The big shots didn't want to walk outside and get wet." Firehouse cynicism had not been among the casualties of September 11.

Babies in strollers made happy noises, gray-haired men and women posed for pictures with their beaming middle-aged children, and friends from the civil service towns outside the city exchanged notes on traffic conditions for the journey home. The event's master of ceremonies, Battalion Chief Brian W. Dixon, demanded order. "All personnel being promoted," he announced, "if you don't find your seats, we'll fill them with somebody else off the list." The firefighters laughed and continued their conversations.

Eventually the plea for order was obeyed, and the crowd stood for the Pledge of Allegiance and the invocation. Reverend John Delendick, one of the FDNY's chaplains, asked God to bless "our brothers and sisters" assembled for their promotions. The inclusive language seemed startling, for in the aftermath of September 11, the FDNY invariably was described as a "brotherhood" or a "band of brothers." But in the assembly this day was a sister, Brenda Berkman of Ladder Co. 12, who was about to become the Fire Department of New York's second female captain. She was wearing a gold lieutenant's ring given to her in 1994 by a friend at Ladder 105, Henry Miller. He was among the fallen heroes of September 11.

The president of the Uniformed Fire Officers Association, Peter Gorman, was the first to speak, and he told the crowd that he wished to single out two members of the promotion class for a special tribute. Firefighter Joseph J. Ginley of Ladder Co. 19, shortly to be promoted to lieutenant, had lost his brother, Lieutenant John Ginley of Engine Co. 40, on September 11. Gorman talked about the family's pain, and its courage. Gorman had been a member of the honor guard that removed Lieutenant Ginley's remains from the site.

Then Gorman singled out Brenda Berkman. Her name, he conceded, inspired "mixed reviews" in the firehouse, but he praised her for being "committed to bringing more women to the fire service" while "maintaining high standards."

"I commend her for the work she has done over the last twenty years," he said.

It was a moment of vindication she could not have anticipated twenty years ago, or perhaps even the day before, her last day as a lieutenant in Ladder Co. 12. It was one thing for Gorman to cite her work in bringing women to the department, but quite another altogether to praise her for maintaining standards—it would be hard to imagine more meaningful words. A group of women firefighters gathered in the back of the room silently nudged each other. They had been vindicated, too.

More than two centuries have passed since Benjamin Franklin wrote of the love firefighters have for each other. In the ruins of the Twin Towers, in the memorials for the fallen, in the embraces and salutes of unchanged rituals, the world saw the power of that love. An act of barbarism had instantly separated time and memory into before and after, but it did not have the power to destroy a tradition of courage and a legacy of sacrifice. Nobody who saw New York's firefighters running toward the burning towers, or advancing on the ruins, or picking their way through the rubble field, will ever forget the triumph of simple heroism over unspeakable evil.

New York's firefighters became a symbol of defiance in the face of terror, an inspiration in a world that has become immensely more frightening and complicated. The world saw how much they loved each other, how much they loved helping others, how much they loved their job. And the light of that love traced a path through the darkness of hatred.

It never wavered, that love for each other, that love for the job. The firefighters of New York experienced firsthand the dangers of a new century on September 11, dangers that added to the burdens of risk they carried into burning buildings every day. But even after the loss of so many friends, even after so many final salutes, even after hearing "Going Home" more times than they could bear, they loved the job, and they loved each other.

Like his higher-ranking brother, Reginald, Captain Vincent Julius has been retired since the mid–1980s, but both of them remain active in the Department's Vulcan Society and as unofficial and extremely energetic ambassadors of the Fire Department of New York. They wear FDNY hats and jackets; they talk about fires and firehouses; they go to conventions not just to reminisce but to plan for the future. The captain is seventy-five years old, three years younger than the chief.

In late May 2002, as firefighters gathered on Long Island for the funeral of Ray Downey, the Julius brothers told fire stories over pints of Guinness in an Irish pub in New Jersey. They talked a little about the racism they faced a half century ago, but most of the conversation was about the joys of the job. They laughed a lot. "It's all about ordinary people who have found a calling over and above what the average person does," Vincent Julius said. "You go into a burning building, down a hallway, you see what we call the red demon, and that red demon's fingers are reaching out for you, and they're saying, 'C'mon. C'mon. I've got something for you. C'mon.' And you put your head down and you keep moving."

Just outside the pub was a landmark firehouse with rigs parked on the apron, and because the Julius brothers are firefighters, they couldn't resist a visit. They looked over the pumper with a professional's eye, noting the differences between the rigs in New York and this one in the suburban township of South Orange, New Jersey. They lit cigarettes, and then walked to Reggie Julius's car. In the trunk were his old boots, turnout coat, and white chief's helmet, the equipment he wore when he worked the pile that was the World Trade Center. Two of his successors as chief of the Twelfth Battalion, Joseph Marchbanks, Jr., and Fred Scheffold, were wearing better coats and better boots but virtually the

Vincent Julius, left, and his brother, Reginald, fought fires in New York from the early 1950s to the mid-1980s. Retirement hasn't ended their connection to the FDNY.

same helmet when they died under the Twin Towers.

His brother crushed the butt of his cigarette.

"You know," Vincent said, "I'm seventy-five years old. I've had a good life, and a good career. I could die tomorrow. But if I do, I'm coming back as a firefighter for the city of New York."

He'd have to wait a while. There's a list for that job, and it's always long.

NOTES

Shortened titles are used for items listed in "Sources," pp. 357–360.

PROLOGUE
xv **Deputy Commissioner Bill Feehan:** Audiotape played at exhibit at the New-York Historical Society, Spring 2002, on the history of the World Trade Center.
xvi **Benjamin Franklin:** Carp, *Fire of Liberty*.

CHAPTER 1:
SEPTEMBER 10, 2001
1 **On the morning:** Author's interview with former commissioner Thomas Von Essen, December 2001.
5 **Battalion Chief John Fox:** Author interview, March 2002.
5 **Bill Bresnan:** Author interview, March 2002.
6 **"Three, two one":** The description of the scene at Engine 73 and Ladder 42 is based on a videotape of the ceremony, provided to the author by Deputy Commissioner Frank Gribbon.
9 **The Department's Daily Orders:** Number 98, FDNY, General Orders, Municipal Reference Library.

CHAPTER 2:
"DISCREET, SOBER MEN"
12 **The Council ordered a tax:** Common Council of New York, Minutes, 1675–1776, Volume 4, 54.
12 **Even then:** Ibid., Volume 1, 187.
12 **In the 1680s New York was a city:** Burrows and Wallace, *Gotham*, 50, 87.
12 **Fifty years earlier:** Costello, *Our Firemen*, 25.
12 **Sensing an opportunity:** Ibid.
13 **This would:** Limpus, *History of the New York Fire Department*, 25–26.
14 **That piece of legislation:** Common Council, Minutes, vol. 4, 82.
14 **As the great day:** Ibid., 122.
15 **A Boston newspaper:** Costello, *Our Fireman*, 26.
16 **Two sheds were built:** Common Council, Minutes, vol. 4, 128.
16 **The legislators instructed:** Ibid., 437.
16 **Indeed, the General Assembly:** Limpus, *History of the New York Fire Department*, 29.
16 **Observing the firefighters:** Carp, *Fire of Liberty*.
17 **Within days of arrival:** Fernow, *Records of New Amsterdam*, vol. 1, 1.
18 **The director general was determined:** Burrows and Wallace, *Gotham*, 43.
18 **"It has been noticed":** Fernow, *Records of New Amsterdam*, vol. 1, 5.
17 **He ordered that:** Ibid., 6–7.

22 **Within a few years:** Burrows and Wallace, *Gotham,* 127.

22 **Nine whites were killed:** Ibid., 148

23 **And any slave:** Common Council, Minutes, vol. 5, 17.

24 **"I depart this waste":** Morris, *Fires and Firefighting,* 39

24 **the council appointed:** Common Council, Minutes, vol. 5, 44.

25 **In the 1760's***:* Ibid., vol. 6, 255.

25 **According to the Common Council records:** Ibid., vol. 7, 345, 358, 370, 394

26 **in service records:** White, *Index to Revolutionary War Service Records,* vol. 6, 2623.

26 **As for private property***:* Theodore Thayer, *Nathanael Greene: Strategist of the American Revolution* (New York: Twayne Publishers, 1960), 107.

27 **Within two hours:** Burrows and Wallace, *Gotham,* 241.

27 **"The deck of our ship":** Limpus, *History of the New York Fire Department,* 64.

28 **"This provoked the Spectators"***:* William Henry Shelton, "The Burning of New York and the Secret Mission of Nathan Hale," unpublished manuscript, New-York Historical Society.

28 **They were spared:** Ibid.

28 **As he watched:** Langguth, *Patriots,* 397.

28 **More than 500 buildings:** Burrows and Wallace, *Gotham,* 242.

28 **Major General James Robertson:** Limpus, *History of the New York Fire Department,* 66–67.

30 **They took great:** Ibid., 78.

30 **This massive rebuilding**: Common Council, Minutes, vol. 1, 201–2.

32 **"for the relief of disabled":** Limpus, *History of the New York Fire Department,* 89.

34 **"It is no longer a doubt":** Ibid., 96.

34 **Nevertheless, a select:** Common Council, Minutes, vol. 3, 662–64.

35 **Before the hoses:** Limpus, *History of the New York Fire Department,* 110.

35 **By the early 1820s:** Jackson, *Encyclopedia of New York,* 409.

35 **One firefighter was fined:** Asbury, *Ye Olde Fire Laddies,* 87.

35 **So popular were the firefighters:** Common Council, Minutes, vol. 12, 774.

35 **Two days later the paper called for:** *Evening Post,* Aug. 24 and 26, 1822.

CHAPTER 3:
A NATIONAL CALAMITY

37 **A European visitor:** Ellis, *Epic of New York City,* 228.

38 **"The frequency of fires":** Nevins, *Diary of Philip Hone,* 15–16.

38 **He and his wife, Catherine:** Burrows and Wallace, *Gotham,* 452.

38 **Mayor Cornelius Lawrence:** Ibid., 595.

38 **One company executive:** New-York Historical Society, *Letters from John Pintard,* vol. 2, 260.

38 **In 1834:** Burrows and Wallace, *Gotham,* 594.

40 **Engraved on a monument:** Costello, *Our Firemen,* 220.

40 **America's Own and Fireman's Journal:** Calhoun, "From Community to Metropolis," 129–33.

40 **With the northern boundary:** Wall, "The Great Fire of 1835"; see also Limpus, *History of the New York Fire Department,* 151.

41 **It spoke of:** Ibid., 143.

42 **None of the other fires:** *Evening Post,* Nov. 2, 1835.

43 **Newspaper reports:** Ibid., Sept. 19, 1835.

43 **"We pity the poor":** *New York Herald,* Dec. 17, 1835.

43 **Forcing open a door:** Limpus, *History of the New York Fire Department,* 151.

45 **Before long, the light from the fire:** Wall, "Great Fire of 1835," 14.

45 **"At ten o'clock":** *New York Herald,* Dec. 17, 1835.

45 **Samuel Swartout:** *American Print Works,* 114.

46 **The horror of the scene:** *New York Herald,* Dec. 17, 1835.

46 **Eyewitnesses described:** Limpus, *History of the New York Fire Department,* 155.

49 **King decided:** *American Print Works,* 88.

50 **Colonel Temple agreed:** Ibid., 103.

51 **"I was concerned":** Ibid., 90–91.

52 **About an hour later:** Ibid., 168.

53 **"The miserable wretches":** Dunshee, *As You Pass By,* 62.

54 **James Gordon Bennett:** *New York Herald,* Dec. 18, 1835.

56 **"Our community":** Wall, "Great Fire of 1835," 19.

56 **Three hundred extra:** C. Foster, "An Account of the Conflagration."

56 **The destruction of New York:** *New York Herald,* Dec. 18, 1835.

57 **The *Herald* reported:** Ibid., Dec. 19, 1835.

57 **Philadelphia's Common Council:** Proceedings of the Citizens of Philadelphia.

58 **From a pulpit:** Muhlenberg, *Rebuke of the Lord,* 6–15.

58 **The Reverend William Ware:** Ware, *A Sermon.*

59 **Commenting on a public:** Wall, "Great Fire of 1835," 14.

59 **The Common Council:** Ibid., 16

60 **"The city of New York":** Phillips, *Speech Upon the Bill.*

60 **"there was no harmony":** Ginsberg, "History of Fire Protection," 198, 199; see also *Evening Post,* Dec. 21, 1835.

60 **The board adopted:** Foster, "An Account of the Conflagration."

61 **They asked citizens:** *Evening Post,* Aug. 31, 1835.

61 **When the men:** Ibid., Feb. 2, 1836.

61 **And they were quick:** Ibid. Feb. 5, 1836.

62 **A little more than:** Board of Aldermen, Proceedings, vol. 10, 171–72.

62 **After listening:** Limpus, *History of the New York Fire Department,* 162.

64 **They did:** *Evening Post,* May 5, 1836.

64 **The assistants already:** Anonymous, "The Truth."

64 **"In a city such as":** *New York Herald,* May 7, 1836.

65 **"Such a nomination":** *Evening Post,* Nov. 5, 1836.

65 **One person who wrote:** Ibid., Nov. 15, 1836.

66 **Unchastened:** Ibid., Nov. 24, 1836.

CHAPTER 4:
GANGS, FEUDS, AND POLITICS

67 **In short order:** Connable and Silverfarb, *Tigers of Tammany,* 143.

67 **At the age:** Hershkowitz, *Tweed's New York,* 11.

68 **He swilled beer:** *Daily News,* March 2, 2002.

69 **Mose was a smash:** *Irish Echo,* Feb. 13–19, 2001. I am indebted to the historian Edward T. O'Donnell for sharing his knowledge of Old Mose.

69 **The majority of firemen:** Calhoun, *From Community to Metropolis,* 140.

71 **A nineteenth-century historian:** Costello, *Our Firemen,* 180.

71 **A thousand men:** Jackson, *Encyclopedia of New York City,* 409.

71 **Costello observed:** Costello, *Our Firemen,* 180.

74 **"The existence of politics":** *Proceedings of the Committee on Safety,* 2.

74 **Worse yet, he said:** Ibid., 12.

75 **"[It] is a fact":** Ibid., 21–25.

76 **The "people of the city":** Board of Aldermen, Proceedings, vol. 18, 400.

76 **In the two decades:** Calhoun, "From Community to Metropolis," 140.

76 **George Templeton Strong:** Ibid., 140

77 **In his study:** Ibid., 138.

77 **Stephen Ginsberg:** Ginsberg, "History of Fire Protection," 44.

78 **Walt Whitman compared:** Anbinder, *Five Points,* 185.

78 **In his book, *Five Points*:** Ibid., 166–169.

79 **When Ireland's potato crop:** Baylor and Meagher, *New York Irish,* 91.

79 **The *American Republican*:** Benson, *Concept of Jacksonian Democracy,* 116.

79 **Those concerns:** Ellis, *The Epic,* 256.

79 **A Catholic newspaper:** *Freeman's Journal,* April 13, 1844.

79 **"blood will have blood":** Ellis, *The Epic,* 256.

79 **After an exchange:** *Freeman's Journal,* June 8, 1844.

79 **When the mayor asked:** Burrows and Wallace, *Gotham,* 633.

79–80 **In case the mayor:** Coffey and Golway, *Irish in America,* 76.

80 **In an acknowledgment:** *New York Herald,* Oct. 15, 1842.

82 **No trace of him:** Costello, *Our Firemen,* 238; *Evening Post,* July 21, 1845.

83 **In an hour-by-hour account:** *Evening Post,* July 19, 1845.

83 **a lone woman walked:** *New York Herald,* July 21.

83 **"They were unwearied":** *Evening Post,* July 21, 1845.

83 **"a new facility":** Ibid., July 22, 1845.

84 **He quit:** Costello, *Our Firemen,* 446.

85 **Costello, the bard:** Ibid., 172.

85 **Writing in 1878:** Tyler, *Reminiscences of the V.F.D.,* 5.

86 **"On approaching the house":** *New York Herald,* Dec. 8, 1852.

86 **By the late 1840s:** Chief Engineer, annual report, 1850, published in the *New York Herald,* Sept. 6, 1850.

86 **a strict set of bylaws:** Fifteenth Ward Hose Company, By-Laws.

87 **A contemporary remembered:** Hershkowitz, *Tweed's New York,* 12.

88 **When he received a report:** Chief Engineer, annual report, 1850.

89 **Kelly was a particularly well-known politician:** Anbinder, *Five Points,* 160–161.

89 **"If my own father":** Chief Engineer, annual report, 1850.

90 **The newspaper noted:** *New York Herald,* Sept. 9, 1850.

90 **Alderman Kelly took pains:** Ibid., Sept. 8.

90 **On September 9, Bill Tweed:** Board of Aldermen, Proceedings, vol. 39, 690.

91 **"reformer in non-reforming age":** Costello, *Our Firemen,* 118.

92 **insurance company-funded Fire Patrol:** Asbury, *Ye Olde Fire Laddies,* 185.

92 **When he delivered his 1852 annual report:** *New York Times,* Sept. 8, 1852.

93 **Of that figure only $100,000:** Jackson, *Encyclopedia of New York City,* 410.

93 **As a result, in 1853:** Chief Engineer, annual report, 1853; see also *New York Times,* Sept. 6, 1853.

93 **From 1850 to 1853, the council:** Ibid.

94 **The school day:** *Evening Post,* Sept. 21, 1851.

94 **Firemen, responding to the false alarm:** Sept. 9, 1850.

95 **"Amid crackling timber":** *New York Herald,* Dec. 11, 1853.

96 **A newspaper reporter at the scene:** Ibid., April 26, 1854.

96 **"I got out":** Costello, *Our Firemen,* 447.

96 **"Is that near you":** *New York Herald,* April 26, 1854.

97 **Howard complained:** Chief Engineer, annual report, 1857.

CHAPTER 5:
WAR AND REVOLUTION

99 **It was a chilly winter's evening:** *New York Times,* Feb. 4, 1860.

100 **Civic leaders like Charles Loring Brace:** Burrows and Wallace, *Gotham,* 849.

101 **A writer in Harper's Weekly:** *Harper's Weekly,* April 1, 1865.

101 **Committee members returned:** *New York Times,* March 4, 1860.

101 **At around the same time:** The account of the Elm Street fire is based on reports in *The New York Times,* Feb. 3–7, 1860.

105 **Within weeks, the aldermen passed:** Limpus, *History of the New York Fire Department,* 222–223.

107 **Decker spoke of the men:** Costello, *Our Firemen,* 406, 407, 409.

107 **Decker estimated:** Chief Engineer, annual report, 1860.

107 **Though the *Times* conceded:** *New York Times,* Dec. 29, 1860.

108 **Decker shared the *Times*' concerns:** Chief engineer, annual report, 1861.

109 **"my young friend":** Costello, *Our Firemen,* 725.

109 **As he heard a ball whiz:** Ibid., 726.

109 **thought the Zouaves were:** Foote, *Civil War,* vol. 1, 80; Limpus, *History of the New York Fire Department,* 230.

111 **Decker saw what was going on:** Chief engineer, annual report, 1863.

112 **The worst riot:** The account of the draft riots is based on reports in the *New York Tribune,* the *New York Times,* and the *New York Herald,* July 11–20; see also Burrows and Wallace, *Gotham,* 889–95; for the report of Decker's quick wit, see Limpus, *History of the New York Fire Department,* 236–38.

116 **Although the number of fires:** FDNY, annual reports, 1857–63.

116 **"New York ought to be" and "New York ranks low":** Brandt, *The Man Who Tried to Burn New York,* 258.

116 **On March 17, 1864 :** Costello, *Our Firemen,* 784.

116 **Chief Decker soon:** Chief Engineer, annual report, 1864.

117 **"The Common Council":** Ibid., 1865.

117 **"[I]t is absurd:** *New York Times,* Jan. 30, 1865.

118 **on the evening of:** Brandt, *The Man Who Tried to Burn New York,* is a fine study of the Confederate plot.

118 **"It is a revolution"***:* Costello, *Our Firemen,* 794.

119 **"The Legislature has":** Chief Engineer, annual report, 1865.

119 **"preventing thousands of helpless":** *New York Times,* March 31, 1865; see also Chief Engineer, annual report, 1865 (Decker's final report).

119 **fire commissioners published plans:** Limpus, *History of the New York Fire Department,* 247.

119 **volunteers took a vote:** Ibid., 247.

120 **He remained bitter:** Chief Engineer, annual report, 1865.

120 **Each company:** Ibid.

120 **criticisms leveled by the *New York Times* :** The *Times* editorials of May 6, 1865, and June 22, 1865, pointedly summarized the newspaper's point of view.

CHAPTER 6:
"A DUTY, NOT A PASTIME"

121 **The city surrendered:** Costello, *Our Firemen,* 811.

122 **Of the 4,000:** Ibid., 834.

122 **Of the eighteen who quit:** Ibid., 827.

123 **Bonner's family fled:** Costello, *Our Firemen,* 932

124 **John Bresnan's family:** Ford, *Third Alarm.*
124 **"narrow ways":** Burrows and Wallace, *Gotham,* 698.
124 **"the most degraded heathen":** Anbinder, *Five Points,* 241.
125 **Not surprisingly:** Metropolitan Fire Department, annual reports, 1865–66.
125 **Such absences:** FDNY, annual reports, 1880, 1881.
126 **In another drastic change:** Metropolitan Fire Department, annual report, 1868.
126 **"Under the present system":** Ibid., 1867.
126 **The Academy of Music:** Burrows and Wallace, *Gotham,* 765; *New York Herald,* May 23, 1866.
126 **A performance of *La Juive*:** The account of the Academy fire relies on eyewitness reports in the *New York Herald,* May 23, 1866.
128 **873 fires in New York:** Metropolitan Fire Department, annual report, 1868.
129 **By the time:** Costello, *Our Firemen,* 838.
129 **Shaler paid astonishing attention:** Ibid., 843.
130 **He had his son:** Hashagen, *Distant Fire,* 12.
131 **allies in place:** Allen, *New York: A History,* 169.
131 **The fire insurance industry had to lend:** Limpus, *History of the New York Fire Department,* 262.
134 **Paul Hashagen, firefighter:** Hashagen, *Distant Fire,* 35.
134 **"Great numbers":** Limpus, *History of the New York Fire Department,* 273.
136 **accused his counterparts:** Metropolitan Fire Department, annual report, 1869.
136 **"[The] people of":** The account of the Brooklyn fire is based on eyewitness accounts in the *New York Times,* Dec. 6–12, 1876.
139 **the Department's commissioners declared:** FDNY, annual report, 1879.
139 **To complement Hoell's tutorial:** Ibid., 1883.
141 **They clearly could take a hint:** Ibid., 1886.
141 **Included among the department's general orders:** Ibid., 1888.
142 **One of the most prominent voices:** Burrows and Wallace, *Gotham,* 979.
143 **In 1866, the average property loss:** FDNY, annual report, 1888.
143 **The number of fires was on upswing:** Ibid.
143 **One nineteenth-century observer:**

Costello, *Our Firemen,* 881.
143 **from 1877 to 1882 fires in dry-goods district:** Ibid., 880.
143 **the plan of a New York civilian:** Stevens, *Fire Protection in the Dry Goods District.*
144 **Department was more than 75 percent Irish:** FDNY, Roster, 1888; author's tally.
144 **In the mid–1880s:** Ibid., annual report, 1885.
144 **Three of the four:** Ibid., roster, 1888.
146 **Generations of young Irish Americans:** Ibid., annual report, 1894.
146 **He got her out of the building:** Ibid., 1888
147 **"When the fire was over":** Ford, *Third Alarm,* xix.
147 **Chief Bresnan seemed to regard:** annual report, 1893.
148 **But even such measures:** *New York Times,* Feb. 8, 1892.
149 **Tenement fires in the late 1880's:** Tenement House Committee, *Report,* 221.
149 **Many of the fires:** FDNY, annual report, 1893.
149 **"Such shafts in case of fire":** Tenement House Committee, *Report,* 269.
150 **"made it his business":** *New York Herald,* Dec. 31, 1894.
150 **"He knew the botany of a fire":** Ford, *Third Alarm,* xvii.
150 **In the first six months of 1894:** Tenement House Committee, *Report,* 14.
150 **One such blaze:** Ibid., 224.
152 **Bresnan had barely returned:** *New York Times,* Dec. 30, 1894; see also Ford, *Third Alarm.*
152 **The fire in Cassidy & Sons:** *New York Times* and *New York Herald,* Dec. 30–31, 1894.
153 **Chief Bresnan had many friends:** *WNYF,* April, 1953, 21.
153 **His grandson, Bill:** Author interview, April 2002.
153 **Members of the Tenement House Committee:** *New York Herald,* Dec. 31.
153 **Filled with tables and statistical analysis:** Tenement House Committee, *Report,* 270.

CHAPTER 7:
VERTICAL CITY
155 **Just after midnight:** *WNYF,* centennial issue, 1965, 25.
156 **As recently as 1896:** Ibid.
156–157 **On December 31, 1897:** FDNY, annual report, 1898.
157 **More than 300 buildings:** Burrows and Wallace, *Gotham,* 1050.

158 **He had joined:** Limpus, *History of the New York Fire Department,* 294.

158 **At three o'clock:** The account of the Hotel Windsor fire is based on reports in the *New York Times,* March 18, 1899.

161 **Croker's apprenticeship:** Burrows and Wallace, 1104.

163 **The day before Bonner left:** *New York Times,* May 1, 1899.

163 **"I have no ambition":** Croker's comments appear on a variety of Fire Department plaques and official documents, and are read at official FDNY functions.

164 **"There was no politics in it at all":** *New York Times,* May 1, 1899

164 **"never took such punishment:** Hashagen, *A Distant Fire,* 259.

165 **"Gentlemen," he said:** *New York Times,* Oct. 3, 1930.

165 **"That floor won't hold you, Cap":** *WNYF,* first issue, 1984, 11; see also Hashagen, *A Distant Fire,* 260.

165 **In one of his special orders:** FDNY, Special Orders, Feb. 1, 1905.

167 **On January 6, 1907:** *WNYF,* third issue, 1967.

169 **When the new system was finished:** *WNYF,* Centennial Issue, 1965, 27.

170 **"They are fireproof":** *New York Times,* March 26, 1911.

170 **The Fire Department asserted:** FDNY, annual report, 1910.

170 **The business leaders:** *New York Times,* March 26, 1911; see also *NYT,* Jan. 14, 1912.

171 **"the place looked dangerous to me":** *New York Times,* March 26, 1911.

171 **H. F. J. Porter:** Ibid.

173 **"a man's body come crashing down":** Stein, *Triangle Fire,* 17.

173 **"no apparatus in the department":** Ibid., 18.

173 **The city's coroner:** *New York Times,* March 26.

174 **"Look around everywhere":** Ibid.

175 **The Department was given permission:** FDNY, annual report, 1912.

176 **one significant loophole:** Ibid.

176 **Equitable Life Assurance Building:** The account of the Equitable fire is from the *New York Times,* Jan. 10–11, 1912; see also Hashagen, *Distant Fire,* 197–198.

179 **The following Sunday:** *New York Times,* Jan. 14, 1912.

179 **13,868 fires in 1911:** FDNY, annual report, 1911.

180 **"Fools must no longer be allowed":** *New York Times,* Jan. 14, 1912.

180 **"Without exaggeration":** FDNY, Report on Incendiarism, 4.

181 **cigarettes on the sweatshop floor:** FDNY, annual report, 1912.

181 **"it is not a fact, as charged":** FDNY, annual report, 1914.

183 **When the Department turned out:** See "Firefighting in New York," vol. 2, a video series available through the Ahrens-Fox Video Library.

CHAPTER 8:
AMERICAN COLOSSUS

186 **The firefighters he served:** Hashagen, *A Distant Fire,* 310.

187 **"There's nothing to that story":** *New York Times,* Oct. 3, 1930.

188 **talking about the nickname:** Limpus, *History of the New York Fire Department,* 328.

188 **Four hundred homes were destroyed:** *New York Times,* June 16, 1922.

189 **"I've got work to do":** *New York Times,* July 19, 1922; see also Limpus, *History of the New York Fire Department,* 323.

191 **Fireman William L. Pratt:** The account of the Ritz Tower fire relies on the *New York Times,* Aug. 2, 3 and 4, 1932.

194 **The number of firefighters rose:** FDNY, annual reports, 1920, 1930.

194 **By 1936, the Department had 6,717 fire-fighters:** FDNY, annual report, 1937.

194 **FDNY to shrink by half:** Scher, *New York City Firefighting,* 38.

194 **In a memo to the mayor:** Heckscher, *When La Guardia Was Mayor,* 159.

194-195 **He launched a campaign:** Kessner, *Fiorello La Guardia and the Making of Modern New York,* 344.

196 **When he appointed Chief of Department McElligott:** Limpus, *History of the New York Fire Department,* 332.

196 **What, he asked:** Heckscher, *When La Guardia Was Mayor,* 240.

196 **As La Guardia ran for a second term:** FDNY, annual report, 1937.

197 **Their workweek was cut:** FDNY, annual report, 1940.

197 **In a letter:** Fiorello La Guardia, Papers, roll 20, documents 334–35.

197 **La Guardia's efforts won him the support:** Ibid., document 342.

198 **a letter he sent to Governor:** Ibid., roll 182, document 250.

198 **Colonel Arthur V. McDermott told the mayor:** Ibid., roll 20, document 292.

199 **By April 1941:** *WNYF,* April 1941.

199 **On one occasion:** Packard, *La Guardia's Fire Chief,* 150.

199 **All suffered from dysentery:** Ibid., 33–40.

200 **number of fires declined:** FDNY, annual report, 1942.

200 **ship fires:** WNYF, April, 1945, 8.

200 **"fatheads":** Packard, *La Guardia's Fire Chief,* 168.

201 **first large fire of postwar New York:** The account of the Washington Heights fire is based on stories in the *New York Times,* Dec. 13–16, 1946.

202 **Adolph Joseph Popper joined the Fire Department:** The account of the reunion between Adolph Joseph Popper and Chief Kinnick is contained in FDNY's institutional history, commonly called its "Millennium Book," published in 2000.

203 **Wesley Williams:** Biographical information on Wesley Williams is from material at the New York Fire Museum; see also *Daily News,* Feb. 1, 1989; and the Vulcan Society's Web site, www.vulcansocietyfdny.org.

205 **Other forms of harassment:** Reginald Julius and Vincent Julius, author interviews, May 2002.

207 **firefighter appointed in 1952 earned:** Fireman Neil Duggan's appointment papers, in author's possession.

207 **loosening of residency restrictions:** FDNY, Engine Co. 57, journal, 1943, showed that all forty-three members lived in the city; by 1954, about a quarter were living on Long Island.

209 **"The house is built on top of a hill":** Smith, *Report from Engine Co. 82,* 51–52.

210 **"more than 700 pieces of apparatus":** FDNY, annual report, 1953–54.

210 **Firefighting in New York:** FDNY, annual report, 1956.

210–11 **"how we can live with our newest menace":** *WNYF,* July, 1959, 4–6.

211 **Thousands turned in their papers:** FDNY, annual reports, 1960, 1961.

212 **"I was newly married":** Larry McCarthy, author interview, March 2002.

213 **soap factory in Masbeth:** *New York Times,* Oct. 28, 1962.

214 **city's fire fatality rate:** FDNY, annual report, 1962.

214 **Conditions when right:** This account is based on the *Staten Island Advance,* April 22,

1963, and the author's personal observations of that fire.

CHAPTER 9:
THE WAR YEARS

218 **the annual number:** FDNY, Operational Reference, 196.

219 **Vincent Dunn:** Vincent Dunn, author interview, April 2002.

219 **Engine Co. 18:** *New York Times,* Oct. 19, 1966; memoir by Joseph D'Albert of Engine Co. 24, *WNYF,* second issue, 1973.

221 **Lieutenant Dunn and Engine Co. 33:** Vincent Dunn, author interview, April 2002.

221 **waited on the street:** *New York Times,* Oct. 19, 1966.

223 **Donovan never saw the abyss:** Ibid.

224 **"This was the saddest day":** Ibid.

226 **Every year of the 1960s:** FDNY, Operational Reference, 196.

226 **Bullets were fired:** Ibid., "Millennium Book,' 114.

227 **"Nobody was going to look out for us":** Lawrence McCarthy, author interview, March, 2002.

229 **"great pride in devotion to duty":** FDNY, "Millennium Book," 120.

230 **Meanwhile, a dozen firefighters:** *New York Times,* June 19, 1970.

230 **Three hundred and ten civilians died:** FDNY, Operational Reference, 196.

230 **At around noon:** *New York Times,* March 7, 1970.

231 **"These are urban guerrillas":** *New York Times,* March 13, 1970.

231 **the busiest firehouses were responding:** FDNY, Operational Reference, 196.

232 **"[I]f we had responded":** *New York Times,* March 7, 1970

232 **number of false alarms would grow:** FDNY, Operational Reference, 196.

232 **At the headquarters of Rescue Co. 2:** Peter Hayden, author interview, February 2002.

233 **"Kids do this a lot":** Smith, *Report from Engine Co. 82,* 15.

234 **Through the summer of 1970:** FDNY, annual report, 1969.

234 **After several contentious bargaining sessions:** *New York Times,* Nov. 2, 1973.

235 **With great fanfare:** Ibid., Nov. 17, 1973.

236 **"the firemen's traditional dedication to duty":** *New York Times,* Nov. 6, 1973.

236 **"Don't mess with the Taylor Law":** Edmund Staines, author interview, February 2002.

237 **Larry McCarthy picketed:** Larry McCarthy, author interview, March 2002.

239 **About 4.2 percent:** Based on FDNY figures; see Vulcan Society Web site, www.vulcansocietyfdny.org.

239 **striker versus nonstriker:** *New York Times,* Nov. 7, 1973.

242 **In fact, they had voted against the strike:** Ibid., Nov. 18, 1973.

242 **"If he lied":** Ibid., Nov. 19, 1973.

242 **"one of the most destructive acts":** Ibid., Nov. 30, 1973.

242 **body blow to the morale:** Dennis Smith, Al Washington, Larry McCarthy, author interviews.

242 **"the whole episode":** *New York Times,* Nov. 19, 1973.

243 **Firefighters were awarded a $700 a year raise:** *New York Times,* Dec. 2, 1973.

243 **Tom Cashin:** Tom Cashin, author interview, March 2002.

245 **several dubious records:** FDNY, annual report, 1974–75.

245 **John Fox:** John Fox, author interview, March, 2002.

246 **When firefighters reported for duty:** *Daily News,* Jan. 26, 1976.

246 **the South Bronx was a modern no man's land:** *WNYF,* fourth issue, 1975.

247 **tenants standing on sidewalk:** Peter Hayden, Dennis Smith, Author interviews.

248 **school near Yankee Stadium caught fire:** *New York Times,* Oct. 13, 1977.

249 **Though number of fires actually declined:** FDNY, Operational Reference, 196.

249 **Afterward, Celic was reminded gently:** Staten Island Advance, Aug. 8, 1995.

249 **Celic and the firemen of Engine Co. 15:** *Staten Island Advance,* Sept. July 3–10, 1977.

251 **the lights went out:** Time, July 25, 1977.

251 **Larry McCarthy:** Larry McCarthy, author interview, March 2002.

252 **During the worst of the war years:** FDNY, Operational Reference, 196.

253 **fire in a Waldbaum's:** *New York Times,* Aug. 3–5, 1978.

255 **number of fires dipped:** FDNY, Operational Reference, 196.

CHAPTER 10:
A BATTLE FOR INCLUSION

258 **The possibility of women:** *New York Times,* Oct. 8, 1974.

258 **pick up a dummy:** United Women Firefighters Papers, Department of Personnel Documents, box 1.

258 **Lorraine Cziko:** Lorraine Cziko, author interview, May 2002.

259 **"if men want to try this job":** *New York Times,* Sept. 8, 1977.

263 **only 89 showed up:** *New York Times,* March 6, 1982.

263 **Brenda Berkman:** Brenda Berkman, author interview, April 2002; see also United Women Firefighters Papers, Department of Personnel Documents, Box 1.

264 **Berkman filed a complaint:** The documents for *Berkman v. The City of New York, et al.* are archived in the United Women Firefighters Papers.

265 **"separate bathrooms, showers and living facilities":** *New York Times,* Jan. 5, 1978.

265 **"bone in your throat":** Ed Koch, author interview, May 2002.

265 **demanding higher salaries:** *New York Times,* July 1, 1980.

266 **tenement on West 151st Street:** *New York Times,* July 2, 1980.

267 **Two days before he was sworn in:** Charles Hynes, author interview, May 2002.

269 **carry a 210-pound mayor:** Ed Koch, author interview, May 2002.

269 **What was even more shocking:** *New York Times,* March 6, 1982.

269 **a new physical exam:** Debovoise & Plimpton, letter to all plaintiffs in the class action suit, Aug. 4, 1982. United Women Firefighters Papers, box 1.

270 **In the new test:** Ibid. Sept. 23, 1982; also Brenda Berkman, author interview, April 2002.

270 **"The City of New York formally acknowledges":** *New York Times,* Sept. 23, 1982.

271 **"If the Union":** Nicholas Mancuso, letter to Brenda Berkman, Sept. 28, 1982, United Women Firefighters Papers, box 1.

272 **She was assigned:** Brenda Berkman, author interview, April 2002; see also United Women Firefighters Papers, box 1.

272 **by turning inward:** Brenda Berkman diary, United Women Firefighters Papers, box 3.

273 **same story for Lorraine Cziko:** Lorraine Cziko, author interview, May 2002.

275 **"I'm gonna tell you motherfuckers":** Reginald Julius, author interview, May 2002.

275 **Cathy Riordan:** Cathy Riordan, author interview, May 2002.

276 **Susan Byrne:** Susan Byrne, author interview, May 2002.

276 **Al Washington:** Al Washington, author interview, May 2002.

279 **"on the day of the exam":** *Newsday,* July 29, 1999.

280 **fire was a potential tragedy:** FDNY, Operational Reference, 196.

280 **Bill Bresnan:** author interview, March 2002.

281 **the Happy Land fire:** *New York Times, Daily News,* March 26, 1990.

CHAPTER 11:
A NEW WORLD

283 **World Trade Center bombing:** The actions, thoughts, and comments of John Fox, Peter Runfola, Ed Staines, Bill Bresnan, and the members of Rescue Co. 5 as reconstructed here are based on their interviews with the author in the spring of 2002 and on Ed Staines's notes and incident report for the World Trade Center bombing, which he generously shared with the author. The incident report contains individual statements from Firefighters Foley, Modafferi, and Tripoli.

284 **Initial reports from the field:** The summary of conversations between arriving units and the dispatcher is based on a recording of radio traffic on Feb. 26, 1993 (in author's possession).

293 **number of annual emergency responses:** FDNY, Operational Reference, 196.

293 **"The Fire Department's basic function":** *New York Times,* March 13, 1995.

296 **Watt Street fire in the West Village:** *Daily News,* March 29, 1994; see also Michael Daly, *Daily News,* March 29–May 10, 1994, a series of columns written during Captain John Drennan's forty-day ordeal that offered moving insight into the lives of firefighters and their loved ones.

298 **"My husband lived for forty days":** *Newsday,* Jan. 9, 1999.

299 **Susan Blake:** Susan Blake, author interview, May 2002.

CHAPTER 12:
SEPTEMBER 11, 2001

301 **account of World Trade Center fire and collapse:** The stories, words, and thoughts of Bob Bohack, John Fox, Pete Hayden Bill Bresnan, Susan Blake, Peter Runfola and Paul Washington are based on author interviews conducted in the spring of 2002.

303 **The annual total of civilian deaths:** FDNY, annual report, 2000.

307 **film crew:** I am indebted to the work of two French filmmakers, Jules and Gedeon Naudet, whose harrowing video of the attacks was broadcast in spring 2002 on CBS. Some details and snippets of conversation from the command post are based on the footage they shot. Chief Pete Hayden was visible and audible throughout much of the footage from the command post.

310 **Lieutenant Chuck Margiotta:** *Staten Island Advance,* Nov. 1, 2001.

315 **Father Judge was lying:** Smith, *Report from Ground Zero,* Hayden and several other 28–35.

318 **Berkman walked toward the smoke:** Women in the Fire Service Web site, www.wfsi.org.

CHAPTER 13:
GOING HOME

323 **Battalion 58 in Canarsie:** John Fox, author interview, March 2002.

323 **John McAvoy:** *Staten Island Advance,* Sept. 21, 2001.

325 **Of the 341:** Statistics culled from newspaper lists of the dead.

325 **One hundred and forty-five:** *Irish Echo,* Nov. 21–27, 2001.

326 **"Everybody was hoping":** John Fox, author interview, March 2002.

326 **Susan Blake:** Susan Blake, author interview, May 2002.

326 **Reginald Julius:** Reginald Julius, author interview, May 2002.

328 **"as [a] result of injuries sustained":** FDNY, General Orders, Sept. 13, 2001.

329 **details of October 5 funeral:** Eyewitness report by author; see also Thomas Cullen's obituary in *Staten Island Advance,* Oct. 30, 2001.

332 **Assistant Deputy Chief Gerard Barbara:** *Staten Island Advance,* Sept. 28, 2001.

332 **Firefighter Brian Cannizzaro:** *Newsday,* Jan. 22, 2002.

332 **Firefighter Francis "Frankie" Esposito:** *Staten Island Advance,* Oct. 30, 2001.

332 **Lieutenant Paul Mitchell:** Ibid., Oct. 30, 2001.

332 **Firefighter Sean Hanley:** Ibid., Sept. 17, 2001.

332 **Mark Whitford:** Ibid., Sept. 30, 2001.

333 **Thomas Sabella:** Ibid., Sept. 29, 2001.

333 **Joseph Ogren:** Ibid., Sept. 25, 2001.

333 **"It is a privilege":** Monsignor Joseph Murphy, author interview, November 2001.

333 **the house needed a new roof:** This account is based on author interviews with Cosmo DiOrio, Gerri DiOrio, and Dennis Taaffe in November 2001.

EPILOGUE

337 **A quarter century after:** Lorraine Cziko, author interview, May 2002.

339 **"could never bring back":** *Wall Street Journal,* March 7, 2002.

339 **The Department lost:** FDNY, Operational Reference, 1–5.

340 **Hundreds more new probies:** Vincent Dunn, author interview, March 2002.

340 **Dunn's report:** It is available on his Web site, www.vincentdunn.com. A letter Chief Dunn wrote to Homeland Security Chief Tom Ridge is also available on the site.

341 **morning of May 2, 2002:** Author' eyewitness account.

344 **Julius brothers stories:** Author's reporting and interviews.

Sources

Primary Sources

American Print Works v. Cornelius W. Lawrence. Supreme Court of New Jersey, Essex Circuit. New York: Collines, Bowne & Co., printers, 1852.

Anonymous ("a late member of the Fire Department"). "The Truth." New-York Historical Society.

Board of Aldermen. Proceedings, 1836–1850. New-York Historical Society.

Chief Engineer. Annual Reports, 1850–1865. New-York Historical Society.

Common Council of New York. Minutes, 1784–1831. 12 vols. New-York Historical Society.

_____. *Minutes of the Common Council of New York, 1675–1776.* 8 vols. New York: Dodd, Mead, 1905.

Fifteenth Ward Hose Company. By-Laws. New-York Historical Society.

Fire Department of the City of New York. Annual Reports, 1871–2000. Municipal Reference Library, New York.

Fernow, F., ed. *Records of New Amsterdam.* 7 vols. Baltimore: Genealogical Publishing, 1976.

_____. An Operational Reference. New York: Fire Department of the City of New York, 2002.

_____. Company journals, various years, 1880–1965. New York Fire Museum.

_____. General Orders, various years. George F. Mand Fire Department Library.

_____. General Orders, September 13, 2001. Municipal Reference Library, New York.

_____. Journal of Protection Engine Co. 5, the Bronx, for 1895. New-York Historical Society.

_____. Register of the Fire Department of New York, 1880. New York Fire Museum.

_____. Report on Incendiarism in New York City, 1912. Typescript. Municipal Reference Library, New York.

_____. Roster of the Fire Department of New York, 1888. New York Fire Museum.

_____. Special Orders (various years). George F. Mand Fire Department Library.

Foster, C. "An Account of the Conflagration of the Principal Part of the First Ward of the City of New York." Typescript. New-York Historical Society.

Jacobus Stoutenburgh's will, filed 24 Jan. 1770. New-York Historical Society's Abstracts of Wills, vol. 8, 85. New-York Historical Society.

La Guardia, Fiorello. Papers. La Guardia Community College.

Metropolitan Fire Department. Annual Reports 1866–1870. Municipal Reference Library, New York.

Pocahontas Fire Engine Co. 49. By-Laws, 1836. New-York Historical Society.

Proceedings of the Citizens of Philadelphia, Baltimore, Boston, etc., in Reference to the Great Fire in the City of New York, 1835. Typescript. New-York Historical Society.

Proceedings of the Committee on Safety, Appointed by the Public Meeting of Citizens on the Subject of Fires, 1840. New-York Historical Society.

Staines, Captain Edmund. Incident Report for Feb. 26, 1993. Notes in author's possession.

Stoutenburgh Family Wheel. New-York Historical Society.

Tenement House Committee. *Report of the Tenement House Committee of 1895, Delivered to the Legislature on Jan. 17, 1895.* Albany: James B. Lyon, State Printer.

United Women Firefighters Papers. Wagner Labor Archive, New York University.

SECONDARY SOURCES

Allen, Oliver E. *New York: A History of the World's Most Exhilarating and Challenging City.* New York: Atheneum, 1990

————.*The Tiger: The Rise and Fall of Tammany Hall.* New York: Addison-Wesley, 1993.

Anbinder, Tyler. *Five Points.* New York: Free Press, 2001.

Asbury, Herbert. *Ye Olde Fire Laddies.* New York: Knopf, 1930.

Baylor, Ronald H., and Timothy J. Meagher. *The New York Irish.* Baltimore, Md.: Johns Hopkins University Press, 1996.

Benson, Lee. *The Concept of Jacksonian Democracy.* Princeton: Princeton University Press, 1970.

Brandt, Nat. *The Man Who Tried to Burn New York.* Syracuse, N.Y.: Syracuse University Press, 1986.

Burrows, Edwin G., and Mike Wallace. *Gotham: A History of New York City to 1898.* New York: Oxford University Press, 1999.

Calhoun, Richard Boyd. "From Community to Metropolis: Fire Protection in New York City, 1790–1875." Ph.D. dissertation, Columbia University, 1973.

Carp, Benjamin L. "Fire of Liberty: Firefighters, Urban Voluntary Culture, and the Revolutionary Movement." *William & Mary Quarterly* 58, no. 4 (October 2001).

Connable, Alfred, and Edward Silberfarb. *Tigers of Tammany: Nine Men Who Ran New York.* New York: Holt, Rinehart & Winston, 1967.

Coffey, Michael, and Terry Golway. *The Irish in America.* New York: Hyperion, 1997.

Costello, A. E. *Our Firemen: The History of the New York Fire Departments.* New York: Knickerbocker Press, 1887.

DeForest, Robert W., and Lawrence Veiller. *The Tenement House Problem, Including the Report of the New York State Tenement House Commission of 1900.* New York: Macmillan, 1903.

Dunshee, Kenneth H. *As You Pass By.* New York: Hastings House, 1952.

Ellis, Edward Robb. *The Epic of New York City.* New York: Old Town Books, 1966.

_____. *The Millennium Book.* New York: Fire Department of the City of New York, 2000.

Foote, Shelby. *The Civil War: A Narrative.* Vol. 1. New York: Vintage Books, 1958.

Ford, James L. *The Third Alarm.* New York: Brentano's, 1910.

Freeman, Joshua. *Working-Class New York.* New York: New Press, 2000.

Gillingham, H. E. "The First Fire Engine Used in America." *Bulletin of the New-York Historical Society* 20 (July 1936).

Ginsberg, Stephen F. "Above the Law: Volunteer Firemen in New York City, 1836–37." *New York History,* April 1969.

Ginsberg, Stephen F. "The History of Fire Protection in New York City, 1800–1842." Ph.D. dissertation, New York University, 1968.

Hashagen, Paul. *A Distant Fire: A History of FDNY Heroes.* Dover, N.H.: DMC Associates, 1995.

_____. *Fire Department of the City of New York Commerative Edition.* Paducah, KY: Turner publishing Co., 2000. (This volume is referenced as the FDNY's "Millennium Book.")

Heckscher, August. *When La Guardia Was Mayor: New York's Legendary Years.* New York: Norton, 1978.

Hershkowitz, Leo. *Tweed's New York: Another Look.* Garden City, N.Y.: Anchor/Doubleday, 1977.

Jackson, Kenneth T., ed. *The Encyclopedia of New York.* New Haven: Yale University Press, 1995.

Johnson, Gus. *FDNY: The Fire Buff's Handbook of the New York Fire Department 1900–1975.* Belmont, Mass.: Western Island, 1976.

Kessner, Thomas. *Fiorello H. La Guardia and the Making of Modern New York.* New York: McGraw-Hill, 1989.

Kirtzman, Andrew. *Rudy Giuliani: Emperor of the City.* New York: William Morrow, 2000.

Koeppel, Gerard T. *Water for Gotham.* Princeton: Princeton University Press, 2000.

Langguth, A. J. *Patriots: The Men Who Started the American Revolution.* New York: Simon & Schuster, 1988.

Limpus, Lowell M. *History of the New York Fire Department.* New York: Dutton, 1940.

Morris, John V. *Fires and Firefighting.* New York: Bramhall House, 1953.

Muhlenburg, William Augustus. *Rebuke of the Lord.* Jamaica, Queens, N.Y.: I. F. Hones and Co., 1835.

Nevins, Allan, ed. *The Diary of Philip Hone, 1828–1851.* 2 vols. New York: Dodd, Mead, 1927.

Nevins, Allan, and Milton H. Thomas, eds. *The Diary of George Templeton Strong.* 4 vols. New York: Macmillan, 1952.

New-York Historical Society. *Letters from John Pintard to His Daughter Eliza Noel Pintard Davidson, 1816–1833.* 4 vols. New York: New-York Historical Society, 1940–41.

Packard, Kathleen Walsh. *La Guardia's Fire Chief.* New Albany, Ind.: Fire Buff House, 1993.

Picciotto, Richard. *Last Man Down.* New York: Berkley Books, 2002.

Phillips, Stephen Clarendon. *A Speech Upon the Bill for the Relief of the Sufferers by the Fire at New York.* Washington, D.C.: National Intelligence Office, 1836.

Scher, Steven. *New York City Firefighting.* Charleston, S.C.: Arcadia Publishing, 2002.

Slayton, Robert A. *Empire Statesmen: The Rise and Redemption of Al Smith.* New York: Free Press, 2001.

Smith, Dennis. *Report from Engine Co. 82.* New York: Saturday Review Press, 1972.

_____. *Report from Ground Zero.* New York: Viking, 2002.

_____. *Song for Mary.* New York: Warner Books, 1999.

Stein, Leon. *The Triangle Fire.* New York: Carroll & Graf/Quicksilver, 1962.

Stevens, Francis B. *Fire Protection in the Dry Goods District.* New York: D. Van Nostrand, 1884.

Still, Bayrd. *Mirror for Gotham: New York As Seen by Contemporaries from Dutch Days to the Present.* New York: New York University Press, 1956.

Tyler, James. *Reminscences of the V.F.D.: From Fire Laddie to Supe.* Bay Ridge, N.J.: n.p., 1878.

Wall, Alexander J., Jr. "The Great Fire of 1835." *Bulletin of the New-York Historical Society* 20 (April 1936).

Ware, William. *A Sermon Preached on the Sunday Succeeding the Great Fire.* New York: Charles S. Francis, 1835.

White, Virgil D., ed. *Index to Revolutionary War Service Records.* Waynesboro, Tenn.: National Historical Publishing Co., 1995.

WEB SITES

Chief Vincent Dunn: www.vincentdunn.com

Dennis Smith: www.dennissmith.com

Fire Department of New York: www.nyc.gov/html/fdny

Lower East Side Tenement Museum: www.tenement.org

Uniformed Firefighters Association: www.ufalocal94.org

Unofficial Fire Department Web site: www.nyfd.com

Women in the Fire Service: www.wfsi.org

Vulcan Society: www.vulcansocietyfdny.org

AUTHOR INTERVIEWS

Captain Brenda Berkman
Firefighter Susan Blake
Lieutenant Bob Bohack
Firefighter Mike Bonner
Firefighter Bill Bresnan (ret.)
Firefighter Susan Byrne (ret.)
Deputy Chief Tom Cashin
Firefighter Lorraine Cziko (ret.)
Firefighter Cosmo DiOrio, Gerri DiOrio
Firefighter Damien Duggan
Firefighter Neil Duggan (ret.)
Deputy Chief Vincent Dunn (ret.)
Battalion Chief John Fox
Firefighter Tom Golway (ret.)
Deputy Commissioner Lieutenant Frank
    Gribbon

Assistant Chief Pete Hayden
former Commissioner Charles Hynes
Battalion Chief Reginald Julius (ret.)
Captain Vincent Julius (ret.)
former Mayor Ed Koch
Volunteer Firefighter Bob Leonard
Lieutenant Larry McCarthy
Firefighter Cathy Riordan (ret.)
Lieutenant Pete Runfola
Firefighter Dennis Smith (ret.)
Captain Ed Staines (ret.)
Firefighter Dennis Taaffe
Firefighter Frank Tomaselli (ret.)
Former Commissioner Tom Von Essen
Firefighter Al Washington (ret.)
Captain Paul Washington

INDEX

References to illustrations and photographs are in boldface type except under those headings. All references to streets are for Manhattan. All references to fires are for Manhattan unless otherwise indicated.